First Ladies of Disco

ALSO BY JAMES ARENA

Fright Night on Channel 9: Saturday Night Horror Films on New York's WOR-TV, 1973–1987 (McFarland, 2012)

First Ladies of Disco

32 Stars Discuss the Era and Their Singing Careers

JAMES ARENA

Forewords by Gloria Gaynor *and* Claudja Barry
Afterword by Harry Wayne Casey (KC)

McFarland & Company, Inc., Publishers
Jefferson, North Carolina, and London

LIBRARY OF CONGRESS CATALOGUING-IN-PUBLICATION DATA

Arena, James, 1960–
First ladies of disco : 32 stars discuss the era and their singing careers / James Arena ; forewords by Gloria Gaynor and Claudja Barry ; afterword by Harry Wayne Casey (KC).
    p.   cm.
Includes index.

ISBN 978-0-7864-7581-0
softcover : acid free paper ∞

1. Disco musicians — Biography.   2. Disco music — History and criticism.   I. Title.
ML394.A74 2013   782.42164092'52 — dc23   [B]   2013020986

BRITISH LIBRARY CATALOGUING DATA ARE AVAILABLE

© 2013 James Arena. All rights reserved

No part of this book may be reproduced or transmitted in any form or by any means, electronic or mechanical, including photocopying or recording, or by any information storage and retrieval system, without permission in writing from the publisher.

Cover artwork: Paul Tams

Manufactured in the United States of America

McFarland & Company, Inc., Publishers
Box 611, Jefferson, North Carolina 28640
www.mcfarlandpub.com

I'd like to dedicate this work to my loving mom, Evelyn, who selflessly lugged countless dance records from all corners of the globe back to my anxious, waiting hands in New York for many years when I was younger. She knows how much this book, this music and these women mean to me.

This book is also dedicated to each of the amazing ladies profiled herein.

And to Andrea True. Wherever your spirit is soaring, thank you!

Table of Contents

Acknowledgments ix
Foreword by Gloria Gaynor 1
Foreword by Claudja Barry 3
Preface 7
Behind the Scenes 13
Dancing in Heaven 31

The First Ladies of Disco

The Andrea True Connection	41	Kelly Marie	152
Claudja Barry	57	Maxine Nightingale	156
Pattie Brooks	64	Scherrie Payne	163
Miquel Brown	71	Wardell Piper	170
Linda Clifford	75	The Ritchie Family, 1975–1978	175
Carol Douglas	83	The Ritchie Family, 1978–1983	183
Yvonne Elliman	89	Barbara Roy (Ecstasy, Passion & Pain)	190
Rochelle Fleming (First Choice)	93	Pamala Stanley	197
Gloria Gaynor	100	Evelyn Thomas	203
Debbie Jacobs-Rock	111	Jeanie Tracy	210
Madleen Kane	117	Anita Ward	217
Evelyn "Champagne" King	123	Martha Wash	224
Audrey Landers	130	Carol Williams	231
Suzi Lane	137	Jessica Williams	237
Cynthia Manley (Boys Town Gang)	143	Norma Jean Wright	244

Afterword by Harry Wayne Casey (KC) 249
The Flip Side: Recommended Listening 251
Index 255

Acknowledgments

I was blessed with help throughout the making of this book and I am thankful for all of it! First and foremost, I extend my heartfelt gratitude to each of the 32 extraordinary artists who patiently endured repeated delving into their lives and memories and who selflessly supported the development of this work. Few words can express my gratitude for their kindness and the trust they placed in me to tell their stories. Each of these performers is intelligent, insightful and vital, and I quickly discovered that their music is but one side of their remarkable personas. I hope everyone who enjoys this book will be better able to appreciate each of these women as extraordinary human beings!

I'd like to extend a warm embrace to Linda Clifford. She was the very first artist to grant me an interview, and had she not followed up our conversation with an email to her fellow performers and associates encouraging them to participate, I might still be struggling to make this book happen. A big hug to the phenomenally supportive Jeanie Tracy, who went above and beyond to patiently introduce me to everyone she possibly could. I am truly starstruck when it comes to Audrey Landers, an artist for whom I have tremendous admiration and who sent me into orbit by sharing a special lunch with me in New York City while I was working on this project. I can't thank enough the always uplifting Cynthia Manley, an artist (and now a friend) who stepped in numerous times to keep the ball rolling and always saw the big picture. Dodie Draher kept me laughing, and I am very grateful for her assistance (including the introduction to Felipe). It was profoundly heartwarming to have the constant — and I do mean *constant*— support of Carol Williams and Carol Douglas, who treated me like family and never allowed me to underestimate the value of this work. My thanks to Maxine Nightingale for giving me a helping hand in securing contacts and for giving me one of the most enjoyable rewrite sessions of the project. Debbie Jacobs-Rock was as kind as human beings come, and she prayed for the success of this project — that's how I know this book will be a hit. I am grateful to have enjoyed the warm southern charm of Anita Ward, whose humility and grace were very inspiring to me. Barbara Roy and Rochelle Fleming eagerly granted me two of my earliest interviews, and I thank them for building my confidence tremendously. My thanks to the wonderful, charming Evelyn "Champagne" King, who contacted *me* when it should have been the other way around — and who made me feel like a friend. I must thank Miquel Brown and Kelly Marie for expediting our overseas interviews and for representing Britain's finest disco divas so well. Thanks to Evelyn Thomas and Jessica Williams for sharing their stories with me so frankly and unconditionally trusting my intentions. I am so grateful to Norma Jean Wright for her friendship and constant support of this project. Thanks to Wardell Piper, who has one of the most positive attitudes I've ever encountered and who helped me to build my own. My sincere appreciation to Martha Wash — who could easily have declined my offer to participate but didn't. I am very grateful to the lovely and charming Madleen

Kane, who doesn't usually grant interviews, yet took a chance on me and was extremely warm. Thanks to Suzi Lane for her great enthusiasm and never holding back. Pattie Brooks, Yvonne Elliman and Scherrie Payne have my sincerest thanks for being great women and consummate professionals who opened their hearts to me. And a special thank you to Cassandra Wooten, Cheryl Mason-Dorman and Gwendolyn Wesley who thankfully introduced themselves to me at the very last second and added immeasurably to this work.

I'd like to extend a special thank you to the remarkable Gloria Gaynor, truly the "Queen of Disco," who selflessly contributed to this project. She took the time from her extremely busy schedule to give me what was likely her billionth interview and to write her eloquent foreword for this book. This endeavor would not have been complete without her participation and support. I express my most sincere gratitude to one of the greatest disco legends, the beautiful and amazing Claudja Barry, who not only wrote an uplifting foreword herself, but also shared her friendship with me. It was a privilege to have Harry Wayne Casey, a remarkable and true pioneer of disco, provide an afterword for this book, and I am deeply grateful to the great KC for his courtesy.

I am obliged to these highly dedicated, genuinely caring artist managers and representatives: Troy Bronstein, Stephanie Gold, Stephany Hurkos, James Washington, Dwayne Taylor, Amy Willis and U.K. connections Paul Tams and Rebecca Hough. A very special thanks to Paul for his incredibly energized vision, talent and artistry that graces the cover of this book and captures so well the spirit I tried to achieve. I'm also exceedingly grateful to the following honorable, accomplished, and selfless artists and music professionals: Hazell Dean, Tom Moulton, Felipe Rose, Carlton J. Smith, James Wirrick and Michael Zager. Each of these wonderful people enthusiastically and actively participated in the development of this work. They shared their time, knowledge and unique perspectives, relentlessly secured contacts and photos, and they helped me meet every challenge I encountered. These remarkable people were instrumental in documenting the important stories herein, and this book would never have been a reality without their unyielding support!

A special thank you to the amazing George "Iz" Correia for his tremendous encouragement, enthusiasm and diehard assistance (from the very start). I must thank Rick Gianatos for his relentless and determined efforts to help me with this project as well as his positive attitude and friendship. My sincere gratitude goes to Tom Hayden for generously sharing so much valuable information with me and for connecting me with Madleen. Thank you to Michael Williams for sharing his resources, knowledge and passion for disco with me. Thanks to Sandy Galetovick for relating her warm memories of Andrea True. A special thank you to Eddie O'Loughlin for helping me to get this book noticed.

Thanks to Sophia Arteaga, Jason Dunphy, Denis Kohler and Kristin Sheerin for their invaluable technical assistance and support. I'd like to acknowledge Discogs (http://www.discogs.com) and Joel Whitburn's *Billboard's Hot Dance/Disco 1974–2003* (2004, Record Research Inc.), which were most helpful as data verification resources. A very special thank you to Tony Capullo, who inspired me from day one and helped me find the "yes" attitude I needed to succeed with this project. "The statue was always there."

I was lucky enough to also have friends and family who were very supportive of this project. They include Elvis Bramble (thank you so much for your loyal friendship), Trudie Eppich, Jeremiah Freeman (a truly great artist), Brenda Manzanedo, and Robert and Maureen Arena. And a big shout-out to John Russell and Joe Grimaldi for sharing the nightlife and living the disco era with me! What a blast we had!

Thanks to anyone I may have left out who gave me much-needed encouragement.

Foreword
by Gloria Gaynor

I am very glad to see this book written and published. It contains the stories of the struggles and triumphs of the women who embodied one of the best-loved genres of music to date. I consider it a privilege and an honor to be counted among them.

Disco is the first and only genre of music, in the history of music, to be embraced by every nationality, race, creed, and age group — and these women have helped to make it so. Disco music had the potential to be used as common ground to bring people together who were locked in conflict, but it was never used as such. This is a loss to the world. Many of the women featured in this book are still performing and pleasing crowds across the globe and doing a wonderful job at it. They are a testament to the strength and fortitude of women in general.

I can only hope that the new generations of female performers have the strength of character and real talent to have their music and careers thrive and survive in the same way for at least as long.

Gloria Gaynor, best known for "I Will Survive," "Never Can Say Goodbye," "Let Me Know" and "I Am What I Am" (photograph by Troy Word, courtesy Gloria Gaynor).

Foreword
by Claudja Barry

Perhaps we did not achieve the impossible, but we certainly changed the status quo. It was the time of big hair, tight satin pants, hot dance moves, the velvet ropes of Studio 54 — and then we added "More, More, More," "Love to Love You Baby," "I Will Survive," "Right Back Where We Started From" and so many, many more wonderful songs. Can you see where I'm going with this?

During the mid– to late '70s and early '80s, disco music had highly talented and absolutely committed artists. At a time when the earth was once again in crisis, they created worldwide moments of joy. In an industry where you're only as good as your last hit, there was a group of women who, on the whole, didn't have huge crossover pop records. Gold- and platinum-selling albums were not unheard of, but it was not the norm. But these special ladies were trailblazers, standard bearers, and they *are* performers who, to this day, are revered and emulated. They turned the beat around, but were not a staple of pop radio or late night talk shows or even MTV. Yet they made their mark, and it stands today.

It would take quite a while to list all these women's accomplishments, and still longer to note all of the career

Claudja Barry had two Billboard Hot 100 hits during the classic disco era, "Dancin' Fever" in 1977 and "Boogie Woogie Dancin' Shoes" in 1979 (courtesy Claudja Barry).

highlights of the artists featured here. But I can assure you, it would be time well spent. They made the disco era magical, and their contributions to the music industry were outstanding. They played a significant role in shaping the music scene as we know it today. For a certain segment of the listening public, and perhaps critics of the music, disco is still not always considered a positive word to describe this genre. Enter stage right: Madonna, Whitney, Gaga — and suddenly the music *is* legitimate again. Almost immediately it became cool to have disco music (renamed dance music) on mainstream radio and television again.

"Down and Counting," "Don't Leave Me This Way," "Coming Out of Hiding"—these are just a few of the anthems that you can draw on when you are down! They not only describe the human heart and the emotions of pain, loss, and triumph, but also the music form itself. The music *did* survive and stayed alive—vibrant, exciting, motivating—and it spread joy among a host of new devotees. Growing up, maturing (if that's a better word to describe what happens with time), is beautifully illustrated by the first ladies of disco who tell their stories here. They are definitely survivors, champions in life and heroes in time. Perhaps they did not go to war and earn medals, but when their fans tell them the stories of how a particular song helped them get through a bad time or gave them the courage to face their fears, or that their music generally just made life a bit easier—those words are the medals of honor in their lives. Their music made them strong!

Many of our friends and fellow performers are gone. But they are not forgotten, and their music lives on. There has been much joy, and also a mountain of pain and disappointment, in some of the lives of the divas that you will read about in the following pages. They were down, and just when you thought they were out came the shout: "I will stand!"

Their music sometimes wasn't given the status of a "Stairway to Heaven" or any other classic rock-pop song, but their music will always be a part of history. Not that they did it on their own. The producers were paramount in giving opportunities for all these women of disco to shine. Some of the magicians were Giorgio Moroder, Tom Moulton, Gino Soccio, Larry Levan, Jurgen Korduletsch, Bobby Orlando, Cerrone and Nile Rodgers, among others. These guys had the vision, and these women gave life to their words and music. And the songs endured. Google any of the artists in this book and you will see many remixes and alternate versions of their songs made years later. Many new hits have been composed from lifted parts of the big disco-dance hits of the era. I am sure you have heard "Get It on Tonight" by Montell Jordan—this song was built totally from a disco song called "Love for the Sake of Love." I should know, because it's my song! Montell went on to sell millions. Disco fluff? *Hmmmm* ... opinions can change ... *and how they've changed!*

After the joy of the disco era, it seemed, for a time, these ladies were the only ones at the party. Major venues closed; agents and managers went on to other artists. Some disco artists went on to other careers, but for many the music was paramount. So they kept going, sometimes even with big successes! Mostly, I think the music kept them going. And now, at last, this book gives these wonderful women the recognition they deserve and have earned.

Everyone loves to reminisce, go back in time, pore over old family albums and listen to the good time music of days gone by. This book will be a collective reminiscence, but it won't stop there. It will evoke the past, let you relive it and then make you look at the present—so you can take on the future. As for the first ladies of disco—*they ain't done yet!*

I am delighted to have been a part of the disco era—a time when the performers in this book and I had so much fun and showed the world how much excitement music could add. We celebrate James Arena for undertaking this effort. In writing this book, he has given a capsule biography of each of the participants and, perhaps, shared some revealing anecdotes from each of our journeys. In the panorama of changes that have occurred for all of us, there are qualities that remain constant: our commitment to excellence as performers and as women, our concern for our fans and our regard for our music. We want to maintain what is good and enduring about the music of the past — even as we move forward to face the promise of the future. As wonderful as things were in the good old days, there are even better, more challenging, more rewarding and more exciting days to come!

Preface

My baptism in disco came quite by accident; I didn't even know what it was 35 years ago. I was a 17-year-old nerdy kid and, very late one Saturday night in 1977, I was watching TV and waiting for my favorite horror film show, *Fright Night* (on New York's WOR–TV), to start. It was hard enough to stay awake at that hour, but I soon discovered I'd have to wait an additional 30 minutes for my beloved show to begin. The station had added a surprise program to their lineup. My first reaction was "Oh, what the hell is this?!" Then it happened. Over a thumping beat, the program's announcer said, "From Miami Beach and Ft. Lauderdale, Florida ... the disco capital of the world ... *Disco '77*!" Taking the stage (in a small but flashy-looking club called Pete 'n' Lenny's) was singer Andrea True, wearing a sparkling burgundy sequined dress and lip-synching her guts out about the joys of dancing the night away in the Big Apple. The song was "N.Y., You Got Me Dancing" and from that moment on, I was hypnotized — instantly addicted to a sound I had never heard and an energy that absolutely made my heart leap! "Holy cow," I thought, "this is great!"

This was disco!

I didn't realize it at the time, but I had just discovered a new music genre that had begun to sweep the nation — actually the world. For many, it was irresistible music with the power to make one not only relish the hook of its pop-soul sensibilities, but *move* — dancing with a new kind of urgency and with a rhythm that had never been felt before. For some of us, the music had the ability to elevate our mood and change our entire outlook on life. It was new, fresh, exciting and fun. It was sexy, dangerous and inspiring. It was the sound that was revolutionizing fashion, liberating the oppressed attitudes of a generation and profoundly affecting the lifestyles of millions. For a few short years, the phenomenon of disco absolutely dominated pop culture. This fresh, new music genre gave birth to an army of new vocalists, morphed the careers of gospel and R&B singers, expanded the chart-topping potential for pop and even some rock stars of the day and revived interest in artists whose careers had faded. It created a fresh cash cow for record labels and expanded their opportunities to sell vinyl, if not always through album sales, through the emergence of a unique singles format that could theoretically increase the once-modest profit of the 7" 45 r.p.m. record (until labels were forced to contend with the compensation demands of music publishers). The more expensive 12" single, featuring extended versions of the hit song and, later, the revered remix, was a revolutionary development.

Male artists and groups like The Brothers, B.T. Express, Disco Tex & The Sex-O-Lettes, Barry White, Harold Melvin and the Blue Notes, Van McCoy, Carl Carlton, Eddie Kendricks, The Trammps, Bohannon and KC & the Sunshine Band dominated DJ playlists during disco's earliest days (and nights). But soon the ladies took over. The female vocalists that became synonymous with disco were an extraordinarily talented group of women who gave the music a mix of elegance and gutsy fire. Among them were The Andrea True Connection ("More, More More"), Claudja Barry ("Boogie Woogie Dancin' Shoes"), Pattie Brooks ("After Dark"), Miquel Brown ("So Many Men, So Little Time"), Linda Clifford ("If My Friends Could See Me Now"), Carol Douglas ("Doctor's Orders"), Yvonne Elliman ("If I Can't Have You"), Rochelle Fleming of First Choice ("Dr. Love"), Gloria Gaynor ("I Will Survive"), Debbie Jacobs-Rock ("Don't You Want My Love"), Madleen Kane ("You Can"), Evelyn "Champagne" King ("Shame"), Audrey Landers ("Manuel Goodbye"), Suzi Lane ("Harmony"), Cynthia Manley of Boys Town Gang ("Remember Me/Ain't No Mountain High Enough"), Kelly Marie ("Feels Like I'm in Love"), Maxine Nightingale ("Right Back Where We Started From"), Scherrie Payne ("I'm Not in Love"), Wardell Piper ("Super Sweet"), both incarnations of The Ritchie Family ("The Best Disco in Town," "Put Your Feet to the Beat"), Barbara Roy of Ecstasy, Passion & Pain ("Touch & Go"), Pamala Stanley ("Coming Out of Hiding"), Evelyn Thomas ("High Energy"), Jeanie Tracy ("Time Bomb"), Anita Ward ("Ring My Bell"), Martha Wash ("It's Raining Men"), Carol Williams ("More"), Jessica Williams ("Queen of Fools") and Norma Jean Wright ("Saturday"). If there was a "Glitter Ball of Fame," these names would be prominent among the sparkling panels. These are some of the extraordinary women who proudly put their hearts and beautiful voices behind disco's greatest hits and who kindly shared their stories in this book. As the esteemed Gloria Gaynor and Claudja Barry duly note in their forewords, these women are survivors.

The explosion of disco encompassed not only the energized music, but also the venues that supported the sound and the popular culture that the genre spawned. Much has been written about the clubs that gave rise to the music these women sang. Branded as hedonistic hook-up and drug-peddling joints by some, for others they were a place to let off steam, socialize and dance to a beat that made everyone feel alive and forget whatever troubles were besetting them. The most publicized clubs — Studio 54, Regine's, Copacabana, Paradise Garage and Xenon, among many others — were bastions of the elite, the brightest stars and über-celebrities of disco's heyday. The music initially emerged from the danceable soul tracks popular in the clubs that catered to African Americans and Latin Americans. A short time later, it exploded in the homosexual and underground watering holes of New York and San Francisco and began a sub-revolution in the gay, lesbian and transgender community that would foster a newfound sense of freedom and pride. It put pounding beats and superior voices behind the unstoppable rise of a culture determined to break down the walls of suppression and discrimination, which the minority populace had endured for, well, centuries. The gay community, unquestionably over the years, proved to be the most loyal of disco's fans and advocates. The music became a soundtrack of hope through the devastation of the AIDS crisis for that same legion. But until that horrific scourge became an acknowledged national crisis, the straight community was equally interested in sharing all the fun the queers were having, and the ripple effect on disco was both startling and extraordinary.

While the disco music landscape became littered with a plethora of faceless studio acts and silly, comical material like *The Ethel Merman Disco Album*, "Disco Duck" and "Disco Lucy" (which, while sometimes amusing, unfortunately also contributed to a lasting negative impression of the genre), many brilliant compositions demonstrated the music's depth and power, such as Candi Staton's "Victim," Donna Summer's "Sunset People," Labelle's "Lady Marmalade" and Machine's "There But for the Grace of God (Go I)." Finally, Hollywood glamorized the music and nightlife tsunami with the movie *Saturday Night Fever* and its bestselling soundtrack. Then, after a frenzy of disco *everything*, the nation and the media grew bored and annoyed with the very overkill they had helped create.

Disco and some of its vocalists survived, prospered in Europe (where the music never receded) and muddled through the reversal of fortune in the U.S. Retreating slightly back to its underground origins in this country for a time, the genre successfully reinvented itself with a new, more encompassing name: *dance music*. Smaller independent American record labels embraced the genre while the majors figured out their next move (which was to start producing — you guessed it — more dance music). With its slow but eventual respectability re-established to some degree by the mid–'80s, the dance genre continued to produce club and crossover smashes, blurring quick categorization boundaries with its rock and new wave hybrids, funk and R&B jams, electronica, electro-swing, hip-hop derivations and, most closely resembling its original style, Hi-NRG and house anthems.

Today, these music classifications coexist peacefully, with brilliant, energized works scalding the airwaves and dance floors (though perhaps fewer tracks stand out as readily identifiable classics of the genre). Modern dance music has evolved into a model that now focuses on the mixers and production teams for all but a handful of vocalists. However, there are still a few contemporary singers who've deservedly secured the diva title: In-Grid, Mylene Farmer, Kate Ryan and Adele (give a listen to the remixes of "Skyfall" if there's any doubt) out of Europe. Here in America there's Jennifer Lopez, Rihanna, Kristine W., Kelly Rowland, Nicki Minaj and Lady Gaga (check out the melding of Amii Stewart's "Knock on Wood" with Gaga's "Born This Way") to name a few. It's easy to imagine the latest hits of these ladies coming out during disco's heyday. Today's pop music *is* dance music, as many industry notables in this book will attest, and few Top-40 songs are released without club-targeted remixes. Many of today's songs freely borrow from the original disco era, whether in style or through the sampling of hooks, choruses, vocals and rhythm tracks. The conclusion that much of disco's original material was, in fact, *good* music is inescapable. It worked then, and it still works today. Just ... don't call it disco.

The disco music birthed generally between the years 1974 and 1984 was created by many enormously skilled and talented writers, producers, musicians, engineers and mixers who had largely been in the industry long before the revolution began. For some, their hard-knocks training and love of the craft was a part of their souls well before disco presented them with an opportunity to reach the mainstream. Others came on board as disco exploded onto the scene, affording them an opportunity to add their fresh artistry to the mix. Many of the vocalists who made now classic disco hits had distinguished careers in R&B, jazz, gospel and soul. For the female artists who wore the so-called disco queen crown for any portion of their career, disco became something of a winning lottery ticket ... at least for a time. Their voices, which had sometimes languished in obscurity, brought them to the front of the line. When these women sang, they unleashed a passion and power that could only have come from experience — and it was palpable. They have that in common. Their voices became as much a part of the musical experience as the beat that was driving so many feet to the dance floor. Yet, except for a seemingly universal respect and love for the late gender-blurring disco artist Sylvester (James) that most of these women possess, each of these ladies is distinctly individual. Each singer has her own fascinating story to tell, and I gave these women free reign to do so. What they say here is what they want the world to know.

It may seem conspicuous that some artists synonymous with disco and unquestionably major pioneers of the genre are not included in this volume. As you might expect, some artists were unavailable, unreachable or uninterested in participating. Regardless, the contributions to disco of the missing-in-action were enormous, and lack of visibility here is by no means a commentary on their amazing talents, accomplishments or legacies.

Although this project largely focuses on the living, it is important to remember those disco artists who made a lasting contribution to the genre and have passed on. No exploration of disco could ever be complete without noting the accomplishments of Laura Branigan, Loleatta Holloway, Viola Wills, Vicki Sue Robinson, Karen Young and the illustrious and celebrated diva who became synonymous with the genre (and vanquished any of its limitations)—Donna Summer. It was my hope that Donna would provide commentary on her fellow artists, whose fame and accomplishments were sometimes eclipsed by her own spotlight. Fate decided otherwise. The news of Donna's passing stunned the world on May 17, 2012. However, her distinguished life is highlighted in the *Dancing in Heaven* section of this book, along with the careers of some other departed artists. A less-prolific singer, Andrea True, who died in comparative obscurity in 2011, was originally intended to be the sole subject of this work; the details of her fascinating personal story had oddly remained untold. As I researched her time on this planet, some little-known information, insights and rarely heard particulars were revealed by friends and associates of True that make for intriguing reading (and are included in a special chapter for her). When hopes of working with Andrea on an actual biography were dashed, the need for a more comprehensive volume to preserve her story and those of other artists who pioneered the disco frontier became apparent.

Asking what contribution these women made to disco is like asking what purpose brick and mortar served in building New York City. But I wanted to learn more about their lives and careers and how they faced the challenges of maturing. They gave me this insight—and much more—in interviews conducted between February and October of 2012. They are the best possible ambassadors of disco—the women who breathed life into the music. They are the reason disco still fascinates after more than three decades. These ladies gave it their all and wanted very little in return: a fair paycheck and the satisfaction of seeing an audience happy. Regrettably, some of these artists received little more than the fleeting joy of the latter over the course of time, enduring some of the financial pitfalls of life in the recording and entertainment industry. Others prospered and navigated their personal paths in ways that brought continued success. Some are conservative women with strong religious convictions whose recollections show a great sense of faith. A few of these amazing singers relate their extraordinary experiences with eye-opening candor, sass and sharp humor. However, whatever my conversations with these vocalists reveal, I can tell you they never once appeared in any way resentful or bitter about any of the difficulties, challenges or injustices they may have experienced. That may be a reflection of their professionalism and upbringing, which many of these ladies have in common. Or, maybe they just *are* truly happy to have been a part of this era. Though acknowledging their ups and downs, successes and missteps, they often dismissed the inequities in their careers with a simple "That's life" philosophy. They all showed tremendous humility, and they all embraced their music history, accepting of all that encompassed it. Each of them lived up to their end of the original bargain and delivered immeasurable joy to the masses, come what may. They gave us the music to associate with the happiest times of our lives and the inspiration to get through the worst.

There is a danger in being too nostalgic; it can color the past and keep one from appreciating the present. However, this book is much more about celebrating the past rather than pining for its return. Just as the doo-wop and '60s superstars received their accolades, it now is time to acknowledge the joyful sounds that the remarkable women assembled here brought to the disco era. Quite simply, life was (and is) *tough*, and these women make it easier by bringing people together with their music. *First Ladies of Disco* is something of an official declaration of appreciation for what they have accomplished and the examples they have set. This book is a very humble and decidedly inadequate love letter to each of these magnificent women. It's an apology for a "Here today, gone tomorrow" society that often forgets those who paved the way. It is an acknowledgment that these ladies continue to bring joy and are still very much in the game. Many of these dynamic women are continuing to release new songs and albums that stand up to anything offered by their contemporaries.

The work you hold in your hands is a heartfelt thank you to these amazing women whose records and performances defined an entire genre of music and who never failed to leave us wanting, as Andrea True sang so earnestly, more, more, more!

Behind the Scenes

The amazing women who forged the disco music genre have worked with some of the music industry's most esteemed professionals. These experts encompass a diverse range of renowned notables from the performance, management, production and composition sides of disco and dance music. They each possess formidable credentials, remarkable knowledge of disco's history and unique insight into the workings of the world in which these women have flourished (and in which they continue to market their skills today). They have been individually asked to give their responses to a series of questions based largely on some key points common to many of the featured performers' lives and careers as recording artists. The professionals include:

Troy Bronstein: In the mid '80s, no nightclub was a hot spot without a constant stream of A-list entertainers parading through its doors and onto its stages. "As a waiter in a large Southern California club," Troy says, "I had the good fortune to become a liaison between many of these performers and the club, and, in doing so, established great friendships with some of the hottest names on the charts. With the encouragement of several of these performers, I formed the T-Best Talent Agency." His company has become one of the largest independent talent agencies in the world, representing more than 100 acts, including artists from the disco era and current DJs. Bronstein has also added a management division and created an independent record label (House of Hustle and Pride Records) and has worked with Cher, Tina Turner, Bette Midler, Chaka Khan, Deborah Harry, Jennifer Holliday and the Pointer Sisters. Bronstein also handles several top comedians and models.

George "Iz" Correia: "As a huge lover of music since my infancy, I had always dreamed of working with the artists whose music blasted out of my stereo!" says George. "I started in the entertainment business doing freelance work with a friend of mine who worked for Emmis Communications. Their properties included jazz station CD 101.9, hip-hop station 97.1 and R&B station 98.7 KISS–FM in New York City. I would help come up with production concepts and organize various community outreach events, concerts and parties for the radio personalities. I was summoned to book various recording artists for some of the events, and many of the artists complimented me on how professional the events were and how well they were treated. This led to many friendships and management opportunities with some of the women featured in this book." Correia launched Show Iz Entertainment, which offered artist bookings and personal-road management services. He works actively today with various R&B–disco artists, including Rochelle Fleming of First Choice, Linda Clifford, Barbara Roy of Ecstasy, Passion & Pain and others.

Hazell Dean: Hazell, widely revered as the "Queen of the British Clubs" and the "Duchess of the Dance Floor," scored a succession of massive club and dance hits in the mid '80s (following the original disco era). Many of her dance-floor classics crossed successfully onto the U.K. and European mainstream charts. Though she didn't have her first hit until 1984, she started working as a singer and songwriter as far back as the '70s. After numerous recordings in the northern soul style, she eventually started veering towards dance music. Dean's first big hit in both the U.K. and the U.S. was the double A-side dance smash, "Evergreen"/ "Jealous Love." She topped the charts on both sides of the Atlantic a short time later with her electrifying Hi-NRG recording of "Searchin' (I Gotta Find a Man)." By the end of the '80s, Hazell was the reigning diva of British dance music thanks to a slew of hugely popular singles, among them "Whatever I Do (Wherever I Go)," "They Say It's Gonna Rain" and the Top-Five Brit pop smash "Who's Leaving Who." Many of Dean's biggest successes were produced by the legendary Stock-Aitken-Waterman and PWL production teams. She was voted best female performer by the prestigious Club Mirror Awards and best live performer three times by the Federation of American Dance Clubs. Commenting on her numerous career highlights, Dean says, "There have been so many amazing moments. I had the pleasure of introducing Gloria Gaynor on stage at 'The Fridge' in Brixton, and I have performed at the legendary Studio 54—and you can't get more disco than *that*!" Since the early '90s, Hazell has concentrated her energies on both production and songwriting, while continuing to record hit dance music, including a 2012 remake of Sharon Redd's disco evergreen, "In the Name of Love," and Laura Branigan's "Shattered Glass." Reflecting on her remarkable legacy, she says, "By the industry, I would like to be remembered as a professional. By the public—I want them to have enjoyed my music and to know me as a nice person. Simple!"

Stephen Ford: "I got my start in music management working for one of the best managers around—Bill Sammeth—who trained me and was my mentor," says Ford. "At the time, Bill managed Cher, Joan Rivers, Olivia Newton-John and KC and the Sunshine Band. I always wanted to work for Cher. I always thought she was cool, creative and did things her way. She didn't care what people thought, and I liked freethinkers like that. It was my dream to work with Cher, and it all kind of started when I was working on the 1987 Academy Awards, where she was nominated for *Moonstruck*. I was with her the entire time of the show, and I learned how to be around celebrities. I think she saw something in me and liked the way I took care of her and [she] mentioned it to Bill. He then offered me an opportunity to work with him—and that was really my big break. Cher showed me you don't survive in this business for nearly 50 years without being driven, focused and knowledgeable about who you have around you and what your talent is about." Today Ford books veteran performers such as Thelma Houston, Anita Ward, Maxine Nightingale and Yvonne Elliman, as well as comedy stars, R&B legends, circuit DJs and *American Idol* contestants.

Rick Gianatos: The name Rick Gianatos was one of the most important and respected in music production during disco's heyday. A pioneer DJ who helmed the turntables of the most prestigious clubs and an innovator of one of this country's earliest disco remix services, Gianatos was instrumental in breaking many of the genre's earliest classics. He became well-known and highly respected as one of the era's most sought-after remixers, transforming the musical works of countless artists into all-time disco classics. Among his most celebrated achievements were Gene Chandler's "Get Down," Front Page's "Love Insurance," Edwin Starr's "Contact," Shalamar's "Right in the Socket" and "The Second Time Around," Carrie Lucas' "Keep Smiling," 5 Special's "Why Leave Us Alone," Loleatta Holloway's "That's What You Said," Pamala Stanley's "This Is Hot" and KC's "Give It Up" and "Are You

Ready?" Other major acts he's worked his remix magic on include the Gap Band, the Whispers and Yarbrough & Peoples. Gianatos' remarkable creativity has extended into the 21st century. Under his independent imprints, Altair Records and Nu & Improved Records, he produces artists Scherrie Payne, Pattie Brooks, Freda Payne and Linda Clifford, as well as rising new dance-music star Kim Yarbrough.

Tom Hayden: The founder and president of TSR Records, Tom's successful label product was among the most sought-after music in the history of disco and dance. His resume is rich in hands-on experience. "I got into the business in 1972 working at 20th Century Records," he says. "I worked my way up in the company handling artist relations and climbing to various label positions. I started an in-house disco department at 20th Century and, to this day, there's still a debate as to whether we had one of the first 12" records to ever come out on the market — Bob Crewe and the Eleventh Hour's 'Hollywood Hot' back in 1975. We also had the Ritchie Family's 12" single, 'Brazil,' that same year. In 1977, I left 20th Century Records and started my own independent promotion company called Tom Hayden & Associates. Our first project was CJ & Co.'s 'Devil's Gun,' which went on to hold the number 1 position on the *Billboard* disco chart for five weeks. We had a string of successes, and, in '79, we took out an ad in *Billboard* magazine touting that we had promoted between one-fourth and one-half of all the records on the disco chart that year. I was very young back then, in my early 20s, and we had a blast! I was awarded best independent dance promoter numerous times at the *Billboard* disco conventions. We were handling dance promotion for the Rolling Stones, Barry White, The Whispers, Shalimar and on and on. Those were good days!

"After the 'disco sucks' backlash in 1979, I still saw the power of the clubs, and I started a new label when all the majors were getting out of disco and were thinking it was kind of a negative for them to promote that genre of music. I started TSR Records in 1980 and debuted with Two Man Sound's 'Capital Tropical.' It was a Top-10 dance record, followed by Claudja Barry's 'Work Me Over,' Miquel Brown's 'So Many Men, So Little Time,' Evelyn Thomas' 'High Energy,' Fun Fun's 'Color My Love' and Pamala Stanley's 'Coming Out of Hiding.' We later had success with Madleen Kane. We eventually expanded into flamenco music, alternative rock and jazz. That's where we still are today. But my heart is always in dance music, and if I can find something that I really love, I'd love to sign a great new dance artist," he says.

Tom Moulton: A New York native and former model, Tom is considered by many to be the disco genre's original king. He is credited as the innovator of the extended mix, the 12" single and the man who refined the sound of countless classic disco songs that became mammoth hits. He's worked with nearly every major artist of the day (KC and the Sunshine Band, The Three Degrees, Gloria Gaynor, Double Exposure, First Choice, Van McCoy, Grace Jones, Isaac Hayes, B.T. Express, etc.) and the words "A Tom Moulton Mix" on an album or single jacket became the seal of approval and the mark of excellence for DJs and music fans the world over. Moulton mixed The Andrea True Connection's "More, More, More," The Trammps' "Disco Inferno" and countless other records, turning them into disco crossover smashes. Always frank and holding tight to his convictions, Tom laughs at his fame (with a kind of outspoken humility). He nearly dismisses the acclaim bestowed upon him, saying, "Tom Moulton — a big believer in toilet paper! I say that because I never believed in kissing anyone's ass to get a record or to do anything. I wanted to make it on the merits of the mix. I wouldn't play any of the games. Judge me for what I do, not how

I am. It wasn't about me; it was about the music — *not me!* I'm just the vehicle for it. I liked my music to take the praise and accolades. I tried to do the best I could with what I had to work with. But I don't think it's because of me that it's that way. It's a combination of all of us. It's the song, the performance. It's that combination that turns my creativity on. It's the simple, honest truth. I absolutely believe in that, and I always felt like that. People would say, 'Oh, I can't believe you're Tom Moulton.' You know, my mother used to say that!" he laughs.

Tom reflects on his remixing accomplishments. "I was doing something I loved doing; that's the only way I could look at it. I was shocked that a lot of these records went to number 1. I mean, I was really taken aback by that. I never thought I really 'arrived.' I thought of the music, the artist and then me — in that order. If it weren't for that music and those singers and the songs I mixed, I wouldn't be anything. If you don't have the right tools to create something — good luck!"

Felipe Rose: Hailing from Brooklyn, New York, and of Puerto Rican and Native-American heritage, Rose is best known as the vocalist adorned in American Indian attire in the world-famous Village People, a group eternally synonymous with disco. While dancing at the Anvil — a once notorious gay and leatherman watering hole in the meat-packing district of New York City — in full Native-American regalia, Felipe was approached by music producers Henri Belolo and Jacques Morali to become part of a group they were forming. The producers' inspired idea was to form a disco group that would embody the male stereotypes found in the city's gay district, Greenwich Village. Felipe and the men who were enlisted to form Village People (with cowboy, leatherman, cop and soldier characterizations) became a nearly instant pop, disco and cross-cultural phenomenon. "Macho Man," "In the Navy" and "YMCA" became enormous pop crossover hits at the peak of disco fever, while songs like "San Francisco" and "Fire Island" became empowering gay anthems. Amassing more than 30 gold and platinum records from around the world, the Village People continue to tour. Rose has been inducted into the Native American Music Hall of Fame, actively promotes Hispanic and American Indian cultural awareness and tirelessly lends his name to HIV and AIDS awareness events. In addition to hosting a radio show, he is an ordained minister and a culinary expert. He continues to reinvent himself while remaining a highly visible media personality.

James "Tip" Wirrick: Wirrick began his record-producing and composing career creating songs like Sylvester's landmark "You Make Me Feel (Mighty Real)" and Two Tons of Fun's "I Got the Feeling" during disco's early days. Later, Wirrick created such hits as "Time Bomb" for Jeanie Tracy and "Stranger (In a Strange Land)" sung by Pamala Stanley & Paul Parker. An accomplished guitarist, he also composed songs for Jimmy Sommerville, CeCe Peniston, The Barrio Boys and numerous other artists. His work has been featured in many major motion pictures, including *Beverly Hills Cop* and Robert DeNiro's *Flawless*, as well as the final episode of the classic TV series *Friends*. Today he continues to write and produce music out of Los Angeles through Wirrick Productions, Inc.

Michael Zager: Michael Zager's contributions to disco music are renowned the world over. As a prestigious producer, composer and arranger, his music has also been a hugely successful part of pop history. He has worked with a multitude of major artists, including Whitney Houston, Jennifer Holliday, Luther Vandross and Herb Alpert. Zager made his mark in the disco genre numerous times, helming the enormously popular productions of Cissy Houston's classic "Think It Over," The Spinners' "Working My Way Back to You" and "Cupid" and The Andrea True Connection's "What's Your Name, What's Your Number?" The producer and composer had landmark disco hits of his own with "Do It with Feeling," under the Michael Zager's Moon Band name, and the worldwide smash, "Let's All Chant" as the Michael Zager Band.

"We sold about 5 million copies of 'Let's All Chant,'" Zager says proudly of the classic disco record he made with partner Jerry Love. "It went to number 1 on the pop charts in many countries, but not in the U.S. In this country, we must have sold about 6–700,000 copies, and it reached the Top 20. Jerry Love is still my partner. I met him when he was head of A&R at A&M Records in New York. I used to try to get my artists signed to the label. When he left A&M, we became partners. He used to go to the clubs every night. His main club was Studio 54, but one night he went to Greenwich Village in New York City to visit a couple of discos and check out what the dancers were reacting to. He heard dancers going, 'Ooh-ah, Ooh-ah.' The next day, he told me they were all chanting this phrase on the dance floor and that I should write a song using that sound. I thought he was crazy! I said, 'You have to be kidding; that's embarrassing!' He said they're all doing it, and if I write something and incorporate that sound, they're gonna love it. The reason I added the piccolo-trumpet and classical section in the middle of 'Let's All Chant' was mainly because I was embarrassed! I thought it was so stupid with that 'Ooh-ah' sound in it that I wanted to add something to lift the track musically. I have a classical background and went to a music conservatory, so I was really feeling embarrassed," he laughs. "I wrote it with Alvin Fields, and I told my partner, 'I'm gonna kill you if this isn't a hit!' We released it Christmas week — a time when you *never* release a record. It's the worst possible time usually because so many popular artists release albums during this time period. 'Let's All Chant' debuted at Studio 54, and the record took off like a rocket! We received a lot of club play, and it spread like lightning. We thought it would be a club hit, but it never entered my mind it would be a global hit. I thought it would be a two-month record and that would be the end of it."

Michael's recording awards for producing, composing or arranging include 14 gold or platinum records, Golden Boot Award (France), Europe 1 Award (France), Olé Award (Spain), 2 BMI Citations of Achievement, given for most performed songs on radio in a given year, a Grammy Award nomination for "Cupid/I've Loved You for a Long Time" (performed by the Spinners) and a nomination for producer of the year by the Golden Music Awards, in Nashville. Zager is currently Florida Atlantic University's Dorothy F. Schmidt College Eminent Scholar in the Performing Arts and Director of the FAU Commercial Music Program. He is also the author of two editions of *Music Production: For Producers, Composers, Arrangers and Students* and two editions of *Writing Music for Television and Radio Commercials: A Manual for Composers and Students.*

Q: Were female vocalists better suited to performing disco music than their male counterparts?

Bronstein: "I would say disco was easier for women than men; I wouldn't necessarily say it was better suited to them. Just like anything, if you're going to watch someone perform, a male or a female, you're probably more likely to get into the female. In the club atmosphere, the [male performers] tend to be in competition with each other. You didn't have as many males in this genre as females, unless it was a group. It was more difficult for a male to make it. I don't see issues of masculinity playing into it, though. Look at the Bee Gees. Their music wasn't macho at all. But, then again, [they were] also a group, rather than one guy trying to grab everyone's attention.

"The women who made it big in disco all made their mark in time. They all had their anthem song at that moment that made them the 'one.' They had to jump on it, and then, depending on their 'worthiness'—I'll use that word—that would determine how long they'd last. If you were a one-hit wonder, that's one thing—but if you produced several hits, that would keep you around for a while. The ones who had multiple hits also had just the right backing—the writers and producers of that time. And because they really had talent and could sing and had personality, that was able to carry them onward. For me to work with artists, to sell them, I have to believe in them and know they are going to do a great job in the club and everyone's going to like them."

Correia: "My hypothesis would be that these women found a unique connection—almost a friendship—with the people who listened to disco music. I think women have more flexibility to sing about a variety of subjects. Disco was kind of a free-for-all, and I think it gave women the freedom to sing about various subjects without their sexuality coming into question. There were some male artists that had a big disco following, but I think it was more acceptable for women to sing songs that were sometimes fluffy, about love, dancing—fun stuff like that—and not come across as corny."

Dean: "Oh yes, I do believe female vocalists were better suited to performing disco! Only divas can really do disco, and there is only one reason why—these women were, and are, all *great* singers! I loved disco! Obviously—I was going to discos and working in them too. I was, and still am, a huge fan of Gloria Gaynor. She sang great songs, but more importantly, she has a great voice. I don't know if she or the other [original disco] artists actually influenced me, but I enjoyed their work and the era! Disco [and these women's songs] always will be fun!"

Ford: "When you think of disco, you think of women. You think of Donna Summer, Gloria Gaynor, Thelma Houston, Yvonne Elliman, Evelyn "Champagne" King, Martha Wash. In seeing today how the women have held up next to the guys who were in disco—there's no comparison. The women are such amazing performers. They just still have that 'it' factor when they're on that stage singing their hits. Whereas a lot of the guys—I've noticed they just can't transfer that excitement and stage presence like a woman, like a legend of disco, can. The older the guys get, the harder it is for them to move around it seems."

Gianatos: "I don't feel that women were better suited for disco than male artists necessarily. I can think back to some great dance material by men like the Temptations, and their Whitfield-Strong productions like 'Papa Was a Rolling Stone,' 'Masterpiece,' 'Law of the Land' and 'Plastic Man.' When Eddie Kendricks went solo and came out with 'Girl You Need a Change of Mind' and 'Date with the Rain,' people went nuts over those tracks in the clubs. I would say people reacted to it just as strongly as a female vocalist's hits. The O'Jays, Teddy Pendergrass—my God, both in and out of Harold Melvin & the Blue Notes—as well. If men like that had really full, gutsy vocals that touched an emotional nerve, people reacted to it. Now, on the other hand, except for groups like Earth Wind & Fire and Kool & The Gang with their wild outfits, of course the ladies were the ones with the outrageous costumes and the visuals. The gay community would eat that up, and they loved a good show. It still happens today with Lady Gaga and artists like her. I think musically it's a good voice that makes it all click. But you couldn't get Teddy Pendergrass to wear an amazing outfit—but you could get Donna Summer or Cher to do it up big. The straight community may have appreciated it, but the gay community really reacted to it."

Hayden: "That phrase 'disco diva' came about back then because there were so many disco records with female artists that were hitting the top of the charts. Back in the day, those women could appear at a club and sing three or four songs over tracks and walk away with $4,000 or $5,000. There seemed to be a lot of successful female artists, and a lot of the clubs wanted performers with a lot of energy. Those women could really belt it out and were very passionate about the music. That's probably one of the reasons why women became so revered and appreciated in disco. The formula seemed to be: the right producer, the right song and a female who could belt it out—and you'd have a hit!"

Moulton: "Well, I don't know; women could do a lot of 'cutesie-wootsie' stuff that guys really couldn't. For some reason, high voices always seem to go big on those records. There were a lot of guys like Eddie Kendricks that could also do that and were popular. When you can get up in the range of the strings, the horns—there's something about it! It brings out the excitement in a song. [Male audiences], of course, like women better anyway for singing. They always like the appeal of the way they look, especially if they're hot looking. It was all very visual back then!

"These women were all very individual. It's nothing they had in common. For example, Loleatta Holloway was very churchy—that's why I liked her. And Gloria Gaynor—Gloria was very professional about what she did. I think of her as a really good pop singer. Working with Grace Jones doing 'I Need a Man'—she had done a demo and I had refinished it—and I said, 'Grace, this is going to be the perfect vehicle for you to get the gay clubs!' She asked me why. I said, '*I Need a Man?*' She said, "Whatever it takes!" And I went, 'Damn! Now there's a person with drive!' And I *really* mean drive! Grace had it, Loleatta Holloway did, Rochelle Fleming, Gloria Gaynor, Linda Clifford—they all did. A lot of these women really knew how to push the buttons!"

Rose: "I think it was in part because gay audiences were more into female performers, especially drag queens. Women were sort of a novelty in the gay clubs. It was also easier to promote and sell females in disco as opposed to men. There definitely were more women than men singing disco."

Wirrick: "It didn't make a difference to me whether a song would be sung by a man or a woman. In the early days, my whole focus was just writing and producing. I just wanted to get my songs on a record, and Sylvester gave me my first opportunity to do that. He was signed shortly after I began playing for him. 'Mighty Real' was a classic example of that, and everything I wrote back then was aimed at Sylvester's voice and the girls [Two Tons of Fun] singing background. Most of it—not all of it, but most of it—was with a dance beat in mind. One of my music teachers in college would say, 'There's no inspiration like a deadline.' And that's so true! If you've got an artist to write for and there's a record coming out, my God, it's funny how you'll come up with something. Whereas if you have nobody to write for and you're sitting in a room thinking of a song, you end up thinking, 'For what, for whom?' But if you have a target—once in a while you hit can really it!

"I do feel female vocalists are better suited to disco, but if you follow that with the question 'why,' I'm not sure I can answer. You can cite really fine examples of very strong dance songs that were done by men, but women had a special connection to the genre. Maybe it has to do with the diva image—and I do think they are a better match for this music. But I just can't say why and, as a musician, I should be able to. Maybe you can say that it's hard to sound real macho against a disco beat. I don't know. Adam Levine does a good job of it, but there's very few.

"Jeanie Tracy has been one of the best singers I have ever worked with. Sylvester himself was much more difficult to work with. However, Jeanie was always wonderful, and we are good friends to this day and we try to stay in touch. Jeanie was a blessing to work with, and I wish I had had a hit with her the way I had with Sylvester. She was one of my favorites, no doubt—still is and she still sings her ass off! Her voice was an inspiration because I knew, no matter what I came up with, she could sing the dickens out of it. She could sing circles around it!"

Zager: "A large majority of the hits were made by women. I have no idea why that was. Perhaps because many of them trained in the church and had a powerful gospel sound that fit the energy of dance music. You can find a lot of great male singers like Sylvester and Luther Vandross, but women just seemed to have more of the hits."

Q: *In the course of its history, did disco music earn an appropriate level of respect from the music industry and the public? Has it received proper recognition over time?*

Bronstein: "I think disco and dance music were respected, but I think it's viewed more positively in Europe than here in the United States. That's also true in South America. Disco and dance acts are seen on MTV there. Here in the States, you don't see them."

Correia: "I'm not sure about outside of the U.S, but I don't think disco ever got the respect it should have in this country. Perhaps in the beginning it did to an extent, but it eventually lost a lot of it for a couple of reasons. I think some people turned against it because they simply didn't know how to dance! [laughing] Over the years, people look back at the music and have given it more respect. Music is one of those things you connect with events in your life and the good times you've had. Even if you didn't like some of the songs at the time, I think in terms of it being a reflection of the points in someone's life, it begins to earn respect. To me, disco was always something that people seemed afraid to admit that they liked. Today you have disco revival shows that lots of people attend, and the artists have large followings on social networking sites. I think it shows these women were loved by a lot of people. And I think there are a lot of closeted disco lovers! So, I think the respect is there now, but people are a little undercover about it. Maybe the better word to describe how people feel about it is 'nostalgic.' So much of today's dance music is derived from the music these women made. Although some artists don't like being classified as just disco, many of them are very happy to have been a part of such a big movement."

Ford: "I think disco is recognized and respected by the generation of people who experienced it, generally by those aged 40 and up. They realize its importance. Some young kids are kind of discovering disco today, and that's cool. I think disco *has* stood the test of time. Thelma Houston won the Grammy in 1976 for 'Don't Leave Me This Way,' and here it is 2013 and she's working more than ever. I've always told Thelma she's like a fine wine because she just gets better with age."

Gianatos: "The respect has come very, very slowly since it became 'dance music.' And now pop music *is* dance music. So many of the top songs today are dance tracks — not remixes —

the actual original versions of the song. I don't think there was respect for disco music [during the peak of the genre]. After it became so huge, everybody cashed in. So you had artists like Andy Williams doing a disco version of 'Love Story.' Some of them were fun, but you had so much kitsch in there that, to me, it didn't give the general public a chance to appreciate the real thing. You had these cliché arrangements — that were derivative of the really genuine material — getting too much attention and backed by major labels. I consider *Saturday Night Fever* the turning point. Before that, there was some great music — not even disco. It was very danceable R&B. It was beautiful music that would appeal to anyone to sit and listen to or get up and dance. Before *Saturday Night Fever*, it seemed more like the music was for the sake of the music — a good melody, arrangement, interesting to listen to and fun to dance to.

"After the movie, it seemed like there was too much 'getting on the bandwagon' and putting out tracks with a beat for the heck of it. If disco had gotten a chance to evolve and come out at its own pace, it might have earned its place as a respectable genre. Instead, there was too much of that junk in there that got a lot of press. I think that ruined things and contributed to the 'disco sucks' backlash. I know Pamala Stanley tells the story in this book of how she was in the middle of touring for her *This Is Hot* LP, and all of the sudden EMI Records stopped promoting her. Her album was full of beautiful arrangements and songs — and they weren't for the sake of thump, thump, thump. They were good, danceable songs. Gloria Gaynor, whether she did a cover or an original, always had wonderful arrangements with everyone she worked with. There was truly quality music out there. The general population got exposed to so much crap that they finally asked themselves — what was the point of listening to the genre?"

Hayden: "I don't think the major companies understood disco back then. I think they knew radio and how to break hits on radio. When a lot of these songs began breaking out of the clubs, radio was kind of being forced to play them, and that's when the record companies started taking notice. They backed into promoting disco music. They certainly didn't jump in with both feet at first. They took a wait-and-see type of attitude and when the records sales became so undeniable, that's when they began putting money into it and getting heavily involved in the disco market. I don't think the labels back in the day treated disco artists any differently than any other artists. However, there may have been some discussion of an artist's importance because they were or were not a 'disco artist.'

"Over the years, you can look at artists who have had problems with labels, but in some cases it wasn't the label's fault. Artists sometimes overspend in producing a record and when the accounting comes in, they don't realize that things get recouped against the money they were spending — or their managers were spending. There's all kind of factors that come into play. But to say that there wasn't also some creative accounting going on at times would be an understatement. It's always happened in the business, and that's why you need good lawyers to represent artists and to hope that it doesn't happen."

Moulton: "You're asking the wrong person! I will say simply this — I think a lot of the stuff today is just garbage. I can't imagine the London Symphony Orchestra playing the hits of Eminem. You *needed* music back then. I think that's why I got involved with it. I always liked those songs for the melody and the artist. I think that's what drove me to do the things I did."

Rose: "I don't think disco music ever lost respect. I think it was the excesses that hurt it. When disco peaked, it was just too much. The fashions were insanely fabulous. There was so much sex and drugs, and it was crazy. After a while, I think people had to come down from that. At the same time, the music industry in general also contributed to its downfall. The old-time rockers really hated disco, and they had a hand in it. The whole 'disco's dead' thing started in Chicago's Comiskey Park where people burned their disco records. [It was] sponsored by a rock radio station. Disco didn't evolve and stayed on the high end of a party high that we never got off. We never got off the merry-go-round.

"When the disco backlash hit, I remembered the saying, 'Don't do anything out of anger.' Don't write a song or do a project that you're going to sell to the masses out of anger. It would seem so obvious. With the Village People, we had two double albums out, the *Live & Sleazy* and *Can't Stop the Music* albums, and we sort of took the nosedive. The album that came out after those was *Renaissance*. It was the one where we immediately dropped the images. We unveiled a glam look copying Adam and the Ants. While the music was good, it was sort of like, 'If you're gonna say disco sucks ... well, [this is what you get].' People didn't buy it. They wanted our old look back. But, by then, the music industry had changed so drastically and it was really hard to regain our footing. Thank God we had our international following in over 35 countries, where we were able to keep disco alive!"

Wirrick: "From a composition standpoint, I stumbled upon dance music because it was in vogue at the time. I was working with Sylvester and that was the predominant type of music on the radio and that's what was making the charts. Many of us who were writers were basically mercenaries who would do whatever it took to get on the charts. Respect for the genre wasn't really an issue. At the time, the late '70s and early '80s, that's what people were writing, and that's where my focus was. I learned by listening to what was on the radio and basically would try to emulate that.

"I suppose it came easy for me. You know, a lot of that music was first generated by using a raw beat. In those days, we used real drum loops. By real I mean we actually used real loops of tape because those were pre-drum machine days. You would literally scour records and the airwaves for any section of one to two bars of just drums. You'd find a song that had a two-bar or two-measure drum beat, and you'd literally grab that and record it onto a stereo left and right quarter-inch tape. In college, I learned how to edit those tapes where you could seam them, make the loop and make it sound like someone was playing. That's how we began. You'd find a good beat that you'd like and start working around that. Beyond that, that kind of writing was like throwing noodles on the wall. You'd try progressions, melodies and eventually you'd find something you think worked and you'd go with that.

"To this day, the word 'disco' is shunned by a lot of musical people. For a time, it was treated with disgust. If you listen to songs on the radio today, jeez, half of the Top 10 has a four-on-the-floor beat. They just don't call it disco anymore. If it's got that four-on-the-floor beat — it's dance music. Disco was pooh-poohed by a lot of the rock 'n' roll people back in the day, and it's still mocked to this day. When it is mocked today, it shows me that the people criticizing it really don't know what they're talking about because all you have to do is listen to the radio. In Europe, hits with dance beats never stopped. It's only really come back in this country in the last ten years or so."

Zager: "I don't think that the musician or singer who specialized in dance music ever got the respect he or she deserved, in spite of the fact that many dance productions were some of the most inventive productions I have heard. Jealousy may have played a part in the demise of disco. Many artists were not receiving radio play because they were recording other types of music — so they began 'blasting' disco. Most of the artists who were putting disco music down ended up having their records remixed as a marketing tool and to expand their audiences. I think that was part of it. It's possible the campier songs also contributed to the decline of disco. My goal was always to get played on the radio. I rarely made a record that was just for the clubs. I have always considered myself a pop and R&B producer. At that time, dance records *were* pop records, and you could sell [a lot of them]. Diana Ross, David Bowie — you can go down the line and see how artists were making dance records into pop hits. I think that some of the records at the time were intended for just the clubs, like Donna Summer's 'Love to Love You Baby.' There was nothing to the lyric, but it had such an infectious groove.

"The thing I liked about disco was it was such entertaining music. To be able to hear that music in a club and be able to watch people having a good time was truly satisfying. I really loved it! But disco wasn't just entertainment — look at Gloria Gaynor's "I Will Survive.' Cissy Houston — she would not record a song that didn't have a lyric that didn't mean something to her. If you go through the disco catalog, there were quite a few songs that had meaningful lyrics. But there's nothing wrong with recording songs that are pure entertainment. Not every lyric has to have a message. I loved the music of Chic! They recorded amazing tracks, but their music was simply entertaining.

"I don't find any difference between what's going on now in dance music and what was going on back [in the disco era], except then we used live orchestras and today most dance tracks are electronic. As a professor, I tell my students that during the disco era we worked with some of the greatest musicians and singers in the world. Disco became a dirty word — although it never lost its popularity. It is absurd because many of the most inventive [music professionals] produced, and still produce, some of the most [creative] tracks in any pop musical genre. It still bothers me when disco gets criticized. The only problem I have with today's music that is specifically for the clubs — not pop dance, e.g., Katy Perry — is that many of the tracks don't include vocals and the instrumentals are so repetitive that I become bored."

Q: Were the recording and entertainment industries fair-minded in their treatment and handling of disco music performers?

Correia: "When it comes to the business side of the music industry, it's always been that the manager is looking out for himself and the record label is looking out for itself. I don't think the disco genre suffered anything the people in rock and soul weren't experiencing. The negative side of the business crossed all genres. Maybe when disco took off and became more commercially viable, there were more opportunities to encounter problems with labels and such, but the recording industry has always been a minefield from a business standpoint. The goal was to make money, and the artist's concerns were very low on the totem pole at most of the labels."

Ford: "Frankly, a lot of disco artists from the past have gotten screwed over — somehow, some way. I don't really think the women who represent the disco era really got all the respect [and fair treatment] they deserved. The sad part about the record industry today is it's all about the youth; it's not about the legends as much. Some TV music shows do bring back the legends like *The Voice* and *Idol*, but it's still rare. I think because music is so centered on the Justin Biebers of the world — centered on the youth — that a lot of young singers and fans are not knowledgeable of the legends that paved the way. Which is sad! They don't really know past Justin Timberlake."

Hayden: "The industry can be very difficult [today], and it was back then as well. One of the reasons I started my own label was because of some bad dealings I had with CBS Records at the time. I had a million-selling hit by Patrick Hernandez, 'Born to Be Alive,' which I had signed to CBS. The 'disco sucks' campaign in 1979 happened at the height of the release's success, and CBS kind of backed away from the disco market and shelved all the upcoming releases I had with the label. So I never ended up making the royalties I should have from his record. After getting burned by that, I felt we should work for ourselves, and so I started our own label, TSR, in 1980.

"As an independent label, it was tough to compete with the majors because they had such an army of marketing forces and such control over the promoters out there. They could get adds to radio simultaneously, which would allow their songs to move up the national pop charts. With us, we'd get added to a station in New York, then one in Miami and by the time we'd get added in Chicago, it would drop off New York. If you look back at the charts back then, even though there were many more releases from independent companies like TSR compared to the majors, you'd have a hard time finding many independents that were at the top of the pop charts. We would do well on the dance charts and get regional airplay, but to bring it all together at once was difficult. It was a very political game, and that was life in the music business. The majors controlled the marketplace. It was the same for alternative bands that couldn't cross over, country acts—anything on an independent label had a difficult time getting on the pop charts let alone the top of them."

Moulton: "They weren't fair—where would anyone get that idea?! [The record labels] were out to make money, and the contracts were for them, not the artists. I thought a lot of things were very unfair. People don't realize that creativity is a wonderful thing, but the minute you try to cheapen it or screw around with it, it turns off. It's like flicking a light switch off. Some people can turn it back on and others, like me, when it goes off—I don't want to deal with that particular thing anymore. You know you're really very vulnerable when you are in a creative position, like these women were. People try to take advantage of you or screw you over, and it affects you. The labels don't realize that—they think you have an on-and-off switch. I've seen it happen with artists—once you've burned them, they just don't want to know you or ever do anything with you again. I think back in those days you could always get another singer. Like a factory just throwing them out all the time. No matter how many they churned out, there's a few that really stood out. Look at Rochelle [Fleming]. She's had so much success—she's a great person and a good friend."

Rose: "When we were on Casablanca, Donna Summer and the Village People were the queen and kings of disco. We had a different type of rapport with the music industry and the label. We were promoted like no others. I felt like we were at Motown. You had to be the best to be with Casablanca, with the family. We had access to radio, access to television—Casablanca had an impressive publicity department and had access to every TV and radio show in the country. Again, I look at it and think maybe we had too much of it. Having so much exposure is also bad for a career. I mean, we were everywhere. I was getting sick of myself! Meaning I was watching myself on TV, in pre-recorded New Year's Eve shows, on several TV shows at the same time!

"There were a lot of offshoot, boutique labels [under Casablanca] that had performers like Pattie Brooks, for example. A lot of artists were like Pattie—they did well, but they didn't get the A-list treatment. If you could have club hits, you'd have a nice career. If you had crossover hits and Top-10 hits, then you could have a career that spanned years and years. Gloria Gaynor had a long career in clubs, but it wasn't until 1979 with 'I Will Survive' that she had that explosion and resurgence again and climbed into the higher echelons of the music industry."

Wirrick: "Well, let me answer by saying the success of my song 'Mighty Real' was a huge surprise, and there's an interesting story that goes with it about the industry somewhat related to this topic. We were touring — Sylvester and the girls — in Europe after 'Mighty Real' had become an international hit. We'd play these huge venues and generally after the show, the promoters and the people who knew about the records would come up to me and say, 'Wow, you wrote 'Mighty Real'— you must be very wealthy!' I would look at them with this deadpan look and say, 'No, I haven't got a penny to my name; I'm very poor!' At least half a dozen of them who knew about the process and money involved said to me I needed to look into that when I got home. They'd say, 'If you wrote that song, you should be very well off by now.' So. I got back to the U.S. and I was referred to a music lawyer and went and introduced myself to him with a platinum and gold record in my hand. I said, 'You know, I wrote these songs, and I don't have a penny to my name.' His glasses dropped down on his nose and he looked at me and said, 'You're kidding, right?' He proceeded to find out that the attorney for the band at that time turned out to be crooked, and he stole Sylvester's and my royalties and bought a house on Long Island with the money. True story — and we caught him with his hand in the till.

"He was almost disbarred. He was prevented from practicing law for a couple of years, and he could have been thrown in jail — really. He had to sell the house on Long Island in order to pay Sylvester and I back. We think we were paid about three-quarters of the money that was stolen from us. Supposedly, what happened was, for example, suppose a check for $5,000 came through for me. Well, [the attorney for the band] had told me he was administering my 'publishing money,' but at 22 years old, I didn't know anything about this. So he would get a check for $5,000 and write me a check for $500 and keep the other $4500. I would receive the $500 check in the mail, and I would think I had just died and gone to heaven. I thought, 'My God, I just got a check for $500, and it's just for a song that I wrote!' It was amazing. A year later, I discovered I should have [been paid much more]. So anyway, we got our money in one lump sum instead of [a payment period of] five years or 10 years, which turned out to be a blessing in disguise for me. For Sylvester, not so much, because he spent every penny he had and more. He went out and bought a lot of furs."

Zager: "In my opinion, many disco artists were treated unfairly. Most had to continually have a hit to maintain a career, unlike a Joplin or a Jackson Browne. Those performers had to sell records too, but it didn't matter if they had a hit single or not. They would still draw a lot of people."

Q: How would you characterize the strong connection between disco music and the gay community? How vital has this audience been to the overall success of female performers in the disco music genre?

Bronstein: "As far as having a large gay audience, a fan is a fan, and I don't know any artist who would disagree with me saying that. In my personal view, there are a lot of gay fans for these artists in America, but you go down to, say, South America, and it's all straight people. I've gone looking for a gay audience, and you can't find them sometimes. Predominantly in Europe and South America, the disco and dance artists are doing straight events. Massive straight festivals and such; they're not gay-related at all. These artists can go there for days and do 10 straight festivals. Gay crowds, I have to say, are always the best crowds. However, over in Europe, the straight crowds respond very much like the gay community does here. A lot of disco artists are working in Europe and South America and don't come [to the U.S.] at all."

Correia: "I do think there was an important connection. Blacks and gays were the first people to discover disco music, and gay men have always been on the pulse of anything new and exciting. Take Bette Midler, for example. She had started her career performing in gay bathhouses. In the clubs, gay men were able to relate to these singers and their music, be themselves and be free. I think that's one of the reasons why these artists are still relevant among the gay community — even more so than the heterosexual community who bought the same records. I think gay men developed a more personal connection with these women. I think gay men just connected differently with these artists than the way heterosexual audiences did. I don't think there's a difference in the way people of all kinds enjoyed disco music in the clubs, however. I think the music had the same effect on all the people. If you looked at clubs like Paradise Garage, straight and gay people mingled there all the time. A businessman and his wife would be dancing next to a drag queen. I just believe the gay and black communities were pioneers of the music, and once disco became commercialized and the overkill set in, appreciation for the music may have [receded] back a bit to the gay fans."

Dean: "You know what? I honesty have no idea if there is some deep and meaningful reason for the connection. Maybe it's because the music is bright, brash and camp. Maybe it was the relentless beats per minute. Maybe it's the pure escapism. The gay audience has always loved a diva — Gloria, Donna, Cher — the list is endless. The magic is born from the combination of fabulous songs performed by women with great voices — and some things will never change!"

Ford: "Having such a large gay fan base is a positive for these women. They feel, according to those I've worked with, that it's an honor that they have qualities that gay fans are so enthusiastic about. They're very thankful. What woman doesn't love to be adored, and most gay men know how to adore divas and legends. I think they are all very, very happy that they have this fan base that [has been] so loyal to them after all these years. In many of the package shows that these divas perform in together, you actually get a mix of fans — couples in their 40s, 50s and 60s, and then you have gay fans and then a whole new generation of fans that prefer this music to the music of today. There are a lot of people living for music from the past — in disco, in rock — and that's what they want. The music from the past can really be timeless. I think the sad part now is we're in a time where the legends are in their 50s, 60s and close to 70 years of age. They are still out there and doing it, though, and aging doesn't mean retiring."

Gianatos: "There's always been a tie to great female vocalists even outside of disco — Judy Garland, Edith Piaf and a lot of the divas from back in the day. So I think when dance music started to evolve into its own genre, outside of being just a danceable pop or R&B song, of course gay men were immediately attracted to it. I don't even think it had as much to do with it being disco music as it was the artists — their personalities and energy. By the early '70s, Stonewall had already happened and then there were these clubs that started playing this music — and the gay clubs were always the trendsetters. When I was a DJ in

New York and worked at the Limelight, everybody came to the club, not just gay people, because everyone knew that's where they would hear the hippest music. The gay community that embraced disco was setting the trends that everyone else followed. I'd say, for the most part, I don't think I've ever talked to a straight person that had the intense type of reaction to an artist that gay people did. I don't think you heard straight men or women gush over Donna Summer or Gloria Gaynor. I think there's just this emotional chord that's touched in the gay community with this music and these women. It's emotional ... it makes you *feel* ... it's not arbitrary. It may very well be that female voice on the top of these magnificent dance tracks that somehow makes that connection."

Hayden: "There's no denying that the gay clubs were the front-runners in breaking dance music, especially the Hi-NRG brand. There were so many huge gay clubs that didn't care what was happening with a record on radio. They almost shunned the record if it was a big radio hit. They were more into discovering new talent that wasn't on the radio and taking pride in breaking it first and kind of making it be *their* music. I always appreciated the success we had with gay clubs, and I catered heavily to breaking music with them as well as crossing songs over to a mass appeal audience.

"The gay clubs were the forerunners of making disco happen to begin with. Back in the real early '70s, they were playing 45s before the 12" single even came to the market. Places like Fire Island were very important, and four or five of the hottest DJs would play the clubs out there. If they all played a record one weekend to say a thousand people in each of their clubs, those people would then go into the city and spread the word. You'd sell 40 to 50,000 units *without* radio play. The gay clubs like 12 West, Infinity and all those discos in New York were packed constantly and breaking records all the time."

Moulton: "I never understood why disco is sometimes referred to as 'gay music.' I have trouble understanding that mindset. I've heard people say, 'That's such a gay record.' Well how is it gay? Most of the stuff I've worked on made the R&B charts. I never made 'dance records.' I made records you can dance to. There's a difference. I always try to explain that to people. Why should I make anything only a disco record? You're narrowing your audience.

"When I have been in gay clubs, they are more open than the straight clubs — the way they danced and expressed themselves. In other words, there was no feeling self-conscious. They were there to have a good time and screw everything. I think when they see a lot of these artists like Grace Jones and Linda Clifford, they can relate to them. There's that same kind of mutual connection — 'I'm here to do what I do and if you don't like it, well move on!' It's true! I went to see Grace about 10 years ago at the Roxy. She was two hours late. I was really pissed off and thought, 'Who the hell does she think she is?' And then she shows up and the crowd was screaming and she was wearing this wild outfit — and then the mike wasn't working. She yelled, 'I need a better microphone!' and she threw it at the audience. And I mean she really flung it and hit someone in the head! The guy started screaming, 'Oh my God! Grace Jones hit *me* in the head! Oh my God!' He was so excited that Grace Jones hit him in the head, and he thought she did it just for him. He was screaming that he loved her! I couldn't believe it! The owner came over to Grace and said, 'We're gonna get sued! What are you, crazy?' She said, 'It wasn't working! I need a microphone that *wooooorks*! So I can *siiiiiiing*! That's what I'm here for!' She yells to the audience, 'You want me to sing?' They all scream, 'Yes! Yes! Yes!' I think that's why gay men like her so much! She's like, 'Fuck everything! I'll do everything the way I want and when I want and you're gonna wait for me — and if you're not here, other people will be!'"

Rose: "Disco was taken from the urban clubs to the gay clubs because [the gay community] was the underdog of society. If you wanted to break a new single or an act in disco, they'd take it to a gay club first. That would be the barometer — the test ground to see how successful it would be. Out of that, everyone would report to *Billboard* magazine. *Billboard* would report to radio and suddenly these disco songs were charting. I think if a record wasn't big in [the gay clubs], it would never have made it to radio or crossed over. Also, the record pools were extremely important. You had DJs wanting to pick up records from each other, taking them to Boston, Chicago and Atlanta. I remember that happened with Karen Young's 'Hot Shot.' Everyone wanted to hear her!"

Wirrick: "I can't believe how many gay men have come up to me and said, 'You wrote this song or that song? I came out to that song!' That may have been more than I needed to know!" [laughs] "I am as straight as the day is long, so go figure. I think if you have a concept of what makes dance music work, gay or straight, it doesn't matter. But so many of the producers of that music were straight, and they were just trying to get on the radio. I was never phobic about my audience at all, but I did wonder if my songs could make it, if you will, in the straight marketplace. With the passing of time, they have."

Zager: "If it weren't for the gay community, disco would never have been what it was. Disco music broke barriers from a sociological point of view. There were so many gay clubs at the time, and the music was appealing to this community. It was a great civil rights form of music. The genre never would have reached the heights that it did without their support. [However,] I never specifically kept this audience in mind when I made music. I just made the best record I could make. Making the record danceable was all I was concerned about if I was doing a disco track. I think for a disco song to cross over to all audiences, it couldn't be just a good track or a good remix. It had to be a good 3.5-minute *pop* record."

Q: *Are there still opportunities today for disco's original female performers? Are they still relevant?*

Bronstein: "There are some challenges to booking the women who had hits in the disco era today, but it depends on who they are. If they crossed over, it's easier. Evelyn 'Champagne' King, for example, is working everywhere, all of the time. Whether it's a straight event, a gay event, a black event — it doesn't matter. Her hits are timeless; they're classics! I think these women are appreciated once they are seen today, and I think that's evident by the love they receive when they do perform. Sometimes they don't let 'em off the stage — they just give them so much love. That's a great feeling when you see that happening to them. Sometimes people think that because they don't have a current hit record or they don't have a record label deal, their career is over. And that's not true. You just gotta market yourself to the right people and be in the right place."

Dean: "Are there opportunities? Hell, yes! Of course they are still relevant! I have seen *The X Factor* contestants left speechless after being blasted by the so-called oldies, like myself and Gwen Dickey (Rose Royce). Do we need to compete with the kids? Absolutely *not*! I have nothing to prove. *I can sing!* The biggest challenges to any artist are the changes to one's voice. A trained voice will mellow with age, like a fine wine — and you do get tired."

Ford: "Most of the disco artists need to rely on their hits, because that's what people want. And the way music is today, you're lucky to squeeze one new song in your set — whether it's a 30-minute track show or a one-hour band show. Most fans want to hear the hits from the era that take you back. Thelma Houston, for example, has acknowledged that she may not have had as many songs as Whitney Houston or Dionne Warwick, but what she does sing she makes her own. Thelma, who has been performing over 43 years, is a Motown legend, has 23 albums and a Grammy, and knows exactly why she does it so well. 'Don't Leave Me This Way' was just one song of many accomplishments that just happened to be in the disco era and outshined most of her other work. She is, in my opinion, on a par with Tina Turner when it comes to having the whole package. She knows what to sing and includes songs by other artists from the era as well as her hits that compliment her voice. Maxine Nightingale is another performer in that category. As a disco legend, it's your ability to put a show together where you make the songs your own. And a lot of people only have one hit and, frankly, sometimes they don't have the whole package—the stage presence—and they haven't found the other songs from the era that go along as a nice companion piece to their big hit."

Moulton: "I think they are very relevant today. I mean, they're always working! I went to a couple of big clubs where they had these diva shows. And it always seems so nostalgic because the audience is so mesmerized by them. It's like they're in awe of them. Rochelle Fleming was at a show and started to sing one of her hits and people were singing it louder than she was. I would say that's a testament to their talent and there's a happy association with the songs, especially if it was a big hit."

Rose: "I think most of these ladies are relevant today! Take, for example, Linda Clifford—she looks like a million dollars! And because of radio shows on SiriusXM, Studio 54 and other radio stations, their careers have warmed up again!

"You know, I like my career today. I like being in and out of the music business, in high profile and high definition! I also get to go home and reboot out of it and have a normal life and be my whimsical self. [I get to do] a cooking demonstration and also, as an ordained minister, spread love and the union of marriage. I work on my Native American music and charities and things that I'm passionate about. I imagine many of these women feel the same way. I can't speak for most of the ladies of disco. I do know that Donna Summer was a very successful painter. Gloria Gaynor just recently received a degree in psychology. They are reinventing themselves and staying relevant. I know for the Village People, the philosophy is just to constantly strive to be the best we can be on a stage. The more seats you sell, the happier the promoters are. Gloria, for example, is always changing her show around. She keeps it fresh, and vocally she is probably singing better today than she's ever sung. She keeps presenting herself beautifully in different live venues—it's all about how you present yourself. How you keep coming back and evolving with the times. You have to do your best to preserve what you have."

Q: *What qualities do the first ladies of disco profiled in this book possess?*

Bronstein: "I can put together a show with five or six of these divas and there's no competition—they all support each other. They all cheer each other on. And it doesn't matter who opens and who closes. In fact, a lot of the ones who would normally be the closers ask if they can go on first, so they can make the fans happy and get home. [laughs] Many of these women are like family to me, and they are family to each other. A lot of these artists are helping each other out by doing duets or one will write the song and the other will sing it. They keep each other involved, which is great—and that's family."

Correia: "I think of the strengths and character these women have. Their talent was in the forefront, not their sexuality. They can still sing great! They fought sexism and racism and endured. The bottom line is they let nothing deter them from doing what they loved, and they followed their dreams. They were fighters and were willing to withstand a lot of negativity within the business. And a lot of these women are still singing their hits and coming up with new material. With each negative situation they may have encountered, they learned from it and they kept it moving forward — and I think that's the part that's very inspirational and encouraging. They have amazing fortitude and a passion for their music. I think now that the hard part of their careers, making sure they were having hits and making money, is behind them, they can have fun now. They can enjoy it more now and embrace the basics of why they got into the business in the first place."

Ford: "Humility. Singers in general will never think of themselves as *great* singers, no matter who they are. I've found that they are always very critical of themselves, and they almost never listen to their own music. Each project they do — they kind of leave it behind when it's done and go onto the next. They don't look back too much and always seem to want to look onto the future, the next project."

Gianatos: "The women I am in contact or deal with today — they are beautiful people! The artists I have worked with, like Pattie Brooks, Scherrie Payne and Linda Clifford for example, are professional, come into the studio and do their thing and are just lovely people. They have been affected by some of the things that have happened to them, good and bad. They are survivors, and they continue on. They are real singers — they are not manufactured — and they can go out there live and kick ass. Most of them are troupers and are determined to continue on, have a presence, get their gigs — and I think they are all highly capable performers! I've never had anybody that I've worked with in the whole group represented in this book that I'd ever say, 'I never want to work with that person again.' Every encounter has been beautiful!"

Rose: "To all the first ladies of disco, I take my feathers off to you! I'll say this — if you're lucky enough to be able to roll with the years, it's really an honor to still be in demand. And these women are! We've had some amazing women open for [the Village People]! Loleatta Holloway, Gloria Gaynor, Karen Young, Linda Clifford, the girls from Chic, The Ritchie Family. And Grace Jones — she was for disco what Lady Gaga is today for dance music! It was so complementary for us! Madonna even opened for us with her first single, 'Everybody.' We saw her walk through the lobby, and she had this "I *am* somebody!' kind of look. One of my group members said, 'Oh, she won't last.' I said, 'I think this girl's here to stay!' If anyone studied Donna Summer, it was Madonna. She grew up listening to Donna.

"I would watch these women [who pioneered disco]. Before I went on stage, I wanted to see their craft. I wanted to see how they did it. I wanted to see what separated these women and what made them different. The thing I kept coming back to was just that they had their own different personalities and great styles. They just had ... *something*!"

Zager: "They were great singers! They could have sung anything. They would have been hit artists no matter what they sang. They were ... and *are* ... extremely gifted!"

Dancing in Heaven

Several female artists prominent in disco music have slipped away from us, but no profile of the women who pioneered the genre would be complete without remembering and acknowledging the incredible musical contributions of some of the greatest.

Laura Branigan (1957–2004) A native of New York, Laura began her career as a backing vocalist for Leonard Cohen. Atlantic Records mogul Ahmet Ertegun recognized Branigan's vocal prowess, which he felt made her a shoo-in for pop music success. An early single, "Looking Out for Number One," made a few ripples, but the release of "Gloria" in 1982 was a game-changer. It took forever to climb *Billboard*'s pop and dance charts, but once Laura's remarkably powerful vocals and the irresistible energy of the track (an Italian composition produced by Jack White, who would score hits with Audrey Landers) began getting radio play, the song caught on like wildfire. To follow was a string of dance crossover hits any artist would be proud to have on her resume—"Solitaire," "Self Control," "The Lucky One" and "Spanish Eddie" among them. Branigan became a worldwide sensation and added to her impressive catalogue with the club favorite, "Shattered Glass," a collaboration with Britain's iconic Hit Factory (the Stock-Aitken-Waterman production group that redefined dance music in the mid- and late '80s). The artist eventually moved away from the spotlight and spent much of the '90s managing the demands of a challenging marriage and caring for her husband (who had been diagnosed with cancer) until his death. Branigan began planning her comeback early in the 21st century. However, a twist of fate would result in Laura's sudden passing from a brain aneurysm on Long Island in the summer of 2004. Though her death was a tremendous blow to the dance music community, she left the world something to remember her by—stupendously updated and newly recorded versions of "Gloria" and "Self Control," and the remarkably inspiring Hi-NRG anthem of hope, "The Challenge" (released through Germany's Dance Street/ZYX Records).

> Troy Bronstein: *"Laura was a lot of fun, but she got led down the wrong trail a few times. A lot of people tried to keep her in a box and make her act and do things that weren't always her. She was a great singer though."*

Loleatta Holloway (1946–2011) To say this Chicago native had a magnificently powerful vocal ability would be the ultimate understatement. Trained from an early age in gospel music, she became one of the most euphoric, identifiable and compelling talents in the history of dance music. Though she had previously recorded with little attention, Loleatta's signing to Norman Harris' Gold Mind Records (through Salsoul Records) gave rise to her first major explosive hits in 1976—"Hit and Run," "Dreamin'" and "We're Getting Stronger" from the album *Loleatta*. She sang with the Salsoul Orchestra on "Runaway," another smash in '77. Hit after hit followed as the artist's remarkable voice and the disco genre gained in popularity. Legendary tracks like "I May Not Be There When You Need Me," "The Greatest Performance of My Life," and "That's What You Said" shook the walls of clubs nationwide. In 1980, under the production wizardry of Dan Hartman, the single "Love Sensation" became an enormous and enduring hit, which the singer is reported to have said was one of the hardest songs she ever sang. Loleatta's earth-shattering belting was also incorporated into Hartman's disco smash, "Relight My Fire." Holloway's iconic voice was sampled without proper crediting in a huge hit for Black Box called "Ride on Time," which made it necessary for the singer and her attorneys to take legal action. She was, however, legitimately featured on the Mark Wahlberg-Marky Mark and the Funky Bunch number 1 crossover concoction, "Good Vibrations," in 1991. Loleatta was a featured vocalist on several dance hits throughout the '90s. The artist continued touring and recording up until her sudden death from heart failure in 2011, and she is widely regarded by her fellow singers and fans alike as a truly unforgettable legend of the genre.

Claudja Barry: *"She would enter a room, and you could see the electricity. She had an electrifying personality to match."*

Troy Bronstein: *"A charmer and a voice we're really gonna miss. She was a powerhouse singer and very supportive of a lot of the other divas. A lot of them called her 'momma.' She watched out for a lot of people."*

Pamala Stanley: *"A person very much bigger than life!"*

Jeanie Tracy: *"Now there's a woman who could have told you stories!"*

Martha Wash: *"She was crazy, but she could sing her face off. I loved her!"*

Vicki Sue Robinson (1954–2000) Harlem, New York, was Vicki's birthplace, and she first began getting noticed when the singer joined the Broadway cast of *Hair* around 1970. While doing session work in a recording studio, her voice caught the attention of producer-engineer Warren Schatz, and their association led to 1976's "Turn the Beat Around," which became a disco triumph, a Top-10 pop hit and a Grammy-nominated smash. Vicki's über-upbeat performance of this track in live show, club and television appearances was exemplary of the singer's drive and relentless energy. Her subsequent releases through her long time association with Schatz and the RCA label, such as "Hold Tight" and "Daylight," failed to keep Robinson high on the pop charts. However, her status as a dance diva was highly regarded and lasted well into the '80s. Her albums, *Never Gonna Let You Go*, *Vicki Sue Robinson*, *Half and Half* and *Movin' On*, in addition to being popular club favorites, were always a listening pleasure that featured a mix of ballads, pop songs and danceable tunes. "Act of Mercy," "Let Him Go" and "Trust in Me" were fan favorites, among many more. Vicki returned to her *Hair* roots by participating in a discofied album version of the show that also featured Evelyn "Champagne" King. The performer's later hook-laden club fodder, "Hot Summer Night," "To Sir with Love," "Everlasting Love," "Summertime Fun" and "Nighttime Fantasy," were dance-club staples, and she could be heard among the background vocalists on such major pop hits as Irene Cara's smash, "Fame." That was also Vicki handling the backgrounds on her own "Turn the Beat Around," by the way, which RCA remixed and re-released in the early '90s. Singer Gloria Estefan brought the song back to the top of the charts with her version in 1994. One of the true originals, Robinson was performing and recording great dance music, including her last releases "House of Joy" and "Move On," until she succumbed to cancer at just 45 years of age.

Troy Bronstein: *"A ball of energy! Always a smile on her face!"*

Rochelle Fleming: *"A powerful, short little thing! We did a diva show for KISS–FM. She was a very spicy performer. She went on stage and she didn't quit! Very hyper, very upbeat—which fit right in with my personality. She was a wonderful, uplifting person."*

Gloria Gaynor: *"I loved her; she was an absolute sweetheart! I will never forget that Vicki had a very close friend of hers call me when she was in the hospital to ask me to pray for her. Her friend couldn't get to me until that night, and when I got the message, Vickie had already died. That was horrible. That was really horrible. I was so blessed and honored she would try to find me to pray for her—not that I hadn't been praying for her all along. So, I'm confident that she is in a better place. She was fun to be around—that was her! She was just very bubbly, very positive, very caring, a very strong person. Just loving and just the greatest girl!"*

Cynthia Manley: *"Vicki was very gracious about telling me about songwriting. She told me when she worked on 'Turn the Beat Around,' one of her neighbors or family members would say, 'Drop the beat!' and 'Pump the bass!' and things like that, and she would take all those phrases and built some of that into the song. Her inspiration came from her family and neighbors rehearsing with their bands."*

Tom Moulton: *"I never worked with Vicki Sue; I wished to hell I did. I always liked what she did. She was always full of energy and rarin' to go. And I liked people like that—the energy always comes across in the record."*

Pamala Stanley: *"Vicki and I just loved each other. She was crazy in a good way. A very warm woman and she was full of energy—she was a firecracker!"*

Martha Wash: *"She was sweet. We used to do jingles together sometimes. A really nice, fun, lovely lady."*

Carol Williams: *"Vicki was always full of energy and delightful to be with in a show. She would still be performing even backstage when there was downtime! She would be making up steps and practicing between the shows. I miss her!"*

Donna Summer (1948–2012) Quite simply — there will *never* be another Donna Summer.

Born LaDonna Adrian Gaines in Boston, the first stage of her music career began when she moved to Germany, after being cast to star in the musical *Hair*. Living there for several years, Donna went on to star in other musical productions and sang and recorded backing vocals and demos. While working on a backing session in Munich, she met producer-writer Giorgio Moroder and commenced with her stellar disco recording career. Her stage name was conceived during her marriage to Austrian actor Helmuth Sommer, with whom she had her first child, Mimi. They parted in 1976, and in 1980, Summer wed singer-songwriter Bruce Sudano (of the group Brooklyn Dreams, who were featured on her hit single, "Heaven Knows"). The couple had two daughters, Brooklyn and Amanda Grace, and remained married until Donna's passing.

A distinctive and beautiful entertainer, Summer became the disco genre's most widely recognized female superstar, crossing into the pop market with huge success. Her powerful, expressive, dynamic vocal style (combined with tremendous and undeniable star quality) made her unstoppable. Summer became synonymous with the disco era, yet managed to exceed everyone's expectations and endure decades beyond it. No other artist in disco and dance music received more media attention and a brighter spotlight than Donna—and no wonder. She was the first artist to have three consecutive double albums reach the number 1 position on the U.S. *Billboard* albums chart, and her hit songs, along with those of the Bee Gees (whose Robin Gibb passed May 20, 2012, just a few days after Summer), were credited with bringing disco fully into vogue by the late '70s—and making the intoxicating sound the unofficial pop music of the time. It started late in 1975 when "Love to Love You Baby," a wild, nearly 17-minute orgasm set to a dance beat, placed her firmly on the map.

The New York Times included in her obituary a comment she made to *Ebony* magazine in 1977 regarding the song and the impression it had left with the public. "I'm not just sex, sex, sex," she is reported to have said. "I would never want to be a one-dimensional person like that."

Summer indeed had far more to offer. With three multi-platinum albums, 11 gold albums, 12 gold singles, an NAACP Award, six American Music Awards and five Grammy Awards (and 18 nominations) in the pop, R&B, rock, dance and inspirational music categories, Donna Summer undeniably proved that she was multi-dimensional to the extreme. From the synthesizer masterpiece "I Feel Love," to the unexpected breakthrough triumph "MacArthur Park," to "Last Dance" (from the movie *Thank God It's Friday*, which earned songwriter Paul Jabara an Oscar for best song), Summer was unstoppable. Her groundbreaking association with producer Giorgio Moroder gave birth to the iconic number 1 track "Bad Girls" and a legendary double album by the same name on Casablanca Records in 1979, one of the era's best-sellers. "Bad Girls" was among the crossover classics that many of the vocalists interviewed for this book wished they'd been offered an opportunity to sing. Summer also earned a Grammy for best rock performance with the hybrid powerhouse "Hot Stuff" from the same LP. Later that year, the artist teamed up with Barbra Streisand (who got first billing) for the duet "No More Tears (Enough Is Enough)," which was penned by Bruce Roberts and Paul Jabara, a joint effort between Columbia Records and Casablanca. She moved on to other major labels, and her journey continued with the Quincy Jones–produced "Love Is in Control." Jones tweeted upon her death that Summer was "the heartbeat and soundtrack of a decade." Next up was the working-class women's anthem, "She Works Hard for the Money." In 1989, she collaborated with the celebrated U.K. production team of Stock-Aitken-Waterman for the comeback classic, "This Time I Know It's for Real" (her last single to make the U.S. pop Top 10). In its online obituary, the BBC quoted the song's co-producer, Pete Waterman, as saying, "She was the icing on the cake. We were at the top of our game when we worked with her. She was just fantastic." Summer's fame was an international phenomenon, and her works were widely regarded as mas-

Donna Summer managed to surpass the expectations of everyone in the music industry and, though eternally identified with disco, transcended the genre (photograph by Mark Lidell/Epic Records, author's collection).

terpieces of dance music that managed to please music fans of all tastes and in all corners of the globe. Inevitably, Donna was viewed as the "Queen of Disco" in the eyes of millions (though she had verbally deferred the title to Gloria Gaynor), but she was ultimately truly a pop phenomenon. Among her enormous fan base was a substantial following in the gay community, which had supported her music from the start.

Donna was not always comfortable with her status or fame and was not immune to controversy. The artist, who became a devout Christian during the '80s, received quite a bit of negative publicity for allegedly making an anti-gay remark in the early days of the AIDS crisis. She reportedly denied the accusations and later made efforts to ameliorate the situation, which she described as a misunderstanding. Summer was seen center stage at AIDS benefits in the years that followed. Co-authored with Marc Eliot, Summer's memoir, *Ordinary Girl: The Journey* (Villard), was published in 2003 and is said to have made scant reference to any such difficulties. However, over the long haul, the gay community still largely kept the diva close to their hearts, and Donna's eminence in dance music and general commercial appeal prevailed well into the 21st century, though she was a good deal less in the spotlight. Her 2008 studio album *Crayons* (which had been eagerly anticipated for nearly 17 years) managed to crack the American pop Top 20 and generated further number 1 dance hits like "Stamp Your Feet," "I'm a Fire" and "Fame (The Game)." She released "To Paris with Love" in 2010, which once again returned her to the top of the dance chart. In past years, she received nominations for induction into the Rock & Roll Hall of Fame and was finally inducted in 2013.

The New York Times, in its online obituary for Ms. Summer (written by Jon Pareles), quoted the artist's comments made in 2003. "The music will always be with us. I mean, whether they call it disco music or hip-hop or be-bop or flip-flop, whatever they're going to call it, I think music to dance to will always be with us," said Donna. The BBC's website quoted a 2009 *Windy City Times* interview with Summer in which she said, "I am still working and there are fields that I haven't conquered yet. I won't stop until someone says, 'It's over.'"

Donna Summer died in Florida on May 17, 2012, at age 63 after a reportedly long battle with cancer, a condition she kept largely private. She was buried in Nashville, Tennessee.

Claudja Barry: *"I don't think that we really give enough props, as they say, to Donna. Her contribution was immeasurable. Without Donna Summer, there wouldn't be a Madonna, a Lady Gaga, or a lot of the danceable music that's out there right now. I met her early on in the late '70s in Europe, and I was totally amazed by her accomplishments. She really was a great role model for a lot of people coming up, and the fact that she had that courageous 'I'm gonna make it!' quality gave everybody—well, it certainly gave me—the thought that we are viable artists and we should be respected as people with talent. With Donna, we all were making an important contribution to an industry that was just being born."*

Linda Clifford: *"I have to say that the losses we the world suffered with the passing of Etta James and then Whitney Houston were so difficult to deal with—both of them being incredibly loved by so many of us and so talented. But I must say that hearing the news about the loss of Donna simply took my breath away. I did a few TV shows with Donna—The Midnight Special, The Billboard Awards, etc., but we never got to be close friends. I wish we had been. I will miss her presence on the planet, but, like everyone else, I will dance when I hear that voice."*

Hazell Dean: *"I loved Donna's music. Like Gloria Gaynor, she was one of the artists who summed up the 1970s. She was working with fantastic producers. Magic happens when a great* voice, a great song and great producers come together. I loved her Stock-Aitken-Waterman tracks, too! In fact, the only song I have ever been jealous of was 'This Time I Know It's for Real.' And here's something not a lot of people know — I did the backing vocals on all of the pre-recorded backing tracks used for An Audience with Donna Summer for ITV, working with Clive Scott and Ian Levine."

Dodie Draher: *"The Ritchie Family would like to pay tribute to this lovely lady who made such a huge impact on the disco era and music in general. Although we shared the same record label, we never had the pleasure of working together, but our paths would cross from time to time. She seemed to be very grounded and extremely warm. She left a void that will never be filled. Thank you for your contribution and inspiration. Rest in peace, Miss Donna Summer."*

Evelyn "Champagne" King: *"This was such a loss. Donna Summer was truly a loving soul. I recall meeting her once. It was at the top of both our careers doing a television show, though I can't recall which one, as we were always on the go. She made me feel like we had known each other forever. I just know that she will truly be missed. Her songs and personality were delightful. So, I will say to the 'Queen of Disco' Ms. Summer, we will keep on dancing and singing to your music. Thank you, Donna!"*

Audrey Landers: *"I was so saddened by the news of Donna Summer's passing. She had a spectacular voice and presence. Her music defined an era, yet she inspired artists across all genres. She will be missed."*

Scherrie Payne: *"I couldn't believe that another music legend had passed on so young! Although I know her soul is soaring right now, it's the ones left behind who mourn. I always admired her beauty and respected her talent. She was a great singer and performer."*

Felipe Rose: *"I felt the music industry did not give her the proper respect [upon her death] that they gave Whitney Houston. I don't get it! Her passing was literally like a punch in the stomach. She was always very nice to [the Village People]. I always thought she was beautiful! She walked so gracefully, her voice — there was nothing quite like it. She knew what to give her audience and fans. She had her finger on the pulse. Whether she did rock songs, disco or world music like 'Unconditional Love,' she was always able to blend so many styles. She was able to stay relevant. To this day, I still play her music. On my radio show, we created the Summer on Summer Tribute Mix. We did this special where we asked guest DJs to do mixes of her music with the music of today, like Rihanna, Katy Perry and Chris Brown. I'll tell you — Donna's music mixed so well with the other artists it sounded like it just came out today! Her music will stand the test of time!"*

Martha Wash: *"It was a shock [to hear the news of her passing]. She was still very young. I just met her briefly when she was recording with Paul Jabara, I believe, and we went over to the studio to meet her. I had always respected her work. She was a great singer. I remember when 'Love to Love You Baby' first came out, and they were playing it on the radio. There was this new, unknown artist and 'Love to Love You Baby' was the song and being played nonstop. There was so much controversy because of the way she was singing the song. There was a rumor that she was actually making love at the same time she was recording that song. I thought to myself, 'Hmmm, that would be a little bit hard.' I don't think that was the case, but I knew the Christians weren't too pleased with it. Nobody had done anything like that before. However, it catapulted her to stardom. She seemed like a very nice woman and was certainly very nice to me!"*

Viola Wills (1939–2009) Hailing from Los Angeles, Wills was the protégé of singer Barry White. She first gained the attention of disco fans in 1979 with her smash single "Gonna Get Along Without You Now," released on the Sugarhill label ("Rapper's Delight") in the U.S. In 1980, Wills released arguably one of disco's all-time greatest albums on Ariola

Records, *If You Could Read My Mind*, the title track from which became an enormous club hit and garnered the singer a tremendous gay and international following. Other tracks on the album, including "Secret Love," "Always Something There to Remind Me" and "Up on the Roof" cemented her reputation as a reliable, distinctively voiced dance music diva. Her stellar Hi-NRG remake of "Stormy Weather" in 1982 caused a sensation on the dance floor and gave her yet another signature hit. Viola recorded more hits in England ("Dare to Dream," "Both Sides Now" and "These Things Happen" among them). In the mid–'80s she became known as Viola Wills Ashmun, following her second marriage, and scored club hits with "If These Walls Could Speak," "Space" and "When Will It Be My Turn." She continued recording dance music well into the '90s. Though the artist never attained a crossover hit in the U.S., this kind and versatile performer's legion of fans remained extremely loyal following her death from cancer in 2009, and her music still causes a tremendous stampede to the dance floor.

> Troy Bronstein: *"I managed Viola for a little while. She used to call me 'Troyski!' She was another sweetheart. She was too easy sometimes and let people walk over her. A lot of years went by before she was able to say 'no,' and sometimes she still couldn't say it. She stayed with me for a time when she was [experiencing financial difficulty], and I helped get her back on her feet again. She knew her If You Could Read My Mind album was an iconic record, but she was another one who was a victim of the system and she got ripped off royally. But she was always very excited to perform, always wanted to make people happy and changed her style to accommodate people's needs and wants. She would do shows and then party with the people. The club would be closing, and she'd still be on that dance floor!"*
>
> Pamala Stanley: *"She was so sweet. She was very good on stage, but she was a softer type of person. She was very motherly, and by that I mean one of those nurturing types of women."*

Karen Young (1951–1991) From humble beginnings in Philadelphia, Pennsylvania, Young started off singing TV and radio commercial jingles and providing backing vocals for various production companies in the city. Her work led to a longtime association with producer Walter Kahn and a song that would catapult her to the top of the 1978 disco chart: "Hot Shot." A worldwide percolating disco monster, the song became a classic of the era. While the singer didn't possess the sexy image of some of her fellow performers, she had a powerful voice that was well-suited to the energized material found on tracks like "Bring On the Boys" and the *Hot Shot* album. The club hit "Deetour," on Atlantic Records, written by Alice Cohen and "produced and directed" by Kahn, was a brilliant, unexpectedly mind-boggling and hypnotic journey into spacey trance music (sleaze-disco as it was sometimes called at the time) that lingered high on the dance charts for months in the summer of 1981. Although subsequent releases like "Dynamite," "No U-Turn/Expressway to Your Heart," "You Don't Know What You Got" and "Come-A-Runnin'" kept the singer on rotation on the disco scene for some time during the '80s, she was unable to duplicate her "Hot Shot" crossover success. Young eventually became ill and passed on from the complications of a bleeding ulcer just shy of her 40th birthday. Remixes of "Hot Shot" would continue to sizzle on DJ's turntables long after her death, and the previously unreleased track, "Rendezvous with Me" (originally recorded as a follow-up to "Hot Shot"), was remastered and widely played on the club circuit in 2009.

> Gloria Gaynor: *"I met Karen Young on the Regis Philbin Show years and years ago. She was a very sweet, kind and very unassuming person. And a dynamo as far as performing was concerned—she was a great performer."*

In Memoriam

Izora Armstead (1942–2004) — Two Tons of Fun, Weather Girls: "I Got the Feeling," "I Depend on You," "It's Raining Men"
Jo-Carol (Davidson) (1956–2003) — Modern Rocketry: "Born to Be Wild/Into the Future," "Earthquake"
Eria Fachin (1960–1996) — "Savin' Myself," "Eria's Aria/I Hear a Symphony"
Gwen Guthrie (1950–1999) — "Padlock," "Ain't Nuthin' Goin' On But the Rent"
Phyllis Hyman (1945–1995) — "You Know How to Love Me," "Tonight You and Me," "Riding the Tiger"
Lillian Lopez (1936–2012) — Odyssey: "Native New Yorker," "Use It Up, Wear It Out"
Teena Marie (1956–2010) — "Behind the Groove," "I Need Your Lovin'," "Square Biz"
Phyllis Nelson (1950–1988) — "I Like You," "Don't Stop the Train," "Somewhere in the City"
Esther Phillips (1935–1984) — "What a Difference a Day Made," "Turn Me Out"
June Pointer (1954–2006) — The Pointer Sisters: "Jump," "I'm So Excited," "Neutron Dance," "Dare Me," "Goldmine"
Sharon Redd (1945–1992) — "Can You Handle It," "Beat the Street," "In the Name of Love"
Tasha Thomas (1950–1983) — "Shoot Me with Your Love," "You Put the Music in Me"
Brandi Wells (1955–2003) — "Watch Out," "What Goes Around Comes Around"
Belita Woods (1948–2012) — Brainstorm: "Lovin' Is Really My Game"
Syreeta Wright (1946–2004) — "Love Fire," "Quick Slick," "If the Shoe Fits"

The First Ladies of Disco

The Andrea True Connection

There were a number of strong, visionary women who saw an opportunity in the '70s to advance the freedoms and rights of the so-called weaker sex. Gloria Steinem, Bella Abzug, Billy Jean King, Shirley Chisholm and many others made tremendous strides to mobilize the power of women in business, sports, education and politics. They rallied supporters in huge numbers to fight sexism, symbolically burned bras in a quest for women's liberation, and demanded a closing of the gap between the sexes in their courageous struggle to pass the Equal Rights Amendment. There was another woman who briefly received attention during this era and who took a rather unusual path in entertainment to make a personal statement about living life on one's own terms. Andrea True, who sang disco music while simultaneously appearing in porn flicks, had one of the most intriguing and least-documented stories of the women's movement (a rally that ironically ran somewhat parallel to the ascent of disco). Her rise from humble Tennessee beginnings to adult show-business notoriety, to unexpected pop and dance-floor stardom and then right back to obscurity in many ways mirrored some aspects of the rollercoaster ride of the feminist movement. Andrea's brush with fame was generally and unfairly (not to mention inaccurately) relegated to "one-hit wonder" status in popular culture by the time her career began to wane in 1980. The details of her life have previously been sparsely documented, and recollections from those elusive few who knew her personally have only begun to surface following her death late in 2011.

Born Andrea Marie Truden on July 26, 1943, in Nashville, Tennessee, she was the only child of Frank, an engineer, and Ann Truden. Family friends who recall her Catholic all-girls high-school days at St. Cecilia Academy, an institution dedicated to the performing arts, described her as a talented piano player with the look of a cold, black-haired beauty. It's alleged her favorite color was burgundy. She appeared in many school musical productions, according to a biography released by Talent Consultants International, Ltd. (TCI), in the '90s, and, at age 15, Andrea reportedly produced and hosted her own program, *Teen Beat*, for WTVF–TV (the same station which had launched Dolly Parton). Upon graduating with a music degree from George Peabody College at Nashville's Vanderbilt University, Andrea migrated to New York City to pursue a career in show business.

The details of Andrea's early days in the city have largely remained a mystery. However, it's been fairly well established that she held a variety of jobs in the Big Apple while struggling to get a singing and acting career simultaneously off the ground. Don Kirshner would later introduce her on his *Rock Concert* TV show by saying she had a background in clothing design, modeling and "appearing in movies." Sandy Galetovic met and befriended Andrea True in the '90s. Galetovic says it was True's primary ambition to be a successful singer. "She was proud of her vocal ability. The acting was almost accidental—out of financial need," Sandy claims. True landed a few extremely small, uncredited parts in major theatrical films such as Barbra Streisand's *The Way We Were* (1973) and Liv Ullman's *40 Carats* (1973) and, musically, she may have worked in some capacity with composer Gershon Kingsley ("Popcorn"). She was rumored to have had singing engagements in the famed Empire State Building's Riverboat venue, where TCI reported she received rave reviews and was held over for four weeks. True is also said to have dabbled in writing radio commercials. But the big fame and stardom she sought remained out of her grasp. *The New York Times*, in its obituary for the singer, quoted another friend of Andrea who described her as a free spirit, but one with drive who never stopped wanting to make it.

Andrea True publicity picture, circa 1977, **signed by the artist when her second Top 40 hit, "N.Y., You Got Me Dancing,"** began stirring the masses (author's collection).

Some speculators have suggested it was the result of an emotional reaction to a recent romantic breakup, and others claim it may have been Andrea's attempt to obtain more acting and movie experience. Still a few more theorists have conjectured it was a decision based upon financial need. Whatever her reasons may have been, somehow True ended up in pornographic films. "I had nothing better to do," said Andrea to the *Los Angeles Times* in 1976 (as quoted by *Newsday* in the artist's 2011 obituary). "I had been turned down by an agent for a record deal, and I was tired of working as an extra in pictures." Any would-be entertainer struggling to make it during this era in a tough, economically challenged city like New York may have seen the rising porn industry as a quick avenue to much needed cash and a boost in ... exposure. Andrea is said to have performed in over 40 such films and used a variety of names, including the Swedish-flavored Inger Kissen, Catherine Warren, the eclectic Singe Low and Andrea Travis. Eventually she settled on Andrea True, the not-too-far-off adaptation of her real name, allegedly changed to spare her parents embarrassment. "For one thing, how do you go home and say, 'Mom, I'm in porno movies?'" True told *The Los Angeles Times*.

Under the circumstances, Andrea's relationship with her family may not have been easily navigated. According to Galetovic, Andrea rarely mentioned her parents and would quickly change the subject whenever it came up. Regardless, True quickly managed to become a conspicuous and highly recognizable figure in the city's burgeoning adult-film business and is alleged to have attempted to unionize the industry's stars. Andrea's name was spelled out in large plastic letters on the flashing marquees of New York's X-rated theaters in a town governed by Abraham Beam — the same porn palaces that would be eradicated in just a few decades by Mayor Rudy Guiliani. She was experienced-looking, sexy, uninhibited and she appeared genuine — an undeniable underground box-office draw in this emerging market.

Critically said to be one of her best porn performances, Andrea's role as the title character in *The Seduction of Lyn Carter* (1974) found her portraying a cheating housewife who is strangely attracted to an abusive man that she meets in a doctor's office. The adult films of this time often attempted to bridge legitimate storytelling with sex, giving rise to a period of "porn chic." Directed by Anthony Spinelli, the film nearly plays out as a legitimate drama, with surprisingly long dialogue scenes aimed at capturing the sexual and emotional complications of a modern marriage. Had the film not crossed the line by including hardcore sex scenes, one might easily see Andrea's participation as a solid and successful attempt to hone her acting chops with mainstream potential. However, with other movies bearing titles like *Sweet Wet Lips, Illusions of a Lady, Mash'd* and *Little Orphan Sammy* on her resume, Andrea was still decidedly *anything* but mainstream. For better or worse, Andrea's early porn career was the bridge to her crossover success.

In a 2002 VH1 special promoting the *100 Greatest Dance Songs of All-Time,* hosted by Paula Abdul, Andrea True's disco hallmark, "More, More, More," pulled in at number 45. Not bad for a song which was, at the time, over 20 years old. In the program, Andrea was briefly interviewed and described the song's origins. Dismayed by the Jamaican election of a politician who was reportedly a Castro sympathizer, the United States imposed sanctions on the island in 1975. The Jamaican government's counter-imposition of a ban on asset transfers prevented True from taking her earnings from a television commercial she'd filmed there out of the country. With plenty of cash to spend, Andrea got the idea of turning her paycheck into a song demo, the tapes for which she could take with her. She would effectively launder her money.

Andrea's personal connection to lanky, punkish-looking producer-songwriter-pianist-drummer (and former member of the bands Jobriath and the Creatures) Gregg Diamond (1949–1999) may have evolved from hiring him as a drummer on a failed attempt at an earlier recording. It appears she knew him well enough to ask for his help with her scheme. It's widely believed that Diamond arrived in Jamaica a short time later with a quickly written musical composition in hand. I was able to obtain (thanks to Karim of France's Reggae Museum) an original 7" vinyl pressing of the raw, unmixed "More, More, More" track made by Jamaica's Federal Records, which appears to have been released on the island by Gregg Diamond in 1975, well before remixer Tom Moulton reworked it for its U.S. release. The artist was listed simply as Andrea True and the record indicated it was written, "produced, arranged and directed" by Diamond (release # GD461). The recording had a lean tone and a rather hollow, airy sound that almost gave the impression of musical instruments being played in the back of a big room with the piano and bass largely taking center stage. The opening seconds of the rhythm track in this version evoked shades of Queen's "Another One Bites the Dust." The 3-minute 26-second demo wasn't quite as lush and heavy as the Buddah Records-Moulton mix yet to come, but all the elements of the hit version were intact in a simpler form. True's vocals were a bit muted and given the echo-chamber treatment — but what vocals they were. Breathy, whispering, seductive, ever-so-slightly off key in the cooing segments, they were a remarkably perfect fit for the material. In her VH1 interview, Andrea cringed when discussing her performance, saying she believed the recording was only to be a scratch version and was horrified to learn there'd be no retakes.

Instantly catchy and easily remembered, the song's lyrics seem to unapologetically play up True's porn movie career with references to rolling cameras and some ensuing action. Oddly, the singer seemed to have dismissed any not-so-hidden meaning in the song. "It gets repeated and repeated and repeated. It means nothing," she said, referencing the song's title and lyrics in her interview for the 2005 film documentary *Inside Deep Throat*. Galetovic concurs. "She did discuss the song lyrics with me. It was not meant to be a direct reference to her film work or that industry. It was just something that came out of her mind at the time. She just wanted to hear simple words. [Andrea said] it was kind of a last-minute decision, and she sat there and wrote it quickly. She *was* the lyric writer, and I definitely recall her telling me she wrote it while in the studio in Jamaica." In a 1976 *Rolling Stone* article about True, the singer was reported to have shown staffers explicit photos, citing them as

The risqué French 7-inch single jacket for "More, More, More" makes no apologies for and does little to hide Andrea True's sexier side (author's collection).

examples of her previous career, but assuring them her new song would be a hit independent of her background. In music mixer Tom Moulton's brief experience with the singer, he says he never heard that Andrea wrote any of the lyrics, and he believes that the song's content was less than innocent.

Moulton was already a respected, sought-after music remixer by the time he crossed paths with The Andrea True Connection. He'd worked his magic on Gloria Gaynor's Top 10 "Never Can Say Goodbye" and the Trammps' classics "Disco Inferno" and "Hold Back the Night," among others. He vividly recalls his involvement with "More, More, More." "I was doing a lot of mixing for Buddah Records at the time," he says. "I had gotten 'More, More, More' from [Buddah Records' founder] Art Kass, but I had also heard about it from Jerry Greenberg at Atlantic and somebody at Epic. I told them all the same thing—that Art should be the one to handle it because he's the one who actually sent it to me. I thought the record had something. I liked that sort of hokey Herb Alpert-ish trumpet solo. I thought it was kind of corny enough to really work. Andrea wasn't shopping [the song] around; it was Gregg Diamond doing that. Buddah said they would take it if I mixed the record, but Gregg said, 'No way!' He didn't want anyone to touch it. I said, 'Fine!' I was working all the time, so it really didn't mean anything to me if I didn't mix it. All the labels had said the same thing—they would take it if I would mix it. Well, Gregg must have gone around the block several times and finally got back to Art and said, 'Okay, Tom can mix it, but I have to be there.' I said, 'That's fine as long as he keeps his mouth shut. He can be there. I don't care.' We already [heard] *his* version, and nobody seemed to want *that!* So anyway, we agreed to do it. He had to have a limo to drive him to my studio. I thought he was kind of whacked out—seemed like he was high as a kite. I never saw him doing anything, but he appeared like someone on something. He was sleeping when he arrived. The driver asked if he should wake him up, and I said, 'Hell no! Just drive him around and come back in three or four hours!'"

Tom observes, among other aspects of the track, that it may have been Diamond's intention to have an instrumental version of "More, More, More" as the A-side and the vocal version on the flip. "Anyway, I'm working on [the cut]," Moulton remembers. "It was an eight-track tape bounced up to 16. I was trying to make something out of it. I actually thought [the song was] about the music. That's why I made it so pretty sounding. If I had known what they were *really* talking about, I wouldn't have done the record. Not that I'm saying I'm 'church people,' but I don't like profanity in a record. I just don't care for it. I'm not being prudish or Victorian about it; it's just the way I feel. If you have to [make references to explicit words or subjects], you need to get a lyricist. [The original song recording] was crude. When I say crude, I mean there were a lot of horn mistakes, and it was sloppy. It was like a demo that people kept adding things to. The basic thing about it was it was very *rough*. In other words, you'd have heard the tape and you would have said, 'Okay, that's good, now let's record it for real.' But there's always something about a hook that gets me—that's why they call them hooks. And I liked it. I had heard it and I liked it, and I thought I could do something with it. Andrea wasn't singing much on it. I had to double her vocals and add a lot of reverb on it just to make it, you know, very sweet and dreamy. I really wanted it to be sweet-sounding because I wanted it to be about the music. It took me about six hours to finish it." Moulton confirms the extended dance version was developed first, followed by the edited-down 7" single version.

Moulton recalls, "I never did wake up Diamond. When he came to, I just said it came out good. I went to Buddah Records. Everybody was there, and they listened to it and they applauded. I was really taken aback by that. That's when I first met Andrea True. I said to her, 'Just out of curiosity, I wanted to take a couple of phrases out of the song, and I realized that's the only verse in the song.' She asked me which phrase, and I described the one about the cameras rolling. I'm thinking it means she's being videotaped while dancing to this song. I had no idea who she was. I said it didn't make any sense. 'Well, do you know what I do?' she asked. I said, 'Well, obviously you're a singer.' She proceeded to graphically tell me what acts she performed in X-rated movies! I was gasping, thinking, 'Oh my God, what's my mother gonna think?' I just wasn't brought up that way and, you know, naughty girls are naughty girls," he laughs. "There are plenty of good girls out there, so why do we have to deal with the naughty ones? I have to say, I do think it's funny now. But she was actually very nice. I still have the original tape, and I listen to it sometimes to remind myself ... hmmmm, *that's* what I had to work with! It's in a pile with a lot of other great things." Moulton remembers with a laugh that True declared, "If any stations won't play it, I'll personally deliver a copy of the record to them!" He thought to himself, "I'll bet you will!"

The Andrea True Connection was about to be made. "More, More, More," was initially released in late 1975 exclusively to DJs, clubs and radio stations as a non-commercial vinyl 12" single and was one of the first tracks to be promoted in this format (often credited as the brainchild of Moulton). Today, original copies of this single command hundreds of dollars on eBay. True, just as she'd promised, was reported to have literally walked her discs all over town, visiting venues, DJs and publications like *Rolling Stone* in person to get the word out about the song's release. Clubs were the first to recognize the track as an infectious dance-floor draw, and radio airplay and record-buyers quickly followed suit by the spring of 1976. A quickie pre–MTV promotional video was made of the singer performing the song in a club setting that could be used by television shows when Andrea could not appear live, such as on the U.K.'s important *Top of the Pops* program. Wearing a white suede fringe jacket and hot pants, she stiffly, yet lazily, bopped back and forth as she stared hypnotically into the camera. Andrea seemed to have rather minimal physical flexibility for life under multicolored strobe lights and a disco ball. The artist was said to have had difficulty getting her groove on as far as dancing and moving about on stage were concerned.

The single debuted on *Billboard*'s pop chart early in 1976, and by the beginning of summer, it was a certified smash. "More, More, More" was on steady rotation at nearly every pop station nationwide and, in its six-minute extended version, was well on its way to establishing itself at the clubs as a certified classic. The song peaked at number 4 on *Billboard*'s pop singles chart, number 2 on the disco chart and earned the artist considerable media attention. *Rolling Stone* would later call the record "one of the iconic songs of the disco era." Says Sandy Galetovic, "To Andrea, it was a dream come true. It was the highlight of her life. She said not only did it make her happy, but she was thrilled that it made others happy. She told me what made her the most happy was seeing how many people danced to it. Making so many people happy was like having a power, and she said it was amazing!"

Tom Moulton asserts, "All I know is, I mixed that original record for all the right reasons. I thought the song was very hokey, but there was something about that song that really got to me. I hate to tell you how many people tell me that the song was so important in their lives. You know what my response is? 'You know, I've done other songs?'" he laughs. "'More, More, More' didn't open up any significant new doors for me; the doors were already open.

"My fee back then was $500 a track and a point on the record," Moulton adds. "One point is 1 percent of the record. In other words, I had all the safety nets in place. So, because

Andrea True (center) with her original Connection, a mix of musicians and disco dancers, circa 1976 — note future Kiss guitarist Bruce Kulick at the top (author's collection).

someone offered me better money, I wouldn't do a 'better' mix. I charged everyone the same price so I could be in reach of everybody, and if I didn't care for something, I could say I'm not interested. 'More, More, More,' 'Disco Inferno' and a number of other songs were lucrative for me — absolutely. I never saw Andrea again after [the song premiere meeting at Buddah Records]. I spoke to her on the phone when it charted on the R&B side, which I knew would happen because I made sure that soulful part was there. If there's any soul in a record, I'll find it! She was very grateful."

The song was a huge hit internationally, climbing the U.K. charts to number 5 and scoring Top-10 positions throughout Europe and South America. True appears to have re-recorded her vocals for a Spanish language mix called "Mas, Mas Mas," which blended the original instrumental track and parts of the original vocals with less refined portions re-sung in Spanish. The Latin market single jacket bizarrely featured a picture of True wearing her signature fringe outfit while feeding a small farm animal. According to TCI, from June 1976 to June 1977 Andrea, along with a band and troupe of dancers hired to accompany her (the first Connection), performed over 300 concerts for crowds in the U.S., Mexico, Canada and Europe. She was reported to have performed at the prestigious Venice Music Festival along with Twiggy and Rod Stewart. In her live performances and on record, Andrea seemed set on striking a personal relationship with her audience. "My personality has always been connected to my audiences. Our intercommunication has been, and always shall be, the life-force of my success," True said.

With a *Billboard* ad heralding "More, More, More" as number 1 at a slew of radio stations ("with more hits coming"), Buddah Records quickly went to work on getting an album into production in New York. Gregg Diamond composed and produced all the tracks, which were largely long instrumental concoctions. Andrea was dressed in a decidedly conservative, non-revealing pair of outfits for the record jacket photos (it was said to have been Andrea's idea to distance herself from her porn career), and the album shows evidence of being rushed. Some manufacturing runs featured inaccurate track listings and included an apologetic note (indicating the correct sequence). The album's cuts, though often melodic and beautifully rendered, were not as immediately hook-laden as "More, More, More." Neither were they quite as suggestive (though double-entendre titles like "Keep It Up Longer" kept a sexual theme going).

Tom Moulton confirms the album "was another problem! When ["More, More, More"] started going up the charts, I went to Art Kass and said he really ought to consider an album. He said Gregg was working on one, and I said that was great. I asked if I could hear it and was told that Gregg didn't want me to hear it. I asked how I was supposed to mix it without hearing it and was told [Diamond], again, didn't want me to mix it. I said, 'Oh, no problem!' I didn't care. If someone didn't want me to do something, there were plenty of other people that did! Andrea's song had gone to number 1, and it started dropping. Art called me on a Friday and said, 'Tom, we gave Gregg another $100,000 to finish the album, but he's just not all there. He just wasn't himself. Tom, we really need help! The album is *terrible*.' I said, 'What do you want me to do? I tried to get involved with it, but [Gregg] said he didn't want me.' Art said Diamond *still* didn't want me, but that they couldn't put it out that way. He asked me to save it. I said, 'Oh God, well can I *hear* what you want me to save?' When I heard it, I thought, 'Oh my Lord!' I just didn't know what to do. I kind of liked the songs, but I couldn't tell what was going on. It was a mess. It didn't sound like it was mixed. I tried to make sense out of it, but, mind you, I only had a weekend to do it. Buddah needed it by Monday or they would miss this whole production run thing, and you don't want to lose the sales on an album when a record is number 1. You want to have an LP out there for it."

Moulton expresses his frustration about handling the album tracks. "I loved 'Party Line' and 'Heart to Heart,'" he recalls, "but I really didn't *know* the songs. That's the thing that really aggravated me so much. I needed time to learn the songs. I really loved Art Kass. He was a great record man, and I would have done anything for him. He gave me a lot of good opportunities to mix any records he had that I wanted to work on, and I enjoyed it. And that's why any time he needed help, I was always there for him. But I didn't have any time to get into the songs like 'Heart to Heart.' I would have loved to have gotten into a nice breakdown on that one, but I had to do all these tracks over the weekend and it was so stressful. I didn't want to let Art down, and I really did it for him. I think the reason Andrea didn't have any other big hits off the album was because I didn't have the option to do it right."

Late in the summer of '76, "Party Line," with True sounding more boisterous than breathy, was released as a single and marketed to clubs and radio. Andrea performed "Party Line" and other cuts from the LP on prominent music shows like *Rock Concert* (with future Kiss guitarist Bruce Kulick in her band) as she smiled enthusiastically and gave it her all. Still, she nervously tugged at microphone cords and carefully watched her footing on a confetti-covered floor. While the song fared well in the clubs, the single received a cool reception at radio and with record-buyers, climbing only to the lower regions of the *Billboard* pop chart. The triple-play of the tracks "Party Line/Fill Me Up/Call Me" was a Top-10 club hit, but the album material went largely ignored by the mainstream. The LP was, at best, a modest success, achieving its highest ranking at number 47 on the *Billboard* pop albums chart. In a relatively short time, mired by the inability to further promote any singles, the album was soon featured in record retailers cut-out bins for $2.99.

Despite her newfound success in a legitimate arena, Andrea appeared to have been perhaps cautiously hedging her bets by still appearing in a few porno films while her music career was taking off. These films may have been released or re-released to capitalize on her sudden music fame. Movie posters for some of her X-rated projects boldly proclaimed their star as the singer of the hit "More, More, More." Yet in Andrea True's obituary released by the BBC News, they quoted True in *The Los Angeles Times* interview from 1976 as asserting, "I would be a waitress or a typist before I'd star in another." According to Galetovic, Andrea was not overly concerned about the impact of her adult film ventures on her singing career. "She said at the beginning she was, but after a while she just learned to overlook it and even embrace it. She felt that it gave her 'personality' and even made her story a little more interesting. She found that people were very accepting of her even though she herself wasn't always. She found out later that people didn't really care so much about it, so I think she just learned to accept it. I think where it caused some problems for her was in the dating area. I think deep down inside she wanted to get married and have children and was afraid no man would take her seriously with her background. She never did settle down with anyone or have children—not that she didn't want that, it just never went that way."

Her porn career would not be an influence on her next music release, which would instead focus on the disco scene that had launched her. The single "More, More, More" would be a tough act to follow, and something with a stronger hook than the previous album tracks would be needed to keep the momentum going for True's career as a mainstream star. "N.Y., You Got Me Dancing" was the ticket, a madly paced dance-music triumph again composed and produced by Gregg Diamond. It was a frantic, high-energy blend of keyboards, brass and bass and a celebration of the clubs and city which had made her a star. The single debuted on *Billboard*'s pop chart early in 1977, and its lyrics name-checked discothèques like Regine's, Barefoot Boy and 12 West. Andrea sang confidently and with energy, giving what may have been the best vocal performance of her career.

True sang "N.Y., You Got Me Dancing" everywhere: racetracks, sporting events, concert halls, discos and on television shows like *Disco '77*. Though it failed to quite mimic the success of "More, More, More" and was up against the competing sounds of emerging disco queen Donna Summer and a full onslaught of the genre's newest performers, the song was a decent pop hit peaking at number 27 and number 4 on *Billboard*'s club chart. The track was widely featured, along with her signature hit, on hugely popular commercial LP compilations like K-tel's *Disco Rocket* and Ronco's *Disco Fever*. But it would mark her final collaboration with Gregg Diamond, who went on to more club hits with his Bionic Boogie project, and signaled the beginning of preparations for her sophomore album.

Carlton J. Smith, today a successful international club singer and songwriter who charted in the U.K. under the name Napoleon Soul-O with the dance hit "Excite Me" in 1986, worked in the promotions department of Arista Records (which had picked up many of Buddah's artists for distribution) in 1977. It was the same time that *White Witch*, Andrea's next album, was being prepared for release. He recalls one of her visits to their offices, remembering her as a sharp-looking, well-dressed woman. "She clearly had an agenda," he says. "She appeared to feel that the male-dominated management of radio stations and such owed her airplay, since they had gotten plenty of enjoyment from her porn work." Galetovic does not recall Andrea relating any specific fears about avoiding the so-called "sophomore album jinx," but says, "She worried about her music. She put a lot of pressure on herself."

Positioning the *White Witch* album may have been a challenge for Buddah Records. Gregg Diamond was nowhere in sight, possibly because of Art Kass' reluctance to work with the problematic producer. Tom Moulton also wasn't asked to come on board the project. Tom says, "I had let a royalty check due me for the Trammps album slide because [Buddah Records and] Art were having some [financial] hard times. I wanted to see them go on. Art may have felt awkward about asking me to participate. I would have done it though. It would have been fun."

Up-and-coming production maestro Michael Zager took charge of The Andrea True Connection just before his own single, "Let's All Chant," became a disco sensation. "I became the producer of *White Witch* because of Art Kass," says Zager. "He asked us if we were interested in producing her. I knew 'More, More, More,' but I didn't really know anything about Andrea. We took the project because ['More'] was a great record. I thought we could get a really big hit. I didn't [initially] know Andrea was an adult film star. I didn't know anything about her other than her hit."

Ironically, it was not Zager's first time at the musical rodeo with a porn star. He had produced an orgasmic disco single called "Benihana" for Roulette Records, sung with sultry, frenzied abandon by Marilyn Chambers (1952–2009), the star of the landmark 1972 porn flick *Behind the Green Door*, around the same time as he had worked with True. Says Zager, "I also didn't know anything about Marilyn Chambers. Marilyn's 'Benihana' was an idea we took to 'Rocky' (Hiroaki) Aoki, who founded the Benihana restaurant chain. We went to him and said we had an idea that would promote his chain and that we wanted to record a dance track called 'Benihana,' which means 'little flower.' We wanted him to finance it, and if it became a hit, he'd get free publicity. I thought we should get a beautiful Japanese pop star to sing it and hopefully promote it into an album. Rocky said he had Marilyn

Chambers in mind for it, but I had no idea who she was. He said she was beautiful and could sing. So, he sent her up to our office, and she *was* stunningly beautiful! By then I had found out that she was an adult film star. She was wearing this wild outfit, and you could see right through her shirt and pants. And she had been walking down the street that way with her husband. It was unbelievable! She was absolutely breathtakingly beautiful — just gorgeous — and she was also a very nice girl. We brought in a sax player to play on the end of that record, and we turned the lights down in the studio for Marilyn to do that [orgasmic] part of the song. From what I remember, we told her to do all that moaning while he was playing — and [as a result] he could hardly play! It was really quite funny!" he laughs. "I didn't think [the song] would get airplay, but I thought it would get some club play. I think it did sell pretty well because of the clubs." Chamber's raunchy song managed to get the spotlight in David Cronenberg's mainstream horror-movie vehicle, *Rabid*, which the actress starred in, but it didn't have a prayer of getting on the radio. Zager wisely ignored that approach and the gimmick of Andrea's porn background when plotting a course for *White Witch*.

Michael recalls the early days of the production and working with Andrea. "Buddah and Art gave us no direction or requirements; they left it in our hands. I can't imagine anyone coming off a big hit like 'More, More, More' that isn't nervous about following it up, but Andrea never expressed that to me. We went over the songs for the album, and she agreed on the material. I never recorded anything that an artist didn't want to do. This was true with all the people I produced, because there is no way to get a good performance from an artist if they didn't like a song. She had no objections that I ever heard to recording disco music. It was the height of disco at the time, and she was very pleased with the final product," he says.

"At the beginning, when we went into Columbia Studios," Zager says, "I remember we were recording 'What's Your Name, What's Your Number?' and that she wasn't particularly nice to the engineer, a renowned gentleman named Tim Geelan. I had to come down on her and told her she had to treat everyone nicely or I wasn't going to have anything to do with the project. I honestly don't recall what was agitating her because he was a very calm guy. I couldn't figure out why her behavior was so erratic. She calmed down though and was very nice after that, and we had no more problems." According to Zager, the album took about four months to finish.

In January 1978, the track selected as the next big push for The Andrea True Connection was "What's Your Name, What's Your Number?" a song penned in part by Britain's Roger Cook (co-writer of the New Seekers' "I'd Like to Teach the World to Sing" and Carol Douglas' "Doctor's Orders") and Bobby Woods. A deliciously unapologetic pop-disco confection about spotting someone hot on the dance floor and getting hold of his or her phone number (that reflected the wonderful superficiality of club-going), it was nearly the perfect track for Andrea. True's vocals were in the forefront and strong, and she was now backed by male vocalists. "I thought 'What's Your Name, What's Your Number?' was a really good record, and she did a good job on it," Zager opines. "She wasn't the greatest singer, but she projected 'attitude' in her performances. She had that kind of — what's the word I'm looking for — almost blasé attitude in the way she approached music, and it came across as a hit vocal style. Even though she obviously didn't have Whitney Houston's vocal ability. She wasn't a Jocelyn Brown or a Martha Wash, but she could get the melody across without too much augmentation. By doubling her [voice], she could really sell a song. We had to record numerous takes and make what is called a composite track to get the best performance. We'd do punch-ins (re-recorded selected sections of a vocal performance). It wasn't overly difficult. It was kind of typical of working with a singer with her ability as opposed to someone like Jocelyn, where you get 10 great takes and just use what you want. Or like Cissy Houston ("Think It Over"), who I was producing at the time, which was, of course, also a very different experience."

Although True modestly dented the charts again with the single, it failed to perform well enough to reach the upper regions, peaking on *Billboard*'s pop chart at just number 56. "What's Your Name" was featured on a few mix segments of some TV dance shows like *Soap Factory Disco*, often with the track noticeably accelerated to mix with the faster beats of other bigger hits like Chic's "Dance, Dance, Dance." The *White Witch* album, with its striking cover painting by Ralph Wolfe Cowan of Andrea dressed almost as a Wonder Woman-type character, looked visually sophisticated sitting on record retailers' racks. (At the time this book was being prepared, the original life-size painting used for the cover was available on eBay for $700.) However, the promotional wheels for the project failed to turn as vigorously as they had in the days of "More, More, More."

Zager observes, "I know the song did fairly well, but it never achieved the success of 'More, More, More.' At the time I thought that it should have! If I recall, I believe Buddah Records was starting to go downhill and didn't have the promotional dollars to push it. Disco was very popular when it came out, and I suspect it didn't get the type of promotion that would have made it a hit. I think it should have been a Top-10 pop record! It did well outside of the U.S., but I thought it would be right up there with 'More.' I know the label was having financial problems, but I never knew the extent of it. I believe that's why nothing more came off that album."

Still, TCI claimed True toured extensively for the album, traveling to Canada, Hawaii, Australia, Italy, Mexico, England and Germany to enthusiastic reviews. Though the single cracked the Top 10 of the U.S. club chart, it would mark Andrea's final appearance on any other major music listing. "I didn't know if Andrea True would have a future after our album," admits Zager. "That kind of an artist has to continually have radio hits. I know she was still performing live because I knew her manager." Indeed, a recently secured document dated October 10, 1977, between Andrea and the Vincent Rottkamp Agency shows the artist arranging contractual tour performance payments through at least March 25, 1978.

There had been some rumors True would next release a new album under the guidance of Patrick Adams, who had garnered attention with Musique's crossover smash, "In the Bush," and Adams recently confirmed he did have a discussion with the singer. However, nothing came of it. Many biographies of the singer end her music career with *White Witch*, but True's recording continued, though in almost complete obscurity. *War Machine*, released in 1980, saw Andrea True drop the "Connection" and cut a deal with Italian label Riccordi for a project sparingly distributed in Italy (and possibly Austria). True's international success had been formidable, and the trip to Europe to produce this effort may have been rooted in a belief that her music career could be extended there, where audiences and record labels were far more loyal and nurturing. In their obituary for the artist, *The New York Times* quoted Andrea as saying, "Europeans will support and respect an artist for the lifetime. That just won't happen in America."

In *War Machine*, there's clear evidence of Andrea's desire to change things up, but one has to wonder—what she was thinking? Almost defiantly, not one of the tracks on this album can even remotely be classified as disco. Instead, True delivered a retro-rock, punk-flavored collection that completely smothered any connection the artist had to dance music. TCI described the album as a "classic," saying, "It is state of the art, energetic and forges together rock-and-roll at its best and most vibrant with contemporary sounds." Although Andrea actually seemed more enthusiastic and was vocally competent with '70s rock material, the album suffered from a somewhat dated sound, even for 1980. This radical departure from dance music must have been a confusing and alienating surprise both to those fans who managed to get hold of her scarce new album and the label, which, perhaps unknowingly, had sponsored what ended up sounding like an experimental vanity project (or one produced to distance Andrea from the perceived disco backlash in the U.S.). While only the term disco had really suffered in America and the genre was spinning off a rock-dance hybrid in new wave music, disco was still abundant and selling well in Europe. There, it morphed into the commercially viable italo disco, German dance and house-music booms that would begin in 1982. Any of these new sounds would have been ideal for True and an opportunity to ride out her branding as a flash in the pan in the U.S. Oddly, this fact was ignored by Andrea and her advisors.

"War Machine" was the first single off the album, a fiery, guitar-fused anti-war anthem written by True. It certainly had merit as a punkish shouter with its machine-gun-spatter underbeat. The song had a better engineered sound than any other track on the album and appeared to have been given the most attention. Its video featured True and her band looking almost like the Village People in various soldier and wartime costumes and was interspersed with clips of battle mayhem. But when the video and song went nowhere, the label released a second single, "Make My Music for Me," this time taking a new marketing approach and promoting True on the 45 rpm record sleeve as the "The Dance Queen of the U.S.A." and urging listeners to keep dancing. The cut relates True's struggle with churning out commercial music vs. the music *she* wants to make, an age-old dilemma for many recording artists. In its LP mix, the lightly catchy pop tune had a sing-song sound, but would hardly motivate feet to do anything more than toe-tap and thus the ploy failed. The album reached a dead end, despite TCI describing it as a hit with "top sales reinforcing her popularity."

It has been alleged that with her music career rapidly faltering, Andrea reconsidered returning more actively to porn. But approaching 40 years of age, Andrea was physically no longer what the adult movie industry was looking for, and her name as a disco singer was meaningless in that trade. The music business wasn't being any kinder. In the liner notes of a CD box set of Buddah Records greatest hits, True's singles were mentioned (with the "More" track described as "banal"), along with a cold, single-line update that stated: "She has not emerged in the public eye since." In her 1999 interview with Michael Paoletta for *Billboard*, True was quoted as saying she was relegated to touring throughout the '80s in a variety of other countries because of the fickleness of the American public and a record industry that did not support the careers of artists. However, True failed to mention the mysterious complications of throat surgery that reportedly made it difficult for her to continue singing, as mentioned in her *New York Times* obituary and often in other biographies of the artist. Galetovic does not recall Andrea ever speaking of any vocal problems in her exchanges with the artist. "Her voice always sounded well. The last time I spoke with her was around early 2011, and she sounded great. She never once mentioned to me that she ever had a problem singing. In fact, she'd occasionally just burst into song. She sounded perfect to me — pretty much *every* time I spoke to her."

The *Times* obituary also reported that True had "tried a variety of jobs, including counseling drug and alcohol abusers, telemarketing and real estate management," which Galetovic confirms. Ironically, True's co-star in several porn films, Harry Reems, also pursued a real-estate career following his tumultuous employment in the adult film industry. "When I met her [circa 1996], she was trying random, temporary jobs," Sandy says. "She was having a great deal of difficulty getting the royalty payments from her music that she was entitled to. She really had to fight them and hire an attorney. Eventually she won, late in her life, and they had to compensate her. But for many years she went without the proper payment for that music and struggled financially."

There are a few online anecdotes that bolster the notion True was indeed having financial problems later in life. Despite what sound like hard, lean years for Andrea far removed from the spotlight, the singer's selfless side becomes more perceptible in Galetovic's recollections. She alleges, "Andrea was the type of person who, where some would shy away from other people's problems, she would take them on. A perfect example of this was Andrea's effort to help a longtime gay friend of hers named Michael who had, at some point, contracted AIDS. It was a time when many people were still afraid to be with someone who had the disease, and he was poor and really had nobody. She moved in with him and took care of him until he died and was wonderful with him. It was remarkable. I remember she invited me over to have dinner with him, and she treated him like a normal human being and made his last days, which were extremely difficult due to his temper and complications from the disease, a lot easier. She held her ground. She didn't have an intimate relationship with this man — obviously — it was just simply out of the kindness of her personality. He had nothing to offer her, and she had nothing to gain. She cooked for him. If she bought groceries, she bought some for him as well. She shared whatever she had with him, even with her limited resources, until he died."

What's old became new again by the late '90s and Andrea True, who had vanished below the surface, came up for air. Galetovic recalls Andrea's enthusiasm about a major New York radio station (WPLJ) sponsoring two sold-out disco revival concerts at New York's Paramount Theater at Madison Square Garden. Among the performers were the Village People, France Joli, Evelyn "Champagne" King and, incredibly, Andrea True, reuniting with many of her original band members. I was lucky enough to obtain tickets to one of these shows with the sole purpose of seeing True for the first time. Though I had a less-than-ideal seat to witness the event, especially with a packed crowd of thousands on their feet and dancing around for most of the show, the MC announced The Andrea True Connection to a roar of applause. The band members ran onstage and last to emerge from the wings was Andrea True. A bit heavyset and appearing a touch nervous, with long blond hair and wearing a black fringe leather jacket, black leggings and boots, Andrea True humbly took the stage and thanked the audience for their support. She seemed truly happy and attested to delight at being back in New York. She belted out her repertoire of hits—"NY, You Got Me Dancing," "What's Your Name, What's Your Number?" and "More, More, More"—for what was probably the last huge gathering of those who knew and loved her music. In her interview with *Billboard*, she expressed enormous shock and happiness that so many fans from 1976 had shown up and wanted to know where she'd been. Galetovic says, "Andrea was hopeful this concert might restart her music career."

Felipe Rose (the Native American of the Village People) recalls appearing with her at the show. "She was a wonderful woman, but a much older woman at that time," he says. "The great thing about her was that when she sang 'More, More, More,' she sounded like the record. She was a lot of fun! Sadly, people were saying she didn't age well. But who does anyway? She was a wonderful, dear woman, and I just want to keep that memory of her. She managed to come out and relive some of that old glory, which was great. For years after, I would speak with to her from time to time. It was when those huge cell phones had come out and beepers were big. In the last couple of years, she wasn't feeling that well, and her health wasn't that good. I don't know how I lost track of her, but I guess her life was changing. The music industry had changed so much too, and I know she found it harder to work."

Shortly after the Paramount event, alternative rock group Len began enjoying Top-10 success in the U.S. and abroad with a song called "Steal My Sunshine." Written by Marc Costanzo (with a nod to Gregg Diamond) as a track for the group's third album, the song's backdrop was a small sample from the instrumental bridge of Andrea True's "More, More, More." "She was happy about it," says Galetovic. Len's sampling had ignited quite a bit of interest in Andrea's original classic and as the 2000s began, True's version soon began showing up on the radio more frequently. It was elevated to almost iconic status after being used in television commercials to promote the wildly popular HBO series, *Sex and the City*. (It was surreal seeing Sarah Jessica Parker lip-synch to Andrea's vocals.) It should be noted that as late as 2012, "More, More, More" was being used to even promote Post's Honey Bunches of Oats breakfast cereal in TV commercials (though it was a re-recording by Andrea and not True's original mix) and New York's WCBS news radio station (using the original song).

Immersed in almost as much mystery as her original recording was the subsequent release in 2000 of a CD called *More, More, More (and Other Disco Millennium Hits)* by The Andrea True Connection on a label called Hypnotic, U.S.A. It was, perhaps, True's characteristically go-getter attempt to capitalize on the small wave of resurging interest in her music and may have been the album she told Michael Paoletta she was finishing in her *Billboard* interview. Featuring nine tracks, the disc included six newly recorded versions of "More, More, More," one of which was styled much like Len's "Steal My Sunshine." This version was remarkably satisfying after the stir Len had caused and True, vocoder-enhanced and thoroughly mixed with an ethereal effect, sounded wonderful. No production credits were found on the disc, save for the names of remixers, and there was no message to fans from True. It failed to chart or revitalize the name of Andrea or her Connection.

Around this period, Andrea may have also moved to Florida, where Galetovic says, "She went to work for a company called Jupiter and became a psychic. She was actually very good at it. She was very interested in the zodiac arts. She was very passionate about it and even though it was just a job, she took it very seriously. She took anything she did seriously. Music was her real passion though. She never mentioned any aspirations to be on television or anything like that. She just wanted to sing. She had mentioned interest in writing a book about her life, but I guess she never got around to doing that. She had known so many people; it would have been an amazing book. In her later years, she had health problems and had trouble keeping up the energy she needed to pursue her projects."

After her *Millennium* CD and a few other artists like the U.K.'s Rachel Stevens, Dannii Minogue, Samantha Fox and Bananarama each covered her signature hit (plus a few spotlights on VH1's *Where Are They Now* shows), it was back to porn movies for Andrea True ... sort of. This time she was featured as a participant in the widely regarded documentary about one of the most notorious porn films of all time, 1972's *Deep Throat*. Released by Universal Pictures in 2005, *Inside Deep Throat* detailed the story of how *Deep Throat* was made and distributed and its effect on mainstream America in the era of President Nixon. Although Andrea did not appear in the original *Deep Throat* film, she did star in *Deep Throat II* and had the experience to know what the industry was all about. The NC–17 rated film featured interviews with porn stars of the day and included a brief discussion with True, who said of her music career, "The time was right for a porno star to be a pop star. Who would have ever thought?"

When Sandy Galetovic met and befriended Andrea True in the '90s, she did not immediately know her new friend was the singer behind the hit "More, More, More." "It was several months before she actually told me about it," Galetovic says. "I think she felt her life wasn't as glamorous as it used to be. I got the impression she didn't feel as young and beautiful as she used to be. But I don't think Andrea had regrets. She was extremely positive. I think that's why she was able to help so many other people — the way she had with her friend Michael. She once mentioned to me if I had any money troubles, since she didn't have any children, she'd be happy to turn her royalties over to me. But I couldn't do that. I told her to just enjoy it, go to Europe or finally do more things for herself. She had fought so hard to finally get them. She never wanted people to ever feel sorry for her. She always had a young demeanor about her and very positive energy. She always had a lot of good advice. She had a very protective nature, and she often acted like a big sister to me. Other than the fact she had to really fight to get her royalties paid to her, I don't think she had any regrets about what she did. I feel pretty sure that even if she had never received a dime from her singing career, she would have done it all over again."

She adds, "Andrea was one of those people who was just very high on life. She was just hungry for life and always wanted more, more, more out of it. The thing I liked most about her was this aura she had. Her positive attitude — and her incredible sense of kindness. In life, we all make mistakes and do things we aren't necessarily proud of. In her case, I think she made some decisions that ended up being very public, and it affected some aspects of her future. As individuals, I guess you and I are luckier in that our situations aren't thrown out there for everyone to see as Andrea's had been."

Andrea True died at age 68 on November 7, 2011, in Kingston, New York, just a few miles from the city that had given her stardom. The cause of death was vaguely listed as heart failure. She was cremated and inurnment took place in Cleveland, Ohio. "I felt she still had a lot of life in her and her passing came as a tremendous surprise — a shock," says Galetovic, who had not realized True had relocated to upstate New York from her last address in Florida. It took several days for news of Andrea's passing, announced by the Gilpatric-VanVliet Funeral Home in Kingston, to make some ripples on the net, and surprisingly lengthy obituaries in the Big Apple mainstays *The New York Times, Daily News* and *Newsday* soon followed.

Gloria Gaynor, the only performer in this book (besides Felipe Rose) who ever recalled meeting Andrea (albeit very briefly), says, "She was very pleasant and kind of giggly. I met her in Gregg Diamond's office; I think it was at 405 Park Avenue in Manhattan. She was very vibrant." That's about all the public ever really got to see of True — a fleeting, vibrant glimpse. However, say what you will, The Andrea True Connection was far more than a one-hit wonder. Clearly, Andrea had a dream and a vision and kept going in the face of adversity. She saw her dream become a reality, however quickly her star faded. She was a truly self-made woman, a true honorary New Yorker and a fighter. Indisputably, she is a unique and unusual part of pop music history (whose porn endeavors were barely noticed by the media or music fans and never had much impact on her singing career), and she is broadly admirable for her never-give-up way of life. She ended up doing something few can lay claim to with her lasting contribution to disco music.

Andrea True is often quoted from a VH1 interview as saying, "I wanted to be remembered as someone who brought people joy ... with my music." In this endeavor, she was wildly successful.

Claudja Barry

"I think that had I compromised a little bit more, I could have reached that top level of performers, but, you know, I really actually like me just as I am. It's always nice to look back and see what you've produced. The chronology of life—my life, anyway—is all in album covers and record sleeves, and it really is quite remarkable. I haven't changed that much!" Claudja Barry chuckles. Her songs expertly blended exotic, powerful, distinctively island-accented vocals with the lush sounds of Europe and the pop sensibilities of the U.S., making the artist enormously popular across the globe. Claudja's career has spanned every decade that followed her auspicious debut in the '70s and her hits, highlighted by the unrelenting anthem "Boogie Woogie Dancin' Shoes," are considered undisputed disco classics. She speaks with a confident, articulate voice that is warm with appreciation for her prestigious ranking in the genre's history.

Claudja describes her earliest days. "I must tell you, as a kid growing up, the last of 11 children, by the time they got to me—what I needed and what I wanted were two different things. I got what was left. I always felt that, yeah, I'm gonna have to make something for myself. I always felt I was very talented and I thought there was something special about me, and I wanted to share it—not only with my family but with everybody," she says.

"I was born in Jamaica, grew up in Toronto and I always wanted to emulate the people who I thought were amazing talents of the time. You know—Barbra Streisand, Aretha, Gladys Knight, Nat King Cole—all those folks who were absolutely beyond belief in their talent. We loved those people, and we tried to mold ourselves to be like them. I wasn't born in that 'churchified' background of Detroit. I wanted to study classical music. I grew up with *The Marriage of Figaro*, *Porgy and Bess*, a little bit of classical music, all the evergreens. I eventually went to Vienna to study classical voice and, while there, I got an audition to do a show called *Catch My Soul*—that was a big musical at the time in Europe based on Shakespeare's *Othello*. And I got the part! I went on to Berlin to work in the theater there for two years, and during that time I got a call asking if I would like to be in a musical group. The group turned out to be Boney M. I stayed in Boney M, for a while, but I realized that I was just not a group person. I went on to get a call to be a part of Silver Convention too, which I turned down. I was able to start a solo career with Lollipop Records. Producers Jurgen Korduletsch and Ingo Klingbeil heard me and said, 'Look we have a song by Kim Weston called 'Take Me in Your Arms (Rock Me a Little While),' which they wanted to do a version of for Europe, and I was asked to audition for it. I did and I got the job, and that's how my solo recording career started."

It wasn't long before Barry's career expanded to the international stage. In the late '70s, the singer recorded some of her most iconic disco music with Salsoul Records based in the U.S. Behind the breakthrough was the same producer who recognized her talent early on—Jurgen Korduletsch. Professionally (and privately), they were a team. "Jurgen was instrumental in getting my career to jump off because he gave me the opportunity to come out of the theater, leave the groups behind and be a solo artist. He made the deal, the very first U.S. deal I ever had, with Salsoul Records. I first recorded 'Sweet Dynamite,' and I did it in a couple of takes. One was very rough and raw and street, and the other, the one that we now know, was not as aggressive—but it was still out there. You can really feel something with 'Sweet Dynamite.' I don't know what the quality was that Jurgen saw in me — I wasn't a heavy R&B singer, but I wasn't a total pop singer either. My voice was just very distinct. And I think that's what he liked about it."

In 1976, Barry's Salsoul debut LP, *Sweet Dynamite*, featuring a sultry, confident shot of the artist on the cover, exploded on the club circuit. Mixed by Tom Moulton, produced by Korduletsch and arranged by Jorg Evers (the latter two gentlemen would navigate most of her releases over the next few years), the album spawned multiple disco chart-toppers. The explosive and gritty anthems "Sweet Dynamite" and "Dance, Dance, Dance" established Barry as a force to be reckoned with. The artist followed in '77 with the album *Claudja* (known as *The Girl Most Likely …* in markets outside the U.S.), which included the massive club hits "Johnny, Johnny Please Come Home" and "Dancin' Fever," written in part by Barry. The American album version was again mixed by Tom Moulton and featured playing by some of Germany's foremost musicians, including guitar work by Mats Björklund and the drum and percussion work of Keith Forsey. The artist had found a very comfortable niche in disco.

Claudja Barry publicity shot from the early '80s when the artist entered the era of Hi-NRG music and worked with producer-composer Bobby Orlando (courtesy Tom Hayden/TSR Records).

"I had and have no problem with the word 'disco.' I must say it brings back thoughts of a time that was just fantastic. In fact, it was an amazing time! If you say 'disco' anywhere in the world, it really evokes thoughts of a specific type of music and a specific time in history, music history, world history, fun history — and 'growing-up history' for a lot of people. It is danceable music — pop music. So whoever created the negative vibe for the word didn't really see or anticipate how it would evolve into what it is today. Because pretty much almost all pop music today is dance music," says Claudja.

The game-changing *I Wanna Be Loved by You* LP followed next in 1978. Barry was now signed with Chrysalis Records in the U.S., a label that was experimenting with disco through the release of Amanda Lear's underground odyssey, *Sweet Revenge*, and Blondie's "Heart of Glass." Mixer Tom Savarse was credited on Barry's latest vinyl as the "Disco Consultant," and standing out among track nuggets like the island-flavored "Nobody but You" and the hard-shuffler "Give It Up" was the lead single, "Boogie Woogie Dancin' Shoes." Chrysalis also renamed her album after the track. An uncompromising high-energy confection of German electronic-disco, the track was further pumped with the synthesizer sweetening of Kristian Schultze. "Dancin' Shoes" dominated the top of the disco chart for a large portion of the year as a club smash and was poised to break big into the U.S. Pop 100. Oddly, it ended up only making a modest dent.

"'Boogie Woogie Dancin' Shoes' should have gone a lot farther up the pop charts," says Barry. "Unfortunately, the timing was a little bit strange. Chrysalis was grooming other people, and I lived in Europe—I wasn't in Los Angeles. So, in a way, it was kind of counterproductive for me being so far away. But also, I'm actually quite happy I didn't fall into the L.A. trap, so to speak, and fall into a very competitive and an overly desensitizing situation. I'm not trying to be negative about Los Angeles, but many artists lose their way in L.A. because life becomes more about the lifestyle and posing and less about depth and creativity. Working in Los Angeles can take away a lot of the honesty when you're trying to release the inner soul—which is needed when you sing and write from the heart. You end up not creating what's right for you, but rather what's right for the pop or R&B charts. Like when a singer wants to do a great song just because she wants to. Of course, I was very happy to have reached the successful numbers that we did nationally with 'Boogie Woogie Dancin' Shoes,' but after that release it did sort of became a bit like, 'Okay, we're now in the grind and we're established. Let's keep going.' Instead of creating, we were trying to write for the charts."

Chart-focused or not, the follow-up was a hell-raising, rock-tinged single, "(You Make Me) Feel the Fire," a departure from the melodic style of disco for which she'd become known. The Chrysalis album from which it came, *Feel the Fire*, was also an opportunity for Barry to be more involved in songwriting. The artist reflects with a critical eye on the single and all the tracks that comprise her vast catalog, saying, "Well, sometimes the songs were representative of my abilities, and sometimes they weren't. The successful songs—'Down & Counting,' 'Sweet Dynamite,' 'Johnny, Johnny Please Come Home,' 'Boogie Woogie Dancin' Shoes'—those were all very disco-pop songs. I did a couple of things like 'Take It Easy,' which was a totally different kind of feeling for me. I would have liked to have done a few more songs like that. It wasn't really a soft song; it had a little bit more of a jazz feel to it. I would have loved to experiment a little bit more like that. When I went to the Tokyo Music Festival with '(You Make Me) Feel the Fire,' I just thought, 'Yeah, it's a heavy rock song.' But then to get the silver prize for the song and to clean up with a couple of different awards for it made me realize that I really was blessed to have a wonderful kind of appeal and range and that it was good material."

While the label may have seen potential for Barry to be their own Donna Summer during this period, Claudja says she experienced no insecurity about comparisons to the iconic artist. "I think I was being recognized for my specific sound because I didn't have the same kind of vocals as Donna. My phrasing and sound were very different from Donna's. It is what it is; it was what it was. If she hadn't been there, nobody would have been able to say, 'Oh, she sounds a little bit like Donna Summer.' I don't know who else they would have compared me to. We were totally two different types of performers."

Though an undeniably successful artist in the U.S., Barry says her experience in the European spotlight was exceptionally positive. She says, "I speak German fluently, a little bit of French and a little bit of Italian. I could get around, order my dinner, get to my room and get directions. I find that if you are able to express yourself in the language of the place you are visiting or living in, it really helps you to fall into the feel of the country. I was very pleased with the way I was treated and the kind of enjoyment I had, especially in Germany, which I find to be one of the most fascinating places in the world. Looking at it all now, it's very funny that the times have changed so dramatically. For years you could tour Europe—you could be on tour with a new album almost every summer—and visit the same places because they were *that* comfortable with you. They've seen you, they know your music and they're generous with their applause and support. I think you have to have a certain kind of music to elicit that kind of loyalty in the U.S. It's such a quick society now that I don't know anymore. I saw Willie Nelson at the Beacon Theatre in New York recently and, yeah, you can see he was supported. But I don't know if pop or dance music would be the genre that generates loyalty here in the U.S. as opposed to, say, country music or jazz."

Claudja's Euro-dance formula continued to evolve with singles such as "The Two of Us" (featuring Ronnie Jones) and the 1981 album *Made in Hong Kong*, from which the track "Radio Action" garnered plenty of disco-chart action as an import single. In '83, a domestic mini-album called *No La De Da Part 2* (there was never a Part 1) was released by Personal Records, which featured a modernized electronic break-beat sound on the hit single "For Your Love." Barry also teamed with rising producer Bobby Orlando (The Flirts, Divine, Ronni Griffith) for "Born to Love," "Whisper to a Scream" and the immensely popular chart double-hit, "Work Me Over/I Will Follow Him," on TSR Records. TSR's founder, Tom Hayden, describes the artist as "a very good performer who promoted the music a lot in the clubs. She had a great following, and we were very excited about working with her. It was another Top 10 dance record for us early on."

Says Claudja, "There was always a lot of different people that were involved in the production of my work, but Jurgen Korduletsch must be given kudos. He was a solid producer and songwriter with great taste whose productions stand up in quality today. He surrounded himself with the best musicians: Bobby Orlando, Mats Björklund, Keith Forsey and Kristian Schultze were among the people we worked with. When he needed the soaring sounds of the classics, in came the Munich Philharmonic Orchestra, sparing no expense. The same goes for the studio sound. Only the best would be good enough. Musicland (owned by Giorgio Moroder), Arco, Union and Studio 70 in Munich—where it all began. Flying in from Europe to record at Sigma Studios was not unusual in the '70s. It's true; Jurgen was the go-to guy in the end. He knew what he was doing and did not compromise on anything. Bringing in Bobby Orlando was amazing and his vibe was very interesting. 'Whisper to a Scream'—the things we did together—were fantastic. Bobby was a very, very intelligent musician. He was a great musician. He could write; he could play. But he didn't like being in the front or onstage. He just was really very good about being in the background and getting the work done and creating the music. 'Work Me Over' was my first experience with Bobby, and it was just unreal. To this day, people still want to hear that song ... my goodness!"

A major American label, Epic Records, picked up her next U.S. album, the cleverly titled *I, Claudja* (a takeoff on the popular PBS series, *I, Claudius*). "I didn't really get too involved with the logistics of being on a label because that was Jurgen's job," Barry recalls. "It was his job to get this stuff out on whichever label he could secure. So I was happy with being on a major label because, in those days, they really *did* have the money to spend on videos and to get you out in front of the public and on television, on the radio. So being on a major label is always great—*great when you're hot*. A lot of my work came into being through smaller labels, and that's the experience of a lot of disco artists. The difference was a lot of the smaller labels were managed by people who had been DJs earlier or they had something to do with producing music. They had a feel for it and had a vibe for what club music was about and an ability to try and get it out to a mainstream audience. More passion! Smaller labels were sometimes better for an artist. Now, today, you have to be a completely finished product to even get a deal with a major label, of course. They are struggling."

From *I, Claudja* came several dance-chart smashes, including "Hot to the Touch" and "Secret Affair," along with one of her biggest and most widely recognized hits, "Down and Counting" (whose theme was reminiscent of Linda Clifford's feisty hits). "The pressure was really on to get that 'other' hit," she says, "which we did! We got to number 1 with 'Down and Counting' on the *Billboard* dance chart. And then we were about to hit the pop charts when Sony came in, bought CBS and restructured Epic Records — and I sort of fell through the cracks. The whole restructuring of Epic at the time was difficult for us. Nobody knew what to do with Claudja Barry. Well, she's a black singer, but she's a pop singer signed to the R&B department. 'We don't know what to do,' they'd say. It was a very strange time. Consequently, 'Down and Counting,' which I think could have been a Top-10 pop record, just sort of languished in the twilight zone and by the time Sony started to function as a label, they'd moved on to other artists."

Claudja Barry's name was prominent on a number of single releases in the years that followed. Tracks like "Love Is An Island," a sweeping, ethereal dance journey released by RCA Records, "Tripping on the Moon" (a brilliant, trippy Cerrone composition) and "Poison," which featured the artist as a lead vocalist under the General Base moniker, kept her a club favorite during the '90s. She moved a bit out of the spotlight for a time at the beginning of the 21st century but came roaring back with an independent release in 2006: the pride anthem "I Will Stand." Remixed by prominent DJs Tony Moran, Gadbois and Sugardip, the track returned the singer to the top tier of the dance chart. However, as Barry observes, *only* the dance chart. She recalls, "'I Will Stand' is a *really* great song! It took me something like eight years to get the rights to record the song. I think it went to number 2 on the dance charts. But again, nobody was able to bring it from the dance charts to a mainstream pop label because the money that it takes to bring a record like that out — nobody was spending in 2006. I just felt kind of sad about that. If you don't fit into this tiny little musical category, they won't play you on radio. I don't even know how it's done anymore, but it's very hard to get on the air. You just *can't* get on the air. Thank God for shows like *American Idol*, which discover new voices. The process of getting heard, though, is debilitating. If you're an artist, you probably have a great deal of sensitivity. And the negativity — it's really hard on you. I feel for these kids who are starting out. But you look at Kelly Clarkson and people like her — she believed in her dream and showed you have to keep trying."

Today, while continuing to release new material like "Good Time Girl" (a recent digital release), Barry has an aura of satisfaction about her musical accomplishments. "When I perform, it's understood that I will do 'Boogie Woogie Dancin' Shoes,' but I'm surprised so many people still want to hear 'Down and Counting,' Work Me Over,' 'Sweet Dynamite' and 'Johnny.' 'Boogie Woogie,' 'Sweet Dynamite,' along with 'Down and Counting,' are my personal favorites. I think about a lot of the ladies that were or are in the business, and it's not everyone who has seven or eight albums out during their careers. I was very blessed. My albums had full production and live musicians. It's amazing when I really *do* think about it, and I think the music really still holds up today. I did 'Tripping on the Moon' and performed it live at the Saint with Cerrone, who flew in from Paris. Or when I went to Tokyo and I did the festival with a 70-piece orchestra. It was just phenomenal—you know, I *truly* have been blessed. I look back at those times—and I don't want to sound like I'm tooting my own horn—I sometimes think it really was something special."

She adds, "I've heard people tell me, 'Oh, I came out to this song' or 'Gosh, "Johnny Johnny" was my dream song' and they can remember a relationship that they had at the time or how amazing a song was when they first heard it. Or that one of my songs made some event in their life so fabulous—and I do know there was impact from my music—and the impact was very positive. Some people will try to make disco appear to be inconsequential and something that was not of great value. But that's not true. In essence, disco bridged a lot of hard times that occurred throughout the era, like the AIDS crisis.

"I left Jamaica when I was seven years old, so I left before I was influenced by anything there—whether it was the negativity of the dance-hall music content or the cultural dissatisfaction with personal lifestyle choices. As I look back on my music career, the support of the gay community was crucial on all levels, from audience participation as well as in the corporate structure. These fabulous gay men who embraced me so openly without any reservation—had they not been there, there would not be a Claudja Barry today. Because they laid the groundwork; they made the impact. When I would go to perform for them, it was such an amazing encounter. The feedback, the warmth, the generous applause, just the feeling of being loved and appreciated from the audience made me realize, 'Yeah, I gotta keep going. It's real!' Imagine—The Saint on New Year's Eve packed with 7,000 guys that were responding so loudly and going so crazy you couldn't even hear the music. You go onstage thinking, 'Yeah, I'm doing this because it *does* mean something to somebody!'" Claudja says.

When recalling the greatest highlights of her career, the singer is hard-pressed to identify a single favorite. "The closest thing I can recall to a moment where I thought, 'I've made it,' was probably doing the Tokyo Music Festival and coming in second to Dionne Warwick. Although in my mind, I always wanted to be an opera singer—I wanted to be the next Leontyne Price, you know? I wanted to be the next Elisabeth Schwarzkopf. But the music I made and my turn at bat were so amazing, I couldn't have wished for anything better. I never really thought 'I've made it' at any point. I always wanted to keep going. There were more moments of joy to come, more things to conquer. I was invited to sing for the prime minister of Canada, to sing for many royal houses, for Helmut Kohl, the prime minister of West Germany. Even with all those wonderful events, it wasn't like I ever felt I'd made it."

She adds, "I was the opening performer for Canada's biggest music night—the Juno Awards—that certainly could have been an 'ah-ha' moment! But the icing on the cake was when the governor general of Canada sent me an invitation the next day to be his guest for a dinner that was being given for Prince Charles—who was touring Canada at the time. I had to turn it down because I had a performance in Europe with a signed contract. You see, when I give my word to be there, I'm there. That invitation, however, was definitely a wonderful moment!"

But then it clicks with the singer—the heartflash moment that stands above the rest. "Ah, yes, maybe there *is* one event that really *does* stand out on a personal level. Let me tell you the story! I was working in East Germany at the time at this huge theater called the

Friedrichstadt-Palast and I got a call in the middle of the night from my mother and she said, 'Well my dear, I suppose I must congratulate you because, even though I think that you really should have studied to be a doctor or a lawyer, I hear your music being played at the halftime of the Stanley Cup Playoffs here at the Maple Leaf Gardens. So, obviously, you have arrived, because they *only* play the hits!' [laughing] I think that's perhaps when I realized I really did make an impact. So yeah, I'll go with that — I thought I made it when I heard they played 'Boogie Woogie Dancin' Shoes' at the hockey game halftime. And getting my Juno Award and sitting with the prime minister of Canada on television. There I was and all my siblings saw it, and from then on I was looked at in a different light," Barry smiles.

Some 36 years after making her first impact on the disco scene, Barry accepts the aging process as just that — a simple process. She says, "I don't ever use the 'o' word. I believe the divas and people with good spirits and hearts never seem to reach that point or be defined by that word. About a year ago, I went to Mexico to do a show with Jessica Williams and Cynthia Manley, as I recall, and everyone was saying how we haven't changed. A lot of it has to do with the fact that change sometimes means something's wrong. I haven't really changed inside. And I think that's what people see on the outside. My spirit and soul is still fresh from the time people knew me. I think that's how we should all try to be. It's still Claudja Barry — not some pulled-back creation. Part of how I've stayed sort of sane and was able to take care of my look was that I didn't fall into some of the traps of club life. I don't smoke, I don't drink a lot and I tried to do everything correctly. I tried not to do bad things and not be a horrible person, although sometimes you probably *should* be one. I think that's how I've tried to keep myself together. I don't have any problem showing who I am today, and I set up a website at www.claudjabarry.com, where you can see all kinds of pictures of me."

She proudly adds, "I've done something recently — a documentary film, about music. Our time was a happy, joyous time. The music made the time. I do believe that music is so influential — it influences our spirit in more ways than we actually understand, and that's the focus of this film. It's about my journey as an artist and as a singer, my music compared to the music of today. I've just finished the music for the film, much of which I wrote. I wrote the script and I produced it. I think it's important to do things like that. We can't just sit and wait for people to arrive and present opportunities like that for us. I would say to all the artists in this book — I would love to do a film about the women of dance who were influential in this era. This book represents the core group of women who brought a lot of joy to people and performed a lot of great music. I think what I'm trying to say about maturity and about realizing who you might be, who you were or what your achievements are — you can't stop growing. You can't stop achieving or stop making the music or accomplishing goals. You can't stop polishing who you are, and you can't stop creating new things and new music. Or even just getting out whatever is inside of you to let people know that you are a viable artist — you are real and that there's something behind you. You weren't created in a studio, and you weren't thrown on a stage to lip synch some words for an evening. You have to keep going! It's like this book — the purpose is to make people understand and realize what this music and what these singers mean — that it really was great music and it *is* great music and it should be acknowledged. There were people in this music who were in it for the right reasons!

"You have to create opportunities yourself," Barry says. "There aren't a lot of people out there who both remember disco, were affected by the music and are in a position to make a difference for singers of this genre and era. It's such a joy to be here today and be able to say we really *did* bring something to the table. If you look at what's out there today — and don't misunderstand what I'm saying — a lot of what is presented today as great music is not really even close to being a song. Not like, for example, the wonderful song 'I Will Survive' by Gloria Gaynor," Barry observes.

"It was difficult to achieve success back in the day and the competition was serious, but today it's brutal — just from the sheer volume of the competition. Today, *everybody* is a singer; everybody is an actor. Everybody believes they can write and have a certain amount of entertainment value. But in the end, it's the public who still makes the choice. Again, the public can be manipulated to make them think [they want something]."

The artist's worldwide fan base today is substantial by anyone's standards — the fruits of being an all-time chart-topping champion in disco history. As she constantly looks for new ways to express her creativity, few disco era legends stand a better chance

Claudja Barry is proud of the disco music she made and says, "I have been truly blessed" (courtesy Claudja Barry).

of being eternally revered by the planet's countless disciples of dance music. Claudja Barry has a simple hope and vision of how her name will be recalled. "I want to be remembered as someone who didn't give up! As someone who didn't compromise and did the very best she could in all endeavors — and a person who did the right thing. That's pretty much how I'd like to be remembered ... oh, and that I performed some great music — music that was loved!"

Pattie Brooks

"I thought it was a really interesting song, a lot of fun to do, and it made it to number 1! What more could I ask for?" observes singer Pattie Brooks of her classic disco masterpiece and the *Thank God It's Friday* movie soundtrack favorite, "After Dark." If that sounds rather unassuming, it's probably because the performer is always looking forward, rather than back to the past. Synonymous with Casablanca Records and the energized disco sound at the prime of the era, today Brooks embraces her good fortune and career highlights while showing she's anything but out of the game.

The singer recalls her earliest days. "I'm a military kid from Ft. Riley, Kansas, and I remember from very early on that I loved to sing!" she says. "I just loved it, loved it, *loved it*! I had some classical musical training at about age nine or 10, and I would listen to a lot of jazz — Ella Fitzgerald and Sarah Vaughn and all those people coming through my life. I listened to a lot of gospel too. I think that's why I can do a lot of different styles — because I listened to everything."

Despite always "singing, singing, singing," as Brooks describes her childhood pastime, she didn't have a clear vision she would ever find fame in the industry. "Looking at Dick Clark's *American Bandstand*, I just wanted to dance on that show so badly. It wasn't until much later on that I found myself on it — not dancing on the show — but I sure did *appear* on it! As an artist! But as a kid, I really just wanted to be a dancer on his show — that was the main thing for a little girl from Kansas. My career really started when I got my first audition for vocal work on the Smothers Brothers' TV show, doing demos, that type of thing, and contracting for other people. I started thinking, well, maybe I should really try to get a solo situation happening here," she says.

Brooks' first brush with her disco destiny came from forging a connection with producer Simon Soussan, who was churning out dance music at a breakneck pace. Tom Hayden, later head of TSR Records, handled numerous promotion efforts for Polydor at the time and, in turn, for Soussan. He recalls, "Simon was like the Ford Motor Company of disco records. He had almost a production line and used almost the same kickdrum beat in nearly every one of his productions. He would take it from one record to the next and then add the overlays." Pattie's introduction to the producer's assembly line was, nevertheless, a stroke of good fortune, and, as she shared billing with the Simon Orchestra on *Love Shook* (her Casablanca Records debut LP in 1977 — essentially a three-track album plus a pop medley), she began garnering attention from the clubs. "I had gone to his house to discuss the whole thing because he had heard what I had done in

Pattie Brooks, who was showered with attention after the success of her Casablanca Records single "After Dark," posed for a label publicity shot, circa 1978 (courtesy Rick Gianatos).

numerous shows — I had been singing backup and contracting for Ann-Margret and then I did some work with Helen Reddy," says Brooks. "I had worked with all these different artists doing the background vocals. To be honest, I didn't really even know what 'disco' was. He told me how he was working with Casablanca and Neil Bogart, and he asked me what I thought of that. Well, I was thrilled!" The song "Girl Don't Make Me Wait" off her debut LP peaked at number 2 on the dance chart. The track was originally recorded by a man, Bunny Sigler (a pop and R&B songwriter and performer who helped develop the Philly Sound), and when they covered it with Pattie, they forgot to remove the "Girl." Pattie remembers regularly being questioned about her sexual orientation by fans misinterpreting the song's title.

Brooks became quite familiar with the Casablanca turf, doing numerous backup sessions for many of the artists on the label's early roster, including Donna Summer. Pattie's resume included vocal work on Summer's legendary *I Remember Yesterday* album in '77. Thirty-five years later, the artist's recollections of Donna and the experience evoke a warm response. "Donna was so talented and just really great to be around. I remember doing all the shows to promote the album — *Soul Train*, and I think we did *Don Kirshner's Rock Concert* — it was wonderful," she says, stirring up feelings about Summer's recent passing. "I happened to get up and was having my first cup of coffee, and I turned on the TV and there was *My Wife and Kids* [sitcom], which had Donna's daughter, Brooklyn, playing the love interest. I'm looking at it and said, 'Oh my God, she looks so much like her father!' I started to watch the news and suddenly, 'Donna Summer dies at 63' blurted out and I'm thinking, 'Wait a minute!' It was so surreal to me. I had to sit down. I was just in total shock. I had just seen her last year when we had met at a Hollywood event, and Donna and I sat at a table together. We were talking; we took pictures. I have the last pictures of she and I together — and that was just last year. It was just a very strange place to be when I heard the news because I didn't want to believe it. Well, what can I say? It just flooded back all the good times we had together, the crazy times. She was a funny girl; she was such a joy to be around, and she really was also a great actress. My favorite thing I did with her was backing her on a song she did in a show where she played a bag lady — and Donna actually looked like a homeless woman when she sang it. That was real acting coming out of her.

"She was just really fabulous, and that voice was so powerful!" adds Pattie. "I was so glad for her when she did 'MacArthur Park.' I remember she had apparently raced out from the studio — she came to get me — dragged me upstairs over on Sunset where Casablanca used to be and she says, 'You've got to hear this!' And that's when I heard 'MacArthur Park.' Because up until then, she was always commenting, 'Oh God, when are they going to really hear my voice?' She was always doing this very high, whispery singing — and they did the same thing to me too. They cut us really high, and it was this soft thing with these gigantic productions and these sweeping strings and the whole effect was, I guess, just the style of the era. When I heard 'MacArthur Park,' I said, 'Oh my God, this is it!' I just looked at her and said, 'You are over like a fat rat; let me tell you! This is really going to be something! They are going to see you shine! Like you have never had your day before — you are just really going to have it!' I remember we just played it so loud out of the windows, and it was just amazing! When I saw the album cover and all that, and it just took off, it was wonderful!"

The year following her debut, Brooks scored her own breakthrough hit and the biggest song of her career. "Simon was looking for a singer for another Casablanca project, the song

'After Dark.' We did it at Larrabee Sound Studios in L.A., right there off of Santa Monica. I had seen Donna go through her thing, but disco, what it was, just hadn't really made its mark in my brain yet. Then they took me to Studio 1 and they played 'After Dark.' People went nuts and I thought, 'Oh so *this* is what it's about!' It worked out well. Simon was such a European producer—I think he was Moroccan or something. You know, the thing was I just really went in there and sang these songs for him, but it wasn't like I would have chosen them for myself. When 'After Dark' was given to me, I just sang it down, and that was it—I was never thinking it was going to be a hit. I really didn't think at the time it had the power needed to be a hit in such a big way and have the longevity it has shown with so many people for so many years. But it did!"

"After Dark," with its swirling, synthesizer-fueled flavor and ability to stir the masses, became an overnight club smash and is widely considered the best and strongest track off the *Thank God It's Friday* soundtrack, following Donna Summer's immortal "Last Dance" (which it joined at the number 1 spot on the dance chart). It was the on switch for the floodlights to fall on Brooks, who finally made an appearance on her beloved *American Bandstand* show. "Like I said, my whole thing was—I just loved Dick Clark! I just wanted to be on that show so badly as a kid, and then to actually be on it, twice, was remarkable for me. I had performed 'After Dark' with these feathery fans, and [Dick] was telling me there was an older artist who was a Burlesque fan dancer named Sally Rand. Well, don't you know, I went right home to look up who Sally Rand was and, sure enough, she had used the big ostrich feather fan! She was so beautiful the way she moved the fans, and I had no idea this was coming through in my performance of 'After Dark.' Then I was on the *Merv Griffin Show*, and I think he even mentioned something about the fans too. With the song being such a big hit, all those shows came through—*Dance Fever* and *Hot City Disco*! I brought a mini-version of Vegas right to those stages!"

Pattie, with the backing of Marc Paul Simon, head of club promotion at Casablanca, became one of the first artists to go out and do track shows in the clubs that were more than just an artist going up on a stage and singing to the music. Simon reportedly put a whole show together for her, which they debuted at the Back Lot, a live cabaret venue in the back of Studio One in West Hollywood. In addition to a thematic set, she was outfitted in showgirl style costumes showing off her fabulous legs, and she utilized props such as the elaborate fans. Producer Rick Gianatos remembers his first personal expose to Pattie, who appeared live at the *Billboard* Disco Convention the year of the release of "After Dark." "She was brilliant on stage, all smiles and legs," he recalls. "The kicker for me was a favorite song of mine, written and produced by Bob Esty, called 'The Background Singer.' Pattie had gone offstage and came back trailed by three cutouts of herself and performed the song. The audience ate it up! To see everyone respond so well to a ballad in a dance club at a disco convention proved to me her versatility!"

Pattie remembers, "I had two children at the time 'After Dark' came out, so maybe I wasn't as wild as I could have been during that experience. But the whole time was a lot of fun, and I really got to meet a lot of wonderful people. I'll tell you, I really loved going to Fire Island. I had so much fun and so much time was spent there! I remember Cherry Grove—yeah, that place was great, and we had a blast doing those shows. In fact, Paul Jabara was there with me on Fire Island, and we performed together. That was wonderful. We stayed at a beautiful home there, and Paul flew in and they had this huge—and I'm telling you *huge*—party! He and I did 'Take Good Care of My Baby,' which was on his album at the time. We also performed it on Dick Clark's show. So it's like having some real history with Paul. What was really funny is that later on, I think at one point before 'It's Raining Men' was given to the Weather Girls, he had said, 'Oh, I have this song for you to do!' I don't know if it was the producers or the people at Casablanca, but they didn't think it was the right thing for me at the time and the rest is history. The Weather Girls got it!"

Performing in clubs became the norm under the spotlight, and life on stage had more than its share of odd moments for the singer. "I was singing in New York, I think it was at the Flamingo or the Paradise Garage, one of those clubs, and I'm singing and I'm waving the big fans, and I feel something hit me on the side of my mouth—and it was wet. I'm thinking, 'What the heck was that?' Then, all of a sudden, my lips kind of froze, kind of went numb! When I came off stage, I told one of the managers what happened. He said, 'Oh, I know what that was—you probably got sprayed accidentally or hit when they were flinging a handkerchief around and some of the—whatever chemical was on it—numbed your lips," she laughs. "I remember going to Studio 54, walking in and going into certain dark areas of it, and there were some celebrities off in the corner doing drugs. I won't say who they were, but they were there! And then downstairs was where all the action was on the floor. Well, I can say it was very interesting. A wild party time—people probably having the most fun of their lives at that point!"

None of it rattled Brooks. "When I think back, I realize I was around everything! I was a mother, and I was actually afraid of those things because I didn't know what it was going to do to my voice or any of that. I was just so afraid it would affect the way I would sing, so I just didn't want to get into that, and I knew I had to maintain myself, do the work, have fun and go home. I would perform, I would schmooze just a little bit with everybody and then the next thing I knew, the limo would whisk me back to the hotel, sometimes a gorgeous hotel in New York! I think it was the Plaza or one of those on a few occasions. That was enough fun for me because I really needed the rest in between all that craziness, and if I had been on drugs and stuff like that, I don't know how I could have really maintained my voice and my pitch. I probably would have been exhausted and unhealthy and the whole 'messed-up' thing. I'm so glad I didn't do anything back then. I knew the ones who were partying heavy; they would offer me certain things, and I would say no. One time, I admit I tried one little thing and I remember I said, 'That hurts my throat!' After that I said, 'Absolutely not!'"

The album *Our Miss Brooks* was the final production under the watch of Soussan, and was followed by *Party Girl*, Brooks' 1979 album with a new production team led by Bunny Sigler. Each of Brooks' subsequent albums searched for a new sound for the artist. Pattie recalls, "I think what happened is they were trying to make a transition for me with the *Party Girl* album. Bunny Sigler, who had hits with the group Instant Funk, knew I wanted to sing more R&B and kind of get out of that exclusively disco niche. And then I did an album with Michael Love Smith, which was very pop and R&B. Then it was on to a new label, Mirage-Atlantic, and the LP *In My World* with producer Sandy Linzer. Sandy Linzer had a great pedigree, having written and produced '60s hits such as 'Lover's Concerto,' 'Workin' My Way Back to You,' and, in the '70s, 'Native New Yorker' for Odyssey. He'd also produced the landmark album *Dr. Buzzard's Original Savannah Band*. For me, though, my album was a mixed bag of songs, including a trendy and kitschy song about Dr. Ruth. [He also had me do] a pop song originally done by Petula Clark, 'I Couldn't Live Without Your Love.' It was a write-off album. They just didn't know what to do with it and the album's material just didn't click with me."

Rick Gianatos concurs with Pattie. "I agree that the album was a write-off. My remixing services were very popular at the time, and I loved Pattie's music and was therefore able to see some potential in it. Yes, the album was a mixed bag, but I thought the Petula Clark cover was a potential smash if it were pumped up for the club scene. The shuffle beat was very popular, with dance hits like 'Give Me Just a Little More Time' by Angela Clemmons big in the clubs. I was so sure I could do the same and get a hit, that I offered my services for free to Pattie's manager at the time and to the record company. My pleas fell on deaf ears."

"I think timing has a lot to do with it because at the end of '70s and early '80s, the direction of music was changing," Brooks observes. "They began to burn disco records and all that type of thing. But you know, all the experiences were just great because they made me even more convinced of who I was as an artist, and I found I could do just about anything I wanted — depending on who the producers were. If I could get the right producers that really got into my heart and style, I'd have been set. But I don't think at the time they were really into me *per se*. They knew I could sing, but they just didn't go deep enough to find the right selections for me. It seemed to me, back then, anybody and their mother could get on a disco record with the producers they had out there. They just played a beat, gave you the melody, had you sing it and the record was out. I think for real artists capable of singing really great music, sometimes not really getting the right producers made the experience of performing disco difficult."

The disposability element evident on some disco music releases may have contributed to the genre and its singers failing to receive the respect and recognition they may have otherwise been entitled to in later years. Pattie comments, "I don't know if that whole era was marred by certain things, politically as well as whatever else we were going through at that time, sexuality and the whole '70s thing. I don't know if we artists got the right kind of recognition. We delivered a soundtrack to everybody's life at that time. I see people, and they tell me how much this music meant to them — I didn't even think they were serious or that it had any significance. I didn't realize [the songs] meant so much to other people. When you get that kind of recognition, I say 'Thank you, thank you, thank you!' Donna, Gloria Gaynor, Madonna ... I think there's a certain [level of] recognition with those names — high recognition for them. But for all the rest of us, well, I think it's 50–50 — we got the attention, and then we didn't get it. I think our music was sometimes thought of as fluff or as throw-away music at times. But I think dance music just keeps evolving and going in and out of everything."

Decades after the success of "After Dark," Brooks has remained a busy performer. Her approach to maturation is based on fearlessness and respect for the body and mind. "Don't be afraid of aging!" the singer says. "Don't be afraid of it, and stay as healthy as you can. It's such a mindset. Everything that you do every day — remember there's a purpose when you wake up. There's something out there. Don't just be locked up in your room and sit there and do nothing. You have to get out and rejuvenate your mind and your spirit. You must keep doing what your passion reaches for. Aging is a process, and, I think for me, the inner glow from within you keeps you young and also current. And taking care of your body — you have to take care of your body as you age and do all the right things. Eat the right kind of foods to keep from getting different diseases and problems like that.

"I was reading a book called *Zero Limits* given to me by singer Chris Bennett. I'm not really an avid reader, but one morning I got up and everything was quiet and I read a chapter. I was so taken with this book. There was a mantra in there, and I say it all the time, whether I'm driving, walking, talking to people—I'm thinking it in my mind, it's like in my subconscious. This thing works and it heals and it cleanses your mind, like trying to get you back to the zero limits when you were born—so there's no blocks, so you can do anything you want to do.

"Don't be afraid—you can't be afraid, and you have to get out of your comfort zone. You have to really embrace the changes that happen. But it's okay because all those things are part of the process, and all those things make you who you are. Stay with it and enjoy the people that you meet. Really look them in the eye when you talk to them—don't make all your contact like a nothing kind of conversation. Really look at the person and really hear what they say, and you'll find it so gratifying. That's my spin on life. We are here for such a short time, so, damn it, have a great time!" Pattie declares.

The artist has continued her recording career, reviving her signature hit "After Dark" with new vocals and a floor-filling arrangement by Rick Gianatos in 2006, which featured a staggering assortment of remixes, one of which was done by L.E.X. (who, by coincidence, had their studio in the complex that had housed the Casablanca offices). Rick and Pattie recorded more material, and the club smash "It's All About the Music" was elected to be her next release in 2011. This original song, co-written by Marilyn McLeod (who wrote "Love Hangover" for Diana Ross and "Same Ol' Love 365 Days a Year" for Anita Baker), was a huge club hit that placed Brooks back the dance music charts. In 2013, she teamed with Rick Gianatos for a rousing new high-energy track for the *First Ladies of Disco* album called "I Like the Way You Move." "It's an exciting time because even with the economic downfall, there's still that excitement about club music and to do something like this track has been very cool," she says.

Pattie Brooks ranks among disco's finest talents—a woman whose voice was capable of far more than the confines of the genre but who expanded its dimensions. She hopes that her life and accomplishments, including "After Dark," will be remembered and that people think of her as "*Fun!* That I was fun, that I stayed true to myself ... the path that was chosen for me was fine, and I have no regrets. I really want to see everybody become who they want to be, whatever path they take. Go to the max with it! That's the way I feel about myself. If they can remember me as someone very authentic—that I loved people—that I wanted to see other

"You have to get out and rejuvenate your mind and your spirit," says Pattie Brooks (courtesy Rick Gianatos).

people fulfill their dreams — that is the way that I would love to be thought of. And that I loved my family, loved being me and loved looking in the mirror and saying, 'Oh my God girl, look at you!'" Pattie laughs.

Miquel Brown

Okay, here's the plain and simple truth: sometimes disco cuts right to the chase! In this case, they mixed a frantic countdown, an urgent beat and savvy lyrics about the hedonistic joys of getting laid by sexy male studs with the stunning vocal work of a dynamic singer named Miquel Brown, and they ended up with one of the most popular dance concoctions to ever blast from a discothèque speaker! "So Many Men, So Little Time" placed singer Miquel Brown forever on the dance music map, but it's just one of many highlights from the artist's long and exciting music career.

Born in Detroit on the border with Windsor, Ontario, Canada, Miquel Brown's love for singing manifested itself early. "I started singing when I was about three years old," she says, "and drove everyone crazy! Singing was my passion even then!" Her unique name was derived from her original birth name, Michael (and both are pronounced the same). She emerged a beautiful young woman and, while still quite young, the aspiring artist gave birth to a daughter named Sinitta (who would eventually become a protégé of *The X-Factor*'s Simon Cowell and achieved stardom in Britain as a major dance music artist with the Stock-Aitken-Waterman team in the later half of the '80s. Sinitta scored big with the hits "Toy Boy" and "So Macho"). Brown's early career included appearances in cast shows, including the U.S. tour of *Hair*, a stint in *Bubbling Brown Sugar* and the London production of *Decameron* in 1973. Performing was her entire focus. "I loved both singing and acting equally, and I didn't think of success. I just enjoyed doing what I loved doing," she says. Brown soon added recording work to her resume, with songs such as "First Time Around" creating a buzz in the U.K.

Among her associations was Amii Stewart, who followed a similar stage performance path to success in disco music, eventually exploding on the scene in 1979 with the worldwide number 1 classic disco remake "Knock on Wood" and the internationally acclaimed Italo soft-dance hit "Friends" a few years later. Brown clarifies widely reported inaccuracies about their relationship saying, "Amii is not a stepsister; she is my best friend. There was never any competition between us. I helped get the deal for her to record 'Knock on Wood,' and I had a track on the charts at the same time entitled 'Symphony of Love.'" Brown's hit from the album of the same name was produced and composed by Alan Hawkshaw, who scored a disco smash with "Here Comes That Sound" with his group, Love Deluxe, and had worked with Casablanca Records' Love & Kisses and Donna Summer. "Symphony of Love" was mixed by Jim Burgess and became Brown's first hit on the late '70s club scene.

Miquel had little hesitation about lending her voice to the disco genre. "I didn't feel disco was restrictive in any way. I had studied opera with Fredrick Wilkerson and Jean

Povey and actually thought I wanted to be a female Sinatra," she recalls. She cites Plastique Bertrand, Donna Summer and Grace Jones as the artists she wanted to emulate. By the early '80s, Miquel's path crossed with that of famed British producers and songwriters Ian Levine and Fiachra Trench, who took the singer to the next phase and the ultimate level of her music career. Says Brown, "Ian was a fan of my theater performances and had someone get in touch with me to record with him. I truly love both of them! They're amazingly creative people. The labels put my name out there in a big way, and I am thankful for that!"

"Big way" only scratches the surface of the partnership. In 1983, the team released the song "So Many Men, So Little Time," a track Brown says the duo wrote specifically for her voice. It received a thunderous reception. With its introductory countdown and popping, energized beat, the invigorating tune helped usher in the Hi-NRG sound that revived and furthered the evolution of disco (along with Evelyn Thomas' smash, "High Energy," by the same team). Brown's song became an enormous worldwide anthem. Striking an equally powerful, if campy, chord with gay and straight audiences alike, the song became a club smash in the same way "It's Raining Men" had sent dancers rushing to the floor. The artist says she had no premonition the song would catch on as wildly as it did. "I had no idea it would be that big, and I was shocked at its success," Brown admits. "The beat at the time was great and the counting effect was also good for aerobic classes!" she laughs. "I believe it was a fantasy of both the straight and gay communities to have a one night stand with no strings, which the song exemplified. When I received my first gold record, it made me scream! The first time someone asked for my autograph when I was just out shopping made me think, 'Wow, I better start wearing makeup when I go out! People know who I am!'"

Miquel Brown was ready for the '80s when her single "So Many Men, So Little Time" was released in America by TSR Records (courtesy Tom Hayden/TSR Records).

The song was picked up by West Coast U.S. dance label TSR Records and, according to the label's founder and president, Tom Hayden, it was an all-out smash. He states, "The biggest record for us ever was 'So Many Men,' as far as 12" singles go. It was already released in Europe, and there was a buzz starting to happen on it with DJs in New York and other major U.S. club markets as an import. I was calling DJs every week to find out about hot new product, and I was hearing about this record. I called Record Shack and they said it was available for the U.S. I think, at the time, we paid a lot of money for it. I was generally picking up dance records for about $3,000 to $4,000. I think our first release, 'Capital Tropical' by Two-Man Sound, cost us $1,000 for the rights in North America. For Miquel Brown, I think we paid $10,000 for the rights in North and South America, which, at the time, was kind of high. But it just exploded! Within the first four or five weeks, we were selling 3,000 to 4,000 copies a day of the 12." I think we ended up selling a quarter of a million 12" singles, which was huge!"

"It didn't go as high as we hoped it would on the pop chart though," he admits. "It was funny. We had a lot of pop stations playing the record at different times. If all of them had been playing it at once and we had gotten all those reports in the same weeks, we probably would have had the record in the Top 20 or Top 10 on the pop charts. We were on every station in New York — WKTU, WBLS, Los Angeles and Florida, all the major cities, but all at different times. One city would come off the record, and another would pick up on it. Unfortunately, they just all didn't come together to get us higher on the pop charts."

He adds, "'So Many Men' had been released in England when we took it, and it had been doing okay, but it wasn't a big hit there yet. We really got it onto the charts here and took it to number 1 in the U.S. and produced a video here, which got on MTV and a few other outlets. So it made Miquel a big star, and she was performing a lot. A lot of countries caught on because it was a hit in the U.S. It did very well for us in Brazil, and I think we had a gold record with it in Mexico and I think Canada as well. At the height of all this, Miquel was doing really well, and we had her on tour. The night before a big show at a major club in Philadelphia, we had her take a limo from New York and it was a real rainy, icy winter night, and the limo got in an accident. She got seriously injured. She had to fly back to England and had to recuperate for quite a few months. That, unfortunately, sidelined her right at the peak of everything happening.

"Miquel Brown was fantastic, though!" Tom says. "She would be any place you asked her to be, do anything you needed her to do and was the nicest person. So sweet! She was always sending us notes thanking us — when we should have been thanking her. She was always a great person to work with!"

Many fondly recall the understated, yet sophisticated, artwork that graced the TSR 12" single for this release, which was the polar opposite of the usual beefcake shots that were common marketing gimmicks for dance records of the day. Hayden explains, "I thought it was kind of neat that the cover for 'So Many Men' was a lot of little male icons and the clock in the middle. It seemed to get the point across. I kind of felt a lot of the artwork that was out there at the time was so flashy that it made the records seem hokey to me. So I wanted to do things that were classy, but still got the marketing across. I take responsibility for the art, so like it — I get the credit. Don't like it — I get the criticism. We purposely went for that type of look. It seemed to work and was on display prominently in records stores. Understated or not, I think it got the point across."

The single was followed by a six-track album recorded in London, aptly titled *Manpower*. Hot on the heels of her astonishing success, the Record Shack label delivered the next single, the theatrical "He's a Saint, He's a Sinner." Another Levine-Trench composition, the track was a hit in the clubs, but it failed to ignite the fire of the previous release. Singer Earlene Bentley ("I'm Living My Own Life") contributed backing vocals to the "Saint" song, adding to the sweetness. Another noteworthy cut, the stomper "Beeline," was structured to somewhat emulate "So Many Men." However, Hayden found the efforts less than stimulating. "I was a little disappointed that the album, which we picked up as well, didn't have more hits comparable to 'So Many Men,'" he recalls. "With Record Shack, I found they kind of ran in and produced albums in a hurry and were very intent on getting the advances from all the territories they licensed the singles to. It didn't seem to me that they took the care and effort into getting two or three more good hits on the album. Had they done that, we would have probably done a bunch of albums with Miquel Brown. We probably just broke even on Miquel's *Manpower* album after the advance."

Despite the modest appeal of her LP venture, Brown continued to appear onstage in theatrical productions, while actively promoting her music. Another new album followed in 1985, *Close to Perfection*, which was again produced by Levine. The title track was a popular club hit — creatively different, melodic and slightly softer in its approach than "So Many Men." However, the widespread success of the latter again could not be duplicated. She continued her association with Record Shack and other labels for a time, releasing club hits like "On the Radio," "One Hundred Percent," "One Way Street/Love Reputation" and "Footprints in the Sand." Most of her collaborations were with the Levine and Trench team.

In 1986, Miquel filled in for a pregnant Helen Scott and became a temporary member of group the Three Degrees, promoting the single "This Is the House" across Europe. The singer, who ironically cites the song "It's Raining Men" as a track she wishes she had recorded, returned to Hi-NRG music in the '90s with the release of a cover version of the Pet Shop Boys' "It's a Sin," co-produced by legendary British diva Hazell Dean. This recording saw release in Brazil, Japan, South Africa and the U.K. (through Infinity Records) and has become a cult-favorite cover version among Pet Shop Boys fans. Miquel has spent the last decade concentrating on her family and has maintained her media presence mostly through acting work in film and television. Her most notable recent film credits include *French Kiss* with Meg Ryan and *An American Haunting* opposite Sissy Spacek.

"I don't think people realize we are or were some of the best singers around, even by today's standards," opines Brown. "It helps being a female, because both straight and gay men are usually perfect gentlemen when around a lady. They act accordingly, and I just love them and they know it!" On managing to avoid

Still acting and singing, Miquel Brown embraces her standing as a classic dance music diva (photograph by Francis Loney, styled by Paul Tams).

the drug and alcohol pitfalls of the business, she says, "I was and am still addicted to singing and performing. You can't do that properly off your head, and I guess I've always cared too much for my public image. I wanted to be a role model for the next generation." Her philosophy today is, "Enjoy life, take care of your skin, drink lots of water, seize the day and embrace unconditional love!"

Miquel Brown has made some unforgettable contributions to dance music that ensure her voice will be hailed among the finest the genre has served up. She would like to be remembered "as someone who loved singing and acting and someone who felt very blessed to be allowed to do what she loved most as work. How cool was that? I am honored and humbled to be thought of as a classic dance music diva!"

Linda Clifford

Entering the disco music arena in the late '70s, Linda Clifford possessed the beauty, charm, personality and vocal prowess of a surefire winner. A former Miss New York State, each of her endeavors in the disco genre has been widely regarded as a "classic with class" (an equally accurate description of the singer). All of her hits are instantly recognizable anthems, and there's no mistaking her powerful, energizing, determined voice. Linda's smoky, street-worthy delivery saturated every lyric with a raw authenticity and a dose of urban real-life. "If My Friends Could See Me Now," "Runaway Love," "Red Light" and "Don't Come Crying to Me" spoke to the frustrations, romantic or otherwise, of a legion of fans. She loaned her voice to inspiring, high-energy songs of empowerment throughout the disco era (and beyond) and still actively records engaging dance music today. Without question, Linda Clifford is a true artist.

Like so many great singers of the disco era, Clifford was a product of New York City. She was born in the Bedford-Stuyvesant section of Brooklyn and later moved to Park Slope. "My dad had a great voice but chose to be a plumber since there was no money in music. My mom was a fashion designer—so don't ask me how they got together!" she says with a laugh. Her family included two brothers and a baby sister. Her career as a performer began at the age of four, early by anyone's standards. Right out of the gate, she started making disco connections. "Carol Douglas and I actually started together as child performers at Macy's and on weekly television shows and that sort of thing," she recalls. "It's amazing — there's connections all throughout this whole thing." As a skinny actress in the earliest days of her show business career, Clifford had roles in such films as *Sweet Charity* with Shirley MacLaine and earned "scream queen" horror movie credentials by appearing in the 1968 chiller *Rosemary's Baby* with Mia Farrow and *The Boston Strangler* with Tony Curtis (where she enjoyed playing the role of a "dead girl"). She says, "Growing up in New York as a young child, my dream was really to become a singer. Acting was just something that if it happened, it happened. But I had always wanted to do theater, and I loved performing for live audiences. That was always my goal. The fact that I was able to work with a live band and perform in front of a live audience every night was a big joy for me in my early career. Although

I eventually left New York and didn't get to Broadway, I started touring and felt I was very successful at this phase in my life."

Linda began performing in nightclubs and singing a variety of musical styles. Unlike other entertainers in the early stages of their careers, she managed to avoid being a secretary, part-timing at department stores and other typical jobs, saying, "For many, many years, working clubs was the *only* thing I did. And not always very successfully at times, I might add. You know, you'd go and work your gig, and at the end of the week you'd go to get your money and the manager would say, 'Oh, well, we didn't really make any money this week and we can't really pay you.' I'd be like, 'What?!' And there you are! You've got your whole band standing around, and they've got families." Linda's tone changes from appreciation for the humor of that frustration to cognizance of the somewhat sobering reality of life as a performer. "It's a brutal business—seriously—from the beginning all the way through. It just takes different shapes of brutality as you progress in the business."

"There were so many times," she laughs, "I would take my portfolio and toss it under the bed or throw it in the garbage—and then go dig it out. I'd say, 'That's it! I quit, and I'm never singing again!' You just go through those phases. Then, 15 or 20 minutes later, you say, 'What am I crazy? This is what I live for!' And you go and start all over again. I would say, overall, I did have that never-say-die drive, but there were times it wasn't easy!"

Linda was part of a group called the Jericho Jazz Singers and another called Linda and the Trade Winds. Life on the road scoring gigs was creatively satisfying for the vocalist learning her trade, but it was also physically taxing. "I was working nightclubs for a long time, but after a while you sometimes start thinking, 'Can I get up and do this one more time?'" she says. "When you're doing it six nights a week and you're working six hours a night, that's a lot of singing! It was rare to get home before the sun came up. After a while, that begins to play on you. At some point you start to say, 'Is this really good for me?' Of course, being young and naïve, I didn't realize those late hours at the club were *nothing* compared to what was coming later in my career!" she admits with the vigorous laugh of a club-life survivor.

Clifford recalls, "I can remember one time I was doing a gig up in Anchorage, Alaska, working with my band. I was so sick—I had pneumonia. I was weak with a fever and passing out all the time. I made them tie me to a bar stool so that I could go on. They covered the roping with my blouse so nobody could see it. My guys had wives and kids, and if I didn't perform, we didn't get paid. I sat there, and I sang. Horribly, I would add, but the thought of not doing the show—I couldn't deal with that. When you grow up performing the way I did, working the Catskills circuit and all over New York, I met a lot of people who had been performing for years and years. They approached me with the mantras 'the show must go on,' 'break a leg'—all the stuff that you hear and you laugh about—but it really *is* the mentality when you are living that kind of lifestyle. It's like, 'You've got pneumonia; that's nice—here, put your dress on!'"

She adds, "Some people might say fortunately that attitude is not around so much anymore. But other people might say *unfortunately* it's not around anymore because the work ethic is different now. A lot of things in the business are so different now, and I'm not sure that's all good for the performers. I think some of my training made me a better performer. It made me appreciate my success more. It's like anything that's worth having is worth the struggle to get there. When you get there, you really, really appreciate it. You're like, 'Oh my gosh, look at this!' You worked for it; you earned it. It's not something that someone just handed to you because you looked a certain way.

"It reminds me of that TV show *The Voice*, which I love. Just the fact that the judges cannot see who's performing — that makes my heart sing! When I watch the show, I think about the people that are so talented who are out there and who didn't get a break because of maybe how they looked. Maybe they were a few pounds overweight or maybe they didn't walk the way people thought they should walk, whatever. Those things stopped someone who was really talented from having a career. Unfortunately, we live in a society where people really listen with their eyes. Today, you have to almost be a performance artist to be successful. When I watched the [2012] Grammys and I saw Adele just stand there and sing a song, I said, 'Thank you God!' I was so over this circus performance thing that happens with so many acts. Even if they are really talented vocalists, you don't really hear that because they keep you so busy with the stuff that's going on."

Linda's striking, youthful beauty in the '70s, a combination of warm, piercing, almond-shaped eyes, high cheekbones, luxurious dark hair, a slim athletic figure and an electric smile, were assets to the artist, which she readily admits. "I have to believe my looks had something to do with my success. But I also think being forceful and knowing what you want also had more to do with it. Sort of, 'Desperate times call for desperate measures.' At one point in my life, I was working at the Playboy Club in Chicago with my band, and I had just divorced. I was raising a sister, a foster child and a one-year-old son, and I thought I was going

Linda Clifford stands proudly after scoring the chart-topping disco smash "If My Friends Could See Me Now" in 1978 (courtesy Linda Clifford).

to have to take a job as a waitress because I couldn't take care of these children and handle all this craziness on the salary I was making. I thought, 'I have to do *something*!' I knew there was this record company in the city, Curtom Records, and I just hopped in a cab and went there. I just walked in, and I asked for the owner, Curtis Mayfield. The receptionist asked if he was expecting me," Linda laughs. "He wasn't there, but his partner was and he let me up to his office. I introduced myself and said I was appearing at the Playboy Club, and I would love it if they would come see me and hear me sing. 'I need to be a recording artist!'" Linda chuckles, "If I tried that today, I'd be thrown out on my butt!"

"After I left, I thought I had gone insane doing what I did. Well, amazingly, they showed up. About three nights later — Curtis Mayfield, his partner, and maybe five or six other people. They sat at this big huge table right in the center of the room and I thought, 'Oh my God!' Well, we did our thing and it went great. I did everything from Aretha to Phyllis Hyman to Paul Simon — a variety of different things. Two weeks later, I had a recording contract."

Clifford's 1977 debut album, *Linda*, produced and arranged by Gil Askey (*Lady Sings The Blues*, *The Supremes Sing Rogers & Hart* and Diana Ross's music director for many years), garnered some attention with "From Now On," the funky, uptempo soul-pop single composed by Bunny Sigler. The song held positions on both the R&B and dance charts. Other tracks included renditions of material by Rod Stewart, the Bee Gees and Stevie Wonder. "My first album was mostly covers," she says, "because we really didn't have any new material, and they were thinking we'd try it and see what happens. The album actually got quite a bit of airplay, and people took notice. So, they thought that maybe we should do something else. And that's when 'If My Friends Could See Me Now' came along, a song which really took me to the next level."

Clifford's follow-up album, also called *If My Friends Could See Me Now*, was a smash on the discothèque circuit and crossed over to both the pop albums chart and the Top 10 of R&B. The infectious high energy title track (a mainstay from Broadway's *Sweet Charity* show, which Clifford had once appeared in elsewhere) was a powerful, feverishly orchestrated disco extravaganza. Miraculously, it somehow managed to avoid camp pitfalls thanks largely to Clifford's relentless, stylized vocal enthusiasm and a serious, pumping arrangement. The Jones Girls, who later received their own record deal, provided backup vocals on the track. Invariably, Clifford was compared to Donna Summer, the rising superstar from producer Giorgio Moroder's camp. "I absolutely felt they were trying to mold me to be like Donna. I can't say I wasn't a fan of hers. I enjoyed her music to dance to — I liked to dance a lot. I had even sung her 'Love to Love You Baby' hit with my band before I had begun recording myself. I remember people asking me, 'Sing that song where she moans a lot!' I always said, 'I don't moan for just anybody!'" Linda laughs. "I did end up singing that song often, but I didn't imagine myself singing disco [as a recording career]."

Had Linda followed her initial instincts about doing a disco cover of "If My Friends Could See Me Now," the iconic dance classic might never have been made. "I originally turned down 'If My Friends Could See Me Now' when they came to me with it. I said 'No, that's sacrilege! You can't take that beautiful Broadway song and turn it into disco.' They laid the track down anyway, and when I heard it, I immediately took back what I had said." The track had a power, theme and hook Clifford felt the public would relate to strongly. "I think so many people have someone in their life or in their past that they want to say, '*Ah-ha!* Look at me now!'" she says.

"I did the song, and I had no idea it would take off the way it did. They called me and asked me if I had seen *Billboard*. I said, 'No, I'm washing my kitchen floor!'" she laughs. "They said my song was number 1, and I thought they were joking. I ran out and got the magazine and, sure enough, it was! And then this whirlwind started, and I was going everywhere, meeting the DJs and all the wonderful people who played the song. I was seeing for the first time how people reacted when the song came on. I couldn't believe it—the people dancing, the screaming and the jumping. These people didn't even know I was there with them. The song would come on and the first five notes would play, and it was like people were losing their minds! Studio 54, all the major clubs in New York, Los Angeles—everywhere!" Clifford's stardom spread to Europe as well, where the singer performed on numerous television shows in France, Germany and the U.K. (where the single was a Top-50 hit).

With an explosion of attention engulfing the performer as a pop and club sensation, Linda experienced the moment when she knew she had truly arrived. "I can tell you exactly when that moment was," she claims. "I had hosted *The Midnight Special*, I had done *Don Kirshner's Rock Concert*, and then I got a call to do *American Bandstand*—and *that* was it! I stood on that stage next to Dick Clark! And he asked me, 'What's the most exciting thing that has happened to you in the last two years?' I had been to Europe, done all these amazing concerts, all the things I had dreamed of doing—but I said, '*This* is it!' Because I grew up in New York watching *American Bandstand*, and I just couldn't believe I was standing next to Dick Clark and we were actually talking—like having a conversation in a living room. It was unbelievable!"

This stellar event in Clifford's career trumped even the Grammy and American Music Award nominations she received in 1978, which she readily admits were also career highlights. "I was thrilled about them, absolutely. But I never expected to win the Grammy. They put me in a category with Chaka Khan, Aretha Franklin, Donna Summer and Alicia Bridges," she says. Don't place any bets too quickly on the outcome of that race: "Guess what—Alicia Bridges won!" laughs Linda. Like all polished performers, Clifford smiled and applauded as Bridges accepted her award. "That particular night was filled with so many ups and downs. I was also a presenter with Evelyn 'Champagne' King. We were presenting a Lifetime Achievement award to Isaac Hayes. It's funny now, but it wasn't funny then. Glen Campbell introduced Evelyn and me. At the rehearsals, he kept calling me 'Linda Crawford.' They were holding up these cue cards and saying, 'Glen, just read the cards.' Three times he called me Linda Crawford and said, 'Aaah, don't worry about it. I'll get it right tonight.' Well, sure enough, we're standing in the wings that night, and he introduces us. There was no monitor backstage, so we couldn't hear anything. You just waited for somebody to give you the signal to walk out. So we walked out. Evelyn and I did this whole thing—a little banter between us—and we introduced Isaac Hayes. I get back to my seat and my husband grabs my hand and says, "I'm so proud of you!' I'm thinking, 'What the hell is he talking about?' Then it hit me: Glen had introduced me as *Linda Crawford!*"

Nearly as big a hit as "If My Friends Could See Me Now" and, for many fans, her most memorable, was Clifford's Gil Askey–penned single "Runaway Love," a Top-Three R&B smash that crossed onto the pop chart. It was the first of her songs to slam home the "take no crap" theme that ran through many of Clifford's biggest hits. She delivered her philosophy with a very honest, heartfelt style that helped to make her words ring true. "I really wanted something that would empower women and make them feel their worth," she asserts. "'Runaway Love' was kind of an accident though. It came about in the studio goofing around talking about my ex-husband. It was recorded without me knowing it, with the band laughing in the background. They said to me that it could be a hit. They started playing it back to me and I said, 'Oh no, you can't use that; I'm so embarrassed.' But they said, 'No, it's gonna be great!' Then we started putting verses and choruses to it. And the rap was really off the top of my head. You know, I grew up and I saw things, heard things, saw the issues with women—women being battered and that kind of thing. I really thought this was the way to go. When it was time to do a follow-up—and 'Don't Give It Up' ended up being the song—I was kind of like, 'Okay, here we go again.' But I really *did* want women to hear [these songs] and feel stronger and take more charge of their lives." Clifford feels they are still relevant today, citing contemporary political debates boiling over health insurance rights, abortion and other women's issues. "Here we are today, and we're still dealing with issues over women's bodies, who's in charge, and men deciding whether women should have certain types of health insurance. I mean, come on!"

There is humor in these songs as well, and it's not lost on Clifford. The singer laughs at the references to canines in these tracks. "I love animals, and I especially love dogs. I don't have one right now because our last one passed away a few years ago. It was just so hard. He was 13 years old. You go through that a few times and they become ill—you just start to feel that your heart can't take it anymore. But I *am* an animal lover. The reason I mentioned the dog in the song was because I once got left with a 240-pound St. Bernard that used to drag me all over the street! He was too strong—he would walk *me*!" she laughs. "So, I thought nobody should be left with a dog *that* big."

The *Let Me Be Your Woman* album followed in 1979. The album continued Linda's hot streak with an LP cover accentuating her highly stylized, sensual look. In addition to the somewhat derivative, finger-pointing single "Don't Give It Up" (another Top-20 R&B hit which Clifford co-wrote with Askey), was another unlikely and eclectic disco smash. "Bridge Over Troubled Water" followed in the footsteps of Clifford's "Friends" adaptation and pumped a ferocious vocal performance into a revved-up Jimmy Simpson mix. The track was a high-energy variation on Simon & Garfunkle's soft-rock classic, and it landed Clifford a Top-20 dance hit that fell just short of the pop Top 40.

Quickly following this album came two more efforts from the Curtom Records camp, projects that reflected the label's uncertainty about where to position Clifford. Both vocally strong R&B efforts, the albums seemed to be pulling the singer away from the disco genre. *Here's My Love* from 1979 and a 1980 duet collaboration with mentor Curtis Mayfield, *The Right Combination,* showed Clifford on a more soulful journey that, though often critically lauded, failed to duplicate her previous commercial success. However, the detour soon wound its way back to the dance floor.

In 1980, Linda's career was bolstered after a mandatory switch from Curtom to RSO Records, the pop label formed several years earlier by Robert Stigwood. RSO Records had distributed Curtom, and, at the time, was embroiled in a $200 million lawsuit filed by the BeeGees that was later settled. Stigwood disassociated from RSO the following year, and the label was eventually absorbed by Polygram. Despite the drama, Clifford delivered two major disco career highlights with the record company. The first was the funky number 1 dance-chart smash "Red Light" (from the *Fame* movie soundtrack and composed by Dean Pitchford and Michael Gore). Clifford says she had no wish to sing the *Fame* title track, which was handled by Irene Cara. "I was just thrilled to be part of a soundtrack that was Grammy and Oscar nominated!" she says. Clifford then teamed with producer Isaac Hayes for the album *I'm Yours*, which contained yet another smoking number 1 high-energy dance smash, "Shoot Your Best Shot." Both "Red Light" and "Shot" were mid-charting pop hits, a significant accomplishment during the disco backlash days. Linda describes Hayes as a "down to earth guy and easy to work with."

Moving over to Capitol Records, Clifford became caught in another tug-of-war. Her new label's desire to position her, again, with a more soulful sound jeopardized the security of the pop-dance crossover material that songwriters like Pitchford and Gore had so successfully crafted for her. In the end, both musical styles managed to let Clifford shine.

Linda's 1981 album, *I'll Keep on Loving You,* featured collaborations with arranger Luther Vandross and included the wonderfully heartfelt R&B hit, "I Had a Talk with My Man." The real triumph, however, was "Don't Come Crying to Me." The Pitchford-Gore composition (remixed by Rusty Garner), was a pounding thrill-ride into the swirling electro-pop and synthesizer landscapes that were evolving in the early '80s. The song returned the singer to the number 1 position on the dance chart.

By this time, Linda had earned herself a resume impressive by anyone's standards, but she concurs that life wasn't all fun and cash rolling in. Clifford, like so many others of the era, says she had to fight for royalty income. "I was very fortunate in that for the last 34 years I have been married to a very wonderful man who has allowed me to continue to do what I love to do. But also, if I don't want to do it, I have someone I can lean on. A lot of these girls who were singers that I have worked with, some with kids, had to go out and work *hard*! They *had* to do all these things, and that made it really difficult for them. I really feel in many ways I have been blessed in having this second chance at life with my children and husband. The royalty payment thing would be a real bonus if someone were to say, 'We're sorry, we screwed up. Here's the four million dollars we owe you.' But that's never gonna happen.

"If you write your own songs, there are organizations that watch out for you and protect you," she adds, "but for the artist, if you didn't make your money on your public appearances, then you didn't make *any* money. That was then — I know things are different now. I think today the labels are more careful about how they rip you off. So maybe those things don't happen as much anymore, but you really had to be prepared to make your money in your performances and not expect a great deal of royalty income."

She observes, "Once you catch on to what's happening, you can sometimes have a little bit of clout. Once you have a hit, when you can say that people know you, they know the label because of you — then you can say you want an advance on the next album. That was one thing that worked to my advantage. But there's a limit — you can't walk in and go, 'I want two and three million!' That didn't happen, especially back in the days of 1978 and '79. You might get a little something, but certainly not what you were entitled to and certainly not what you deserved.

"Today, with digital," she adds, "how do you even know what's really going on? Somebody actually gave me a website that I could reference, saying they didn't think I realized how many compilation albums I was on. I typed in my name and seriously — there had to be thousands of albums where my tracks had been used or I had been sampled and they were selling it. And I didn't even know about it! The fact that they are wrongly taking something that is unique to me — my voice — doesn't occur to them, or they just don't care. Sadly, I'm not the only one this is happening to. That doesn't make me any happier, but still. When you start talking about what goes on outside of this country, the thought of having to go to Germany, the U.K. or France and trying to sue someone to get your money — you're kidding. It's ridiculous! They know that, and they go ahead and do what they do because they know it will be so costly for you to go after them — that it won't be worth it in the long run. You'll give it up."

Clifford's recording career continued after leaving Capitol Records. The *Sneakin' Out* and *My Heart's on Fire* albums followed in 1984 and 1985, released by Red Label (a small, independent record company). The albums' standout tracks were the irresistible "A Night with the Boys," which read like a danceable love letter to the singer's many gay fans (and a Top-20 dance hit), and "The Heat in Me." From there, Linda stepped out of the limelight and began raising her family with her husband full-time. "The most important thing I concentrated on most of my life was my family," she says. "That, for me, was number 1. So as much as I loved the performance end of it, if I had to choose, I'd put my children on the school bus in the morning and be home when they got off that bus. And I did that for years. I stopped touring. It was important for me to be there for them. If they were not my kids, I'd want to be their friend. Today, my son is an archeologist—he likes to dig in the dirt. My daughter is working on being a singer and an actress, and she is into theater and living in Los Angeles. I'm very proud of both my children."

By the mid '90s, with her children sufficiently grown, Linda was able to return to music. In her decade-long absence, music had evolved, but her iconic status was still appreciated. While bootleg recordings sampling her vocals abounded, Clifford began teaming with prolific DJs and remixers like Ralphie Rosario and Joey Negro for legitimate releases, signed for a single with the historic (and then recently revived) West End label and racked up more house and club hits in the U.S. and U.K. (including her dance floor version of the song "Going Back to My Roots"). Most recently, Clifford's 2012 single, "How Long," overseen by Rick Gianatos and remixed by a truckload of highly revered DJs, among them David Ospena and the Almighty team out of Britain, has been a big success for the artist.

"Every time you do a performance, you learn something about yourself and your audience," she says. "As you age, there are certain things you know will affect your audience—that will pull them close to you. I just feel that when you are young and you're out there doing it, every time you go out there it's an experiment. As you get older, I don't think it's an experiment anymore. It's more that this is what I've learned, and I'm going to share it with you. I want you to get it. So I think for myself, there was a saying about some beauty product—'I'm not getting older; I'm getting better.' I think that's very true. If you've learned from life and the things around you and your mistakes—and everybody makes them—you just get better. You definitely get better. I'm grateful to have had that opportunity. And I hope to continue to get better!"

Today, Clifford says the biggest challenge of being a performer from the disco era is still centered on the bottom line of the financial statement. Though she's more interested in counting her blessings than dwelling on the subject, she addresses the issue firmly. "I've played a lot of major venues in my day. Even now, I still perform and do different types of shows. I work with dancers and background singers. I do my hits, some jazz, a little bit of everything. But then there are clubs that want you to do your hit songs, and they don't want to pay you. The venue

Linda Clifford attests, "If you've learned from life and the things around you and your mistakes—and everybody makes them—you just get better" (courtesy Linda Clifford).

managers call you up and say, 'Oh my God, you're a legend!' Then they ask you to show up and assume they can pay you almost nothing. The line I usually hear is, 'Why do we need to pay you money?'" Clifford laughs her response: "*Because you just said I'm ... a ... legend!*"

Part of the current dilemma for artists like Clifford may lie in the public's fading memory and their perception of disco as more of a novelty than a serious music genre. Thanks to significant crossover pop hits, Linda has fared better than some singers whose music was limited to club-land. "The first names you think of with disco music are Donna Summer and the Village People," says Linda. "There's no question Donna Summer opened the door. She had been ignored for years before she finally started to have a name in the industry and people, in general, began to respect her. I have performed with the Village People. They put on an amazing show and were — and are — wonderfully talented, still drawing crowds today. Their show is incredible! But you know, many of us had really big hits too, and yet we have to sometimes struggle to find work today. I'm luckier than some. What's that all about?"

Despite the realities of the current industry, she continues to plan ahead. "Actually, I would love to do an album of standards. Some of the old beautiful songs when they were really writing lyrics, and it wasn't about 'do me,'" she laughs. "Beautiful songs like 'In the Still of the Night.' I would love to do that kind of music." Most recently, Linda performed an extraordinary live show in September 2012 at the Park West in Chicago. It benefited Chicago House, an organization that cares for men, women and children with AIDS. "They help by providing housing, food, meds and education. They are simply amazing!" says Clifford. Featuring dancers, costumes and elaborate staging, it was an opportunity to perform a one-woman autobiographical show that left crowds dazzled and appreciative of the singer's extraordinary accomplishments.

Linda reflects on her vast catalog and one of her all-time favorite recordings. "[A song] that I recorded that not a lot of people know about was written for me by Michael Gore and Dean Pitchford. It was called 'All the Man That I Need.' That was written for my husband and I, and I recorded it for my *I'll Keep on Loving You* album. I was so thrilled when they came up with that one for me. When Whitney [Houston] recorded it and made it as popular as it was for her ... well, at first I thought, '*Aaarghh*, that's my song!' But then I got over it," she laughs. "[She sang] a great version. I thought, 'That's our song, and at least now everyone will hear about it.'"

As Linda Clifford's career continues to evolve and as appreciation for her monumental contributions to disco grows at a breakneck pace, there's no big litany of songs or specific highlights from the artist's honored history for which she'd like to be remembered. In fact, what she'd like is very simple. "I would want people to say, 'I remember going to her show and having the best time! She was a lot of fun! She was *fun*!'"

Carol Douglas

"It's so funny! Some people may not remember your name, but they remember your song. I've had people say, 'Oh, I don't know "Doctor's Orders," and then I'll have to sing it. And then they go, "Oh, wow, that's you? I know that song!" So, now, even my grandkids have seen me sing and perform, and they're all proud of me!'" beams singer Carol Douglas. Douglas' position as a disco diva was cemented into place from the very beginning of the genre's launch with "Doctor's Orders," one of disco music's very first pop chart crossover classics. It was just one of many recorded performances by the artist that became a standard of the genre. As one of disco's true originals, Carol Douglas has an unrelenting energy, sense of humor and appreciation for her history that is instantly endearing.

"I've never had a chance to talk about these things, so its fun for me," Douglas, a cousin of Sam Cooke, confesses. "Nobody usually calls you, except at that particular time when you're hot. Here comes *Billboard* or another magazine and then that's it until another album comes out. Sometimes you hope somebody will call because you're still doing concerts and clubs and touring or because you want to say something. So, you know what? I just keep a personal diary! But it *is* fun to talk about those days because it was the best time of my career. It's great to be in the lineup of original disco divas. I think my life would make a great movie or mini-series. All we need is to get Toni Braxton to play me as a young woman. Maybe call it 'The Carol Strickland Story' ... or wait, how about 'The True Life Story of Carol Strickland Douglas?'"

Carol recalls growing up in Brooklyn, where her earliest days were spent pursuing a youthful acting career, singing jingles and finding her niche. "I was a child star from the age of 10. I was at the Apollo Theater and was on the TV show *Name That Tune*. I won one of Hal Jackson's *Talented Teens* contests, and I followed in the footsteps of Patti Duke, Gregory Hines and Bernadette Peters. Our moms were friends, and we would hang out when we were little kids. Linda Clifford grew up on the same block as me, too, and we played with dolls together. I'm so glad she made it big. Our moms used to dress us up together for dancing school in Manhattan, so Linda and I are really close. She was at one end of the block, and I was at the other. Halsey Street—we need to change that name to 'Clifford-Douglas Way' in Brooklyn, New York—and the brownstone houses are still standing! I'm living right around the corner now from the house I originally grew up in. I came out as a singer in 1975 and '76, and Linda came right after me. I kind of envied her—she could always sing, and she was always pretty. She had long hair, and I had hardly any hair. I was always telling my mom I liked Linda's hair. My mom would say, 'What do you want me to do, put a pin in your head and

"Wow, I really accomplished something," says Carol Douglas of her debut disco smash, "Doctor's Orders," seen here in its LP format from 1975 (author's collection).

stick the hair in your scalp? Come on!'" Carol laughs. "I'd invite Linda to come over and play, and then I'd get mad at her beautiful long hair and tell her to get out!" she laughs heartily. "I knew Linda was going to be famous, but with her powerful voice, I thought she was going to be on Broadway or something. Then that perfect song, 'If My Friends Could See Me Now,' landed right at her feet."

In 1974, Carol discovered her own perfect song. Midland International Records was looking for a singer to cover a track originally sung by an artist named Sunny that had been doing well in the U.K. It was called "Doctor's Orders," a hook-filled tune ripe with the fledgling disco sound emerging in the U.S. "My mom happened to see an advertisement in a show business paper back in the day, and I auditioned for the song. They said if I could sing as good as I looked, I'd get a record deal. You know, everybody auditioning in the room was white; the only black person was me. Well, I got the record deal, and that was it — that was the beginning of it all. You know, I called my mom to tell her I got the contract, of course, and I was crying. She asked me why I was crying. I said it was because they told me I sounded white! She said, 'Oh yeah, I forgot to tell you; you *do* sound white.' I was like, 'Why didn't you tell me?'" she laughs in complete amusement. "It was so freaking funny; I have to laugh about it."

"Doctor's Orders," produced by Eddie O'Loughlin, a co-founder of Midland Records (distributed by RCA), utilized the production genius of Meco Monardo and Lou Del Gatto to give Carol's song the disco treatment. Monardo and Del Gatto were part of the same DCA production team, along with Jay Ellis, behind Gloria Gaynor's smash "Never Can Say Goodbye." Though happy to have gotten her big break, the artist frankly admits, "I wasn't really into [the song]. I liked the way I sang it, but it just wasn't the type of material I had been hoping to sing. To be honest, being a black artist, I really wanted a more soulful song than 'Doctor's Orders.'

"I hit the charts, though!" she adds. "I went around the world and performed in many clubs. I had a number 1 album in Japan, and I still haven't gotten there. They sent me an award by Fed Ex," she chuckles. "It was such a whirlwind thing having such a big record, but being a housewife and a mom, it didn't faze me at all — till maybe years later when I settled down and wasn't on the road as much. Then I could look back on it and say, 'Wow, I really accomplished something.' I look at the gold record on the wall — it's really been very exciting. I think it's more exciting now than it was at the beginning. I'm meeting a lot of fans now that like me, remember me — and that's great!"

Instantly catchy, "Doctor's Orders" hit the Top 10 of the pop chart in 1975. The track was in heavy rotation at the clubs, along with Gloria Gaynor's "Never Can Say Goodbye," resulting in both cuts often being cited as the first breakthrough disco crossover songs by women of the era. "It sold 100,000 copies in the first week! How many songs did that?" says Douglas. "I felt the minute I heard the music that it was going to be something, and after hearing my voice on the track, it was even more amazing. I remember they did throw me off when they played me the original European hit version. So I had to approach it in my own way. Almost all of my early hits were European hits. 'Doctor's Orders,' 'Midnight Love Affair,' 'Dancing Queen'— they were all European songs, and I just did the remakes." The label followed "Doctor's Orders" with *The Carol Douglas Album* in 1975, which yielded another Top-20 disco hit, "A Hurricane Is Coming Tonight," a song that also crossed onto the pop charts.

Douglas describes her partnership with O'Loughlin, who was her producer for several years. She says, "Eddie was very nice, but we sometimes had our differences in the studio.

I felt that he had a good handle on my singing career, but I felt a little uncomfortable about being, well, black at times. I think there was some effort to keep me with a certain [white] sound and I wanted to do more R&B. It made me a little uncomfortable, and it made me sometimes dislike some of the songs I did because they didn't want me to sound like ... well ... the way I thought I was supposed to sound. I always thought I was supposed to sound like Stephanie Mills! She was my idol. I always wanted to get a song like hers. But then I came to realize that even if they gave me a song like Stephanie Mills', I wouldn't sound like her. Because I just didn't have that real soulful sound. And I still don't today. It's funny now; I can actually laugh about it today."

"Midnight Love Affair," released in 1976, was the name of Douglas' much-anticipated follow-up single and album. The song, part of the sequenced suite on the A-side of the album, failed to dent the U.S. pop charts, but became an enormous number 1 club hit and standard of the era. "'Midnight Love Affair' was my favorite song, favorite album cover—everything," Douglas declares. "It's a really magical song, and I also became a big star in Paris as a result of it. I met the producer [of the original French version] when I was there, and we had a wonderful time. That was a very good era for me. I did a lot of television. I did *The Midnight Special* with Wolfman Jack and John Travolta, who was also on my label at the time, *Soul Train, American Bandstand, Don Kirshner's Rock Concert* and many others. I met Michael Jackson, and I remember when he said, 'I love your song "Doctor Love."' I had to tell him it was 'Doctor's Orders,'" she laughs. "I also opened Studio 54. I was one of the first or second acts they ever had at the club."

The formula was repeated on 1977's *Full Bloom* album, which included Douglas' remake of "Light My Fire," a dual club hit with "I Want to Stay with You." The artist's disco-fused rendition of the ABBA hit "Dancing Queen" was on every major club DJ's playlist, further cementing her standing as a major disco star. The arrangement influence of Monster Orchestra stalwart John Davis ("Love Magic," "Ain't That Enough for You") was evident on many of the LP cuts and his flair for lush orchestrations was an excellent match for Carol's sweet-sounding vocals. The album, which featured background work by Sharon Redd, also included a take on the Rupert Holmes–penned track "Who, What, When, Where, Why," which Dionne Warwick was adding to her repertoire around the same time. The club gigs came fast and furious, but the singer had little problem handling the nightlife. "The drugs and stuff didn't affect me. It was just going on around me. You know, I was more the mom type, and I had to get home to my kids and watch my children. I did hang out in the clubs sometimes after singing, and I did party once in a while. I guess I was a club person in that respect. But I was home a lot more often, and I preferred to go shopping," she laughs. "That's what was going on in my life."

At the height of the disco era, Carol's star power was evident when the singer's name was prominently seen on the marquee of a nightclub in the film *Saturday Night Fever*. Still, only modest critical acclaim had ever been bestowed upon Douglas' recording efforts, a reality to which most disco artists had become accustomed. In 1978, that changed. *Burnin'*, her next studio set, expanded beyond disco's so-called predictable parameters and featured a proud, bright, close-up cover portrait. It became her most progressive-sounding and highly lauded album ever. Released by Midsong (formerly Midland) in partnership with MCA Records, the electronic drum and keyboard-fused LP was highlighted by a sharp Michael Zager arrangement of the BeeGees' "Night Fever."

Co-producer John Davis' sumptuous (and Grammy-worthy) pop-dance masterpiece, "Fell in Love for the First Time Today," and the thumping, anthemic title track, "Burnin'," were tailor-made for the clubs and substantial hits. The tracks smoothly melded on another non-stop A-side mix. Both the title track and "Night Fever" were Top-20 dance chart hits. Carol recalls of the well-reviewed album, "Cissy Houston sang on the track 'Burnin', which was wonderful, and it got nominated for a Grammy. That was so exciting ... until they *didn't* announce my name. Donna Summer won that year, but that's okay. Really, it was an honor in itself just to be nominated, and it was a major highlight of my career." Ironically, Carol was tapped to sing her own rendition of Donna's hit "Heaven Knows" on a recent album tribute to the late artist.

Though *Burnin'* was a tough act to follow, the LP *Come Into My Life* ambitiously hit the record stores in 1979. The A-side was produced by Greg Carmichael, who was a collaborator with dance production legend Patrick Adams. John Fitch and Reuben Cross (who had written many of Evelyn "Champagne" King and Wardell Piper's first hits) produced the flip side tracks and gave the artist some of that soulful sound she had been seeking. Although some momentum had been lost since *Burnin'*, the frantic lead single, "I Got the Answer," focused squarely on the dance floor. However, the song and the album failed to register strongly with its target audience and became further mired in the disco backlash at the decade's end. Douglas left Midsong and the RCA fold on good terms, however. "RCA was very, very good to me back in the day. I had no problems with them. Everything was always on the up and up, and I have only good things to say about them," she declares.

Carol emerged in the '80s with a fresh, funkier sound that was well matched to the changing times. Though covered at the same time by Prince Charles' favorite girl-group (on their Giorgio Moroder—produced album *3D*), Carol's version of "My Simple Heart," released as a 12" single by 20th Century Records in the U.S., was the stateside club winner. The track was one of the earliest releases from O'Loughlin's newly emerging Plateau production house, soon to be called Next Plateau Records. With his new label, "Eddie O" (as he became known in the business) would eventually oversee one of the biggest record companies in dance music history. "My Simple Heart" was a sleaze-speed floor shuffler that garnered extensive club play throughout the 1981 summer season. Douglas then joined the launch of Next Plateau and released "I Got Your Body" and "You're Not So Hot" in 1982, the latter mixed by Jonathan Fearing. Another single, "Got Ya Where I Want Ya," kept Douglas on the turntables with remixes by John "Jellybean" Benitez. The artist's last full-length album was among her best. *Love Zone*, a highly listenable LP with zero filler, featured full-length versions of her earlier '80s hits. By the end of the decade, she teamed with producer Darryl Payne and co-penned the track "When Love Goes Wrong."

Carol has no hesitation identifying the song she'd like to have been given a shot at and the singer whom she admired most back in the day. "I would have *loved* to sing Diana Ross' 'Love Hangover,'" says Carol. "I finally got a chance to meet her at a birthday party for Burt Reynolds at Studio 54 and she had a beautiful red satin kind of cowboy outfit on with fringe. She was sitting there and these two guys were fanning her and she looked over at me and said, 'You! I want you to come over here and sit with me!' It was unbelievable. My idol was asking me to sit with her. I grabbed her hand and said, 'I just love you.' She said she loved 'Doctor's Orders.' I was so nervous, I said, 'Do you want it? You can have it!'—like I was giving the song away. It was so funny! The next day in the press, they showed her picture with *my* name under it!"

Though Douglas continued actively touring and performing thereafter, her recording career was largely relegated to appearances on compilation albums, and her time was spent enjoying the fruits of her accomplished career. Among her most supportive followers has been her gay audience. She says, "If it weren't for the gay people, there'd be no Carol Douglas. They kept me going! I was always very friendly with people of any kind, and I appreciated everyone. Later on in my career, I have to tell you—I did so many surprise party appearances in gay people's apartments! Everybody was so happy then. To me, to be a part of that was so wonderful—it was like opening a gift. Gay, straight, whatever they were, they accepted me so highly. I miss those days. I miss a lot of that atmosphere. I still have it today, in a different way. I often get shows or events to appear at, and people still come up to me to sign their albums. They are filming me on their cell phones, and it's very rewarding. You know, I see those kids on *American Idol* wanting to make it the way I did, and I wish I could help them to experience what I have experienced."

"I know I'll never stop singing," says Carol Douglas, who regularly performs in disco revival concerts worldwide (courtesy Michael Harkins).

She embraces her experience in the disco genre warmly, including meeting fellow divas Loleatta Holloway and Carol Williams at the very first disco music forum and convention, when they were all pregnant. She doesn't feel the music or its stars have been neglected. Asserts Carol, "I think as long as the singers from the disco era are still performing and radio is still playing our songs once in a while—I feel that we're getting some respect. If I'm on a show with other artists, we're all getting the same applause. We're just there to please our fans. It's a personal choice if someone decides disco doesn't deserve respect. Sometimes even an artist may not want to be associated with the word *disco*, maybe not booked that way—they may want the word 'soul.' I don't know—I think it was a great era and I'm proud of it. If you had hits in that era, you were in the race and you won. If you're in, you're in! It's an honor. Nowadays, it's so hard to make it, and we gotta be grateful and thankful for the time we were on that rollercoaster ride. That's comin' from the heart. I love people to love what I do and who love me. Love is so important! When someone loves your music—that's really so special."

The artist shrugs off issues of aging in the business with an uplifting attitude of indifference. "Basically, I don't really have a philosophy about aging. I think it's more of a destiny. I think you just need to enjoy what you're doing as much as you can when you're doing it. I'm good as long as I'm enjoying what I'm doing. I like doing things myself, and I like being very independent. Being an only child, my mom and dad prepared me for life. And I have good friends. Carol Williams and I are such good friends — we're about the same age and we've known each other 30 years. We're like sisters. I like having connections like that. I know I'll never stop singing. That was my mother's dream for me and that dream came true. I'm planning to do a reality show about helping kids launch singing careers through my Rising Star Entertainment organization, so I got a lot of things in the works. I will always sing. If someone calls me for a show, and as long as I can get there, I'll be there. That's how I look at singing. I don't see myself *not* doing anything ... except maybe *not* cleaning the house too much!" she laughs. Meanwhile, Carol continues performing in disco concerts with her long-time fellow diva friends, effortlessly delivering "Doctor's Orders" here in the States and as far away as France, where songs like "My Simple Heart" and "Midnight Love Affair" cause crowds to roar. Her schedule seems to get busier with each passing week, and the artist seems very pleased by it all.

Carol Douglas' remarkably important contributions to disco are as essential as they are memorable. She helped define the original disco sound and her charming voice and irresistible songs punctuated disco's early days with true grace and elegance. She is proud of her work and accomplishments. Confident, eternally optimistic and absolutely determined, she says, "I'd like to be remembered as a very happy, giving person. And someone who also made people smile. I hope I am remembered as a singer who made people happy doing what I was put on this earth to do!"

Yvonne Elliman

The movie *Saturday Night Fever* was a turning point in disco's history. It brought the music genre and its club culture out from the shadows and turned the stew, for better or worse, into a boiling commercial feast. The BeeGees became superstars and disco, for a time, was truly the in thing. The movie's soundtrack was a sensation, selling staggering numbers and transforming its featured tracks into some of disco's most recognizable hits. Yvonne Elliman's "If I Can't Have You," a passionate, dynamic, uniquely orchestrated pop sparkler with a rolling dance rhythm, was among them. But the performer of the song did not plunge headfirst into the disco pool following her hit, as others had, and she failed to make her presence as well known on the dance floor as one might have expected. Yvonne's absence from the disco party was the result of her initial reluctance to accept her invitation. Her story illustrates that disco wasn't always the ideal genre for every singer and sometimes amazing results just *happened* despite a singer's mindset. However, her talent (and the impact of her rendition of one of the genre's most famous songs) is undeniable. Yvonne reveals that her acceptance of her disco connection has been a personal evolution.

Elliman was an only child who has only happy memories of growing up. "Apparently I'm Irish and Korean according to the Internet, which is totally wrong!" she says. "I'm actually French, German and British and my mom is Japanese. I wish I could say I was born in 1941— then I could really say I look amazing! But I was born December 29, 1951.

It was a great time to be born in Hawaii. I had this idyllic life. My parents never argued. Because I was an only child, my parents would get special things for me like typing classes, Evelyn Wood Reading Dynamics or charm school—whatever. They just would build me up in whatever ways I needed it. They really raised me well. Then you become a teenager, and forget it," she laughs. "You try everything at that point. Drugs, everything. And I guess that's disappointing to a parent to some extent, but basically, here I am today! And I'm glad to be here!"

During her period of youthful exploration, Andrew Lloyd Webber and Tim Rice discovered the singer and invited her to join the cast of *Jesus Christ Superstar* in the U.K. Elliman reprised her Mary Magdalene role in the film version and earned a Golden Globe nomination for her portrayal. The path led her to backup vocal work with Eric Clapton, including a supporting role on his hit "I Shot the Sheriff." Elliman is reported to have been the first woman to share the stage with the rocker, and her gig in his band lasted five years.

Yvonne's unbreakable association with disco, thanks to the song "If I Can't Have You," is a true product of the era. The cut was never officially a dance chart hit, replete with extended versions and remixes, but it still became synonymous with the genre, the *Saturday Night Fever* movie, the LP and the frenzy. The song was produced by Freddie Perrin, who enjoyed a huge string of classic disco hits that included "I Will Survive" by Gloria Gaynor, as well as dance-floor smashes by Peaches & Herb and McFadden & Whitehead. However, "If I Can't Have You," a number 1 U.S. pop sensation, was a mixed blessing for the singer, as was her quick categorization as a dance artist. "I have a lot more respect for disco now than I did then, and I'm much more comfortable with it today. I did love going to the clubs back then. I loved dancing to the tasty stuff. I loved that; I loved dancing up a storm. Donna Summer was wonderful, and I think she had a wonderful voice. I would have liked to have heard more of her outside the genre of disco. I think she could have done some smoky

"I didn't buy any disco records. Not one. And that told me something about myself," says Yvonne Elliman of her reluctance to join the disco revolution of late '70s (author's collection).

jazz and some interesting things. There are a few other singers from that era who I think could have as well. But I guess *me* singing disco was somewhere else in my head."

The uncomfortable shift in Yvonne's career began, ironically, as a new Barry Gibb–penned song, "Love Me" (that had been tailored for her by the Robert Stigwood production house), was making waves in Britain and the U.S. in 1976. She says, "Stigwood had asked Eric if I could sing 'Love Me' in place of 'Can't Find My Way Home,' which was my piece in his show. I was kind of nervous about this because I was like, 'Wait a minute ... those are Clapton fans out there, and they're gonna hear this thing!' You could tell right away that it didn't belong in this show and so why would you do this? I tried to do it; I really did. But I was embarrassed by it. I was never embarrassed before on stage — not even in *Jesus Christ Superstar*, where I sang lyrics about trials and tribulations in 'I Don't Know How to Love Him.' But I was young then. Seventeen — you have small goals. I think you should go with your heart. My manager even said, 'I don't think you should do it.' But you know, you're starving, you gotta eat," she laughs.

"I did the song 'Love Me' twice on Eric's stage, and I just couldn't handle it. I mean, my guitar was taken away and I was being dressed by Raquel Welch's husband and dealing with a whole different set of people, you know?" she adds in a slightly exasperated tone.

"When I was asked to do 'If I Can't Have You,' I was fresh out of Eric Clapton's band. I loved being in his band! That's where my heart was. My heart was in hard rock. I was a Led Zeppelin, Cream, Crosby, Stills & Nash fan, that kind of thing. So, when I was asked to leave his band, it's because my single 'Love Me' was climbing up the charts, and I *had* to leave. Robert Stigwood said it had to be that way and, honestly, I was devastated. And Eric wasn't happy about it either. I took on the disco direction with kind of a 'look what I had to do' attitude. I had to give my jeans away and they put me in satin pants, my guitar was gone — I was kind of floundering a little bit. But I had a voice apparently that went well with Bee Gees' stuff. So I did it. However, I must say, I didn't buy any disco records. Not one. And that told me something about myself. The music that I loved — that's what I would go and purchase."

There's a few urban legends circulating about how the track "If I Can't Have You" fell into Elliman's hands, but Yvonne alleges that she hand-picked it. "Barry Gibb totally denies this ever happened, but Bill [Oakes, RSO label executive], my husband at the time, came home with some cuts from *Saturday Night Fever*. He said, 'What Robert [Stigwood] would like is for you to do one of these songs, 'If I Can't Have You.' But Bill was playing them *all* for me and offering up whichever one I wanted to do. I heard 'How Deep Is Your Love,' but the way they did 'If I Can't Have You' was just so majestic. So big and sweeping and I loved the chord changes. So I said, 'That's the one I wanna do!' They put a bit of a disco thing to it, but it's not a typical disco song. It's not a love song either. Actually, it's very depressing. This person is devastated by not having this love in their life. The horrible pain of not being with the person you want to be with, so that you don't want *anybody*. With this song, it's a sad song, yet so uplifting as a disco song. I don't know why that's okay — but I guess it is. It's funny how people can sing along with the lyrics about the crying and how they can't go on, they don't have the strength, but yet they're laughing and dancing! So, I guess in this case the music is more important than the lyrics in some ways."

Yvonne recorded two albums following her *Saturday Night Fever* success, *Night Flight* in 1978, which cracked the Top 40, and *Yvonne* in 1979, which contained the cut "Love Pains." In 1980, her marriage to Oakes ended, and she married songwriter Wade Hyman the following year. She also recorded the theme to the John Travolta-Lily Tomlin movie,

Moment by Moment. Not a whole lot was heard from Elliman afterward. According to the singer, "You know, that began a time I wasn't allowed to sing. For 20 years, [Hyman] would not allow me to sing. I would sing in church sometimes, which wasn't that often. I went into that marriage because I needed something and fell in love with him. I remember flying on an airplane with the Bee Gees, and I was talking to Robin. I remember saying to him, 'Don't you wanna just find an island somewhere? Go there and just live life simply? Discover yourself again?' For me, all the *Saturday Night Fever* stuff was all just too fast. It was all going too fast, and I was spiraling down with all the cocaine and alcohol abuse. I just felt kind of lost. I wasn't enjoying singing the music that much. It was repetitive, and it wasn't the kind of music that really got me off. I remember thinking to myself, 'What am I doing this for?'

"So, when I met my husband, it was like the family thing. He was really down to earth; it was great. He even bought me a wonderful wedding trousseau — it was halfway see-thru down the front and had wonderful embroidery covering the nipples and I thought, 'Well *this* is very cool.' He wanted me to get married, and I thought ... great! Well, the minute I got married, like the next week, he was like, 'Where's your bra?' I'm like, 'What?' I cracked up and thought he was kidding. He said, 'I'm not kidding. You're in a marriage now; where's your bra?' "Whoooah — threw me for a loop!" she admits. "It was so wonderful getting together, but we were opposites it turned out. I have to say, he was also very loving, and he was damn good-looking — he was an Adonis. But he didn't want me to sing. I got pregnant and had the baby and he said, well, now I'd have to stay with the baby. I had been offered a chance to do Mary Magdalene on the road; they had put together a world tour. It would have been 1 or 2 million dollars — that's what I found out later I would have made. But my husband told them, 'Oh no, she's not interested.' He never even told me about the phone call. So that's what was going on in my life after the *Saturday Night Fever* period. I was kept away from music," Yvonne says. She enjoyed one more hit in the clubs with a high-end remix of her previous single, "Love Pains," by Rob "Scissors" Kimbel for Moby Dick Records in 1982. The remix was especially popular with the gay contingent, who vigorously supported the Hi-NRG releases of the label. But that would be the last commercial release most fans would hear from the singer for many, many years. Elliman went on to raise two children.

Yvonne separated from Hyman around 2001 and returned to the Hawaiian Islands that she loved. With her new beginning, she appears to have made some peace with her disco history. "When I came back to Hawaii, I was kind of a big fish in a small pond. I was this local girl who made good, and people just treated me like royalty. I was like, 'Wow, this is really wonderful.' I could go and play my music anywhere. Musicians wanted to play for free with me and go to the studio with me for free. They just really rallied around me and lifted me up. Then came the offers to go abroad and sing. I have to look at that song 'If I Can't Have You' as my saving grace and the song that carried me through my later years. I always said to myself, if I ever have to sing disco on a cruise ship — that's it! It's the end of the rope!" laughs Yvonne. "Now, I don't think it's such a bad gig at all; I wouldn't mind that! Just sailing along ... it's really pretty nice. I guess it's just age-appropriate."

"I'm not *that* age conscious that I try and look young. I just wear what I think looks good or makes me feel comfortable. I guess it's usually something younger than my age group would usually wear. But I don't deny my age, and I kind of think it's cool to be who I am. I'm traveling now. I'm going to Royal Albert Hall soon. I'm very excited about that. I never got to do that before, not even with Eric. I've done some big disco ball shows in the Netherlands too. Disco is very big over there and in Brussels. I went to this wonderful gay club over there called Blue & Red, I think. People were all dressed to the nines, and it was fabulous. I don't think that happens as much over here. But it's all disco! All these opportunities that allow me to travel again and such are because of disco and my song."

The song is still very much a part of life today for Yvonne. "The way Adam Lambert performed 'If I Can't Have You' on *American Idol* was absolutely phenomenal. I loved it to death! I've also done a blues version of it, and I've performed it here in Hawaii. I get some people mildly talking about it, but then I break into the disco version of it, and then it's all completely like everybody goes nuts!" She laughs heartily. "That is one thing I love about disco music. It is very up! Today it's kind of refreshing because people go back in time, and that was definitely a happier time!"

Yvonne Elliman cares for her elderly parents, records music, tours in disco concerts and enjoys a peaceful life today in Hawaii. A remarkably talented vocalist whose musical expression extends far beyond the confines of any one genre, she is very relaxed about her permanent connection to the iconic song "If I Can't Have You." "I think in my case, the song is more famous than the person who sang it. Especially with the younger generation — they don't know who I am. But I'm grateful though, and it's okay when people don't know my name. They know the song. Maybe I should have called it 'If I Can't Have Stew, I'll Take Beef Curry, Baby!'" she laughs.

"All these opportunities that allow me to travel again and such are because of disco and my song," Yvonne Elliman readily admits (courtesy Stephen Ford).

Rochelle Fleming (First Choice)

When one thinks of the fiery female vocal groups from the disco era, a few celebrated acts quickly come to mind: Sister Sledge, The Ritchie Family, The Supremes, The Three Degrees, The Emotions and, without a doubt, First Choice. Popular since the very earliest days of disco, lead singer Rochelle Fleming and her crew delivered a soulful, energized sound unlike any other ensemble. Filled with lush harmonies and Fleming's earnest lead vocal passion, the group's most-beloved hits ("Doctor Love," "Double Cross," "Let No Man Put Asunder" and "Hold Your Horses" just to name a few) still heat up dance floors decades later. "I'm working a lot now, and I'm so grateful to God and the fans. I'm very thrilled with this part of my life!" Rochelle says of her career accomplishments that have expanded into the 21st century. She is as positive and inspired today as she was from the very start.

"I've been singing since I was four and a half and in the same church that I attend today," says Rochelle. "I was the baby of seven children. My husband and I have been living in this house—which I've been in since I was 14. It's a huge part of my family. A lot of singers were in my family, but I was the one who had what my mother called the 'it factor.' I liked to go out there and do it! My family got behind me and pressed me to do it, but they didn't have to press me too hard because I always like to sing. I really *did* know that one day I was going to make it. From the time I was 12, I was thinking that way. The reaction of the people—I knew I would be a big singer.

"We started off doing talent shows in Philadelphia wherever we could sing, and we would win! People would tell us we had powerhouse voices and we should try to do it professionally. The original group consisted of my friend Annette [Guest] and me. We went to the same high school. We sang in choirs and did a little gospel thing. I told her I wanted to form a group, and she went right along with me. We ended up having four girls. One was Joyce Jones. Another was Wardell Piper, who later went out on her own. She left before all the success started really happening. We kept hearing people tell us, 'Y'all very talented,' so I—the bold little person I was—said we should go see Georgie Woods, a very well known DJ in Philadelphia who had started a lot of groups in the business. We knew once we went to him, something could happen. We barged in and asked for Georgie to hear us. It must have been meant-to-be because he didn't stop us and said, 'Send them right in!' I'll never forget it. He sat back in his chair and said, 'Ok, show me what you can do.' All four of us wound ourselves up, and we sang a capella—none of that track stuff was going on back then. We sang Aretha Franklin's 'Oh Me, Oh My.' When we did that particular song, it blew him away. He said, 'I do not believe you have these powerhouse voices!' From there, he reached right out to [producer] Norman Harris and said, 'I need you to hear these girls!' Norman said, 'No problem; send 'em over. We'll see what they've got!' We went to Norman's home, and we sang and did our thing. He was like, 'What took you so long to come to me?'" she laughs. "Norman said, 'You gotta be managed in this industry. We got a great manager for you—Stan Watson!' He was known as 'Stan-the man-Watson.' We went to his office in Philadelphia on Chesnutt Street, and he thought we were unbelievable. We fell in love with him, too. We needed our parents to sign for us, and the rest, as they say, was history."

Fleming recalls her past with passion and enthusiasm and with a sharp memory for detail, including the particulars of the group's unfathomable meteoric rise on the disco scene. "I love talking about back in the day. I love that time of my life. To be honest, we were all so young. I don't think any of us had any opinions about dance music. We just really enjoyed singing. I don't think we knew the impact or difference of getting into dance music and disco. I don't think we cared that much at the time. As long as we liked the material we were going to sing. It was meant to be—because we all just loved the songs Norman gave us. It was all a great collaboration. Just like the name First Choice. That came about from all of us. We were in Stan's office after the signing of the contract, talking about a name for the group, and I think I said, 'First.' Then Annette said, 'First, first ... girls.' And we were like, 'No, no'—and then Stan said, 'Choice!' That's how the name came up. That's something not a lot of people know—we all thought of it collectively; trust me.

Heating up the early disco scene, First Choice (left to right: Annette Guest, Rochelle Fleming, Joyce Jones) had their act together in the mid-'70s (author's collection).

"We were graduating high school and marching down the aisle. I distinctly remember the kids pointing to us and saying, 'There goes First Choice! "Armed and Extremely Dangerous!" Annette's family, mine—all of the families—were just so excited. Then, when we found out we were going on *Soul Train*, it really blew us away!' We were like, 'Are you kidding me? The big dance show with all the cool people with the big afros?' It blew me away and it still does when I think back that this little girl, the 'little diva with the small mouth' like they used to say, was experiencing all this!" Rochelle quickly confirms the *Soul Train* appearance as the moment when the "it factor" girl and her team had made it. "I would have to say, with First Choice, the highlight was *Soul Train*. We said, 'That's it; we're definitely in it!' Then there was Dick Clark and *American Bandstand*, *Dance Fever*, *The Midnight Special*. And then the *Dinah Shore Show*! We were on with Sarah Vaughan. We sang our hit 'Smarty Pants.' It was such a contrast of guests because Sarah sang 'Send in the Clowns.' Dinah was sweet as pie, Don Cornelius was intimidating because it was like, wow, Don Cornelius and *Soul Train*, and Dick Clark was so nice and gentle. *Dance Fever* was great, too, because we met Merv Griffin. Barry White was on that show, along with Chaka Khan. *Soul Train* was the start, and TV shows came back to back to back — we had no chance to breathe!" Rochelle exclaims.

As sudden and overwhelming as their heated career beginnings were on Philly Groove and Warner Bros. Records (which included the disco Top-10 hit "First Choice Theme" and the club smash "The Player"), the girls were unable to foresee or anticipate the rise of the Salsoul record label, with which they became synonymous. "We had never heard of Salsoul. We went from Warner Bros. to Salsoul. We sure knew Warner Bros., and we couldn't believe that the president of the company at that time had fallen in love with First Choice. We had done this huge photo shoot with them in New York City, and we were so excited about them. Then, boom, like in a blink of an eye, it was Salsoul. Trust me — it happened that fast. We kinda just went with the flow. We did what our manager thought was best. I can't really say that I felt it was a great change. But I want to think that the girls and I felt that Stan knew what he was doing. We found out there were some other reasons why it happened, but its okay — it's all good. It was a blessing. We got to know the Cayre Brothers [Salsoul's founders], especially Tim Cayre, who worked with us closely. The other two brothers, Stan and Joe, were more like executives."

The group's signing to Goldmine Records (distributed by Salsoul Records) redefined the girls' sound. Their groovy, danceable R&B, once so well represented by hits like "Smarty Pants," now gave way to a pumped-up, disco-fueled stream of chart-toppers. "Doctor Love," from the album *Delusions*, became a sensation. With its clever lyrics reminiscent of Carol Douglas' "Doctor's Orders" and soulful, yet accelerated, beat (mixed by Tom Moulton), the song kept them a strong presence on the R&B chart and catapulted them to the top of the disco surveys. "When we recorded 'Doctor Love,' [producer] Norman Harris had a heart problem and was in the hospital for a portion of that work. So, Ron Tyson, who had worked with Eddie Kendricks, helped finish up the song. It was one of my favorite songs. I thought I was done with my portion of the recording, and Norman gets out of the hospital and says, 'Chell,' — that's what he called me — 'I think you can do a better job.' I said, 'You gotta be kidding me!' I was so feisty back then. 'I can't give you anymore,' I said. But he said, 'Yes you can.'" Many years later, "Doctor Love" returned to the upper regions of the dance chart in a 1999 Salsoul-issued remix.

"I just felt they were powerhouse songs and, at the same time, we were growing up. I even started to sing the songs with more conviction. It was definitely a period of transition and growing up," admits Fleming. *Delusions* ended up being a monster album in the clubs, from which tracks like "Love Having You Around" and "Let No Man Put Asunder" became fast classics of the genre.

Rochelle was extremely content with her commercial sound and had no trouble balancing her religious convictions and church life with it. "My mom had told me years ago that 'God doesn't want you to lessen your fun. Be happy. As long as you don't hurt anybody—you should live a good, happy life. Never sell yourself out with the type of music you do. Be careful about what you sing.' We had writers who didn't give us a bunch of junk. The lyrics were story-based. They weren't nasty lyrics. Even to this day, I'm known as one of the church's 'divas.' I said I didn't like that title, but they said they were gonna call me that anyway," she laughs. "Even my pastor was behind me 100 percent. [First Choice's music] didn't conflict with my faith because growing up with the church carried me all the way through my career. And it still does! We never got ridiculed for singing secular music or accused of going to church and flipping and flopping. No one has ever said it to this day. People wanted to dance to our music, not take off their clothes! I just believe that God had a plan for us from the time we were born — and the plan was to wind up exactly where we are."

The club environment's vice-laden trappings left Rochelle unfazed. "First Choice was sheltered from a lot of that," she says. "Sam Watson shielded us from the drugs and bad parts of the business. Even with our musicians — because back then 'reefer' was very popular and if anyone came on high, played notes wrong and such, our manager knew it. He would fine them. Nobody was allowed in our dressing rooms. It had to be approved through him. He was an older guy, and he knew about that element out there. He kept us away from a lot of it. When we sang in those clubs, we were brought right back to our hotel rooms afterwards. It never affected us in any way. We weren't virgins to it — we knew what all the drug stuff was about — but we just were very, very blessed. All of us."

Next out the gate, at the peak of the disco boom, came the album *Hold Your Horses* in 1979. "Double Cross," "Love Thang" and the galloping title track became legendary club anthems and respectably charting R&B hits back when disco songs were able to bridge both genres. Tom Moulton produced many of the tracks with a keen ear for melding the group's soulful sound with dance-floor fortitude. "Hold Your Horses" is often cited by fans as one of the ensemble's most energized and euphoric endeavors, and it remains one of the most unapologetic of their disco-style hits. But Rochelle is more reserved in her opinion of the track. "Speaking for myself, I don't remember feeling that way. I think I just enjoyed singing any good music. There were some songs I didn't like as much as others. Tom Moulton is a huge friend of First Choice and mine to this day. I still check up on him and make sure he's behaving. When he first brought 'Hold Your Horses' to us, the first thing I said — Miss Gutsy — was, 'I don't like that song!' Tom says to me, 'Come on Rochelle; just give it a try.' I gave him the hardest trouble," she laughs. "It's still not a favorite of mine, but I like it a lot more now than I did then."

Moulton confirms Rochelle's initial reaction to the song. "She *hated* doing it!" he says. "I said, 'Rochelle, just try it! I'll tell you if it's any good!' She thought it was hokey, but it was still very soulful. When it actually went up the R&B charts, she couldn't believe it. She said, [as if] in disbelief, 'Hold Your Horses?'" The mix work of Moulton never ceased to amaze Rochelle, who claims, "I admire the stuff that Tom has done! It was good music to begin with, and then to put a spin on top of that and make it even better — it's amazing! I am blown away when I hear the stuff that Tom has mixed, or even when I hear myself sampled today." She laughs, "Well, how many more [samples] can they take? I had no idea how much of my work was used like that, sampling and such."

As far as her experience with record labels and their treatment of the group, Rochelle says, "To be honest, Salsoul has been pretty good. For everything that they have re-released, I have definitely received a [residual] check. I'm pretty sure we didn't know everything that went on, and I'm pretty sure we were kept out of a lot of money we should have gotten.

But I've had songs used in movies like *Summer of Sam*, and I was well-compensated for that. But that's because it was called a 're-recording.' I'm pretty on top of it — about getting paid for the back stuff. 'The Player,' I think, was in the movie *Milk* and 'Let No Man Put Asunder' was in *Precious*. I was compensated for those as well. Sam Watson's attorney — he's in constant contact with me and lets me know what's being re-released, and I will sometimes get a check from him as well — which is something he doesn't really have to do because he isn't my attorney. But I think that's where the blessings come in. If we talk about the sampling and remixes, George 'Iz' Correia, my manager, is working on that. At one point, it used to make me angry. I wasn't gigging, and here they were making the money off my music. We got our props sometimes, like Mary J. Blige when she did 'Let No Man Put Asunder.' She gave me my props, but I didn't get paid for that, and I should have. But its okay, and I'm not bitter about that part of my life. As far as getting stiffed and others lining their pockets, well, back then, we just didn't know.

"We were really, really young. I know some other artists may have been a little bit older when they started having hits than when we were in First Choice. They became savvy about what was going on, and I totally believe they have every right to feel the way they do about injustices. When 'Doctor Love' came out and we started noticing we weren't making any money, that's when we started paying attention. As we got older, we started asking questions, and that's when jaws started getting tight and they didn't want to answer those questions. That's when it all came to a head, in 1979. I did get paid for some things, but I'm sure we missed a whole lot of money. But if you carry that around with you today, you can't move on. Linda Clifford is absolutely right about the business being brutal. I have nieces and nephews who can really shine, and I tell them all to finish college — then come out and sing. But get your education first. You've got to love this business to be in it! For me to go on, I had to forgive a lot of stuff. That's where I'm at now. God has taken care of me, and I'm doing fine."

Shortly after their tremendous success as Salsoul's premier female dance-floor hit-makers, the so-called disco backlash began. "I don't think we worried about it," says Fleming. "We just knew it was a shift. I remember thinking, 'Well, okay, now that they're saying disco is dead, what does that mean? What's next for us?' I knew we were definitely R&B artists, and I never thought, 'God, I'm really scared.' First Choice did come into that era, but we were absolutely an R&B group, and I was just concerned what we would do next. Today I'm known as a dance, R&B, house and disco artist. I do a medley today of the disco hits, and it doesn't bother me to be known as a disco artist. The ridicule disco gets and the way they tore it down at that time makes me feel bad. I have a huge fan base around my disco music. That was a part of my career — then came house and then dance. It's just all wrapped up nicely in a tiny bottle — *me*!"

Salsoul's reign as the leading purveyor of disco music came to an end, and the company folded its recording operations around 1983. First Choice disbanded a short time later. "There were people who said along the way that I should be a solo artist. I always loved being with a group. Six albums and three or four different girls were on each album. I really wanted to hang in there and tried everything I had to keep it going. Eventually, I said, 'I'll just go down with the ship,' because I refused to dive off the boat. It's my baby. It was a little scary when I went out there on my own, but I knew I would be all right."

"I went out on my own in 1986, and I did a tour with the SOS Band overseas to army bases, Guam, Korea, Panama. It was a wonderful tour. Much later, I did a show to help Haiti in New York at Webster Hall a few years ago. Little Louis Vega, Todd Terry and a host of other DJs were there. I never met them and they had sampled me like crazy. It was so funny—I said to them, 'You better cut me a check!' When I did the show and they said my name, the audience went crazy! I can't even tell you how I felt. That was the night I felt my career was rebooted. Mind you, I was the only one of the performers that really started from the beginning. It was mostly some of the new dance artists of that time—Ultra Nate, Sandy B, house music people. I started off with 'Love Thang,' and the people went nuts. The DJs were bowing to me. *Bowing to me!* Nothing has ever happened to me in my career like that! It was the most wonderful feeling I had ever felt as a solo artist. That's when I knew I was never going to stop. I am going to continue to do my thing and be happy as long as God has me on this Earth. And now I'm having fun with it. I'm seasoned now—I have all the smarts with it. With First Choice, we were so hyper and traveling all over and being fabulous. With all that was going on with First Choice, we almost missed it all—we were so distracted. But now I'm actually enjoying it and having a ball. My manager, George, is just the best manager I could have ever picked. We have such a connection. My family loves him, so does my husband—he is a great personal manager. He was a fan before he was a manager, and that's what makes him so good at it." She laughs, "He knows Applebee's is my favorite restaurant and takes me there—and we have a good ol' time."

In retrospect, Rochelle is less than impressed with history's positioning of disco artists and the recognition those who defined the genre have earned. She says, "I totally feel [disco artists] didn't get a fair shake," the singer says. "They weren't fair to them at all. I was at this club with Joceyln Brown and Loleatta Holloway. We were good friends, especially Loleatta. Loleatta—I *still* can't believe she's gone. We were all kind of in the same age bracket, and we were all friends and got even closer when I went out on my own. We're at this club—not performing, just dancing—and they played Jocelyn's song, then a Loleatta song, then 'Let No Man Put Asunder.' The audience was going crazy. And I remember Jocelyn saying to me, "Why y'all get to be the last one!' Loleatta says, 'That's cuz she the *star* girl!' We were all laughing like crazy. The recognition those divas should have gotten—and they didn't get it—and their voices are ... oh, God. They

"The DJs were bowing to me. *Bowing to me!*" Rochelle Fleming beams of a recent concert appearance (courtesy George "Iz" Corriea).

were just like the Whitney Houstons of the world. When they shut disco down, it just seems like they forgot about those disco queens. I think it's horrible. I remember performing with Vicki Sue Robinson and Karen Young, and these were powerhouse singers. It just seemed like when they killed disco, they killed these divas as well. It's a horrible thing. Now, I think they're getting a bit more recognition. Like through this book, for example! I am getting younger audiences and 20-year-old fans. I say that's good because whether you want to label it disco or anything else, a singer is a singer. Talent is talent. Maybe the era's divas are getting now what they should have gotten then. There were so many—Donna Summer, who we just lost. I never met her, but she sure had the hits! One of my favorites by her was 'Bad Girls.' I would have liked to have done that song. I think I could have done a good job. Funky! And Cheryl Lynn's 'Encore'—I would love to do that song, too!"

Fleming says she is standing strong today and very much in the game. "I'm glad my vocals are even stronger now. My stamina on the stage—everything is just working in my favor. And I'm just gonna keep on doing every thing I can do to keep that happening. I just can't wait to do the next thing. My mother used to say, 'Age wears you down.' But I look at Goldie Hawn, Raquel Welch, Jane Fonda, Cher—and proof positive, Betty White. You know what? You do what you can do for as long as you can, and if it makes you happy, that keeps you around even longer!"

She finds it hard to recognize her own place in disco history and to acknowledge her title as a venerable dance music diva. "Let's just say I'm getting used to the idea! George always says, 'I don't think you know who you are!' I have so many problems with the word *diva*. I always say, 'Let me take my time and wrap my little head around it.' I'm getting used to the idea. Let's just say I'm grateful that they want to give me that title. Absolutely grateful!"

Rochelle Fleming and First Choice rank high among disco's essential ensembles and their works stand as prime examples of the genre's most memorable sounds. Reflecting on her legacy, Rochelle pauses and says, "[I'd like to be remembered] for my talent, sense of humor, caring and my loving way—and feel for people in general. For what my music has done and is still doing—it's wonderful. People tell me stories about how they heard my songs and what was going on with them at that time and what it's done for them. I realize how much my music with Norman and a host of other writers did for them. And how much the gift I was given of delivering these songs meant to them. I want to be remembered as someone who made people feel good and helped them let go and just dance and enjoy life—forgetting about the trouble they were going through at the time. That's what my music did for me!"

Gloria Gaynor

"I have to say that the huge success of 'I Will Survive' was nothing that I had ever really looked for or hoped for. The time I spent performing and making a living at what I loved to do was, for me, already a *complete* success! So, you know, everything else was more whipped cream and icing and cherries on the cake. But I must say—it was absolutely marvelous!" Gloria Gaynor observes of just one of her many disco career highlights.

She speaks with remarkable humility considering the enormity of her multimillion-selling signature smash hit. Gloria is synonymous with disco, yet even those who are unfamiliar with the genre know the name of this remarkably enduring, iconic performer. It's a testament to her talent, the warmth and vibrancy of her personality and the legacy of stunning music that she has been serving up to the masses for decades. Her triumphs are remarkable by anyone's standards, including the pioneering of one of the first broadly successful crossover disco singles, "Never Can Say Goodbye" (a remake of an earlier Jackson 5 hit). Gaynor soared to unparalleled heights at the peak of the disco era with the immortal "I Will Survive," but was equally riveting on lesser-known tracks like "This Love Affair," "Part Time Love," "Tonight," "All My Life," "Love Is Just a Heartbeat Away"—songs that were stunningly well-crafted, sophisticated and engaging. She is an American pop-music veteran whose music is enthusiastically embraced here, throughout Europe and beyond. She is as much a part of disco as the glitter ball and the lighted dance floor, but she brings a special and unique warmth, strength and humanity to the genre's history with her own inimitable style. While the singer still enjoys fans proclaiming their love for her music at every live appearance she makes, she has had far greater impact by touching the lives and hearts of literally countless millions worldwide. Gloria Gaynor is the real deal ... the original Queen of Disco.

Like so many of her sisters in the industry, Gloria's rise to fame evolved from rather modest beginnings. "I always liked singing, and I came from a musical family. I had four older brothers and they sang very well, and they had a little quartet, which I wasn't allowed to be a part of ... *because I was a little girl*. I didn't think anyone ever heard me or noticed me singing. I was standing in the apartment building where we lived on the first floor one day, and a neighbor came down the stairs and heard me singing. She got down to the level just above me and she looked over the banister and said, 'Gloria?' She asked if that was me singing. I said yes, and she said, 'Oh my God, I thought that was the radio!' And I thought, 'Wow, I must sound pretty good.' So, that was the beginning. Then my friends began to recognize that I could sing, so I began to sing at school and in the girls' glee club and mixed chorus.

Gloria Gaynor's charm, talent and infectious hits like "Never Can Say Goodbye," "Honeybee," and "Casanova Brown" sent her to the top of the disco charts in 1975, making her one of the genre's most recognizable artists (author's collection).

The teacher noticed me and promised she would put me in the school's group of madrigal singers, but she never did!" Gloria laughs.

Gaynor didn't have to wait long for more meaningful attention to come her way. She says, "I had been sort of discovered by a club owner in my hometown and started working with a band there. We started working around, up and down the East Coast and around New Jersey. I eventually moved on to another group and we did Top-40 music. We put Michael Jackson's 'Never Can Say Goodbye' into the show, and it always got a good reaction from the audience. I was working on getting more into recording, and somebody saw me with the group, took me to Paul Leka at Columbia Records and Paul introduced me to Clive Davis — who was over at that label at the time. Clive had me audition no less than three times before he eventually signed me to Columbia, where he had a couple of writers compose a song for me called 'Honey Bee.' Clive left the record company and left me there. Then my record contract was bought from Columbia Records by MGM Records, and they wanted to put the song out on an album.

"They needed other material, and they wanted a really good title song. I was having such a great response to me and my band's version of 'Never Can Say Goodbye' from our nightclub act that I asked MGM to send someone down to listen to our version. I wanted them to see the response that the audience was giving us to our danceable arrangement because I thought that should be the next single and the album's title song. They came down and they listened, they watched and they agreed! And that's how 'Never Can Say Goodbye' became the title song of my first album. In the process of doing that album and choosing the songs for it, my production team and I came up with the idea of this nonstop, one-song-into-the-other format for side one of the record," Gaynor recalls.

The creative decision to reformulate "Never Can Say Goodbye" as a supercharged dance song in an LP-length mix with the equally energized "Honey Bee" and a cover of "Reach Out, I'll Be There" proved to be one of the most innovative and iconic breakthroughs in disco's history. The LP, produced by Meco Monardo, Tony Bongiovi, Jay Ellis, and Paul Leka for DCA Records Corp., featuring arrangements by Monardo, Harold Wheeler, City Life, Norman Harris and Lou Del Gatto (and mix and sequencing by Tom Moulton) resulted in dance-floor mayhem. "I wanted to give the DJ a way to have a break," says Moulton of the nonstop track sequencing. "Somebody could put the record on, disappear for 18 minutes and the crowd would still be dancing! I always thought we — the DJs and I — were in it together. Us against the world! Because remember, I was in radio promotion and sales, so I knew that system didn't allow for change — this is the way it was. So, you come along with a change and they will try to beat you down. But when you have a way of exposing a product and radio had always controlled it — and now all of a sudden there's another medium and you sell a lot of records without radio playing it — they notice."

"I love to be innovative," adds Gloria, "but sometimes I can get into a comfort zone and not want to move. I was used to a three- or four-minute song. Still, I wanted 'Never Can Say Goodbye' to be longer because I loved dancing, but 3.5 minutes of a record was like the maximum at that time! When I heard the extended version, I got upset in the beginning because there was so much music without vocals. But then a bit later, I kind of tucked my ego away and recognized that it didn't need to be filled with vocals. At least not that much [lead vocal] anyway. So, I began really quickly to like what was done and recognize that it was indeed revolutionary and that the DJs, for one, would love it, and we would get more airplay. They would play it as often they could, so they could get a break from those little cubicles they used to sit in to play the records."

Gloria's debut album cracked the Top 25 and "Never Can Say Goodbye" vaulted to the Top 10 of the *Billboard* pop chart and the number 1 position on the dance chart during the months that bridged 1974 and 1975. "It was absolutely amazing! It was a dream come true—plain and simple. *It was a dream come true!* You look at those charts when you first get into the business, when you first become acquainted with how everything works, and you want to be there. You want to be in that mix. I mean, it's like you have arrived when you get in the Top 10. When you become number 1, you have *truly* arrived. And so, when it happened for me, it was absolutely amazing, and I knew I had arrived and didn't want to leave!" Gaynor beams.

Now fully embracing a highly successful disco formula, the singer faced the prospect of a worthy follow-up album. *Experience* (helmed by the previous production team and duplicating the style, arrangements and sequencing of its predecessor) was released in '75 and was another club triumph, but it failed to spark quite the previous pop crossover excitement. The single "Casanova Brown," a sultry, R&B-fused jam that evoked the atmosphere of late night club love games, still found its way to the number 1 position on the dance chart. Gaynor says she never worried much about the pressures of duplicating previous successes. "You know, I never allowed myself to do that," she says. "My mother told me years ago, she said, 'Honey, even an angel can't do any better than their best.' So, I always made sure that at every performance I was doing my best. At every opportunity I had to choose songs for my recordings, I was choosing the best of the best that was available to me. Producers, arrangers, songs—everything. Once you have done all that, then it's out of your hands and that's it. You just go and hope that the record company has the same work ethic that you do and that they try to get your music onto the best radio stations. You hope they try to use the best promoters they can with the most clout and that they're going to get you the most airplay that they can. You just hope that people really love what you've done as much as you do, if not more, and that you will have a hit. And if you don't, on to the next one!"

The singles "How High the Moon" and "(If You Want It) Do It Yourself" let the singer flex some more muscle on the R&B charts, and the cuts were hot on club turntables. The latter track, an enormously positive and uplifting song about self-reliance, was something of a precursor to Gloria's later triumph, "I Will Survive." She recalls the song as a missed opportunity. "Well, I really liked it. I always did! I was very surprised when I asked the record company in England to release it as a single and they refused. There were retail stores over there taking songs and doing jingles, and they were making huge monster hits out of them at the time. I thought this song would be one of those hits if they tried to sell it for commercials because DIY [Do It Yourself] stores had become very popular. I couldn't get anyone interested." Tom Moulton also recalls the song. "I pushed so hard to have her record it," he remembers. "I just thought it was one of the greatest songs! That was the closest thing to a pure R&B record she ever did—it was so soulful. I mean it always stood out to me ... always."

Polydor Records eventually absorbed the MGM label, and in 1976 they released the album *I've Got You*, whose production and style again mimicked Gloria's previous sets. The clubs favored the tracks "Let's Make a Deal" and the hit "I've Got You Under My Skin." By the time Gaynor's next album was being readied in '77, the previous production team was dropped in favor of a rising star on the disco frontier, Gregg Diamond. Diamond had been enjoying huge hits with The Andrea True Connection ("More, More, More") and his own studio group (Bionic Boogie) and their number 1 disco hit "Dance Little Dreamer." While the *Glorious* album contained a magnificent updating of the venerable *Casablanca* standard "As Time Goes By," arranged by co-producer Joe Beck, Diamond's favoring of instrumental-heavy compositions and diluted vocals (which worked well for a singer like Andrea True) resulted in precious little chemistry between the accomplished Gaynor and her producer. "I honestly don't know how we got hooked up with Gregg Diamond. I only know I wish I hadn't. Oh, he was awful! *Awful!* He was very nasty, condescending and into some things I won't even mention. I will never forget — he wrote a song that he wanted me to record called 'Most of All,' and when he gave me the music, the song only had one line in it — which was the title — and it was just repeated over and over. We recorded everything else on the album, and this was the last song. He told me he was going to write lyrics for it, but he never gave me any. So I wrote some lyrics myself. I called him one day and said, 'Look, we're going into the studio, and I've written lyrics for the song because I know you only did the title. I know you're really busy and you didn't have the time,' and so on. He responded, 'Look little girl, I do not need your pathetic attempt at writing lyrics for my song. I will write the lyrics for *my* song, and I will send them to *you*!' So, he sent the lyrics to me, and all that was on it was one additional line about loving someone like they've never been loved before. Well, we recorded it ... and that's all the words there were."

Gaynor recalls more about the 9-minute, 15-second opus. "Sometime later, I went on a TV show and I was to lip-synch the songs 'Most of All' and 'As Time Goes By.' A producer came to me and said, 'Gloria, I know you were supposed to do two songs for the show, but one of the songs doesn't have the lead vocal on it ... I'm sorry!' They thought that the lead vocal was missing on 'Most of All!' And I never said anything about it!" she laughs. "I said, 'Okay, no problem!' I mean, obviously I'm not the only one who recognized that it wasn't a song. It wasn't my best experience recording an album, but it's okay — I had much better times on my other projects."

Around the same time as Gloria reigned as the official "Queen of Disco" (proudly announced on the back of her *Park Avenue Sound* LP in early '78) another disco upstart, Donna Summer, was climbing her way to the top. Gloria, confident and focused, was undeterred — even when some had begun passing her crown to Summer. "It didn't matter to me at all," says Gaynor. "I'll tell you one of the reasons why. The one thing that may have defused that for me before it even got started was that I was in the hospital and having surgery on my spine — and this was just before 'I Will Survive.' I came out of the hospital on the last day of a three-day disco convention. They were having it at the Hilton Hotel, and I really wanted to go — I really didn't want to miss the convention. So I went on that last day and I'm sitting on the podium, and they announce Donna Summer. She comes up to the podium and takes the microphone and she said, 'Before I go any further, thank you very much, but before I go any further' — and I will never forget this speech, word for word — 'I have to acknowledge a lady who just was released from the hospital from major surgery today, but she decided that she just could not, *not* be here. Ladies and gentlemen, may we really have a warm welcome and huge round of applause for the First Lady of Disco, Ms. Gloria Gaynor!' I was like, 'Oh my gosh, she is so gracious!' How could you have any competitive feelings with a person like that?"

Despite the accolades, it certainly hadn't been all glamour and carefree times for the artist. Gloria endured her share of personal and family issues and her spinal surgery was among the most profound, life-altering experiences with which the singer was pressed to deal. Those traumatic days (before the arrival of what would be her ultimate musical triumph) were enormously challenging. She says, "I had fallen onstage at the Beacon Theatre.

I finished the show, went out for breakfast with the band, went home, went to bed and woke up the next morning paralyzed from the waist down. I had surgery on my spine — they removed a ruptured disc and did a spinal fusion and bone graft. I didn't have any music coming out while I was in the hospital. The record company was getting ready to cancel my contract just before I got into that accident. So oddly, it was my faith in Christ who got me through that. And I believe it was His favor that brought me the song 'I Will Survive.'"

The album *Love Tracks* and the single "I Will Survive" transformed Gloria into a genuine superstar by Christmas of 1978. The track became her biggest hit ever, the most identifiable song of the disco era and arguably the genre's signature moment. "I knew when I heard, or rather read, the lyrics, it was something special. But it started out on a different path. The producers we had chosen, Freddie Perren and his partner Dino Fekaris, originally came to me to record and promote a song called 'Substitute.' They didn't have a B-side yet, but they talked to me about the kinds of lyrics I liked, the kinds of subject matter and the kinds of emotions I like to convey. They said to me, 'We have a song that we've been looking for someone to record, and we believe you're the one we are looking for.' They wrote down the lyrics on a brown paper bag, gave them to me to read over, and I looked at them and said, 'You're going to put this on the B-side of what? Are you nuts? It's a hit song! This is a timeless lyric. Everybody can relate to it.' Because, while I was reading it, I could relate to it after what had happened to me."

"When I was recording 'I Will Survive' and when I was reading the lyrics to it, I was standing there with a back brace that started below my hip and ended right up under my armpit. It's this thick, plastic back brace with three latches across my stomach. I was relating all of that to the song. People had been going around the record company saying, 'The queen is dead.' So that's what I was thinking about when I was reading those lyrics. I was also thinking about the fact that my mother had passed away a few years before that, which was something I never thought I'd survive. So, I'm thinking, if I'm relating these things to this song, everybody will be able to relate something that they have gone through to this song and be able to gain encouragement and empowerment from it. I knew I was right!" she says proudly.

Gaynor wasn't the only one who spotted the potential of "I Will Survive." Independent publicity man Tom Hayden was hired to launch the "Substitute" single when Polydor still had "Survive" on the B-side. He remembers, "I was doing a lot of promotion work and one of my accounts was Polydor, a European company with a strong presence in the U.S. The president of the company actually contacted me and said he had this record by Gloria Gaynor that was doing pretty well in Europe called 'Substitute,' and they wanted to make it a hit in the United States. [The label may actually have been referring to the international success the South African group Cloot was having with their version of the "Substitute" song.] They wanted to start a campaign for it, and Dick Klein, who was in charge of radio promotion at Polydor, told me it was a top-priority record — to let him know whatever I needed. So, I asked for some test pressings of the record, and I sent them out to about a hundred key DJs across the country. I got a call within a couple of days from a DJ in Chicago, Lou Devito. He said he got the record and played it that night at the club, and the floor got packed and everybody went nuts. He had to play it two or three times after that. I said something like, 'Yeah, "Substitute" is gonna be a really big hit.' He corrected me immediately and said, 'No, not "Substitute," the B-side, "I Will Survive!" That's the hit!'"

"I started hearing from others in Boston and L.A., and they all agreed 'Survive' was the hit," he continues. "I called Klein and told him we have to flip this record because everybody is talking about the B-side. He said they couldn't because the song was already out to radio and the label liked the A-side. So they kept promoting 'Substitute,' but people were going into stores asking for 'I Will Survive.' Within about two or three weeks, there was so much of a groundswell that Polydor *finally* decided to flip the record because radio had started playing 'Survive' without them even promoting it. After that, it became a multimillion seller!"

"I Will Survive" received yet another boost on its journey to the multimillion seller level. Gaynor likes to say the song was born in Studio 54. As soon as "Survive" was recorded, she and her management team took it to the A&R department at Polydor, but, like Hayden, she claims they wouldn't listen to her promotion recommendations. She recalls, "[My] team then decided to take it to Studio 54 and have Richie Kaczor, the DJ there, play it. [Accounts vary as to what led to Kaczor's discovery of the B-side 'I Will Survive,' but his first spins of the song at Studio 54 unquestionably helped turn the tide for Gaynor's massive hit, as nearly every DJ in New York immediately followed his lead.] The audience *immediately* loved it, which is most unusual for a New York audience, and days later began to flood radio stations with calls for it. This prompted the stations to ask the record company for 'I Will Survive.'" Gloria confirms Hayden's assertion, saying "Polydor then had to answer with much chagrin, 'You already have it, and it's on the B-side of "Substitute."'"

"Survive" was an astonishing success for Gaynor and her producers Perren and Fekaris (whose production company was aptly named Grand Slam Productions), climbing to the top of the pop and dance charts and hitting number 1 in numerous countries, including the U.K. The song, instantly triggering audience recognition with its famous piano introduction, was recorded as a lean and simple tune without lush remixing. It earned the singer the first and only Grammy award ever bestowed for Best Disco Recording. The *Love Tracks* album climbed into the Top Five of the *Billboard* album chart. Gloria recalls, "I was over in England performing, and my agent came into me and he said, 'Where is "I Will Survive" on the U.S. charts?' I replied that it was number 2. 'Well,' he said, 'no, it's number 1!' The song had reached number 1, but I thought on that week it had moved back down to number 2. Apparently, it had gone back up! So I was in shock, and what was really incredible was that it had knocked 'Do Ya Think I'm Sexy?' by Rod Stewart off of the top of the chart! I remember thinking that was pretty amazing ... really! It was all such an awesome experience. It was again, another huge pinnacle in my career and just a magical time." Polydor released only one follow-up single from the LP. The funky cut "Anybody Wanna Party?" was a momentary minor hit (by comparison) on the pop, R&B and dance charts, but it would be months before the frenzy caused by "I Will Survive" abated.

Late in 1979, Gloria released her much-anticipated follow-up, the album *I Have a Right*. However, caught in the disco backlash, the album (again produced by Perren and Fekaris) languished in the mid-regions of the pop albums chart, and the "Let Me Know (I Have a Right)" single, which was critiqued by some as being too derivative of "I Will Survive," fell shy of the Top 40. Though the clubs responded to the single and Gloria's hot disco reworking of the Broadway classic "Tonight," some momentum had been lost. Gloria took it all in stride. "Well, you know, if I bowed to pressure, the stress of coming up with a follow-up to 'Survive' would have been very intense. Again, I'm always thinking of doing the best I can with what I have to work with. That's all I can do, you know? And

I leave the rest of it in the hands of God. I mean, He's done great by me so far. There was no sense in doubting Him then or now. You just keep your mind on the fact that you are blessed to be doing what you love to do and making a living at something you love. It's that simple. I just kind of always tried to keep my feet on the ground, recognizing that at any moment it might have *not* been me. It could have *not* been what it was. It's just a blessing." (Enjoying one of Gaynor's tour performances for the *I Have a Right* album in a half-filled theater, I recall the singer observing the modest attendance and, undaunted, proudly saying, "That's okay; you're the cream of the crop!" The crowd roared with approval.)

Gaynor never rested on her accomplishments. She contributed the song "Love Is Just a Heartbeat Away" to the disco horror film *Nocturna* late in '79 and continued recording throughout the '80s. The 1980 LP *Stories* was critically lauded and contained a marvelous, retro-pop, gospel-tinged composition titled "Ain't No Bigger Fool." Parting company with Perren and Fekaris, she recorded her final Polydor album, the suitably titled *I Kinda Like Me* in 1981. It boasted a modest R&B-club hit with "Let's Mend What's Been Broken," produced by McFadden & Whitehead, and featured a number of tracks that had been written by Gaynor. In 1982, the artist moved to Atlantic Records for a self-titled one-off album (though it fell under the radar) that many consider among her best. The collection featured Gaynor singing a variety of styles, including softer music and ballads like "Even a Fool Would Let Go," which she delivered in a mesmerizing, sophisticated style. She opines, "I like disco music very much because I truly love dancing, but I prefer singing ballads. So throughout my career, I have always been disappointed that the record companies have always refused to release a ballad as a single from my albums."

Helmed by a wide variety of producers, the *Gloria Gaynor* album also included her funk-dance take on the Diana Ross and the Supremes classic "Stop, in the Name of Love." "I think I did a fantastic job with it," Gaynor says with pride. "It was later released on a *Best of Gloria Gaynor* album at the same time that Diana Ross had done [her version of] 'I Will Survive.' I suggested to the label that if they release and promote 'Stop' right now, while Diana was trying to promote 'I Will Survive,' the DJs will have a field day pitching us up against each other, and we will *both* have hits. Well, they failed to seize the moment. It's one of my favorite songs to do on stage. Kool & The Gang arranged it — they did such an awesome job with the arrangement and the background, I almost didn't even need to sing," she chuckles. "I loved that version, and still I do it today in my show. Audiences enjoy it very much."

The audience Gaynor connected so well with was, and remains, as diverse as any artist could hope for. She had her mainstream followers thanks to crossover hits like "Never Can Say Goodbye" and "Survive," and she had amassed a huge gay following that was enamored with her club hits. As a devout Christian, the gay fan base the singer enjoyed may have seemed like a sizeable conflict of interest for the singer, but not so, says Gaynor. "I had and have no problem with it whatsoever. I'm a Christian, and that means I follow Christ. If you know anything about His life, it was the religious people that accused him of going into the worst places and hanging out with the so-called worst people. What *they* thought were the *worst* people. I carry, for my responsibility, the same message that He carried, and I try to carry it to anybody that is willing to hear it. Because there is not one person on this earth that doesn't need that message — and that includes the gay audiences. So, my purpose for singing now is to use my music as a vehicle to share the love and the knowledge of Christ. Now, that is, with anyone who wants to listen to it.

"At the beginning of my conversion to Christianity, I started going to a church whose congregation did have issues with me," Gloria adds. "They didn't ostracize me, but they did talk to me about performing secular music. I was steered in a different direction. God sent me to the church I go to now, and I've been there since 1988. He literally sent me to that church. If I told you the series of events that got me there, you would probably believe as well as I did—*yeah, that didn't just happen!* Too many Christians bury their gift and talents in their pursuit of spirituality, and what God wants them to do is turn their talent over to Him so He can sanctify them and send them back out into the world to do just what I'm doing. Use those gifts and talents to draw people to Him. So, that's what I do. There is no law against love, as the Bible would say, and I'm coming with pure and honest love. I think when you come at it that way, either people don't like what you're saying and don't like *that* you're saying it ... or they *do* like it. I think that some people have a very difficult time, and they may walk away; they may not listen. But I also think if you approach these people the right way, they have a difficult time rejecting you completely."

As she suspected, Gloria's faith was never a problem for her gay following. The community could not have been more delighted by her high-energy version of "I Am What I Am," a Jerry Herman composition from the show *La Cage Aux Folles*. The track, produced by Joel Diamond, was lifted from her 1984 Silver Blue label LP, *I Am Gloria Gaynor*, and peaked at number 3 on the U.S. dance chart (and nearly cracked the Top-10 pop chart in the U.K.) "Joel Diamond picked me for that song. He called my manager, and then we went and had a meeting with him about doing it. He said he had gone to see *La Cage Aux Folles* and he heard the song in the show, and right away got the idea to do a disco version of it—and he thought of me. He played us a version of what he wanted to do with it, and I thought it was a great idea. That's how we hooked up." The song has been an anthem in the gay community ever since.

Gloria found renewed success in the U.K. and Italy in the years that followed, following the path taken by many disco performers who enjoyed the exceptional loyalty of European audiences. *The Power of Gloria Gaynor*, a bestselling U.K. collection of mostly pop cover songs and *Gloria Gaynor '90*, featuring newly recorded Italian house-music versions of her biggest hits, kept Gaynor in the limelight overseas and created an import demand for the artist's work here in the U.S. "I Will Survive" returned once again to the Top Five on the pop chart in the U.K. in 1993, thanks to a Phil Kelsey remix that took the country by storm. Sounding stronger than ever by the mid-'90s, the singer started recording albums back on her home turf. She secured renewed club interest with the CDs *I'll Be There* and *The Answer* on Radikal Records and published her biography, *I Will Survive* (St. Martins Griffin), in 2000. The book detailed her most personal thoughts and didn't shy from addressing some of the darker elements of the singer's past, including battles with alcohol, drugs and issues of weight. Despite the endeavor's success, she wasn't about to live in the past, and, striking while the iron was hot, she released a two-disc album called *I Wish You Love* through BMG-Logic in 2002. The set brought Gaynor right back to the top of the dance chart with the singles "Just Keep Thinking About You" (a hit for Tata Vega in disco's early days) and the modern classic "I Never Knew," which crossed over to *Billboard*'s Adult Contemporary chart. The Aussies gave Gaynor a chance to sing the type of soft music she'd been longing for when her ballad, "The Power of a Woman in Love," climbed their pop singles chart in 2006. They later voiced approval of a reissue of her "I Am What I Am" classic by sending it soaring back up the same chart. The year 2007 saw the artist featured as a guest on D.O.N.S.' "Supernatural Love" dance hit, and, in 2009, she released a 30th anniversary version of her immortal "I Will Survive," which put Gaynor squarely back in the media spotlight.

The singer has a seasoned perspective on the music business and is truly a veteran of the industry in which she has worked nearly her entire adult life. "There are positives and negatives in everything," she says. "Unfortunately, I think that the music business has turned far to the negative because I think it's become way too money-oriented. It seems the record companies are far more interested in packaging a performer than they are in what's in the package. The young artists today, I believe, are being done a great disservice because they are not being allowed to bring their talents to full fruition before they are shoved out there as stars. Some of them are lucky enough to get people around them who are interested, but, you know, now there's no A&R, no Artist Development department, there's no more career development. There's just branding. So you don't really get people in the industry itself that are interested in the artist. They are all just interested in making money — however they can make it. The cheapest thing you can give the public [while charging] the most amount of money seems to be what they are going for.

"The other thing that the public is being robbed of, in my opinion, is the spontaneous creativity that can only happen between live musicians working together and inspiring one another. Techno music is not a problem for me, but I think there should be — and I always try to do it myself on my recordings — a combination. The best of today — the best of yesterday. But too many people are just doing this technological stuff, you know, altering people's voices and such. God forbid somebody had to sing on a stage and sing a capella! There are not a lot of them that could do that because they've been selling packages, not talent. And then you have all the great undiscovered singers with fantastic raw talent that are never given a chance.

"One thing that has remained the same today as it was 50 years ago," Gloria adds, "is that the music business has always geared itself towards the younger generation. For some reason, people in the music business think young people are stupid and we can just give them anything, and they will love it. I understand that people cannot buy what they don't know about. People can only choose from what they hear, what they are allowed to hear, what's being made available to them, what's being shown and exposed to them. Once in a while, you see someone break through that barrier. Proof of what I'm saying is Adele. Record companies used to say that nobody wants to hear all those lyrics in our songs. Nobody is interested in that, and kids only want to listen to hip-hop. Yeah, they do want to hear hip-hop. I'm not denying that they want to hear that, but they are not so narrow-minded that they wouldn't like different kinds of music if we would just give it to them. But the fact that Adele won six Grammys tells me there are people who appreciate other types of music — music with meaningful lyrics."

While she says she isn't nostalgic about the past, Gaynor feels there is still a place for the women who performed great disco music. She believes they still have what it takes, if given half a chance. "Absolutely these women are relevant! It's always been that way with these ladies. They have to give themselves to the young crowd, and they should never assume that the young people don't want to hear what they are doing. You know, they just are never given enough opportunities to be seen and heard. Some people assume that once you're 30, especially nowadays, because you're not willing to get naked, you're boring; you're passé. You only get seen and heard if you have a string of number 1 hits that haven't stopped yet. Trust me, if Beyoncé's record sales ever start going down and-or her figure starts to spread, she's going to be considered yesterday's news. They are not going to consider that she still has a fantastic voice, still has access to great writers, that she's still able to do her amazing performances. They are going to say, 'She's over 30, she's over 40 years old, and she's done.' Because that's what they always do," Gaynor alleges.

"I think we have to try and be our best. It applies to me as well—my attire, my makeup, my hairstyles and in my music. I try to stay as current as I can. I try to walk a fine line between being current and age appropriate because I know I can't be out here doing hip-hop and bouncing up and down. It's like you are 45 years old and you have a kid that's 18 years old—he doesn't want you talking that street talk; he doesn't want to hear you acting that way. Come on, nobody's going to think I can get away with that, and they won't appreciate me trying to be that way. Just being relevant and knowing what is going on today without trying to pretend or fool anybody into thinking you're still 22 or 24 years old. I said it a long time ago—*'I am what I am!'*" she says with confidence.

Gloria continues to move forward with her life. While embracing her remarkable past, she strives to do more in the present. "In January of 2012, I finished college. I earned a bachelor's degree in psychology with the purpose of opening a healing, learning and recreational center for teenage parents in my hometown, Newark, New Jersey. When I first started college, I was thinking very ambitiously to get this center off the ground [in 2012], but now that I'm seeing how difficult it is to get the ball rolling on it while I'm still in my performing career, I'm thinking 2013, 2014 may be more realistic. There's a lot of work to be done and a lot of obstacles to overcome, especially with the economy being the way it is now," she observes.

"I said it a long time ago—*'I am what I am!'*" proclaims Gloria Gaynor, who is now also the holder of a bachelor's degree in psychology (photograph by Troy Word, courtesy Gloria Gaynor).

Gloria Gaynor is more than a survivor. She has struggled through her share of deeply personal crises, endured, prospered and, through it all, entertained millions with her powerful, distinctive voice. Her superlative legacy in disco remains undisputed, and her crown as its preeminent queen stays firmly in place. As her faith in God and her compassion for others continues to grow, she hopes that her ideals and aspirations, above all else, are remembered. Says Gloria, "I would like to be remembered as a person and as an artist who inspired people to follow Christ. My purpose is to share the love and knowledge of Christ, and I'd like to be remembered as someone who did a good job at that!"

Debbie Jacobs-Rock

"Thirty something years later, I think history played out the way it should have!" says Debbie Jacobs-Rock, a native of Baltimore and the vocalist behind four of disco's biggest and most irresistible smashes: "Don't You Want My Love," "Hot, Hot (Give It All You Got)," "Undercover Lover" and "High on Your Love." A protégé of the highly lauded producer Paul Sabu, Rock (gaining fame largely under her maiden name, Debbie Jacobs) was a club sensation, whose powerful jazz-trained voice became forever connected to energized disco. Putting her formidable performance skills to the side, Debbie proudly moved on to serve an important social cause in the second half of her life, but she revels in the memories of being a disco star.

"How do I tell the story?" she begins. "It's the story of a young little African American girl that grew up in a church, getting off my mother's knee at three years old and getting into a choir that was filled with teenagers and adults — and being able to hold my own! It's that little choir story you hear so much about that many African Americans had back then. I guess I loved singing, but I didn't look at it as if it was a [ticket to stardom] type of thing. That's not a bad goal, but there were other things I wanted as well. So, I became part of a jazz band and, in a way, I thought of myself as just an instrument — my vocals were no more important than the bass player or the drummer. It was like, 'How do we get it in and make the song work?' That's always how I viewed myself until a man named Tom Cossie introduced me to record producer Paul Sabu. He was in the studio on the West Coast with a young lady and they were trying to get their first album done, but she had fallen in love with Paul — so nothing was going right there. Tom had told him about me and described me as this girl from the East Coast that he thought would work well with Paul. They flew me out there and I guess — as they always say — the rest is history."

Paul Sabu, later an Emmy-winning singer-songwriter-producer-guitarist, was a young rising star on the disco horizon, making dance records for himself ("Rockin' Rollin' Disco King") and notables like Ann-Margret ("Love Rush," "Everybody Needs Somebody Sometimes"). He went on to work with David Bowie, Madonna, Shania Twain and a profusion of prominent rock artists later in his career. However, at this point in time, the maestro was looking for his next disco hit. "Paul's dad was 'Sabu, the elephant boy' from the old '50s movies," recalls Debbie. "Paul was very charismatic, and he was good to look at — beautiful! I saw him, met him and thought this was the most handsome guy I'd ever seen in my entire life, and yet he was humble and said he really wanted to work with me! Remember, again, I'm a young girl from Baltimore, and I just had the church-jazz sound. With disco — and I understand this now — they weren't interested in how pretty I could sing. It was more important that I could sing specific notes — that I could I sing exactly what he was telling me to sing. I was part of what they were trying to produce as a sound. I had to learn a whole new style of singing almost overnight. And that was not easy. Paul was always focused and really a super genius who paid great attention to detail. He'd have the violin section actually in the recording studio for the orchestrated parts of the music that he wrote. So when you listen to my first album, those aren't all artificial instruments — Paul used the real thing! It was really a phenomenal experience."

Undercover Lover, Debbie's debut LP released on MCA Records in 1979, was a club sensation. The title track was a catchy, blistering number 1 boogie-woogie hit, along with the equally razor-sharp "Don't You Want My Love," and proved the performer's unique range and raw, earthy vocal style were ideally matched to the energized genre. "Much later on," she says, "I got an opportunity to come back and we cut that bad boy ["Don't You Want My Love"] with two of the most awesome DJs (Rosabel) in 2000, and it went to number 1 again! It was meant to be, just the way it went down. So, [just like back in the '70s] it's about putting yourself in the hands of people who understand what is going on and letting them guide you. I would not have been able to say back then, 'Okay, I'm going into the studio and will cut a disco record' the way it needed to be sung. That was Paul and his talent back in that day."

The experience of becoming a disco star with multiple hits left the singer in nearly a state of disbelief. "I think what we had in that era was special and unique. We had an ability to impact audiences without having to use a band—we could take our music in our pockets. So, that meant that maybe five of us could hit a stage, and we could all do tours and we could have familiarity with each other—and we could connect with the audience. I must say our [most enthusiastic] audience was primarily the gay community. And I have to put that out there. They were so appreciative of our music—it made us work even harder in so many ways. To get on a stage—like at Studio 54, The Saint, or remember the White Party—oh my God! Imagine being able to go up a scaffold at Studio 54, not being able to see or hear anything and have the curtains open up. Suddenly, I'm in front of 4,000 screaming individuals that are not only out there for me, they are out there having fun, living life! My husband and I have been married for 30-something years, so he was around with me. I remember he said to me, 'Deb ... sing!' because I was so overwhelmed and just standing there in awe."

An observer once told Debbie Jacobs, seen here around 1980, to get on the stage and start a fire—and that's exactly what she did with the disco classics "Undercover Lover" and "High on Your Love" (courtesy Debbie Jacobs-Rock).

Debbie reflects on the ways her life was impacted by immersion in so many aspects of the disco culture. "I think about Martha [Wash] or Jeanie [Tracy] or Linda Clifford, Sylvester and Cynthia Manley! They lived all that. All of us experienced that high in itself. It was just a total, total high. And we got paid to do it! Okay, I should just speak for myself. I think one of my favorite starstruck moments was opening for Grace Jones in Miami! Grace is someone who can sing! If you've ever seen Grace perform in a disco club, you know it's dramatic. Grace would just stand up there, and this silhouette would be seen. She would bang on some cymbals for about five minutes and you could hear a pin-drop. She would sing three or four songs, but for the most part her show would be mesmerizing drama. I once asked her, 'Grace, why don't you go out there and show them what you got?' Grace would say, 'They did not come to hear me sing. They came to see what will be the most outrageous thing that I can do!' And she was right! So, in many ways, people got paid for different reasons, and she was just somebody that people just loved for what she presented.

"I was living that little singer's dream, saying wow — I can ride in a limo, stay in a five-star hotel and they pay me to get up there and sing a couple of songs. As a jazz nightclub singer, I didn't have people directing me or doing makeup and all that stuff. You are there in that jazz club from 9 P.M. to 2 A.M., and you got paid $50. With disco, it wasn't so much about who you were; it was about the music, the hit song and it was about dancing. With disco, you could hop several clubs in one night. You could do the clubs in New Jersey to start, maybe the teen or youth clubs, and then the limo would take you to the Garage in New York. There were people that were paying us anywhere from $3,000 to $5,000! Girlfriend was *very* appreciative and was like, 'Is there anything else you need me to do?' she laughs.

"My mother was someone who was very religious and my dad, being a singer, was a bit of a bad boy. So back in the jazz clubs, it was what it was. I think there are many ways to look at the sex and drugs and all that comes in any music genre you're in, including disco. Gay clubs were gatherings of people, no different from any other. People are people. They are going to have all the bad things just like any other gathering — so I never judge people. My mother raised me to never judge people. But I did experience a certain stigmatism — a former preacher at my church would say, 'Okay, now she's out there in that world doing blah, blah, blah, so she's not a part of God.' My mother was worried too until a counselor helped her realize that there was a reason I was doing what I was doing, and she didn't have to worry about me. And it kind of helped me too. I never really saw myself as a 'diva' until someone pulled me aside and said, 'Look they paid $20 to see you sing. I understand you like being the girl next door, but when you get on that stage you need to start a fire up there!' Point taken!" Debbie concedes.

The time came for a follow-up to Jacobs' stellar debut, and a good release strategy was critical. Somewhat luckily still signed with major label MCA for her next production, 1980's *High on Your Love*, Debbie faced the challenge of commercial success in a domain that had become considerably more hostile towards disco. "Knowing what I know now and looking back," she remembers. "I can truly say I don't think I was interested so much in concerns about crossing over and having a big hit more than I think I was in having fun. And that's the most honest statement I can give you. If a lot of us could go back and focus on the business side or the right people that could kind of make sure that all the pieces were tight — that's a different story. I have no regrets or anything. Yeah, if I could go back and recoup dollars, renegotiate contracts and things of that nature — well, of course, hindsight is 20/20. But I know, at the end of the day, there were a lot of people that were never lucky enough to get the opportunity that I had to cut records. I got to travel and meet so many different people, and I thank God for those opportunities. For those things that didn't happen or that were negative — hey, I let them go. I'm at peace with my life."

"High on Your Love" was still a major club success despite the disco backlash, giving the artist yet another number 1 dance hit. A remix of "Hot, Hot (Give It All You Got)," a song which had first appeared on her debut album, also hit the top spot. The sharper, harder sound of "High on Your Love" (no doubt influenced by producer Sabu's affection for rock and a reflection of the times) gave dancers the edge they were looking for to replace disco's sweetness. Says the artist, "I don't know whether or not I can honestly say that I was concerned about [the growing negativity towards disco] when it happened because, again, I was enjoying everything so much. A DJ in Chicago told me that for maybe three months straight he had played 'High on Your Love,' and the audience made him play that sucker every single night because they were doing line dances to it! Again — a tribute to Paul Sabu! Paul would say, 'This how I want you sing it,' and he orchestrated all of that song — and I have to give him credit for that! I could go in and sing gospel and I would not need direction, but with disco I needed the guidance. But *now* I can do it. My voice is the perfect voice for it now!" she says with a confident smile.

Though the album was her last full-length set, she continued to lend her voice to other dance releases in the years that followed. One such project was a recording that put her music at odds with that of another rising diva, Viola Wills. "This was the dirt," the singer confides. "Artie Jacobs from Miami, no relation, came to me and said, 'We have this song, and we just want you to cut it.' When I heard 'Maybe This Time,' I was like, 'Oh my goodness — sure!' It was a sure fire hit. He had kind of explained something that had happened with Viola Wills, [with whom] they had some kind of falling out. They wiped away her vocals altogether from the recording, and I came in and sang it. I honestly don't know all of what happened — the who, what, where, when — but it was a strong enough situation where Viola took them to court and had our recording blocked. It blocked the version I did with them from coming out, but it didn't block me from singing it. So, what I did was to go back into the studio and re-cut a new version of 'Maybe This Time' and made it my own — and it became an underground hit. It was all kind of tragic because I think both our versions could have happened without the drama. The drama happened, however, and it is what it is."

Now known as Debbie Jacobs-Rock, the singer recorded a few more singles in the '80s that saw club action, including the dance hit "Doctor Music," a Paul Sabu and Rusty Garner collaboration, and "In the Heat of the Night," a collaboration with British producer Ian Anthony Stevens (Angie Gold, Hazell Dean) and singer-songwriter Paul Parker ("Right on Target"). "Oh, Paul Parker was another hunk — there was Paul Sabu and there was Paul Parker! Paul — oh my God — that's my Marlboro guy! He would just drive people crazy. Not only was he good looking, he was, at the end of the day, another humble human being. I had an opportunity to record with him when I was a little older, a little more mature, and I was allowed to kind of give more input that reflected who Debbie was. And Paul talked me into being a little racier, especially if you think about some of the lyrics in 'In the Heat of the Night' — he was good for it! I got to spend more time working with him than I did with my first two albums in a production sense. It was more of a relaxed atmosphere, and we got to play around with styles. That's after the [disco] crash and all the backlash things were happening, so our music was not really picked up anywhere. That's when we became more like underground artists."

A medley called "Forever" followed in '88 along with a high-energy venture on Megatone Records produced by Nick John called "I Need Somebody." "*Miami Vice* with Don Johnson was on TV at the time, and I was asked to come down to perform 'It Should Have

Been Me' at the *Miami Vice* Fourth Season Gala. That was a great song, and it became an underground hit that I was able to do in the clubs. I wasn't having the big record sales, but I was able to survive and make money that way," says Rock.

It was some time before Debbie returned to the spotlight with the Rosabel CD retake of "Don't You Want My Love" in 2000. "I dropped out of the music business full time and pursued other adventures. Once you are in that disco world, people tend to not see you unless you have really good, strong management or money behind you. It's hard to get new material or to be able to cross over to other music styles. There were also big changes going on at the time. By the end of the '80s, AIDS was becoming a major issue. At that time, in the clubs, we saw the stigma and how people were being treated. And when I say 'we,' I mean we as entertainers. There was no government funding for this illness in those days. So we would try to raise money in the city — do an extra show or something and raise money and leave it with some clinic or some community organization that said they were addressing the crisis.

"I will never forget it — I saw a copy of *People* magazine where I saw a little boy who had AIDS and I said, 'Wow, this is attacking children,' and I went to an organization here in Baltimore and I told them I wanted to volunteer. I'll never forget it — I walked in and said, 'Hi, I'm Debbie Jacobs and I'm a recording artist.' It was a gay organization that helped people with HIV and AIDS and I'll never forget the little guy at the desk that said, 'What do you want? Help with your faltering career?' From his point of view, I was *not* one of those top-of-the-chart recording artists, and he may have seen me as wanting something other than what I really wanted to do for them. It hurt my feelings, and I have no hesitation about saying that. It's one of those stupid things that happen in everybody's life and I thought, 'Okay, I'm going to have to come at this another way,' and I went out and raised some money.

"I went down to a clinic that was working to diagnose children. I went with two people — some call them drag queens, but I respect them and prefer to call them female impersonators — and they went with me in full gear. The check we brought was pretty big, and I started volunteering every Wednesday. I found a whole new world. I thought I was only going to be working with children, but then I began working with all kinds of people, including many black people who couldn't talk freely to their doctors. It's that communication gap, you know, where you can't say certain things to your doctor. Because they were hearing so much about how bad AIDS was, and being diagnosed and having children, it was a very dark place for people to be in. Now, 25 years into handling the program and seeing some of those same people whose children have now just graduated from college and are nurses and have careers like that and are doing phenomenal things — it is wonderful! Playing a small part in it was exciting and very humbling to me. My husband is Ronald Rock — we just call him 'Rock.' I really have to say, if it had not been for him, I would have not been able to do all this social work. There were many, many people that helped this evolve into what it is today. I'm just lucky and, like I said, I'm blessed, and it's been a great life. I don't regret anything! Maybe for about five years of my life I wouldn't ever talk about Debbie Jacobs, the recording artist, but now — to use the singer side of me to get done what needs to be done — I'm okay with that!" she declares. Debbie is currently executive director of LIGHT Health & Wellness Comprehensive Services, Inc., (*http://www.LIGHThealth.org*) formerly known as Baltimore Pediatric HIV Program, Inc.

Debbie's contributions to dance music continue to be appreciated by fans worldwide. She says, "I've met a lot of people over the years as a recording artist and singing, but when

I came back to it in 2000, it was like a reunion. So, I got a chance to go back across the country and hear how my music has impacted the lives of my fans. I didn't know my albums were on CDs—I thought they were all on vinyl until someone walked up to me off the street and put the CD in my hand for me to autograph for his friend who was sick with complications from AIDS. I also didn't know that anyone knew that Debbie Jacobs was Debbie *Rock*. And discovering MySpace and Facebook was also an eye-opener! It took me over a week to catch up with responding to everybody who had contacted me on [the Internet]."

The performer, though no longer in quite as bright a performance spotlight today, has learned to navigate the process of maturing along with her fellow artists. "My wonderful husband and my daughter, Ashley Nicole Rock, are both the loves my life and have played major roles in my music career. Ashley has been helping with the business end of my career since she was 13 and has now grown up in my footsteps to work as a clinical director of an adult HIV specialty clinic. My husband is five years younger than I am, and we've been married for 32 years," states Rock. "He still says I'm his queen, and that's all that matters. So it doesn't matter if the hair is going and you throw a wig on top of it. You try to look good, and you try to feel good about yourself. And you do what you want to do in life. I'm strong and have faith in the Lord and, I don't know, I think different people have different philosophies about it. I'm not really in the limelight anymore, where I have to focus so much on looks. If the bags are showing under my eyes, then I try to use some tricks of the trade. I think I would be kidding myself if I said I wake up and look in the mirror and don't sometimes see that I'm 56. You're not 26 anymore, and you've put some extras on. But at the end of the day, you thank God you have those aging challenges because some people don't get them. If you have eyesight, hearing—all those things we take for granted—there are plenty of people who don't have them. I really can't say that I stress over aging—you just have to suck it up and go with it."

Debbie offers a philosophy she has come to embrace. "I'll share with you something

A legend in disco, Debbie Jacobs-Rock is executive director of **LIGHT Health & Wellness Comprehensive Services in Baltimore** (courtesy Debbie Jacobs-Rock).

that someone wrote," she says. "Ever since I read it, I find it comforting to share it with others, as I feel very much the same way. 'I love my life. Like a string of colorful beads, the days of my life follow one after another. Every bead, every day, contributes to the whole. As I reflect on the days of my life, some may seem brighter or more colorful than others; some may appear cracked or chipped, yet each day is precious. I have been strengthened by challenge, broken open in crisis and sustained through it all by God within. I have been humbled by my errors and encouraged by my successes. I've been blessed by family and friends as we've lived through times of joy and sorrow. For every loss I've grieved, I have been blessed by a time of love. I have no regrets. I love my life!' It ends with Psalm 23:6, 'Surely goodness and mercy shall follow me all of the days of my life.'"

Debbie Jacobs-Rock hopes that her work at LIGHT and the services she has provided to people in need will be her primary legacy. As for her legendary performances of disco music, she observes, "People sometimes came out to get away from whatever awful things were happening in their lives in the hope that they just could forget it for a while. My job as a singer was to make that experience happen! So at the end of the night when someone said that they were able to feel good about themselves and enjoyed themselves, I guess I was able to say to myself, 'Job well done!'"

Madleen Kane

Many Americans may recall seeing Madleen Kane for the first time performing on the TV show *Solid Gold*, when her smash hit, "You Can," had begun climbing the U.S. pop charts. Aloof, sexy and mysterious, Kane was an enticing vision. The public found themselves hypnotized not only by her exotic blonde beauty, but by her captivating, whispery voice and the haunting Giorgio Moroder composition she sang. For some time, she had been an international media-darling, a jet-setting Elite model and one of disco's sexiest premier songstresses. A mysterious figure with an exotic accent, she intrigued music fans throughout disco's peak years (reaching the dance-chart Top 10 with almost all of her major releases). Madleen looks back on her remarkable career with a sense of accomplishment.

"I was born in Sweden and my father was a Swedish Opera singer, so I grew up in a music environment. I always wanted to do it—become a singer myself one day," says Madleen, a striking-looking woman who had quickly caught the eye of German fashion magazines while still in her teens. She eventually was the focus of several *Playboy* feature spreads. "When I started out, I was 'Ms. Sweden' and that lead into being a model, which lead into music. And then CBS wanted to sign me, so I made a demo for the *Rough Diamond* album." CBS Records released the album in France in 1978, where it caught on quickly throughout Europe. Warner Bros. picked up the LP for distribution in North America. The beautifully orchestrated title track and "Touch My Heart," mixed by Jim Burgess, quickly reached the Top Five on the American dance chart and stayed a fixture on the list for nearly six months.

Kane adds, "We did the first album in Paris [at Gang Studios], and I signed with

Warner Bros. in the U.S. Jean-Claude Friederich was my producer, and he was also my husband. He passed away some 10 years ago. He had a very intuitive concept of me as a singer. But, you know, I had my own ideas too. As the artist, I was deciding the type of material I wanted Paul and Lana Sebastian [composers and co-producers of Madleen's early work] to do for me, song and lyric-wise. I felt it was very important that I had a say in what my music would be. Also, at that time, we were using real musicians—violinists, pianists, guitarists—to create a very special sound. I just want to point out that when we recorded *Rough Diamond*, I think we had something like 40 violinists. Today it's all very different and, of course, computerized. I believe in all my albums, except perhaps the last, we used live musicians. It was amazing, that time, and I really loved it! Although it's hard to pick my favorite [LP], I actually would say *Rough Diamond* is probably the one. Everybody remembers that album, and that is something I am very proud of."

Paul and Lana Sebastian were accomplished European composers and arrangers with a knack for lush, disco-oriented, pop-friendly productions. While scoring cross-continental disco hits for Theo Vaness, they enjoyed great crossover success in the U.S. with Leonore O'Malley's song "First Be a Woman." Their

Madleen Kane (seen here around 1981) possessed extraordinary beauty and her success in modeling segued into a stellar music career which yielded the disco hits "Forbidden Love" and "You Can" (courtesy Tom Hayden/TSR Records).

cohesion with Madleen was ideal, and Kane was very comfortable forging a career in disco under their musical guidance. "I felt disco would be a good fit for me because I loved to dance—well, that was different. I studied ballet for 10 years," she says. "But I always loved the uptempo sound of disco music and the writers that I had—they were just incredible! Most of the music I recorded was uptempo, especially the hits, with the exception of a few songs like 'C'est Ci Bon' on the first album. I recognized my songs as being something special because they were saying something. In that disco time, I loved that I recorded lyrics that meant something. It was not just the boom, boom, boom, like a lot of the music that was out there. Who knows when you are recording something if it will be successful or not, but I wasn't too concerned—I just knew that the music I was making was very close to my heart."

Following her initial success, the artist says she was keenly aware of the expectations placed on her to deliver a worthy follow-up. "Of course, there is always the pressure when you release a song or album because you never know if it will become a hit or not. You have to choose the right songs and sound and hope that people will like what you've chosen. Yes, there certainly was pressure!" she admits. *Rough Diamond* was just a warm-up, and Kane had no trouble duplicating its success. The LP *Cheri* followed in 1979, again on the Warner label in the U.S., and it contained remarkably well-conceived songs that became front-line disco classics. "Forbidden Love/Fire in Your Heart," a monumental piece of music and a brilliantly artistic production arranged by Thor Baldursson, was remixed by Jim Burgess (as a single) and excited dancers worldwide. It scalded the dance charts and became an undisputed highlight of the era. "'Forbidden Love' is one of my favorite songs because of all the musicians [involved in its creation], you know, and that it's so dramatic! Oh, it takes you away! It's wonderful; it's mesmerizing! It was like a symphony on *Cheri*—I always called it a 'symphony.' It was very exciting to help with the arrangement, and I think the beauty of 'Forbidden Love' made me want to be involved in it."

Madleen says having creative involvement in her projects was of the utmost importance to her. "Oh yes, I had some [creative control] on some of my albums and I was very involved—let's put it that way," she asserts. "I helped write some of the lyrics. I always tried to be a part of the whole process—music, mixing, everything. I was always in the studio, even if it was not my time to sing."

As a singer with an attractive, edgy and glamorous look, Kane recalls (with amusement) some of the reactions her beauty inspired. "There were some times when the way I looked became a problem for me in my music career," she says with a hearty laugh. "There were two women in France that wouldn't be on the same TV show as me, back when they had variety shows. They wouldn't be on the same show because of me—because I looked too good. Oh well!" she laughs. But to characterize the golden-haired vocalist as simply "a look" would be to greatly under-appreciate her abilities and talents, which took her to numerous countries at the height of her career. "I was usually very comfortable wherever I was. I appeared in 40-something countries, and I did work internationally quite a bit. I did a Toyota commercial in Japan, and then I had my own variety TV show in France. I also did a lot of work in South America and Argentina—variety shows. I speak a number of languages—French, English, Swedish, Spanish, Danish, Norwegian and some German—which helped me greatly."

Tom Hayden promoted Madleen's work following her Warner years. He recalls, "I started working with Madleen in 1978–79, after she had already put out her Warner Bros. albums, which were big hits on the dance charts. Her executive producer and husband at the time, Jean-Claude Friederich, had met me at the *Billboard* Dance Convention, where I had just won an award for best dance promoter. They had a new album they were shopping around and were looking for a deal. I was doing some work for Prelude Records and got them to release it." The album was *Sounds of Love*, a club mainstay in 1980, and it moved Kane closer to the electronic dance music that was rapidly progressing in the post-disco era. Arranged by Greg Mathieson, the set brought Kane back to the dance charts with the pulse-pounding, harder-edged single, "Cher Chez Pas."

Madleen's musical evolution with Paul, Lana and Jean-Claude continued to be a successful partnership. Hayden describes Friederich as "a very interesting character! He made a lot of his money in the '70s. He owned a huge advertising agency in Yugoslavia and was printing fashion magazines for companies in France, The Netherlands and a few other countries. He was so successful, and that's how I think he came to meet Madleen, who was a model. He was also dabbling in music and promoting concerts in Europe. He made millions from selling his ad agency and had a brilliant idea to get his money out of France when the socialist government was about to take over. He bought a bunch of vacation properties in San Diego, California, during the Carter administration at a time when there was a big oil shortage. Nobody was driving down there because of the gas shortage, and he bought the properties up very cheaply and got all these wealthy Europeans to invest in these units. He ended up doubling his fortune!"

By 1981, with the disco landscape reinventing itself, it was decided a new, fresh sound was needed for the artist. She was taken under the wing of famed producer Giorgio Moroder, who was entering one of his most prolific production periods. Madleen remembers, "I met Giorgio Moroder through Tom Hayden. I got to meet him at his studio up here in Beverly Hills. So, I went up to his house, I met with him, we discussed the opportunity and he shared some music that he had written. I listened to it eagerly. He said he wanted to produce me. I was very excited about it! Oh my gosh, he wrote 'You Can' for me — I mean some really beautiful stuff— and, of course, I was aware of the great things he had done with Donna Summer. You know, I think we both were in Japan together around 1980, Donna and I, and we were singing together in Tokyo at a huge festival. We had such different voices though. She had that lovely song 'Last Dance,' which was kind of similar to 'You Can' because it starts off slow, then builds. I would have liked to have sung that song, but it would have been completely different, you know? So, I knew her very well, and I'm sad she passed. Giorgio had made great music with her, just as I admired the music he had done for me. I always had my own style, and I always did what I thought was good for me. I never tried to imitate anybody. I know there were quite a lot of women out there competing for that sound."

Don't Wanna Lose You on Chalet Records was Kane's fourth studio album and with Oscar and Grammy-winning Moroder producing and writing most of the tracks, the artist's legacy in club-land was assured. Containing multiple hits, the collection kept the singer on active DJ rotation for months. The set was led by the number 1 dance chart smash "You Can," which had enough hooks to get the pop market's attention as well. Says Madleen, "It was a very nice song. It started out really slowly, and then it builds up to such a powerful melody! I was very pleased with the album *Don't Wanna Lose You*. [Giorgio] was very pleasant to work with. He had a house in Aspen, and he had a studio here in Beverly Hills. So we did some work here, in his studio, then we went to Aspen to do some tracks there. It was a very good experience."

Tom Hayden remembers, "I had started to distribute Chalet Records through my TSR label. Jean-Claude and I actually became partners. We then put out the *Don't Wanna Lose You* LP and it did really well, and we had a couple of number 1 singles off the album, including 'You Can.' It was easy to step into working with Madleen because she already had a good, established name in the marketplace. She had a great track record, so our goal was to just produce a good album we could be competitive with. 'You Can' became a gold record in Canada. I believe it was nearly gold in Mexico and it was number 1 on the dance charts in the U.S. It sold very well here and crossed onto the pop chart, but not for as long as we would have liked."

The album yielded more hits in the clubs and on the dance charts, with the rock-fused and hard-edged "Playing for Time" and the equally hook-laden companion piece, "Fire in My Heart," among them. All featured the familiar, razor-sharp thump that Moroder was incorporating into the music of the Three Degrees, Irene Cara (a short while later) and other acts at the time. Despite some reports that Kane was not a very visible promoter of her music and limited her personal appearances, Tom says the artist was out there and dependable. "If we needed Madleen to support her single on radio or perform at the clubs, she'd do it. She was probably a little reluctant on some levels, and that may have come with having had a bit more of a privileged life. However, it never seemed to stand in the way of her doing club shows. In Florida, she was in high demand and often appeared at the Backstreet and Limelight clubs, as well as in New York and L.A. She was out there, but she probably didn't tour as frequently as someone like Pamala Stanley. I was with her on many club dates, and she'd sing live over tracks. She did have a bit of an accent. I think it was sometimes harder for her to perform as easily as acts who spoke fluent English. Because of that, we'd use softer vocals mixed down on the track so there was kind of an echo effect, and it sounded quite good and the shows were great. Clubs booked her numerous times and always wanted her back. She always got a very good response.

"When we were out on the road," he continues, "she used to get some guy groupies who were obsessed with her! I remember one time she was performing in Boston and this guy was just so in love with her, sending flowers and champagne to her hotel and wanting to meet her — just going nuts. We set up a meeting for him to meet her because he was so obsessed and he was a friend of the DJ. When he met her, he was absolutely speechless! We had a lot of security, but it was just funny how passionate some fans are about their singers. Madleen was very nice about it, very cordial and appreciated the fans that made a fuss about her. I've certainly come across a lot of artists who couldn't care less about their fans, but Madleen really appreciated them."

After a brief hiatus, Madleen returned to dance music for 1985's *Cover Girl* on TSR Records, her last studio album, which featured material by up and coming Hi-NRG vocalist Paul Parker. "Giorgio was kind of busy, so he was not an option for my next album. I think he was working on a movie or something and I had to get out a new album, so I found Ian Anthony Stephens," says Kane. "He was very successful in England, and I got in touch with him. I did like what he and Paul Parker wrote for me. Even though I didn't think it was one of my best, there was some stuff on the album that was pretty good. I helped out a lot with that album as well. I went to London and I stayed there for about three months — something like that. It was the first time I believe I was fully using electronic instruments instead of real musicians. I think we used a guitar for 'real,' but other than that, it was that highly computerized sound. You could hear the difference, if you know music, and that it had a lot of electronics in it," Madleen recalls. With shades of the successful Moroder style incorporated into their sound, the singles "I'm No Angel" and "On Fire" were moderately successful Hi-NRG hits for the singer (though they fell short of the dance Top 20 for the first time in her career), and by the time the album's potential had been fully exhausted, so was the artist's desire to continue her music career.

Madleen and Jean-Claude broke up and the artist remarried. She quietly concentrated on being a mother and exploring semi-retirement from the business, letting the limelight dim. "I decided to have a family and I felt, at that point, it was now or never — so I just took some time off. I guess my interests just began to evolve. I had three children — a son, Oliver, who is now 25, a daughter, Alexia, who is 24, and a daughter Stephanie, who is 22. My son is going to be an architect and my daughter is going to be a psychologist. My youngest daughter is a model. I started to paint and I started to do a lot of horseback riding — and, yes, being interested in other things as my children were growing up. I believe there's a chapter for everything. I had my chapter as a singer and in entertainment, and now I'm into other things. I think, you know, I started out so young, and I did what was right for me at the time. By the way, I try to take care of myself and I still try to always look my best," she laughs with confidence.

As for Jean-Claude, Chalet and TSR Records, Hayden says it was an amicable dissolution. "Jean-Claude had the idea of wanting to go in more of a rock and pop direction with Chalet Records, and I wanted to go more towards dance. So we decided to break ties professionally, but we stayed very good friends over the years, and I continued to rent my office space for TSR from him. After that, I started having hits with Miquel Brown and Evelyn Thomas. I wanted to stay in the area I knew best, which was dance crossover material. Then, about 10 or 12 years ago, I approached Jean-Claude about doing a 'best of' CD for Madleen, the *12 Inches and More* collection, which gathered together all of her hits beginning with the Warner Bros. days. It was quite successful."

Kane's career was stellar by anyone's standards, a fact that prompts the singer to reflect on her long and regal history. "I guess when I [want to] look at my career, I can always go look at YouTube—that's one way I can see it," she observes. "But today, I mean after so many years—yes, I do think I contributed something to pop and dance music. Because people today, for one thing, they still like me—not only as a singer, but also as a person. I would never disregard my fans—I always kept a connection and appreciated them. I have many great memories of that time. I have to mention when I was singing in Italy—that was a major eye-opener for me! In the arena, there were thousands of people and they were all holding candles, and it was gorgeous! I looked at this person with me from backstage and said, 'Oh my God, there's no way I can go out there!' I was so scared ... and I had a whole show to do! So I pulled myself together and thought, 'Okay, all right, let's see what's waiting for me!' The crowd—they were screaming! I said, 'Oh, my God, how am I going to handle this?' But you know, once the first note came out and my musicians started, all the fear goes away—the frightening thing, the stage fright. That was an experience of a lifetime—right there in Verona, Italy!

"I do believe that our music is coming back," Madleen adds.

"I would never disregard my fans—I always kept a connection and appreciated them," says Madleen Kane looking back at her fame (courtesy Madleen Kane).

"The music that we had in the '70s and in the '80s *is* coming back. We started it, you know, so we should be rewarded for it, recognized for it in some way. Because it goes in a circle and music today reflects our music. I have to tell you one thing—I don't like hip-hop music. But, if it's more up-tempo, like Rihanna, for example, her music is like a combination of disco and hip-hop—you can see elements of our music in there. So, I do believe that we should be recognized as the ones who started it because it's coming back again. Would I ever perform again? *Never say never!*"

Her philosophy about maturing is direct and simple. "You have to feel very confident about yourself and, also, you have to try to be happy. You know, you have to keep laughing, being happy and not be afraid to grow older. I still feel I'm still very young. You have to take care of yourself and be nice to other people, because it always comes back to you. Being a good person to other people is so much better than being a bitch—excuse my language—and having that kind of philosophy in your life is important. For example, if I had interviews and appointments, I was always on time. I never made them wait and so on because I understand they were working too. I've always been liked by the people in media because I've always been nice to them. I've never been a brat. It is simple—just be nice to people and also take care of yourself. What you eat, what you put on your skin—you know, all of that stuff. I go to gym, work out, I walk. I am lucky enough to live next to the beach, so I walk on the beach and swim. I don't have one wrinkle on my face, and I haven't had anything done! I am spiritual, and I try to be very grounded."

Madleen Kane is a true champion of disco and one of the original heavy-hitters who made the genre exciting, glamorous and intriguing. She may rightfully be considered one of Sweden's greatest exports and her chart-topping musical contributions were highlights of the era. She personified the glamour and excitement of a music genre that entertained literally millions. How does such an accomplished woman want to be remembered? "Wow, that's a tough one," she chuckles. "Well, let's see ... I want to be remembered as a sweet, nice person and a person who cared about others. I hope that I gave a lot of people some joy in their life and that they enjoyed life more by listening to my music. Yeah, that's what I hope!"

Evelyn "Champagne" King

"I must say I appreciate it so much—being thought of as an artist from the '70s. This era will never die, and this is a goal of mine!" proclaims Evelyn "Champagne" King. Crossover hits like "Shame," "I'm in Love" and "Love Come Down" had a mesmerizing effect on club-goers in the disco era, as gyrating dancers by the millions howled in approval for her thunderous beats. For years, King was at the top of disco's hottest A-list and her earthy, soulful vocal style was an integral part of the some of the genre's most credible works. She continues today to be one of disco's most in-demand performers and looks back at the era with immense enthusiasm and joy.

Though one might expect the artist to have relegated the details of her humble beginnings to the back burner of her memory, King conveys them with a fresh sense of excitement. "I was actually working, cleaning up with my mom at Sigma Sound Studios. The day I had gone in there my sister had taken ill, and I was filling in for her. My mom had said, 'All I want you to do is go in there and clean the offices, clean the hallways, clean the bathrooms — you know, do what you have to do and then we're out.' Okay?" Evelyn chuckles. "I got discovered just vacuum-cleaning and singing a Sam Cooke song. I was just singing while working, and it was just a normal thing for me. I was singing about how a change was gonna come, not expecting anyone to show up because my mom said no one was supposed to be there. But, T. Life [the producer, also known as Theodore Life] was there, and he heard me singing and he said, 'Uh, are you here with anyone? Was that you singing?' I actually said, 'No,' like I didn't hear anybody — you know, like it wasn't me! With an attitude! I was totally shocked that he was standing there before me because there wasn't supposed to be anybody there. I told him my mom was there, that she was just around the corner. So he went around to talk to my mom, and he just came back and said, 'I am wondering when we can started recording!' I said, 'Yeah right' and just kept vacuuming.

"It's kind of like a Cinderella story. That's a fact! And here I am today. I was already happy, content with my band, you know? I was in a local band, so I was happy doing what I loved anyway. I thought my life was just going to be working with my local band, happy with that, and we would just be doing nightclubs and the block parties that they had back in the day," Evelyn says, smiling matter-of-factly. "I had always wanted to be an actress, but after singing with my band, I then thought, 'Nah, I'm doing this ... something that is *me*!' So, really, I was happy.

"I had been singing in that band since I was 14, and I was going on 15 at the time. I've had to correct many people, including the producer and one of the writers of 'Shame,' and keep reminding everyone that I was 15 when I recorded that song. Wow!" She chuckles at the memory. "I was 16 by the time it went to number 1. First, let me tell you — John Fitch and Reuben Cross — those are the two names to remember because they were the writers of 'Shame.' John, Reuben, T. Life and I went to T-Life's house — his living room. T. Life or John had a guitar — I'm not sure who starting playing the song 'Shame' — and they just told me to go ahead and sing. You know, 'Sing it down for me one time.' And they just went crazy! We recorded it. Then it took them almost a year to get it out — it seems to have been left on the shelf for a while — and then it was finally put out and I ended up having a number 1 all over the world. It was just incredibly surreal — you just can't believe something's going happen like that. I was a teenager in high school, and I wasn't thinking of anything other than being with my band in South Philly. I was enjoying just trying to be a young girl. But when the song just took off like that, I was totally shocked because I heard myself! I passed out when I heard myself!" King admits with another laugh. "I was just so in shock! It was like no way, 'Oh my God!' There I was, traveling at 16 years old and I haven't stopped since. I'm totally blessed. The era — that time with that disco music — was so much fun, and it took off like crazy. It was the right time and the *perfect* time for me."

"Shame" became a signature song both for King and the disco explosion, vaulting to the Top 10 on both the disco and U.S. pop charts. Her debut album on RCA Records, *Smooth Talk*, quickly broke into the Top 20. "Shame" was chased by an equally rhythmic follow-up single (the youthful "I Don't Know If It's Right"), which made the artist an R&B chart favorite and an international hot commodity. Thrust into the limelight and performing in clubs virtually non-stop, King faced the challenges of becoming worldly in a hurry. She says, "I felt it was strange. I was 16, and I was in these clubs. But my parents were there

Evelyn "Champagne" King, by the time this photograph was taken around 1986, maintained one of disco's most accomplished careers, highlighted by the classic song "Shame" and number 1 dance smash "I'm in Love" (author's collection).

with me, so I was okay. My mom and dad — they were my road managers — they were just there every step of the way. *Every step of the way!* All up until I was a bit older, but they never failed to take care of me. No one can ask for something better than that — to have your parents there, guiding you and supporting you and loving you! They were always trying to make sure that they kept me well grounded. And they *did* do that for me. They kept me away from the drugs; they kept me away from all of the craziness. Don't think I didn't see it all, but I didn't have to be involved in it. And yet, at the same time, they made sure it was my choice, if you know what I mean?

"I saw so much; I was in shock! Mind you, I was out there clubbing with Grace Jones, Alicia Bridges, Frankie Valli, Donna Summer — there was a lot of us from that era! I was always at Studio 54. Wow! The Palladium, The Garage, all those places — you know there was a lot going on ... oh my goodness. It was like my mouth was left wide open, shocked from what I was seeing. I was also in awe because I was a fan of the singers who were there with me, and I had dreamed to just do what I was doing — to get on the stage and show what I loved to do."

With her sudden rise to fame, Evelyn bypassed much of the usual day-to-day life an ordinary schoolgirl might have experienced. The artist says, "I wasn't in school anymore by this time; I had to have a tutor. I was living from my own tour bus. Even though I was just a teenager, sometimes Evelyn *was* in charge because I was in front. I didn't know very much, but sometimes when my mom and dad couldn't go with me and I had another road manager,

I had to take charge. I also knew that I was paying everybody. It was so, so wild. But I did feel like I was missing out on some things a teenager would be doing. One time, we were going on tour and I looked at my mom. She was in the back area we had on the bus with a big TV and everything. I looked at her, and I just started crying. She asked why I was crying. I said, 'I don't know if I want to do this.' She said if I didn't want to do it, we could turn right back around. 'We can turn the bus around, and we can go home,' she said. Then I just looked at her and said, 'No, we can go; I love to sing.' She said, 'Just so you know, if you ever feel like you want to stop—we can stop this.' And I just continued. She said to me, 'The stars will always be up there, but they do fall down. Stars do fall down.' I'll never forget her words. 'Don't ever think you're ever better than anyone else.' I keep those words with me to this day—they've been with me ever since I began."

Dating opportunities were decidedly limited, says King. "*Ahhh* ... not really a whole lot of them," Evelyn laughs, "not with my dad there! He was very protective and wanted to make sure I was concentrating on my work that I loved. Just like a boxer who doesn't go in the ring in the right state of mind because he had a fight with his girlfriend. You have to concentrate. It was kind of tough at times. I guess [I experienced] puppy love sometimes—that's what we called it back then. But it wasn't that important to me. I knew when I was on that stage, I felt I was in God's hands—and I still do. He would make sure I had whatever I needed to keep me smiling and make me feel happy and alive. That's all that mattered."

Her recollections of those early days remind Evelyn of her parents' devotion. "My dad had on a denim outfit with bell-bottoms and my face printed on the back of his denim jacket. He had a cane at the time, and he had a bag that we called 'the mail man bag.' He had all our pictures in there. He would have my albums in there; I mean he just would have everything! He was just very proud of his little baby daughter. My mom, well, no one messed with 'Mamma King,'" she says with assurance. "She would just let you have it!"

According to King, issues of color and sexism were rarely visible to her. Matters of cash were another story. "I didn't look at the color thing because I wasn't really paying any attention to it. I just thought of myself as a young, single, female artist. I was just trying to be in there with all the others. I had to travel with so many male groups: Parliament, Funkadelic, The Commodores, The Gap Band, groups like that. I even did a show with Tower of Power—I mean actually just me, no other women, just me, at the Round in Baltimore—and I'm very proud of all that. Well, we had horror stories too. Actually, it was more about fear than horror—to be out there on the road and people not giving you your pay. My dad wanted to shoot half of them!

"You would arrive at the venue and even before you would do the gig, you'd pull up with your band, and they just didn't have the money. Oh—and I'll never forget it—my dad and I were on the tour bus, and we saw the promoter running out the side door of the club. We were wondering why he was running—it was because the audience was inside waiting and he didn't have *our* money! You know, we'd have situations like that. You'd see people load their guns, ready to shoot each other because of money. *Not cool!* The audience would start to boo us because we'd have to go on and explain the show wasn't happening. They'd think it was our fault. Then I'd have to run—it was like, 'Let's go!' The things we had to go through back then were very scary, and it was out of our control—we're the ones that were just doing the performance. We weren't the ones doing the business end. The audience doesn't know that. Your fans just, you know, they want to see you!"

Despite the strong support network rallying behind King, the pressure to deliver more hits was ever present. In 1979, she released the album *Music Box*. "I felt the pressure, but I thought it's really not all up to me. It's also up to the producers and songwriters," King recalls. "I had that in the back of my mind — if I'm singing good enough on the first album, then I knew it had to be up to the songwriters and the producers to keep giving me the right new material. The second album didn't do as well, but it could have been the way it was marketed. Also, the era was changing. You know, as far as I'm concerned, it went by so quickly — I put out my second album and then the backlash hit, [but my label said] 'Okay, she's good enough to keep.' I was with RCA Records for years, but then it was like they got other artists and they threw them on top first. In fact, they were always working on getting new ones, and that's just the way it was back then. It wasn't always about your music. Your fans are always going to be your fans, and they still love you no matter what. That's not the case with labels. I realize that more than ever now, much more then that I did back then."

Music Box, which yielded a modest hit with its shuffling, soul-fused title cut, had enough muscle to earn the artist another gold record. The album also featured backing vocals by legends like Luther Vandross and Irene Cara (well before their careers took off), but Evelyn wasn't given the opportunity to engage with the performers. "When [my producers] did the studio work," she says, "I never knew who was in there until afterwards. I didn't have to — the artist didn't have to be there back then. They just had arranged it where I would come in and sing. They have the music and the backgrounds already done. Everything was already pre-produced, and all I had to do was come in the studio. So, I never got to see anyone until my later years. I went in, I could do my work in one or two takes and I was done. T. Life will tell you he was in awe all the time. When I came in, we never even rehearsed. I would just sing it down and they were pleased! I would do a lot of my little ad-lib things, and they would go, 'Whoa, where did that come from?' I was so, so skinny, but this sound right here in me — it was like coming out of a 500 lb. person," she laughs.

The final album collaboration with T. Life, *Call on Me*, followed in 1979, and it yielded another strong dance hit, "Let's Get Funky Tonight." By 1981, when Evelyn released her *I'm in Love* LP, the dance landscape had changed considerably. The sugary sound of traditional disco had morphed into the early stages of high energy music. The style of R&B-tinged disco that King had perfected had progressed to a funkier dance hybrid. Steamrolling onto dance floors, multiple charts and crossing over to the mainstream Top 40 once again, the single "I'm in Love" propelled the artist right back into the spotlight in well-timed syncopation with the trends. Up-and-coming producers Morrie Brown, Kashif and Paul Lawrence Jones took the singer in a new direction. Says Evelyn, "My whole thing was, I was a big believer in making sure others were heard because they had a different sound. I don't just like listening to just one type of music. And it was always nice to have people notice that I worked with a variety of different producers and songwriters. I loved it when people would say, 'Wow, we didn't know that was you!'

"I'm not going to say my new producers were a better fit than, say, T. Life; I'm going to just say they were a good match for the time. 'I'm in Love' came out at just the right time. It was like, boom, she's back, you know? I guess that's what the people were waiting for. 'Let's see if she can get into what's going on now'— and I did! It's just like starting over fresh — you have to move on a little bit. If you keep staying in the same area, if you sound the same all the time — people can get bored with that. I was very pleased. They made sure that Evelyn hit the top spot again! It was just fun. I mean, everybody did what they had to do, and they just said, 'Bring it! Just do what you do Evelyn, that's all!' I said okay and I went in there and did the song, and it turned out great!"

The "I'm in Love" video brought King firmly into the dawn of the MTV age, but the singer was not inspired by the visual results. "Well, at that time, I personally thought the ['I'm in Love'] video could have been better," King opines. "To me, it seemed like it was just pulled together. I thought I had a nice look, but I guess I am remembering that I had wanted to be an actor as well and wanted to play the role of what I was singing—as opposed to just dancing on a set. Even by then, we already had seen so much dancing on video. I had said to them before it was put out, 'I don't know guys. I think this should be where we are acting out the part,' and they said, 'Don't worry; it's going to be fine.' Regardless, the song was big no matter what. Now 'Love Come Down'—I thought *that* was a cool video! It was telling a story!"

"Love Come Down" took King right back up to the number 1 spot on the R&B and dance charts in '82 and once more into the Top 20 on the pop side. The album, *Get Loose*, went on to be the artist's best-selling LP. With another chart victory and stride forward for King's longevity, the artist's association with the RCA label continued well into the '80s with the albums *Face to Face*, *So Romantic* and *A Long Time Comin.*' She amassed numerous chart singles and retained a strong club following. By the end of the decade, she finally left RCA and joined the ranks over at EMI Records, where the single "Flirt" was a major soul-fused hit in 1988. King continued performing into the '90s and released another album, *I'll Keep a Light On*, on an independent label. In 2007, Evelyn received great reviews for a new digital LP called *Open Book*, which brought her back to club-land with the single "The Dance." She has remained a major attraction at disco diva shows and continues to earn star billing at revival events like the celebrated Disco Ball.

Her overall impression of the record industry and her experience in the business is measured today. "I think [the labels] should have done more," she says. "It was like they were always searching, you know, so quickly, for new artists. They put you on the back burner for a while and would say, 'She'll be fine; let's go work on the next artist.' So, I think there could have been more attention paid towards longevity. I was happy overall, but I know a lot of us did not get what was due to us. At that time, when my label started losing touch with me, I still had the voice, so I didn't see the problem. I felt it was on them. And I *still* have the voice—and it's even stronger now. I think they lose when they just bypass the artist that they already have going and just jump to other artists so quickly. A lot of us just had to sit it out, waiting to get a new deal. They did it to Natalie Cole and many other artists at that time."

She adds, "A lot of us failed to get what was due us financially back then and are still trying to find it today. A lot of us are not in our own homes, or don't have our own cars, or don't have the things that the fans think that we have. But when we get older, we hopefully get wiser. Sometimes, there's nothing wrong with turning the page backwards just to try to follow up and make sure that you're getting something that you worked for—do you understand what I mean? Some people just close the door. I don't want to be the one to just close the door, and I end up being the one who just talks to other divas and says, 'Did you ever get paid for this or that? Did you try?' and that sort of thing."

Despite any injustices, a review of Evelyn's career still leaves her with a sense of astonishment. "It was just so exciting to hit the stage and really watch the people sing with you, with your song. That is something that is so unbelievably beautiful—to have someone in the palm of your hand. It's like they're all in my living room with me, and we're sitting around having some popcorn and drinking some wine—I'm not gonna say beer because I don't like beer as much as I like wine," she laughs. "We're chillin' out, and it's almost like having a slumber party with your fans. I've never said that until now. But it feels like that. I've never actually had a slumber party, but I imagine it's that way. I just got off doing a show recently, and I'm telling you it really feels that way. I just did Redbank, New Jersey, and I almost wanted to cry. First of all, I got to see my baby brother, one of my baby brothers, and it's just tough when you don't get to see your family often and it feels like you live on another side of the world. I'm in California, and they're in New Jersey, New York and Atlanta. They're spread all over — even Connecticut. Just to see my brother and his wife and just to know that, okay, I did something good enough for my brother and my family to be so proud of me and come to see me.

"Those things mean so much in your heart because you know that you didn't fail your parents. That is my utmost goal in life. It's just making my parents proud. They're gone now. I even lost a child of my own in '89. That's very hard. It's just that you're humbled and grateful for the life that you still have. I have a husband that loves me very much, and I still have some family members living. Like my mom said, 'Stars do come back down, and you're no better than anyone else.' I'm a person first before I'm an artist," King declares.

As a hugely successful performer primarily associated with disco, Evelyn is now in the esteemed position of maturity to measure the recognition that her efforts and those of her fellow disco pioneers have received over the years. "We've been slighted over the years, in my opinion, and we've been only brought to light again once you started to hear rappers and remixers having us in the back of their music. That's the only time a lot of us started getting work again. I'm not going to say it's just me, but a lot of us started getting work again when we were heard on new performers' songs. We were pushed to the background for quite a while. I have nothing against what the hip-hoppers and rappers do, and I thank them for having me guest on their work and showing that they appreciate us. I don't like the disrespect on some of the [songs] or how they put out all of their stuff. But that's everywhere. Everybody's not going to like everything you put out. But when it comes to a lot of things like the bad language or calling women out — that's not my type of thing to listen to. I just think that we artists of the disco era have to stay focused and keep letting them know we still got it and that we haven't lost it! We have to let everyone see that we're still out there, and we still work! When I get up on that stage, I work twice as hard as when I was a teenager because I'm in my 50s. You know, sometimes they think we're ancient. I'm like, 'Oh, okay, right...' I let them know I'm not just a '70s disco artist — I'm the '70s, '80s, '90s and 2000s ... I let them know that I'm still going!

"I exercise and dance every day," she says, "I just get on with living the life. At the same time, what makes me smile a lot is looking back at pictures of the past. We should be proud — proud of coming from where we came from. Sylvester, Martha Wash, Jeanie Tracy, all the others, all the people from that dance era — we were *disco*. Later on, it seems like the less you actually sang — the less work and more chanting — [the more] you were considered dance music. I mean, if I sang less, my songs would be considered dance records. But when I did 'Shame,' that was a totally cool disco song. I personally think disco should've been respected more. Today, music is available only by what a few people sitting in their corporate offices decide should be available. They're not really going out and buying it. Our fans should be deciding and have more of a choice. I love that they have the People's Choice Awards and MTV viewer awards and all that. But what happened to our era of music? When are we going to see an award show for us? We're the ones that should stand up and say this music you hear today is a result of us back in the day. We're the ones that brought today's stuff all to life!

"They are much more receptive to us in Europe," King adds. "They appreciate the music, our sound, and they listen to everything. They care more about sound and what the artist is bringing to the audience and to the stage. It's easier to keep your fans there. Here in the U.S., sometimes they nitpick too much. You know— 'You have to be skinny; you can't be too fat; you can't gain any weight or you can't do this or that.' 'No, you won't look right on TV;' 'No, you don't sound right anymore.' You can't get sick; you can't be human. Am I right? Now, the thing I have to say is—I love the fact that I still have fans here in this country and abroad. But when I've done shows, I've heard, 'Evelyn "Champagne" King? She's still around?' You know, that's so weird and disheartening. The fact is I *do* still work all the time! It's just that they're not paying very much attention because they're still thinking that disco, well ... that was it— it's over. But you know what? It *wasn't* the end!"

Evelyn "Champagne" King says assuredly, "I let them know I'm not just a '70s disco artist—I'm the '70s, '80s, '90s and 2000s.... I let them know that I'm still going!" (courtesy Stephen Ford).

Evelyn "Champagne" King continues to make her presence known and her remarkably honorable legacy and vocal talent rank among disco's all-time greatest. She keeps it real when describing how she'd like to be remembered by her fans. "Remember me as someone bubbly, fun, loving ... *and that she loved to drop it like it's hot!*"

Audrey Landers

In 1978, if they weren't getting ready to hit a disco, millions of Americans across the country were fixated on the tube every Friday night for the CBS prime-time soap opera *Dallas*. In the midst of J. R. Ewing's oil-field shenanigans, Bobby and Pam's struggles to stay morally chaste and Cliff Barnes' underhanded dealings was a beautiful young blonde character named Afton Cooper, an aspiring singer. Turns out the actress who played that dramatic role so well, New York State–born Audrey Landers, really *is* a singer and one who, rather amazingly, built an accomplished acting career while simultaneously being a pop- and dance-music star. Though not an artist who often comes to mind when reflecting on classic dance music, Audrey's hits in the "disco-fox" category (a summery, disco-style also known as "Schlager" or "sugar" in German) were important contributions to this sub-genre that evolved from a melding of German-Austrian-Swiss folk music. Think "Edelweiss" with a disco beat. Combining a voice that was an engaging mix of passion and innocence with equally enticing acting skills was a feat in itself. Yet Audrey's story is all the more remarkable because of her stunningly successful dual career paths, forged relatively independent of each other, on two separate continents.

Anyone scanning the *Billboard* international music charts for the latest up-and-coming hits in 1983 would have seen the song "Manuel Goodbye" by Audrey Landers climbing the Top 20 in Germany. That music fan may have wondered if this was the same celebrity he or she was viewing on *Dallas, The Love Boat* and *Hollywood Squares*. It certainly was, and her splashy first chart-topper, an English-language, lightly danceable tune about the pain of leaving a lover became an international sensation. The song began Landers' long and highly successful international journey, a career that was marked with multiple European gold records. Amazingly, few people in this country were ever aware it even happened.

"It was kind of crazy," Audrey recalls. "I was pursuing my career in the entertainment industry, as a singer *and* as an actress in *Dallas*— both on parallel tracks. These days, that's pretty much expected. However, in the '80s and '90s, that was not an option — not in the U.S. I guess I was ahead of my time. Back then, in America, there was a very distinct delineation. If you were a TV personality, the music business wasn't open to accepting you as a musician or recording artist. I couldn't understand the resistance because I had begun my career as a singer and songwriter. I had my first hit record when I was about 14 years old on Epic Records in the United States. Music was my first love. The acting career was an offshoot of the music. But the music business wasn't quite ready for that in the United States." Landers' first recordings were country-flavored tunes produced by the late, legendary Buddy Killen and included "Apple Don't Fall Far from the Tree" and "You Thrill Me." While a teen skating in roller rinks and enjoying disco songs by Donna Summer and Gloria Gaynor, Landers had no idea she'd eventually share the same charts as the iconic divas, albeit far from home.

"I began songwriting at 11 years old. I really did want to be a singer. I had just written one of my first songs, and I got a chance to sing it on the *Merv Griffin Show*. It wasn't until I got on that show that I got an agent. She was with a big agency, at the time it was called CMA, and that's how I got signed. She saw me as a singer, but signed me as an actor, and she sent me out for an audition on a soap opera, which was *The Secret Storm*, and I got that part. Because music was such an integral part of me and my creativity, the writers caught onto that and had me play a singer-songwriter on the show. So, at that early age, I began writing the songs that my character would sing. Then I moved on up to another soap opera called *Somerset*, and my character did the same thing. Then again came *Dallas,* and the producers wrote me in as a singer for that ... and that's when I had my second opportunity to record in a much bigger way."

Bigger is an understatement. Audrey's 1983 debut album was called *Little River* (released on the major German record label Ariola, a division of the huge Bertelsmann entertainment

While captivating TV audiences on *Dallas*, Audrey Landers launched a hugely successful singing career that culminated in the international hit "Manuel Goodbye," seen here in its German and U.S. promo 7-inch single jackets from 1983 (author's collection).

conglomerate). The album yielded the somber but popular rhythmic title track that introduced her to Germany and then a follow-up, "Manuel Goodbye," which became a blockbuster. Landers says the song was originally intended to tell the story of a fisherman's son saying goodbye to his father, but it was wisely re-envisioned and rewritten by the singer. The tune vaulted up Germany's pop charts and quickly spread to neighboring countries. "Manuel Goodbye" was produced by veteran hit-maker Jack White, a man whose credits included Laura Branigan's earlier chart-topping dance classic "Gloria" and Jermaine Jackson and Pia Zadora's "When the Rain Begins to Fall." "It really is a fascinating story, and it was very exciting for me," Audrey says. "Jack White was a German producer who lived in the States in L.A., and he was producing Laura Branigan at the time. He was a big fan of *Dallas* and saw that I was singing on the show — and he saw that I actually *could* sing. He approached my mom, who was my manager, and we had a meeting and he said, 'Would you want to record something for Europe?' I said 'Absolutely!' Since I was also a songwriter, it was an added plus. And this is how all my songs began — many starting from long-distance calls on the phone! He would hum for me, like hum to me two or three bars and go 'la-la-la-la,' literally, and he would say, 'I want the title to be "Manuel Goodbye."' I would say okay, and I would go and write it. He would pick English song phrases that he felt were easy enough for people who spoke foreign languages to catch onto and sing along with. I have to say, quite often I thought they were inane! *I really did*. Would I ever in my life really write a song called 'Honeymoon in Trinidad?' It had its time though. He was so successful as a producer, and he knew what his audiences wanted. Although throughout the years, I always felt I was sacrificing my art a little, okay? I really did. But I said to myself, I have to look at this in another way — look how creative this is to make a song that I would actually like to sing out of this material."

Not only did Audrey have a passionate voice that was well-suited to the Euro-pop and disco-style songs she was singing (however sweet they may have been), she was also a beauty.

Landers' appealing cover-girl looks were a formidable asset for the rising star. Just as they had helped bring sex appeal to *Dallas* and made the singer a shoo-in for the film version of *A Chorus Line*, the artist looked equally attractive behind the mike and on album jackets. "Looking back, I certainly don't see my appearance hindering my career. I think it's always been a blessing for me. I think when you're young and looking at yourself, you see all the faults. You don't look at what's good. Other people say, 'Oh my God, look at your figure, look at this, look at that,' but, as a younger woman, I used to say, 'Oh, look at this—this isn't right,' whatever. I rarely saw the good; I was so critical of myself. I never felt that I was a sex symbol. As a person, I never saw that and found it surprising when anyone would write something like that about me. It certainly would guide my career in a certain direction though."

"Manuel Goodbye" enjoyed huge success in Europe and momentarily drew the attention of U.S. record label Curb-MCA. A rarely seen 7" promotional single of the song was prepared, but the track was never actively pushed to domestic radio or retail. (Its distinctly European sound was probably deemed unmarketable for U.S. audiences.) "It was barely released in the U.S.," she says. "I don't even remember ever promoting it. It's kind of a blur in my memory. I don't ever remember it being released here."

Despite the lack of visibility for her burgeoning music career in America, the German label quickly chased "Manuel Goodbye" with an even more danceable, romantic and irresistibly breezy single. "Playa Blanca" was the perfect getaway song for her European audience. The disco beat-fueled song completely captured the longing and passion Alpine audiences had for tropical, sandy beach destinations like Mallorca and Ibiza. A video was made for the track that Landers describes as a harrowing ordeal aboard a large, old-fashioned sailing vessel that foundered off the Canary Islands. The song was, again, a multi-country Top-Ten hit for Landers. While she appreciated the success and the emotions her danceable music was tapping into with her fans, she didn't always fully connect with it herself. She asserts, "I didn't always make the kind, or write the kind, of songs that I would have liked to sing, certainly for American audiences. And so, there was 'Honeymoon in Trinidad,' and I had a song called 'Santa California.' I said, 'Jack, it doesn't mean anything. It doesn't have any meaning. Can't it be called "Santa Barbara" or the name of a place?' He said, 'No, it means "Saintly California."' I said, '*Okaaaay?*' And then I would have the challenge of writing lyrics. I did have to sing them after all, and I wanted to like the songs."

The frustration of seeing the cross-genre and cross-continental success other artists working with White were enjoying registered on Audrey's radar. "It *did* bother me that Jack was having crossover hits with Laura. That's what I meant by being so stifled in my creativity. I mean my style of singing—I was more of a blues, rock 'n' roll singer. I always felt like, 'Why can't we do just one thing differently, just one song on the album, Jack?' And he just wouldn't ever, ever do it because he'd say, 'Look, this is what's successful,' and that's where he wanted to stay with me as an artist."

Though she longed for a more diverse sound, Landers continued her association with White and Ariola Records and continued racking up hits, establishing herself as a major player in the disco-fox genre. While most of her material stayed true to White's vision, there were some modest variations in song style with each of the singer's subsequent LP collections. Two Top-20 albums in Germany followed: *Wo Der Sudwind Whet* (*Where the Tradewinds Blow*), which featured the aforementioned songs and a duet with Latin sensation Camilio Sesto titled "Mi Amore," and *Weites Land* (*Far Away Land*), a more country-themed collection which had among its highlights an irresistible country-dance hybrid, "Tennessee Nights (Mama Chiquita)," and an astonishingly triumphant and moving light sounds song, "To All the Survivors" (which Landers describes as one of the few American-sounding tracks she had the opportunity to record). White also let the artist cut loose on the pure dance hit "Jim, Jeff & Johnny," which, in an extended 12" version from the LP *Paradise Generation*, was very much Branigan-esque.

"As an artist signed to a label — and maybe it's changed over time — I didn't really have a whole lot of say as to the style they would choose," she says. "Often the labels would just pair you up with the writers they had publishing deals with or co-production partners that would do the tracks. Although I would write some of the songs and they'd be in a certain genre when I wrote them, I didn't really have any control as to how they would be produced. It was the label's choice."

By the late '80s, Landers was ready to part with her production team and start making music that was closer to the style she desired. Moving to the German WEA recording company, she teamed with producer Christian deWalden. The producer had worked with a wide variety of artists, from Euro-dance legend Amanda Lear (whose deWalden-produced single, "Wild Thing," was an underground disco hit), to crooners like Anne Murray, and rock icons Cheap Trick and Bad English. The result was the sophisticated album *Secrets*, which looked and sounded different from anything the singer had done before. The explosive dance track "Never Wanna Dance (When I'm Blue)," which was remixed and released in an extended 12" version, and several additional singles in the rock and dance genres followed. Says the singer, "*Secrets* was a lot closer to what I wanted to do. But then the label didn't want to promote it too much. It was successful though, I have to admit, and I did love that album. He was a new producer for me, Christian, an Italian who lived in the States and with whom I am still friendly. The fit was right. I really did love that album."

Sharing her English-language success side by side with foreign language vocalists on European charts, dance floors and radio was not uncommon. English, French and Italian songs mixed comfortably in these open-minded countries where language wasn't a barrier. Says Audrey, "At the time, all the labels wanted me to sing in English, which I was more than happy to do. What they would then do is take their German artists and let them do covers of my hits in their language. I was more proficient a songwriter in English, my native language. I think I co-wrote eight out of 10 songs on every LP. So singing in other languages wasn't even an option in my recording career with Jack White. It was only in more recent years that I did that a lot more."

After *Secrets*, Audrey recorded the album *Meine Traume fur Dich (My Dream for You)*, which included an earnest rendition of ABBA's "Fernando," a reggae-Lambada dance-remake of "Sun of Jamaica" and a jolting dance-floor smoker called "Shadows of Love." From there, the artist moved to Polygram and released the LP *Rendezvous*, which yielded a self-penned hit called "Monte Carlo." She also released two dance singles (under the moniker of Rock Candy) with her sister, Judy Landers. The lush and heavy "Hurricane Man" and the percolating electronica number "Teach Me How to Rock" fared well in Germany and Belgium. With the raising of her family becoming a priority, Audrey put any further recording on hold for several years.

"I had given up the European career for a while because I simply couldn't commute like that anymore and, honestly, I'd been there and done that," she laughs. "And for a lot of years, I was raising my children and wanted to focus on my family. So I took some time off from the overseas work, and I focused on writing and co-producing an award-winning children's musical TV series with my mother, called *The Huggabug Club*, for which I wrote about 150 songs! Then a record company approached me a few years ago and asked if I would do a comeback. I talked with my mom and we said, 'What's gonna make it special ... why? Why would I start this up again?'"

She found the answer to her question by accepting an offer to record in the German language and set her music career back in motion around the dawn of the 21st century. Her return was marked by a stellar performance on a duet with one of Germany's leading schlager stars, Bernhard Brink. "Heute Habe Ich An Dich Gedacht" ("Today I Have Thought of You"), which brought the duo to the top of the German charts. "It was a nice experience. The song was beautiful, and for the first time, I sang a little bit in German. I got such a great response from the audiences there. I think that gave some of the labels the idea that I should be doing more in German. I do speak German and my great-grandparents spoke German, so it's not as foreign as it would seem. There were two reasons why I started recording again. One, I would do some of the songs in German or French or other languages. And, additionally, my son Daniel was about 9 years old and he was an aspiring singer, and we said we'd do some duets. So that's how I got back into it. I had the stipulation that I could record here where I live in Florida during the hours that my children are in school," she confesses with a laugh. "I wasn't in the frame of mind that I could be commuting every other week to do a concert or TV show or stay in Europe for any extended period of time."

Audrey began recording solo albums again: 2005's *Spuren Eines Sommer* (*Traces of Summer*, also released under the name *Dolce Vita*) and *Spuren Deiner Zartlichkeit* (*Traces of Your Tenderness*) released in 2010. The latter contained a hot Lou Bega-styled dance track called "Sommer Meer und Sonnenschein" (*Summer Sea and Sunshine*), which recalls the tropical flavor of her earlier smash, "Playa Blanca." But as welcome as these recordings may be for Landers' fans abroad, they also illustrate the challenges of being a cross-continental recording artist. She says, with a touch of irritation in her voice, "With all these hits I've managed to have, to make any money is a joke. I find hundreds of my titles being sold on major digital platforms, and yet it's impossible to collect any royalties. They're all out there under strange label names that I've never heard. It's a crazy world! I try to learn from my experiences, especially so that I can give proper guidance to my son Daniel. He's a great pop-rock songwriter and singer. He just turned 18, and he's a serious musician. He studies classical composition and theory. We've traveled a lot together, and he's done many shows and concerts in Europe. He has been offered record deals in Europe, but after having had my own challenges with overseas labels—well, I can't allow that to happen to his career. I want to be sure that he will have the opportunity to express his own unique creative style. He's just so darn good." Daniel Landers has begun to carefully launch a pop career in Europe, appearing on *The X-Factor* and successfully releasing the hit singles "Find Another You" and the dance-party anthem "Sleep All Day."

Meanwhile, Landers looks back fondly on all of her musical experiences. "It was a wonderful, wonderful time in my career and life, and I loved it. I loved everything—the creativity, the dual lifestyle and sort of being like a rock star. In Europe, I had fans camp out in front of my hotel, and then I'd come home and would do *Dallas*, which was a whole different kind of celebrity. I have no regrets; I have learned a lot. I have been so blessed."

As Landers reprised her Afton Cooper role in the TBS revival of the *Dallas* series in 2013, "Manuel Goodbye" turned 30 years old. The artist proudly considers it her signature song. "It was a definite turning point in one aspect of my career. If you go to Europe, they call it an 'evergreen'—a standard in Germany and in many countries. It went gold in a lot of different countries. It sold something like six million copies throughout the world!" The song credits officially note a suspiciously long list of composers, but rightfully and accurately include Audrey's name among them. "When all was said and done, I got very little for it. I was one of six writers, but I had no publishing rights on it. But that's really okay, you know? It was still an amazing time and an amazing experience," she beams.

Audrey seems comfortable with the balance of her career experience and life as she lives it today. "At this stage in my life, after having taken off a beautiful decade so I could raise my boys and not miss that chapter in my life—that was my choice in my career—I look at where I am now sometimes (I'm in my 50s) and I say, 'I am where I am.' And it's a great place to be in life. I would love to do some more music. But the style would have to be very different. I think the record business is very different now, especially if you're not a top pop artist. I think it's great that there are other outlets and opportunities for people to hear your music. Social media has created so many more possibilities. My *Dallas* fans have been asking me for years why I won't do an album of songs that I performed on the show. I've been toying with it. As soon as I get my son a little bit more settled with his career path, and I don't have to be so involved, then I will begin thinking about those things. (Audrey finally released a new album containing her music from the *Dallas* show in 2013 called *Dallas Feels Like Home*.)

"I just did a benefit show in Florida," she says. "They asked me if I would lend my name to a fund-raiser for a concert venue and arts center. I said absolutely, and then we had a meeting and it turned out to be a two-hour 'Audrey' show!" she laughs. "So I had to create a show, which I managed to put together from my other work, drawing from my performances in Vegas, Atlantic City and the styles that I enjoy. I love to do songs from the Great American Songbook. My style is very classic—I also like gospel and blues and that sort of era. So, it's not like I'm trying to be Katy Perry. I'm very comfortable singing, and I get to sing from my heart. I'm just not appealing now to the 14- or 18-year olds. I have endless energy ... thank you, God! Maybe it's because I have had two boys."

The artist always took a

"It was a wonderful, wonderful time in my career and life, and I loved it. I loved everything—the creativity, the dual lifestyle and sort of being like a rock star," says Audrey Landers (courtesy Audrey Landers).

grounded, stable path, even in her younger days. Her confidence has positioned her to continue to reinvent herself as a performer, songwriter, actress, clothing designer, entreprenuer and advocate for such causes as animal-abuse prevention. "Can you imagine how boring I must have been to the media?" she chuckles. "I think the media looked at me and said, 'Oh my God, there's nothing to write about.' I was raised that way. I'm so corny; it's silly. I look at my career as the icing on the cake. My life — my family — is the important part, and the career was just that little piece that made it more fun and amazing. I was blessed to have strong family support when I was growing up and building my career. My mom has been my manager and mentor. I never looked at anything like drugs and such as a temptation. It was nothing that ever appealed to me. I'm kind of a healthy-living person, and I like being in control. I might even be a little bit of a control freak," laughs Audrey. "I would never want to take anything that would make me have less control of my senses. And I'm blessed with enough energy to get me through whatever I need to get through if I just have a cup of coffee."

Audrey Landers is an atypical star whose talent transcended many forms of entertainment across the globe. "Manuel Goodbye," and her uplifting music here and abroad, is something about which Audrey remains very modest. "It really did open up doors to the world for me, and it was just fun. And to this day, whenever I go to Europe, they always ask me to sing 'Manuel Goodbye'— and it's being accepted by a whole new generation now. So, it's really interesting, and the fact that it's still relevant 30 years from when it was born is really incredible. It was definitely an exciting time, and it was a great beginning. Every time I hear that song's introduction, I get butterflies in my stomach! I would say thank you to anyone who remembers me for it, listened to me and enjoyed my music — because my music is a little piece of my heart. It was an honor that I was able to share that with so many people."

Suzi Lane

It's rare that an artist's first record becomes a number 1 hit and a classic as fast as Suzi Lane's "Harmony" did back in 1979. The conception of international maestro Giorgio Moroder, "Harmony" became an immortal club smash. But the song's all-too mortal singer was only able to enjoy her newfound fame and spotlight for a brief moment before fate turned her world upside down. Perhaps not so ironically, Suzi found harmony with her challenging circumstances over time. She triumphantly emerged from the ordeal confident that she was ready to revive her career with the same kind of energy that had heralded her arrival.

Immersed in a world of neon entertainment from an early age, the artist says her career path was inevitable. "Well, I live here in Las Vegas and, growing up here, you get to see stars at their best. The main thing was I always knew what I wanted to do going all the way back to the age of nine. As I was growing up I had a cousin who was with the Checkmates with Sweet Loui and they were performing at the Hilton here in Vegas — my sisters and I got to perform with them. So, I've really been performing and singing on a professional level for a long time with my sisters until the age of 17. Living in Las Vegas, the choice of performing really intrigued me, and I guess it was natural that I was drawn to entertainment," she says.

"Living in Vegas allowed me to be around people like Diana Ross—literally in her presence. Being in the presence of Sammy Davis Jr. and Bill Cosby, who's like a second father to me, was amazing. I was exposed to a lot of amazing people," Suzi reflects. "I knew [entertaining] is what I wanted to do; I knew I had the talent. But it was hard because there were so many professional people in Las Vegas, and they really didn't recognize the local talent and the realness. My sisters and I always called ourselves 'diamonds in the desert,'" she laughs.

The sparkle Suzi possessed eventually got noticed. She remembers, "I have a friend by the name of Bob Rafleson. He was a huge movie producer who worked on *Stay Hungry, The Postman Always Rings Twice* and *Five Easy Pieces,* and I've known him since I was about 16 or 17. While at his house one evening when I was about 20, I made a big entrance down one of those grand stairwells in his house not knowing he had company downstairs. I would perform for Bob and just act silly with him—so I come sliding down the banister with my eyes closed singing 'I'm Every Woman.' I know that sounds crazy, but we would do things like that—so here I am at the end of my performance and I open my eyes. Well, the company he had was Marissa Berenson, Elliot Gould, Susan Sarandon and Jack Nicholson and out of just sheer embarrassment I just kept performing and acting like they were my audience. That night, Bob said they loved it and they all had a great time. I went back to Vegas the day after, and I get a call from Bob and he says, 'You know you're a star!' I said, 'What the heck—I've *always* been a star—didn't you already know that?' He tells me Marissa Berenson, who was a friend of Giorgio Moroder at that time, thought I was amazing and she wanted to take me to meet Giorgio. Well, I didn't even know who Giorgio Moroder was! Bob said I had to be ready in just four hours. He flew me to L.A., and I was driven to the Beverly Hills Hotel. I go to the restaurant with Marissa Berenson and there was Giorgio Moroder. And I still wasn't really sure who he was. I sat down with him, he talked to me and said, 'I don't even need to hear you sing—Marissa told me you were singing 'I'm Every Woman' and how amazed she was by you.' He said, 'Let's go into the studio and see what you can do.' So, needless to say, we left the

"[Donna Summer] thought I was beautiful and she said, 'Always keep your head on straight and don't lose your soul,'" recalls Suzi Lane of the time when her disco debut, "Harmony," reached the top of the chart in 1979 (courtesy Suzi Lane).

restaurant, and he played a piece for me and I kind of hummed it a little bit. In exactly seven days, I was in the studio with a new haircut — I mean it went into a whirlwind! Marissa actually changed my complete look. It was just amazing!"

Lane made her recording debut on the Elektra Records LP *Ooh La La*. The album yielded a number 1 disco classic with the funky title track and "Harmony," a riveting journey into the type of high-energy electronica that Moroder had pioneered with Donna Summer. "We recorded right there in Los Angeles, at Rusk Recording Studio in Hollywood. We were in Los Angeles for most of the recording, and the last part of it we did in Germany. Then we came back to States. I didn't know the level to which the song and album would go. I was just going through the first steps, and I knew that it would probably lead to something else. That's how my career has always been. I could put my foot on one stone, like Michael Jackson did in his life, and then I'd put my foot on another stone and something else would open up. And that is exactly how it happened. I had no idea. As a matter of fact, I met and found out about Donna Summer at that time. I met her at the studio while I was recording 'Harmony' and she would smile and wave. She was like ... *a star*! She came in and was very down to earth, and she told me I was going to be great. She thought I was beautiful and she said, 'Always keep your head on straight and don't lose your soul.' That was the first and last thing I remember her ever saying to me."

"Harmony" eventually became a sensation on the club circuit and dance radio began placing the cut in heavy rotation. "The funniest thing was," says Lane, "I was in my car driving up Hollywood Boulevard on my way to my condo in L.A., and I heard the song and had to pull over because it was so weird — it was as if time had stood still! I heard the song blasting and I had a friend in the car with me and I remember screaming, 'That's my song! That's my song!' I was on a cloud! It was amazing to hear it — it felt like I was outside of my own body, and I just sat there and enjoyed the moment. I *really* enjoyed the moment! I think that first of all, that amazing bass line — it just grabs a hold of you. *Ooh, La, La* and 'Harmony'— they basically hit the market and let you know it's okay to be whoever you are. Just be you — gay or straight, whatever. It's all about harmony and bringing us together. I think it was more of a unity song. When you really think about the word *harmony*, it's a multitude of notes, a multitude of voices, perfect sync. I think mainly the reason it was a hit was because people came to respect each other for who they were at the time because that song said it's okay."

Ooh La La is hailed by many as an iconic disco album. The project was significant for Lane on numerous levels. "After I finished recording it, the best part was when my album was about to come out — the name of it was to be my real name, *Suzi McDonald*. But when 'Harmony' [looked like it could be a] hit, they started discussing if we should go with Suzi Lynn — that's my full first name. But they thought people might confuse me with Cheryl Lynn who was also breaking around that time. So we came up with the name *Suzi Lane*. My album is the only album in the history of recording — and I'm going way, way, way back from what they tell me — that was actually broken at the Cannes Festival, which is normally only about movies. We had a yacht in Cannes — a beautiful hotel, everything there — and that's where we held our release. My album took off first in Europe. Here in the States, there wasn't a lot of appreciation for it at the very beginning. After it started hitting in Europe so heavily, I came back to the U.S. because I had a request by Frankie Crocker at New York's WBLS station. When he met me he said, 'Today I'm going to make you a star!', 'Did I know what that meant? *No!*' she laughs. I walked into the studio with him, and he proceeded to do the interview there. That was my first step back into the States to promote the album and from the moment that the lines opened and he said, 'This is Suzi Lane and this is "Harmony,"' that was beginning—and it took off."

Recalling the striking and artistically erotic album artwork, Lane says, "When I actually did that album cover, to be perfectly honest with you, that was supposed to be a test shot—and when I say a 'test shot,' they were checking for lighting. If you look at the album cover, it has a lot of shadows because they actually wanted to set the lighting. But it ended up being that they loved that one shot to go on the cover. It was perfect for the *Ooh, La La* title, the spreading of the fingers, the cupping of the breasts and the shock value."

With her breakout success, the fun began. "I was in Germany, and they had a show like the *Ed Sullivan Show* with a lot of different artists that were from all over Europe. I actually performed on the same stage as David Bowie, who I loved! For many, many years, David Bowie, to me, was the most amazing performer around. Even though he was a rock star, when I met him he was more than what I thought he'd be. First of all, I loved his music. He was a single father in that era and raising his son. After doing that show in Germany, he took me, the whole crew—and also the Manhattan Transfer—for dinner at a restaurant. He just shut it down for anybody that wasn't with the private party. To sit down and talk to him and learn a little more about the music business—it was phenomenal. He loved 'Harmony' and he loved *Ooh, La, La,* and one of the things that he said to me that night—and it's weird because it echoed what Donna said—was that there would be a lot of pulling on me. He said I was very, very talented and that I wasn't only talented, I was beautiful on the inside and out. He said this is not a business that allowed both, that I should try not to lose it by all means possible—and that I should protect my spirit. And for me, that was another big *ah-ha* moment."

With so much good fortune at last in Lane's hands, the unthinkable occurred. She pauses and, taking a breath, recalls, "I had been doing a lot of touring and was on my way home to spend time with my mother, my sisters and family. My sister Paula picked me up from the airport, and we were driving home. I don't remember exactly what happened, as there are a few blank moments in here, but there was a car that came out of the desert that I could see out of my peripheral vision—kind of like he was weaving in the desert area. You could see the sand blowing in the wind, and then he roared into the middle of the street and hit me from behind. The impact sent me through the windshield, and when my sister hit the brake, the seat belt yanked me back. The broken glass didn't only tear my face, it ripped all the skin almost off the entire left side, my ear, my hair, my lip, everything. It was horrible."

Suzi was blessed to have a rock solid support system and slowly fought her way back from this horrific event. "The first thing that helped me through it all was my family," she says. "My mother and my sisters were there. Outside of that, I prayed a lot and I know that if it had not been by the grace of God, I would have lost my mind. I remember—although my father was not always with us—he came to my hospital. He was a very reserved man; he would never show his feelings. I mean it was hard for him to say, 'I love you,' even when you said it to him. But he came to the hospital and I saw his face, his reaction to the way I looked. I went to the bathroom, and I saw my face—I literally went numb. I think that, for those years, I stayed numb. I got a call from Stevie Wonder, and he was reminding me about his accident and told me I was going to be okay. Frankie Cocker called. Everybody wanted to come see me. But I needed to heal first. One side of my face was Suzi; the other side of my face was this monster. How did I deal with it? I basically just had to numb up—and when I say numb up, it almost brings tears to my eyes because I don't remember a lot. I just had to shut down," she says, pausing with emotion.

"So consequently, I was homebound for a very long time. Because it's so hot in Vegas, they wouldn't let me go out in the daytime because they were afraid the heat would destroy the raw skin and I would lose movement in my face. For about three years, I was not allowed to come out except to go to the doctors late in the day. I was supposed to have surgery, but my body healed naturally from my mother's prayers and, frankly, aloe vera. She put lots of aloe vera on my face. After that, to be perfectly honest, when you've been a hermit for so many years and trying to heal, I just lost touch with everything. I never ever got to really take care of me or my emotional response. About the fourth year after the accident, two of my sisters, Jerushia and Maria, both moved to New York. They were modeling and Maria was also acting, and they told me come out. So, I sort of pulled myself together. I went to New York to spend some time — at least to get out of the house and get used to being back around people. It's really strange when you've been in an accident and you've been away from people. It's ironically as though somebody pulls your skin back and all your senses are exposed, like the sound of cars, the door, everything — it makes you rather jumpy. And of all places to go, I go to New York. One day while there, Jerushia said she needed me to bring her a bag of makeup and it was only around the corner, so I knew I would be fine. I got up and I took her the makeup and when I walked in — it's just like everything else that happened in my life — everything in my life has been instantaneous, especially when it comes to my career. Jerushia was shooting for *Essence,* and the people there were asking who I was. *Boom*, my career started again! They wanted to shoot me and booked me for a whole day. I joined Cuington Model Management [and soon after] Ford Modeling came calling. Then my career took off — my second time around. I got contracts with Lane Bryant and Hanes."

The artist reveals that a follow-up album (*Savage Gold*) was planned, but never materialized. She continued to persevere. "It was a tough time, but you know what they say — tough people make it through tough times, and a change in your perception will lead to success. And I have to say, I had to be really tough. There are times you don't want to be tough, yet you find you have strength in you that you never really knew existed. The accident made me appreciate beauty and what I looked like then — I never realized how special I was before that. But more than that, I was able to see how the body rejuvenates itself. I was taught to be beautiful inside first and the outside will reflect beauty. During the healing period, I didn't see it that way, [I just] felt a lot of pain. Now I am glad I have gone through everything I have experienced. I do remember the song that would have been the single [for my second album] very, very well. 'Vampire'— hot, hot, hot, strong bass, violins — I love violins — and a sexy sax. I wrote the song, so I will add it to my next project."

Lane looks affectionately back on the disco music genre that launched her, but wonders if the artists from that era are given their due. "I think because they put the name *disco* on it, it hasn't helped artists from that era gain respect and recognition. Dance music has been around a long time, and when they ended up putting a title on it, it's like erasing the importance of what we do as artists. Back in that era, they were treating artists like meat. 'What's the next piece of meat you have on the slab?' And it was up to us to try to figure out how to market ourselves after that. I know that we *did* bring a lot to the market because disco did come into vogue, and the music business was really saturated and they made a lot of money because of us. As far as being respected as singers, as performers, I just don't think we got our due. I think of Chaka Khan — she's looking awesome and she got some respect. But Chaka never really got what she *should* have gotten. I look at it now and see that it's turning around. We're coming back again, baby! This is our second time around, and I think we are coming back smarter, coming back stronger, and we are not going to be as naïve about the business as we've been before. I think, if nothing else, we learned from rappers and this younger generation that we don't have wait for somebody to put our music out. We don't have to wait for anybody to say when our albums can hit the stations. I mean, look at the artists now. There are so many different avenues to go through and now they are coming after us. But now they are going to have to cough up what they didn't pay us before because a lot of us didn't get paid the way we should have," Suzi argues.

"I loved disco and would have liked the opportunity to sing more songs from the era. I always loved Donna Summer's 'On the Radio,' and I always thought I could have done a great job with that song too. That diva was amazing! I'm honored that I was recognized for being a part of disco with such fierce divas for what I *did* do. As I said, I was a young girl that was acting crazy and somebody saw talent. I don't want to dwell on what I missed out on all the time—if you do not appreciate what you get and keep looking over your shoulder, you miss the blessings that are right in front of you. So not only am I a diamond from the desert, but I'm a diamond that's been shining and is ready to work again! As far as my career is concerned, I plan to perform for a very long time. I'm working on a show here in Vegas with Pattie Brooks, Chris Bennett, Billie Kaman and other performers that are willing to merge jazz with disco. I want to keep growing and creating. Eventually, I want to produce, direct and also be able to instill in actors and singers the sense that they *can* have longevity. I don't think we have enough of that ... well, in the disco era we didn't. In the years before disco, they actually took artists and not only trained them, but they gave them the tools to be able to have longevity and to know who they were. I want to bring some of that back."

As Lane enjoys renewed interest in her music legacy and continues to promote her talents, she also has made a point of giving back. "I'm the volunteer vice president of the Hands of Comfort Foundation, and if anyone wants to know something about it, they can go to the website, which is www.handsofcomfortfoundation.org. It's a foundation that deals with all types of trauma. As a matter of fact, I am a trainer and I man the phones, the comfort lines. As an entertainer, I have sung about it—now I put my talent to use in the

Says Suzi Lane of life in 2012, "I am blessed with the gift of resilience. I am blessed to be able to recreate myself" (courtesy Suzi Lane).

community changing one life at a time. I wish there was something like it when I was going through the accident, just to have someone you can pick up the phone and call. We deal with all types of trauma—whether it's thoughts of suicide, bullying, loss of your job, being discriminated because you are black, gay or straight—it doesn't matter. We open the door to everyone. Everything is done free. We try to make it free so that everyone can get the help they need. Last year we had four-time Grammy winner DeeDee Bridgewater, Chris Bennett, Yashi Brown [Michael Jackson's niece] and others to help us celebrate at a gala we held. You would be shocked at the people who come to us for help. We get professional people, nurses, teachers—people are people and we all need help sometimes. [Someone to] just listen and be non-judgmental. I think of myself and a lot of times I needed to just talk—and not to someone in your family that is emotionally attached. I think it would have made my healing happen a lot faster, too."

This artist, a fighter and survivor, is determined to make a difference. "Bottom line with Suzi Lane," she declares, "I am blessed with the gift of resilience. I am blessed to be able to recreate myself. After I started modeling again, I actually had a different appreciation for life. I am an entertainer at heart! So don't ever count me out!"

She would like to be remembered "as someone who loves deeply and cares that mankind and this world is left better because of my efforts through love—someone who thrived in music and someone who had a huge heart. I have a saying that is very important to me: 'When anyone says *no,* turn the word backwards and the word becomes *on*!' Only you can change your perception and your thinking and thrive! I believe that everyone deserves a second chance, and if I can extend my hand in any way, I would love to always be the extension that helped someone through to a moment of happiness. If I could say just one more thing to everyone—deep inside, the only thing you can give—and the best thing you can give—is yourself. Suzi Lane wants to be one of those people who desired to give her best at all times and tried to show others in the world that it was okay to be you!"

Cynthia Manley (Boys Town Gang)

If you were exploring disco music and self-identity in the early '80s, chances are you stumbled upon a very underground-looking 12" single (or 2-track album depending on your viewpoint) called "Crusin' the Streets" by the Boys Town Gang. Featuring a snapshot cover scene of San Francisco's Castro Street intersection with a decidedly hyper-masculine atmosphere, few people would have guessed just how unusual and remarkable was the music contained on the vinyl inside. On the record's A-side was an extraordinarily fresh, hip, full-length dance update of "Remember Me/Ain't No Mountain High Enough." The B-side featured a pseudo-gay porn movie soundtrack, graphically enacting life "Cruisin' the Streets." Clearly, boundaries were being broken ... *big time*! The unusually rough-and-ready voice behind this extraordinary release belonged to Cynthia Manley, a relentlessly energetic woman whose determined attitude and wicked sense of humor are very much alive and well today.

"I came from a large family," Cynthia recounts. "My mother got me singing in church almost as soon as I could talk, and that's where I did my first solo when I was six years old — up in the balcony. I come from a humble background. Later on, I was working in a gentleman's clothing store to pay for college. While I was working my way through [Sacramento] City College, I was rehearsing in a garage and was heard by someone who offered me a paying singing job. Maybe for like a year, I stuck with my original dream of being a third grade teacher, but it was real quick that I discovered I liked all the attention and the excitement of singing, entertaining and traveling. So, when all that started workin' for me, I put everything into being a singer.

"I eventually decided I was ready to run off to L.A. to be a star. I went out on the road with a cover band and was hired as a background singer. One of the guys in the band had a house in L.A. and I said, 'You know what? We need to quit this band and move to your house in L.A. and become stars!' Every time I did a recording, I saw it being the number 1 hit in the world, and I was always optimistic and saw myself being the next Chaka Khan. I never saw myself as a mediocre musician; I always saw myself as a star! There's so much rejection in this industry that you really had to have a strong sense of self — of your dream — and you needed the ability to grab an opportunity. You needed a freedom from fear so that when you saw an opportunity, you jumped at it instead of running away from it. You gotta have a certain amount of balls to be in this industry, and I think part of that comes from liking yourself and believing you *are* a diva. If you don't believe it, how can you convince other people?"

Cynthia wasn't particularly cognizant of disco music opportunities; however, like any aspiring singer, she looked for work where she could find it. She found herself in the hands of dance music maestro Bill Motley and Moby Dick Records. She says, "I was always into R&B — James Brown, Aretha, Otis. I also loved Jimi Hendrix and Janis Joplin and would buy all their songs and sing them at top of my lungs. I didn't know anything about dance music. I'd always been on the R&B and rock side of things. Bill Motley was, as legend goes, auditioning hundreds and hundreds of singers. He was down here in L.A., and I knew all the musicians he was using to do the tracks. They did all the musical parts of the Boys Town Gang, and anything Bill produced, these guys did the music for it. So, Bill was apparently bitching, 'Is it *that* hard to find a cute little white girl who can sing like a black woman?' — that kind of thing. The band said, 'Have you tried our singer, Cynthia Manley?' So I got the audition because I knew the band. I came in at kind of the end of the process. I went in, sang it and got paid $300."

She describes the event as a very satisfying introduction to disco. "I sang 'Ain't No Mountain High Enough,' and he had a rough track of 'Can't Take My Eyes Off of You' and I sang 'em both. I was only there maybe an hour because I was very familiar with the songs already. I think he made me do it about three times, and I thought it was delightful — it was fast! When Bill did that 126 beats-per-minute on 'Ain't No Mountain,' that was considered really fast. Not the case anymore, but at the time it was a whole different thing. I still sang in an R&B style, 2–4 feel. I was thrilled with it — it was happy music. Singing it — you couldn't sit still. My first experience with disco was ... *I loved it*! But, don't forget, my first experience with disco was singing a hit record! What's not to like?" she laughs.

"I don't really remember why Bill chose the song 'Ain't No Mountain,'" Cynthia ponders, "except that one time when I played in Boston, I stayed in this very swanky hotel suite. Bill asked if he could stay with me. I said sure — we enjoyed partying together and the suite was paid for by the club, Pipeline, who hired me. Seems Diana Ross was in that same hotel, and we got to meet her. Bill was like an excited little girl about it! So, I think [the song] was his first choice because he *absolutely loved Ms. Ross,* and it was a great song.

"I got a call a couple of months later, and the guy on the phone said, 'Are you the Cynthia Manley who sang "Ain't No Mountain High Enough"?' I said yeah, and he said, 'Well, you just made dance music history by entering at number 69 on the national *Billboard* charts. You got a hit record!' Apparently, at that time, nobody had ever entered the club chart at higher than that. It was a

The original Boys Town Gang *Cruisin' the Streets* LP from 1981 featured and launched the disco career of Cynthia Manley and was an iconic breakthrough for the gay community (author's collection).

record-breaking event for Bill Motley, and for me, as a newcomer, it was unbelievable! Today you can buy the slots, but at that time in dance music it was all about the dance floor packing up when the DJ put the record on. It was all about audience participation and how the music mixed well. Bill was one of the first to do an independent record distribution, so those guys made a fortune and actually created a pretty much 100 percent gay distribution network. They sold the record in every gay record store in the country. It worked big time."

Manley had no concerns about reinventing the Motown classic. "I wasn't worried about comparisons to Diana Ross. Diana's voice was so sweet and gentle, whereas my voice was way more balls to the wall. There was no comparing the two styles. If anyone mentioned Diana at all, they'd say she must love me — always in a kind respectful way. I loved her as a diva, but I preferred the Arethas and Chakas — I liked that '*grrrrrrrrr*!' Diana had more of a '*purrrr*,' and I was a growler. I just sang the way I was comfortable. I never saw Bill again after that until he wanted to do 'Cruisin' the Streets.'"

Gay lifestyles, especially in the sexually explosive environs of New York's meat-packing district or Frisco's Castro Street region, had never been the uncensored subject of a song before, save for casual references in early Village People releases. "Cruisin' the Streets" took the bull by the horn (or choose your own phallic reference). "Bill needed another song to go with 'Mountain,'" Cynthia recalls. "I believe 'Crusin" was a Bill Motley original song, the only one that he wrote that he put out. It was way, way before the bruha over *Brokeback Mountain.* Bill knew he had a hit [with "Mountain"] and would need a B-side. And he said there's only one person for that — that *sassy* Cynthia Manley! It was obviously a gay anthem and really one of the first of its kind. It was loud, gay and proud!"

The artist recalls the making of the explicit song. "We recorded that whole thing in a bathroom here in L.A. It was hilarious, and when I first heard it, I said, 'Bill, you can't expect me to sing this!'" she divulges with a laugh. "The thing I remember most about it was that rap thing. I just remember we were talking in his living room. I used the bathroom and was singing in there, and I was like, 'God, the acoustics are great in the bathroom, and we should do it in here!' So they told me to come back in an hour, and in the meantime they had set up all the microphones in there, three in different spots and told me to stand in the middle and read the script, which they had given me earlier. As soon as I read it, I knew the story and I believed it — the whole scenario. It was no muss or fuss; I just got into character, and it happened. Imagine my surprise when, as a joke, I put in that stuff about that big sausage, and he actually left it in the record! You can only imagine how horrified I was at the time. I got paid and walked away!

"You know, not only was I not familiar with dance music, I had never been around gay people before. So, of course, the first time I was flown out to do a show — it was to the Pipeline in Boston, I think, a huge club. They said, 'We'll give you $10,000' and blah, blah, blah. But I just really had those two songs. At the club, they put me up on this cherry-picker and moved me out over the crowd. To look down and see over 7,000 screaming, half-naked — and in some cases fully naked with body paint — handsome men, I was in heaven. I was getting the gay connection fully, and I was just looking down saying, 'Oh my God, am I gonna have fun tonight!' I had such a good time, and I asked if I could sing it again in a half-hour. The crowd went crazy, and the owner was thrilled — it was just amazing! So that was my first show in the gay community, and I thought I'd died and gone to heaven. The gay men gave me all the instructions in diva-hood because they had it down more than anybody I knew. They taught me how to strut my stuff," credits Cynthia.

Fellow disco diva Jessica Williams ("Queen of Fools") became something of a mentor for Manley. She laughs, "This little incident led to a life-long friendship. We're on a plane, and she looked at me and said, 'You're Cynthia Manley.' I said, 'Yes, and you're Jessica Williams, the queen of fools.' And now she's really looking at me critically. I'm not getting a hate vibe, but I'm getting a real head-to-toe checking out. She goes, 'Do you *not* shave your legs?' I said, 'Well, I'm blonde, why would I?' Then she says, 'Oh my God — and you don't shave your armpits!' And then she saw my nails weren't manicured, and she looked at my feet and said, 'I assume your toenails are not done either.' I said, 'What do you mean by done? Of course I clip my toenails.' I was a hippie; what did I know? She said, with her finger up in my face and a two-inch finger nail, '*This* will never do! Oh my God, girl, do you understand you are getting ready to perform for a bunch of beautiful gay men? Do you know what that means?' I said, 'Well, no, but I hope they like me.' Jessica said, 'Well they're *not* gonna like you because they won't be able to get over the fact that *you don't shave your legs*! They will talk about your nasty legs and armpits and nails until the day they die! As soon as we get off this plane, we're taking you to a spa, and I'm giving you a makeover. You got any money? We're gonna need at least $500 to a $1000! No friend of mine is going on stage looking like this!' I said, 'We're friends?' She replied, 'If you can make yourself presentable, we can be friends!' Jessica took me to a beautifying place and, three to five hours later, I walked out of there ... *divafied*! It was all Jessica Williams' doing! She wasn't trying to be mean. She was being a big sister, and everyone on my team was so grateful to her because nobody could get me to do that stuff. Love that woman!"

Cynthia struck up friendships with many other dance artists along the way, including the iconic Sylvester. "I did lose a lot of friends to AIDS, and that was horrible — Sylvester being one of them," she remembers. "I have great memories of him. He was a very kind man, a bigger-than-life bitch, and whether he was sitting at a piano or trying to help someone, he was just a kind man. He taught us all how to do it. There was no bigger diva than him. We all watched in awe as he did what he did. He stole every stage he was ever on. Because he was just too much — none of us ever wanted to ever fucking open for Sylvester," she laughs. "He liked my spirit and voice. We were at a gig in Miami or Ft. Lauderdale, a Jerry Lewis telethon event. There were a bunch of us — Jessica Williams, Vicki Sue Robinson, maybe Jo-Carol — I can't remember everyone. Sylvester got a gig at a rooftop restaurant playing Marvin Gaye, Aretha, old R&B songs. And he asked me to join him — of all those divas there, he asked me! I worked a three-hour piano bar with Sylvester, and he would do these riffs and harmonies around me that were just mind-boggling! He was not only a showman; he was an incredible musician. I didn't know him as well as some of the others did, but I loved him."

Manley embarked on a devoted love affair with her other gay friends and fans. "I know more about my gay guys than I do any man I ever loved! I got blowjob lessons from gay men!" she laughs proudly. "I was performing at the Russian River Resort and the place has, kind of sheltered in the back, three hot tub jacuzzi-type things. It was three or four in the morning, and we were high and drinking, of course, and I decided to hit the jacuzzi. My assistant, Nancy, decided to go with me, and she was a very straight little girl. She was glued to me. When she saw all those naked men, she said, 'Oh Cynthia, let's just go to bed!' I said, 'Are you kidding me? I'm not leaving this — this is fun!' So, I see all these naked men and I shout, 'Hey gents, diva on board, don't mind me ... I just need to relax.' They start posing and strutting for me and gave me applause, and it was all in fun. Nancy had her eyes closed, saying, 'I just can't be here; this is too weird!' Then I see this guy giving another guy head and I said, 'You know what? I hope this doesn't insult anybody, but who better to give blow-job lessons than a guy! Would you guys mind showing me what you're doing with your tongue, your teeth, your hands? Can I get up close and watch?' Well, you would not believe it! These guys get up in front of my face like two or three inches away from me so I can see what's going on and show me how they were doing everything. Oh my gosh — what a lesson! It's just one of those fabulous things that happened with my gay brothers. Not one of them was like, 'Get out of here; you don't belong here.' I had more cocks in my face — I was taught so much and they were just loving it! They said after these lessons, every man would be chasing me — straight men will be lining up at my door. And let me tell you, over the years I've gotten nothing but praise! I know it's tacky, but a girl has to be proud of a few things she does well!" Cynthia laughs vigorously.

Unsurprisingly, Manley's equally ballsy pair of club cuts on Moby Dick Records never made the radar of less open-minded mainstream radio programmers, and crossover success eluded the artist. "There was some desire to cross over onto the pop chart," she says. "The pop charts were where you'd get on TV and all. In the dance market, your audience was predominantly gay at that time, but thank God because they were a very, very supportive group of people. At that point in the '80s, more and more people were coming out, and they stuck together. The guys — it was more guys than lesbians — were a tight, tight community. A big part of it was the dance music and the spiritual side of it. There was no judgment in their community. It wasn't like today, where people in general don't care who you're sleeping with as much."

The Boys Town Gang was fronted by different lead singers on follow-up singles and albums. Following her auspicious debut, Cynthia took her talents to other labels, including Atlantic Records. Notable releases from the period included an electric, high-powered remake of the Holland-Dozier-Holland classic "Back in My Arms Again" (performed in a style similar to Kim Wilde's material), a major club hit in 1982. She observes, "If I had to do it all over again, and I knew then what I knew now, I would have stuck with Bill Motley. I was Bill's star, and I would have been treated a lot better. The problem was that Bill was offering me $200 a week and limousine service and telling me he'd make me a household name. And I was already making five grand a week and told him that wasn't working for me. So, really, we had a stupid argument, and if I had sat down with him and not gotten angry about it, I'm sure we could have worked it out. I had some hit records afterward, though. Atlantic Records had Laura Branigan, and they had the strongest dance music department. It was a no-brainer going with them. I didn't have to hustle for that at all because they came to me with a silver platter — I had a built-in fan base. It wasn't much of a gamble on their part, but they never did commit to an album. I thought by going to Atlantic, I could get an album and record some of the music [styles] that I also enjoyed. Atlantic released, I think, four singles from me, and that was it. But in the '80s and early '90s, I was signed to no less than five major labels — so I would get the advance money from anywhere from $25,000 to $100,000 and do a record or album. Then, whoever signed me would get fired or transferred to another label. And if an exec signed you and moved, your project got dropped — and that happened to me several times."

The excesses of the industry and times were very much a part of Manley's wild ride, and she is frank about recollecting it. "Sex, drugs and disco!" she proclaims. "One of the more outrageous things I ever saw — and in retrospect I thank God I didn't jump in and I just watched — was an orgy in New York. I think it was a gig where I opened up for Donna Summer at Studio 54. There was this big party after the show. Donna was, of course, very straight-laced; she wasn't there. It was basically like, 'Leave your clothes there, and come on in.' I was never shy — I had a cute little body — so I got naked and draped a towel around me and went into the 'fun room,' as they called it, and got my mind blown! So, yeah, I witnessed a gay orgy with about 30 people just screwing anything that came close to something else. And I was always a little coke-head, unfortunately. When you're on cocaine, you feel invincible, and so I would do things I probably wouldn't have otherwise. For instance, I was working a show with 1,500 people around a pool, and at the end of the show, I dove in. My stylist, my hairdresser, my make-up artist went into conniptions! I probably didn't make great business decisions, but I *did* make great decisions when it came to my audience."

Cynthia adds, "I certainly wasn't the only one doing cocaine, but a lot of the [female artists] in the circuit did come from church backgrounds — and I grew up a good little Christian girl, too — but for me, as soon as I went out on my own, I found God in the trees and the flowers. I always tried to be a good person in terms of right and wrong and not hurting other people and that sort of thing, but I *was* wild. And I was a free sexual spirit. I mean, I never did it with a gay guy, but I definitely had my threesomes and all of that — and you never really do things like that unless you're high. You can try to convince yourself you're having fun, but unless you're really fucked up, you're really lying to yourself. We'd be up on stage in the middle of performances, and the guys would hand up caps of cocaine to us. We'd snort it and keep performing. Nobody was hiding it. We had silver chains and spoons around our necks. It was something we flaunted; we weren't ashamed of it. Some artists were more like me and some were more conservative and 'churchy,' for lack of a better word. Actually, I do know how to say it — they were a little *classier*," she laughs. "I was well-mannered, but I wasn't a lady. Most of those women didn't cuss, drink, screw strange men — I did *all* of that stuff. I was kind of the bad girl of the circuit."

The singer vividly recounts more adventures with a laugh. "I do remember a wild story that happened at a huge Studio 54 type of place where I was doing a show," she says. "I don't remember where it was, but I had a big hit record at the time. My record was number 1 on all the regional charts and was climbing on the national *Billboard* charts. At the club, they always had your name on your dressing room — they treated their divas well back then — and they said to me, 'Cynthia, why don't you go into your dressing room and get settled,' and they pointed to the door with my name on it." Manley says she was startled to discover singer Grace Jones in her room, who appeared equally displeased to be caught off guard. "She jumped up and said, 'Who the fuck are you!?'" Cynthia recalls. "She was like six feet tall and wearing seven-inch platforms. I just had these little flat shoes on, fresh from the airport, so I came up to her waist. She was this huge Amazon-like woman, and she says, 'What the fuck are you doing in my dressing room!' So I pump my 5'2" self up, throw my shoulders back, toss my hair back and I say, 'I'm Cynthia Manley and what the fuck are *you* doing in *my* dressing room!' And she came at me — like to attack! I kind of bent down and rammed her in the belly with my head, and I caught the momentum so perfectly or she would surely have killed me. I knocked her down! So, thank God, my road manager and some guy in charge of the place came in the door at that point. At least Grace and I were professional enough and went along with the 'is everybody okay in here' thing. But she looks at me like she's gonna *kiiiiiill* me! I said, 'Oh yes, everything's fine. Looks like Grace is in the wrong dressing room. You might want to show her to *her* dressing room.' And that was that!" she laughs proudly.

Manley wrestled with her personal demons, got the upper hand and moved on with her career. She reveals, "I kicked cocaine in December of '89, and it took me a couple of years to get my head back on and recover from the fact that I had been really wealthy and I had spent all my money. I was a crazy girl. When I got clean in '89, I eventually started working with my band again, and that's when I started doing corporate work — Microsoft, Coca Cola — they'd fly you in and have you do corporate retreat gigs. And then I started doing my own CDs. I don't have any complaints at all. I never received any money from my work with Boys Town Gang, except the $300 for 'Ain't No Mountain' and maybe about $150 for 'Cruisin.'' I really don't remember. I didn't see any other money from those recordings, but I did get to tour all over the place. But I signed a contract that let that happen, so I can't blame it on the label. I can't say I have any ill will towards any of my labels. I was treated nicely. And I made great money touring."

The feelings the artist has about her career are grounded in equal appreciation for her adventures and the achievements she had along the way. Says Manley, "I don't feel that I missed out on anything, and I feel like I've lived the most incredible life. I have not yet crossed over to those pop charts, but I think I got all the recognition I deserved. Again, until 1989, it was just one great big party. I didn't care about anything but that when people came to my show they had a good time. That was the only thing I gave any thought to. Anything I didn't get from the business was because I wasn't paying attention and I didn't care. As long as I had money in my pocket and could feed my nephews and nieces and start college funds for them, I was happy. I tried to do a lot with the money I made. I've never been married or had children, so it's allowed me to be more generous with my sisters and their kids. I don't think I've been mistreated any more than I might have deserved. Let's put it that way.

"I was asked for ID at liquor stores and bars until I was 45," she continues, "so I've always been blessed with a youthful look. I have Indian blood, so I have good skin. Plus, having never been married or had kids, I don't have those kinds of stress lines. But no matter how good you look, there's menopause, and it just kills all of us whether we want to talk about it or not. It's a very difficult transition. I've read three books on it just to try to understand it. This is something I usually share with my closest friends, but I think it's very true. Aging—when you are a person whose always gotten a lot of attention and been pretty—and that's not meant to sound arrogant, but I was blessed—I think it's harder. I know that sounds horrible, but if you never had a lot of men flirt with you or beauty has not been one of your tools, you don't miss them so much when they're gone—if that makes any sense. Most of the divas always had that tool to work with, and I think it hits us really hard. I mean, I'm much nicer now—I'm kinder, I'm much more observant, more apt to shut up and listen and compromise. In my 20s, it was, 'Fuck you—it's my way or no way!' And that was no way to live. Most of us performers from that era aren't competitive now at our ages. Now we get jobs from each other. Now we call on each other and try to help each other out. At a certain point, we all become responsible for each other and we all rejoice in each other's success. Because that means there's room for us to have another success ourselves. Getting older ... yeah, it's a tough one, a *really* tough one, and it is a youth-oriented business. But there are times when its okay being older and you don't go through as much angst and drama. But aging—if anyone tells you it's not hard, honey, they're lying. It's a kid's business, and I think all of us are looking for ways to stay in the industry with that cross to bear.

"I'm blessed with an optimistic personality, and I think in the music industry, some people got more beat up than I did—and I'm still in it. I think for me, business people that were mean to me—and of course there were a lot of them—I didn't figure they deserved too much of my energy or attention. I didn't care if the business people didn't like me, and I realize that attitude didn't serve me well. But what hurt me was if an audience member said something mean. It hasn't happened often. Recently, in the last five years, somebody wrote 'great song' about a piece I wrote called 'Sunshine Hotel,' but said, 'Why are you using the old ladies to sing it?' I had gotten tons of great feedback from everyone about that song, and that one [negative comment] was like, 'Ouch!' Why couldn't he have stopped with 'great song?' The 'old ladies' he was referring to were me, Jessica Williams and Anita Sherman. I was like, 'Dude! These "old ladies" you are talking about have all sold millions of records and traveled the world making people happy, and all you've done is sit at your computer being a hater!' But you know, to keep up with it, you have to stay positive in this business and believe that what you're doing is in some way contributing something positive to the world around you and put everything you got into it!" says Cynthia.

"I'm still making records. The Europeans, thank God, they don't care so much about age. So, I have a record deal out of Switzerland on Purple Music, and I'm working on a project with them and writing some songs. So financially and careerwise, I'm still very active. I'm looking to start my own label. With the Internet the way it is, you don't have to have a million dollars to start a label. You hook up with Soundcloud, Amazon and iTunes and you've got an instant distribution system. I know all the promotional companies. This is what I do—I can't just curl up and die. It keeps me vibrant and pays my bills—it's my job. Growing old sucks, but you just have to figure out how to work with it. It's better than the alternative! Your attitude has to be, 'Let's go for it!'" In 2012, the artist successfully

Cynthia Manley's philosophy in the 21st century is "[You have to] believe that what you're doing is in some way contributing something positive to the world around you and put everything you got into it!" (courtesy Cynthia Manley).

began marketing her industry street smarts and developed an instructional-educational video package for anyone in the music business (or who wants to be) at www.youwantto-bearockstar.com. She recorded "Can't Take My Eyes Off of You" in 2013, a song she was to have sung with Boys Town Gang. "I always loved the song and felt it was as good a time as any to lay claim to it!" she says.

Cynthia Manley hopes the remarkable energy she has delivered through her voice (and continues to share with audiences today) will retain a warm spot in the hearts of her fans. She says, "I'd like to be remembered as a great entertainer! I want them to say, 'When Cynthia went on stage, she gave everything she had to make sure the audience had a good time!' I've sung with cracked ribs, pneumonia, a broken leg, and I've sung though it all. I would like to think that, no matter what, anyone who came to see me perform walked away with a smile on their face and that for those few moments I took them on a vacation. They weren't worried about their mortgage, their son in Afghanistan or how they were gonna pay their bills—all of that stuff. It's my job to make sure that all goes away for a few minutes. Life can be brutal at times, and I think that's the joy we all get from music ... God, I'm getting teary-eyed. Where the hell is that coming from?"

Kelly Marie

"After having several successful hit records in Europe and being well known over there years before the hit 'Feels Like I'm in Love'—and to be told that you are then number 1 with such an amazing song in your own country *and* America—is an absolutely amazing feeling! That's when you feel you truly have arrived, and all the hard work was worth it!" So proclaims Kelly Marie of topping the charts on both sides of the Atlantic with her signature dance classic. In the summer of 1981, there wasn't a club, lounge or party in the New York area (or the rest of the U.S. for that matter) that wasn't playing the sparkling, bubbling and hook-laden dance-smash "Feels Like I'm in Love." With its retro-disco style and soaring, pop-ready vocals by a mysterious artist (who was unknown on these shores), the question on everyone's lips was: "Who is *Kelly Marie*?" For fans of the song here in America who still may be unfamiliar with her story, the singer is more than anxious to fill in the details.

Born Jacqueline McKinnon in Paisley (located in the west-central lowlands of Scotland), Kelly says, "I've always loved to sing from the age of three years old. My mother said I could sing before I could talk. I never ever dreamed of becoming a recording star. I just knew from an early age that all I wanted to do was sing in front of an audience. I always knew that singing was in my blood! I lived to sing! I never ever thought about being famous—only about the absolute joy of performing for anyone who would listen."

Kelly received quite a bit of publicity after appearing on a televised British singing competition show called *Opportunity Knocks* (a forerunner of *American Idol*), and her vocal power and range caught the attention of the Pye Records label. She began recording under the name Kelly Marie in 1976, releasing songs like "Who's That Lady with My Man" (a Top-Five hit in France). Her earliest music was mostly upbeat pop with a bubbly, tambourine-fused beat that offered shades of the sound to come. Her 1977 hit, "Run to Me," which firmly moved the singer into the disco genre, was an international favorite and formally introduced her to the U.S. disco charts. The follow-up, "Make Love to Me," was covered in America by Helen Reddy and thus prevented Marie from making yet another dent on the U.S. charts. Though she languished in modest fame in Europe for a time, the artist soon caught the worldwide break of a lifetime.

"'Feels Like I'm in Love' was written by Ray Dorset of Mungo Jerry fame, who was on the same record label as me," Kelly recalls. "The song was actually written with Elvis Presley in mind." While it's hard to imagine how Presley's interpretation of the song (which was originally written in 1977, the year he died) might have sounded, it became the perfect vehicle for Marie. "When he didn't do it, it was played for me, and I went into the studio and recorded it. The rest is history!" she exclaims.

History took a bit of time to unfold. Released in 1979 and produced by Peter Yellowstone, who had been working with the singer for years, the song became a modest hit in South Africa and caused a bit of a stir in her native Scotland. However, "Feels Like I'm in Love" failed to immediately get the attention of the Brits. The clubs came to the rescue, and a slow buzz began to build around the track thanks to a highly charged dance-floor reaction to the song. By the summer of 1980, the Pye label re-released the song, and it shot up to the number 1 spot on the British pop charts. The track reached the Top Five in Germany and crossed into numerous other territories. "I felt absolutely elated; I just couldn't believe it! I was overjoyed and very thankful to everyone who played the song and believed in it—and me!" Marie gushes.

The cover of the 1981 U.S. album *Feels Like I'm in Love* did little to alleviate the mystery of who Kelly Marie was, but the smash disco single of the same name provided the singer with enormous international recognition (author's collection).

As a dual hit with another track called "Loving Just for Fun," "Feels Like I'm in Love" (remixed by Bobby "DJ" Guttadaro) blasted up to the Top Ten of the dance chart in the U.S. by the following summer. CBS' Coast-to-Coast Records released an album in North America in 1981 called *Feels Like I'm in Love*, which contained both the hits. The title track remained a sought-after single for several weeks and flirted briefly with the pop chart thanks to its sing-along lyrics, infectious beat and Marie's irresistible charm. The sugary smash hit was a crowd-pleaser on dance floors on both sides of the Atlantic, securing Kelly's chart presence for several months. Although the singer says she did not recognize the potential of the song while recording it, she now identifies the primary qualities of the hook-laden disco hit. "I think it had an irresistible dance beat, and the catchiness of the song is what made it so amazing for both gay and straight audiences to love and enjoy," she says. "I could sing anything, so any genre of music was easy and a joy for me. Ballads, rock, country and western, disco—I loved all music. I was happy to have such a huge disco hit. It made my name all over the world!"

The artist promoted the album in the States, giving fans on this continent a rare chance to see her in action. "I did do a Coast-to-Coast label tour in the U.S. I had a great time in America! But, you know, people are people wherever you go—Europe, the U.S. and the U.K. They are all lovely people, and I'm lucky to have had great audiences to perform for," Kelly says.

It was no easy task to create a follow-up track as instantly accessible as her mega-hit. The U.K. would be the first audience looking for it and "Hot Love" and "Love Trial" on Calibre Records would try to deliver the goods. The tracks were again produced by Yellowstone. Kelly recalls, "I didn't personally feel any pressure [to have another big hit], but I am sure the record company did. Businessmen always do. If you love singing, you carry on performing. I never sang for the fame, not even the hit records. I sang because singing is in my soul, hit records or not." While both aforementioned releases were modest hits in Britain, the material fell short of creating the media and record-buying frenzy created by "Feels Like I'm in Love."

Regardless, her success had been substantial enough to pave the way for a stream of remarkable (and now legendary) British Hi-NRG dance singles that made Kelly Marie a major club music name in the mid '80s. As she worked with new producers, her sound became sleeker, and the productions reflected the energized direction the era's music had taken. Her final release for Calibre, "I'm on Fire" in 1984, ushered in a long string of classic, savvy floor-thumpers that were released by the famed British dance label, Passion Records. Hits like "Hands Up," "Halfway to Paradise" and the brilliant "Don't Let the Flame Die Out," produced by Nigel Stock and John Davies, became synonymous with the type of British post-disco music that was thundering across clubs throughout Europe and the gay watering holes of America. She next tackled the Patrick Hernandez classic "Born to Be Alive" with stellar results. Marie enjoyed a club hit with "Stealing My Time" (highly interchangeable with Eria Fachin's nearly identical U.S. smash, "Savin' Myself"), under the production hand of Ian Levine. "Feels Like I'm in Love" even received a retread from the PWL team, though the artist, astonishingly, never had the opportunity to work directly with famed producers Stock-Aitken-Waterman (Kylie Minogue, Samantha Fox, Jason Donovan, Sabrina Salerno, Hazell Dean). "I never had a favorite producer, and I loved working with all the producers I ever recorded with," Kelly says. "They were all great and talented in different ways. I was never asked to work with Stock-Aitken-Waterman. 'Feels Like I'm in Love' was re-recorded with the PWL record label, but there was no other involvement with them on my part."

In the '90s, Marie shifted gears and began raising a family that included six children, which placed a hold on her recording career. She says, "I got married just after the huge success of my records, and I was trying to juggle motherhood and married life. So career choices had to take a back seat as you would expect." However, by the end of the decade she would be back on the music scene with her highly lauded album *Disco Queen* on Academy Street Records. Numerous tracks off the disc created a sensation in the clubs once again, including an update of the Corrs' "Runaway" and Ike & Tina Turner's "River Deep, Mountain High." Teamed in 2003 with Britain's other disco upstart, Tina Charles, the duo recorded a remake of Lulu's "To Sir with Love" and Kylie's "Your Disco Needs You," all masterminded by music and TV producer Paul Tams. The success of the singles led to Kelly and Paul recording *Kelly Marie—Applause,* a whole album of their favorite songs from film and stage musicals in a Hi-NRG style. Tams says that of all the classic artists he has worked with, Kelly Marie was his personal favorite, and if he wants someone to record a TV theme or eventually feels the time is right to record another album, he'd have no hesitation to knock on Kelly's door.

Marie became a British media sensation in 2005 by appearing on the TV show *Hit Me Baby One More Time,* singing her signature classic and performing her own take of Britney Spears' "Oops I Did It Again." In 2012, the British Almighty label released an explosive and well-received remix of her "Born to Be Alive" cover, while a newly updated version of "Feels Like I'm in Love" (nearly an annual tradition) made its way to a *Mad About the Boy* compilation and once again reminded audiences of the timelessness of her irresistible classic.

With her vast experience in the highs and lows of the recording industry and life, Kelly says being a maturing diva from the disco era hasn't presented her with too many difficulties. "It hasn't been too much of a challenge in respect to my ability to perform, but it could certainly be a challenge when it came to chasing royalties and monies owed from various people. All I was ever into was singing and doing what I loved. I also had absolutely no reason to fall into the traps of drugs and things like that. And as far as aging goes, I'm just as beautiful now as I was then—and the work is still pouring in!" she laughs. The performer, who cites Gloria Gaynor's "I Will Survive" as a song she'd have loved to sung herself (calling it "an awesome song, a classic"), continues to perform today in the U.K. and is still doing shows in locations throughout the world, including a recent gig in Beirut.

Kelly Marie says she is "massively proud" of her ranking as a classic disco diva (courtesy Paul Tams).

Kelly considers the level of recognition she and other singers of the disco era receive today, acknowledging her own good fortune. "In a here today, gone tomorrow culture," she says, "yes—I do think generally we get our share of respect. They're still playing our music nearly 40 years on. However, there are some people looking at the music and the era and at my past that haven't had the courtesy to always acknowledge my success or have, at times, used my success to make money for them."

She describes herself today as "happy, content, blessed, grateful! I'm happy in my own skin. I love being a wife, mother and grandmother to my four grandchildren. I am still lucky enough to be given the opportunity to perform where and when I wish to and on my own terms. There's not that many that can still say that after the nearly 40 years since I had my first hit in France. My aspirations for the future are to remain happy and healthy and to continue singing for as long as people will listen."

Kelly Marie's vocal charm and talent can be assessed in one word: addictive. She says she is "massively proud" of her ranking by many as an important diva from this historic period and to have been the vocalist behind one of disco's all-time classics. Kelly declares, "I would like to be remembered as a good wife, mother and grandmother that always put her family first, but, along the way, helped create one of the biggest disco hits ever. Not bad for a wee lass from that small town of Paisley, Scotland!"

Maxine Nightingale

"Fans still want to hear those great dance songs, no matter what anyone else does or says! That's what they want to hear. Disco is one of the most lasting forms of popular music we have. People *still* love it! No matter what else we performers who had disco hits do, we are never going to connect stronger with anything else. I feel we should be very grateful that we have that connection and that we in turn connected with so many people," says Maxine Nightingale with a charming British accent. Her hugely popular crossover smash "Right Back Where We Started From" was one of the earliest nuggets of the disco era, and it quickly became one of the most massively played feel-good pop songs of the decade. The success of the track was just one of many highlights in the artist's long and proud career, which she happily looks back on with great enthusiasm.

"It was obviously my destiny to be a singer," she says. "Everything just kind of led from one thing to another. When I was 13, my friend and I stopped by a nearby house where people were rehearsing a band called Unisound. We went over there one night, and they asked me to sing with them. Well, I ended up becoming part of that band. Then we eventually played dance clubs, and one of the managers liked my voice and he paid for a demo. He took the demo to Pye Records in London. The president of Pye, and my first mentor, Cyril Stapleton, really liked it and so that's how I made my first single. I made a bunch of singles as a teenager. Then I joined the show *Hair* and I did [*Jesus Christ*] *Superstar*, and I did a lot of recordings—backup work in London."

Maxine recalls the origins of the recording that put her on the map. "A particular friend who was a songwriter, Pierre Tubbs—he worked at United Artists Records in London—asked me if I would do a demo of a song he had written, 'Right Back Where We Started From.' I did the demo, and he loved it! I guess he took it straight to United Artists Records, and they loved it too. They paid me 100 pounds (about $200) to do the demo. This was obviously a different time in the record business, because they didn't need to pay me further, but they did offer me an advance and a contract to finish recording the single. So, we started working together, and it went like that. The record started going up the charts in England and then," she chuckles, "it all was kind of like a raging river—there was no stopping it. Boom! I was always in show business—I couldn't help it—it was my fate! My dad was a singer, but my mom really didn't want me to be one because she had a lot of bad experiences trying to raise a family with a husband in show business. She was worried about the lack of security, so I promised her that if I didn't become a star, then I would give it up. And then I *became* a star—and I *couldn't* give it up!

"So, they put the record out over here in the States, and by then it was 1976, the bicentennial year. I guess it came out the year before in England. I came over in March of '76 for kind of what you'd call pre-chart promotional work, just TV and some touring. By the summer, the record was number 1. I came to Hollywood, and really it was just such an amazingly fun time—indescribable how happy that time was. It was kind of like living in the movies, for me anyway! I used to love the Elvis Presley movies as a kid because they were so glamorous, and I felt like I was in one."

"Right Back Where We Started From" soared to the number 1 chart spot in numerous countries (just shy of that position on *Billboard's* Top 100 Singles in the U.S.) and also

Maxine Nightingale, seen here circa 1976 (when "Right Back Where We Started From" had become an international disco smash), says of the song, "It all was kind of like a raging river — there was no stopping it" (author's collection).

became a tremendous club favorite. The album of the same name was a grab bag of pop, disco and R&B, of which the singer says casually, "I was okay with it. My first album had a lot of songs which I really enjoyed doing, and it wasn't bad. John Lennon's 'Bless You,' Ray Parker, Jr.'s 'You Got the Love' and a few others on there." But the title track was something extraordinary. Maxine believes the power and longevity of the song lies in its highly uplifting energy. "I would actually pinpoint it as being such a happy, positive song. It is a joyous song that doesn't have a particular story to it, so everybody attaches their own story to it, their own happy memory. As I said before, so many people, *so many*, have come up to me and said things like, 'Thank you! That song was at my wedding, my graduation, my college graduation,' or 'I always remember that summer, and that song reminds me of that wonderful time in my life.' So I think people just enjoyed being happy and identifying their feelings with 'Right Back.' Last year we did a disco show at the Hollywood Bowl and it was amazing to just see the fans' faces, cheering there, just jumping up and down—singing every word. You know that people *lived* the song in a very important way in their life. So, I think that's what it was—it's just pure happiness and a song that everybody loved. I was very lucky to have been the one who recorded it.

"It's just remarkable to see people jump on their feet because of my music. The music connects them to their childhood, their youth, and they can't help themselves; they just feel happy. You know, like they did when they were young. Whenever people say to me, 'Oh my God, we danced to your song at my high school graduation' or any of those similar, really important, happy transitional occasions—what could be better? What could be more of an honor than to see that you are really connected to these people?"

Maxine recognizes the smash as a true early disco classic. "In England," she recalls, "there was a certain style—they called it 'northern soul'—and that was the feel that Pierre, the writer, was putting in to it. Here's the interesting thing—in every case with music that comes from England but is a U.S.-based hit, I always call it a *synthesis*. Literally—a synthesis. A synthesis comprises the thesis and the antithesis. In this case, the thesis comprises black American music and the antithesis would be English music. What is real English music? Folk music, church music, etc. Couldn't be more different. But, put the two together and you get the synthesis. And with black American music, when that synthesis came over to England, it was very, very interesting to all these young English musicians. So, it's their style or their version of American music. The synthesis came back to America and people called it the 'English sound.' That's what so peculiar," she chuckles. "The Beatles music is the synthesis of black American pop music and English music, right? So, I feel that was what was happening with 'Right Back.' When I came to America, people really had a hard time with me—they didn't think I was English. They were very surprised when they heard my voice. In England, people thought I was American. I actually became a U.S. citizen two years ago, so now I'm *really* an American."

As a woman of color singing outside the box, Nightingale found herself in the tricky world of fitting into pop music parameters. "For me, being a woman of color from England was more of a problem here in America because I was not accepted by the black community. They didn't think of me as black. I wasn't black enough. And the record companies would say this too. But if they tried to put me in the white category, they would say, she isn't white enough ... *arrrrgh!* President Obama, really, really experienced this whole thing. What it does to you is it takes you beyond race. I've always been an outsider. When I was growing up in England, my dad was the first black man in our little town. My sister, brother and I were the only black children in our school. We were the only black children in the whole town. And the funny thing was, when we were kids, we were absolutely adored. We were the first. It was only later people were like, 'Okay, okay, that's enough,'" she observes with a slightly reluctant-sounding laugh. "For me, being from a white and black family — my mom being white, my dad being black — it had a really curious effect. I remember having a conversation with my dad when I was maybe 10 or 11, and he stood in front of me and told me not to trust white people. In my head, I was thinking, he's out of his mind because my mamma was white — and at that moment I realized that he *was* crazy — I realized that the whole thing about race struggle is *crazy*. And it really helped me to get beyond it. I never believed in it; it made me simply be more myself. Being an outsider made me an observer. I'm a philosopher at times, and I'm really interested in how things develop and how they become the way they are and so on. Yeah, life is difficult, but I don't think it's more difficult for one person more than for another. We all have our own unique torture chambers that we create just for ourselves! I also want to say life is incredibly beautiful!"

Whatever "categorization dilemmas" the artist encountered, there was no denying the remarkable achievement that was her success in pop and disco. "That summer, the summer of '76, was an enchanted summer," recalls Nightingale. "I did concerts with — oh my God — Frank Sinatra, The Beach Boys, so many artists. They had all these bicentennial celebrations going on, and I was just so lucky to be there. I was in Washington, D.C., performing with the Beach Boys and Sinatra, Three Dog Night, Santana, Boz Skaggs! My brother was there on stage with me, so that was fun, and it was also new to be in the spotlight so much. To be at the top of your game in that new situation was just — I don't know — better than any video game! It was just perfection. I guess sometime during that year, I brought my mom over, and that was so brilliant too. I remember we went to dinner with the record company people at the beautiful Chasen's restaurant in Beverly Hills. My mom's kind of hard to impress and, as I said in the beginning, she wasn't so fond of show business. There she was sitting next to the president of the record company, Artie Mogull, right in the center of this great place and looking at the pictures on the wall of Dean Martin and Frank — it was something else! And she *was* impressed!" Maxine beams.

Following up her enormous smash hit, which had been boosted tremendously by being prominently featured in Paul Newman's movie box office smash *Slap Shot*, presented Nightingale with pressure familiar to many artists. "I wasn't particularly worried about having another crossover hit, but just a good follow up — yeah, that was on my mind. There were all sorts of things going on. The business part of it was hard. Coming from England, where the record business was really a cottage industry, a relatively small business, when I got here it was a very different story. So, that was hard for me and for my people. My manager at the time — he had a nervous breakdown! He was one of the guys at United Artists. It doesn't matter if I say that now because United Artists doesn't even exist anymore. But, believe you me, there were some intense days, and there were some tough people we had to deal with. In the end though, I really came to admire many of those people. Some people sort of painted them all black and said they were all very bad and they pressured people horribly. Well, they did, but they were business people at the top of their game. And, my God, they were running the music business! These guys were the sharks of the music business. Walter Yetnikoff, all the people over at Warner Bros., Teddy Templeman, Bob Krasnow — those kind of people — I can't remember all their names. Eventually they were pushed out by the money men, who drove this business into the ground. It was a very sad day when that happened, a very sad day.

"The fact is," Maxine continues, "it would have been better for me if I had more powerful representation because, basically, these guys just needed people at their own level to deal with. Otherwise, they would just steamroll over you. They certainly weren't angels and, of course, you need people that are tough at the top of the business. It's only in retrospect that I see that. At the time, I didn't like any of them at all, but truth be told they *did* give me something I never would have had otherwise — name recognition. At that time in the '70s, record companies would give out huge advances that would be used to pay for everything to do with going on tour — so it was absolutely exciting. Later, they would ask for all the money back — not so exciting! Having survived and lived to tell the tale, so to speak, I don't blame any of them at all for the way they handled things. I'm more grateful to have been there, to have these wonderful memories, to still be relevant, just in the world of music, because of everything that happened at that time. It's really how I feel now."

Nightingale adds, "At that time, it wasn't always easy to manage what was going on. Oh my God, I remember one time I did an interview with a guy from the *L.A. Times* and, as you can hear now, I guess I didn't hold much back. I probably said too much. But this guy, his name was Dennis Hunt — oh, he made mincemeat out of me. He called his article 'Nightingale's Melancholy Song,' and he printed all the things I had said about all my frustrations and difficulties with the record companies. Well, can you imagine what the record company thought of that — I was in so much trouble!" she laughs. "Now I say it doesn't matter — let them say what they want. Hey, I'm still here. What I discovered was, in the end, in this business, the real value, the real necessity for an artist, is to come through it all. You have to be able to come through it. Do you have the goods? Are you talented enough to stand up on the stage and to just deliver? The most important thing to do was to just perform. I could always perform well, and I still can! I didn't need the records, the studios, as much as some people did. I love to be on the stage and exchanging that energy with the audience."

After her breakout success, the artist released a series of albums in the U.S. on various labels, always keeping her presence in the clubs balanced with a broader pop sensibility. *Night Life* followed in 1977, led by the singles "Love Hit Me" (a major hit in the U.K.) and "Will You Be My Lover," which was targeted as another high-energy disco vehicle. "'Will You Be My Lover' was a good song, but it didn't really suit me," she believes. "It was originally a man's song I thought, and my producer brought it to me and we did it. I just remember that it came out just before 'Lead Me On.' Well, it's water under the bridge now, but I wasn't sure at the time it was the best song for me."

In 1979, Maxine bucked the disco trend by scoring a number 1 ballad in the U.S. with "Lead Me On," which went far to dispel any notions that the singer was just a one-hit or one-genre wonder. "My producer, Denny Diante, insisted that I record it. He was sure it would be a hit, and he was right. I must admit, I didn't see much of a future in it, but it took off on its own. It later reached number 4 on *Billboard's* All-Time Adult Contemporary chart."

Recording in the following decade, one of her most noteworthy albums was *Bittersweet*, released in 1980 on the RCA label. The collection featured the remarkably powerful dance cut "Never Enough," which began as a sweeping ballad and progressed into a pounding floor-filler. "My brother, Glenn Nightingale, worked with me on that track," the singer says, "and my brother was in my first band. We are very close, very tight and we were both here in 1976 for that wonderful time. We have strong links. He played with the Gap Band, then went back to England and played in Boy George's second band, and right now he's playing with Bryan Ferry. He's a very accomplished guitarist and writer and we loved working together. Glenn's another person that understood me absolutely, and I never had any trouble working with him. He was on that album and wrote, as I recall, a few of the songs and did some backup vocals and guitar work. Those were some happy times, and that was a great album for me."

Following a brief move in 1982 to Highrise Entertainment Records for the *It's a Beautiful Thing* album, which kept the pop-dance formula on track with such songs as the uptempo "Stand Up for Your Heart" and the popular R&B duet with Jimmy Ruffin, "Turn to Me," the singer slipped off the radar. "It's true," she admits. "I did drop out of sight. I was experiencing another business dilemma that was really unfortunate. I had a lot of trouble with being allowed to choose whom I wanted to work with. It ended up that I was kind of blacklisted. Blacklisted may be too strong a word. I couldn't get a deal because I didn't want to work with the people A&M Records, who were negotiating my next project, wanted me to work with. They offered me a deal, but the deal was contingent on me working with a certain producer, and I wasn't allowed to change that. Think about it ... who wants to be forced to work for your entire career or long periods with one person — or one person who is not of your choice?

"Now my husband records with me, and he understands me very well. It takes a certain type of man to understand a powerful woman. I remember there was a saying that Barbra Streisand's husband, James Brolin, said about living life with Barbra. He said Barbra likes to wear the pants in the family, and then he said something like, 'Okay, fine, she can wear the pants.' I thought to myself, 'He's a really secure man!' I remember those days being very frustrated in the studio because I was not treated well. I remember Pat Benatar writing and talking about this, too. It was a battle to remain a nice person because they had this preconceived idea that if a woman knows what she wants, she's a bitch. It doesn't make sense. It puts you in an uncomfortable position because I'm the kind of person that doesn't want to see anybody made to feel small. I'm just trying to live my life, do my best work, and I don't want to have to be unpleasant.

"So, by the late '80s, I was working on a cruise ship for a while, then I worked in Europe again, where I made another record around 1986, *Cry for Love*. Then, in the mid-'90s, I guess it was kind of the beginning of the retro era, wasn't it? They started going back and having more retro concerts. And from then on, everything was fine again. So, from that, I learned the only thing necessary in life is to persist and to survive. Life is such a strange thing. When you are young, you kind of want to break all the rules, but the rules, moral codes and the honor code — they are all so important. You never know what is going to happen next — you really, really don't."

The singer reflects, "In 2011, I performed at the Hollywood Bowl in a disco show with Thelma Houston, Kool & the Gang and the Village People. I was standing on stage performing to a huge crowd of people, and I'm going to start doing 'Lead Me On.' I started to give a shout out to my own two granddaughters, who are out there in the audience watching me. As I'm giving it, I'm thinking, 'I am so lucky! My family is in the audience. Let's see, I'm 59 years old and my own grandkids are watching me still performing at one of the world's greatest venues — how lucky is that? What could be better?' I remember taking the girls backstage after I had finished performing. So, there they are with me — the two girls, who were 10 and 11 at the time. And they were both very much into dance, and they're watching Kool & The Gang's dancers who were limbering up from the side of the stage — and just their faces, their excitement! They were looking up at these 6-foot dancers, stretching and stuff, and I just thought this is so nice to be still relevant, to be still watching all of this and doing all this stuff after all these years. It's like I've had these bookends in my life. All those great experiences at the beginning and now what's been happening lately. Bookends. I guess it's not over yet!" Nightingale declares.

Maxine describes another memory with a renewed jolt of enthusiasm. "It is very important to me, and I've got to tell you about this one! When I was a kid, growing up — and, as I said, I was in this little group — we would go and buy what we called 'imports.' We'd buy the 45s of all of the great soul singers: William Bell, Isaac Hayes, Otis Redding, Judy Clay. I remember looking at these singles, these 45s, and seeing the names of the writers I'd read about. Isaac Hayes and David Porter wrote all these incredible songs like 'Wrap It Up,' 'Hold On, I'm Coming,' 'Tramp' and 'Soul Man.' If you can imagine, many years later, after working on a cruise ship, I came back to Los Angeles and I have a show with ... *Isaac Hayes*! I remember being on stage and we did 'Déjà Vu,' which he wrote. It actually *was* déjà vu because all those years before I had seen his name on those Stax singles. The way we did it, I sung the first verse and then he came out after the second verse and all the girls screamed, right? But singing with Isaac, I was thinking, 'How did this happen? This little girl from Chaplin Road in London, once just looking at those singles and now I'm on the stage singing with Isaac Hayes.' Life is so amazing and magical! How much great stuff is going on all the time, and we get bored sometimes of the everyday? But, you know, it's a pretty incredible life we have here."

Though reticent of the magic that can be the human experience, Nightingale is well aware of the challenges of aging. "You have to be conscious; you have to stay conscious of life going by and get whatever it is you supposed to get out of it at every different stage," she says. "I'm not saying that one can face everything that comes with equal enthusiasm because, obviously, it's hard. Getting older is very hard! But what I figured out is that old age and getting older has a particular specific purpose — there is a quality to be gained from it, which can't be gained at any other time. That quality is humility because the nature of youth is arrogance and power. You start off mistakenly thinking you create your own body and you are the source of everything that comes from it. But when you get older, all of those things, one by one, get taken away. And you're still in there. And then you finally realize, oh, you are the *recipient* of all those things, not the *creator*. So that's the important lesson to be learned in old age. And humility, that very nature, is not very comfortable. Nobody wants to be humble until they have to be, whatever they say!

"I've always thought that my job is to communicate with the audience, and, as I get older, I get better at it," Maxine Nightingale reveals (courtesy Maxine Nightingale).

"I am happy where I

am today. In a way, I'm glad that I didn't become so famous that I couldn't enjoy life and be a real person as well as a celebrity. All of the abilities, all the knowledge that I've gained from suffering at times—I wouldn't and I couldn't possibly change any of it because it has brought me right here! I'm lucky enough to still be living a great life. Whether you're a teacher, a writer, a singer, at this point—the more experience you have, the less effort it actually takes. So it becomes kind of like play time. You know, when I get on stage, I have almost all my attention on the audience now. I can relax. The singing—I don't have to worry about that; that's done. But now it's just about having fun and playing, so that is a bonus to me to be able to do that in this point in life. I'm very interested in philosophies and religion, and I have a very big family. I have seven grandchildren, so I'm always busy. I'm always either taking the kids to Disneyland or wrapping presents or I'm on the stage. I sleep a lot in between—I'm always exhausted! I'm married to the gym! Oh, my God, what can I say? I've had a wonderful time, and I'm still having a wonderful time. I'm just here to find out *why* I'm here. That's always been my motto when I get confused. I always ask myself, 'Why am I here?' The answer is—I'm here to find out why I'm here."

Maxine Nightingale, now living in Los Angeles, remains one of the disco genre's most distinctive and distinguished vocalists. She has some dreams she'd still like to fulfill and a wish for how she hopes her career will be remembered. "I've always thought that my job is to communicate with the audience, and, as I get older, I get better at it. You can really feel it when you connect with the audience. It's like an electric shock, and at the same point that you feel it, the audience feels it! So I really want people to remember that my job was to remind them that they are alive—*they are alive*! They are not spectators. They're part of the whole thing. I'm very privileged to do that, and I'd like them to remember that and to remember me, I hope, as a great singer. When I'm gone, I want them to say, 'She did it best!' Before that happens, I really, really, want to sing my favorite songs—the standards I started out singing in my teens. I really knew a lot about this music. I want to do that again, and I really want to sing those songs at Carnegie Hall. And when I do sing those great songs with an orchestra at that wonderful place, I will be ... *right back where I started from!*"

Scherrie Payne

She was a member of the last formation of the venerable Motown group the Supremes (whose '70s disco hits were early classics of the genre), an accomplished songwriter, a vocalist who transformed the rock staple "I'm Not in Love" into an '80s dance classic and a diva often referred to as "the little lady with the big voice." But Scherrie Payne still insists, "I wish I had done a bit more—I didn't do enough! I didn't take full advantage of the '70s and '80s, but it was still just a really great time!" The sister of singer Freda Payne ("Band of Gold"), Scherrie's equally luminous career and unique vocal prowess stand on their own merits. She recalls her beginnings with detail and a smile.

"When I was younger, I would go down into my basement or my 'rec room,' as we used to call it, back in Detroit. We had a lamp with colored bulbs in it, and I would put on records of my favorite singers like Billie Holiday and Gloria Lynne. I would pretend I was them while shining one of the lights on me, like I was in a nightclub," Scherrie chuckles. "I would just sing my heart out, but I never really took it seriously. I went off to college, Michigan State, and, before graduating with a Bachelor of Science in Medical Technology, I sang on and off campus with this little jazz band. Probably if someone had taken me under their wing then, it would have been great — but I was too timid I think to jump out on my own."

"I was actually teaching school, and my sister Freda had come home to visit from New York. She had just signed with Invictus Records, which is the company that Holland-Dozier-Holland had formed when they left Motown. She had gone to school with all of them — Eddie, Brian and Lamont. She was talking to Eddie on the phone, and I was playing the piano in the living room — and playing very loudly on purpose," she laughs. "Eddie called me to the phone and asked me what I was playing. I said, 'Oh, just a song that I wrote.' And I said I had a ton of others. He asked me if I wanted to audition for his company. I think I said something like, 'Sure, I don't care.' So, he sent a car around, and they took me over to Lamont's house and I sang. I played maybe four or five of my songs, and then I signed a contract the next day! They said they would form this group around me because they had enough lead singers. They already had Freda, Laura Lee and the Honey Cone — they had just signed them. So, they brought in Ty Hunter, who was a fabulous singer and

This rarely seen photograph of the recording session for the "I'm Not in Love" single in 1982 includes (left to right) Edmund Sylvers, Mary Wilson, Freda Payne and Scherrie Payne (courtesy Rick Gianatos).

friend of Lamont, Edward and Brian's, and they added two other members to the band, Pearl Jones and Larry Mitchell, and called us the Glass House. That's how I got started professionally."

Her career might have begun sooner and with a bigger bang had a potential hit single not slipped through her fingers. "I recorded 'Want Ads' first, but it was in the can for about a year," she says. "One day, I was in the studio and Barney Perkins, the engineer, played it and said, 'Wow, I haven't heard this song in a long time,' and it wasn't until near the end that there was a lick that was a little different from what I had done. Turns out it was Edna Wright from the Honey Cone. I didn't know they had given [the song] to them. Edna said she had told me she loved the song and that I supposedly said, 'You like it? You can have it,'" Scherrie laughs, "I don't remember saying that, but that is what Edna recalled. So I can't dispute it. So, anyway, she got it, and the Honey Cone of course had a number 1 million-seller with it. It was fate.

"Glass House and I put out the song 'Crumbs Off the Table,' and when it came out, I had to quit my job because I could see things were going to happen. Although they didn't happen quite as quickly as I would have thought, it was a beginning. God has a plan for everything. So, I just went along with the flow." The song was a fairly big hit for the group, but Payne needed a bigger break in order to reach the next level.

"Back in '73, Lamont Dozier was my boyfriend, and he had traveled out to California on business. While he was there, he ran into Mary Wilson at a party. She told him that Jean Terrell had just left the Supremes, and they were looking for a new lead singer," Scherrie recalls. "And naturally, he told her about me. So she called me and we talked, and she asked me to send some pictures. At first, she thought it was Freda he was talking about, and I had to clarify that no, it's her sister. I sent some pictures and I think one of the albums from the Glass House, and she called me two nights later. She asked if I could come out here to California that Saturday. Later, I thought, 'Oh my God, am I crazy joining the Supremes?' I got so scared. My mother had to give me this pep talk and so, of course, I went along with it. On a Saturday morning, I was taken to the airport and headed to California. I was picked up, and we went right to Mary's house and started rehearsing for a gig, which was the following Saturday. I think [it was] the New Mexico State Fair. It all happened that fast!

"I was excited, but at the same time—I have to be honest—I felt a bit like I wasn't worthy. I remember when we were walking into the event some people thought that I was Diana, and they were calling, 'Diana!' I'm like, 'No, I'm not Diana, I'm just Scherrie.' I was feeling like I sort of left them disappointed, the fans, being new to the group. That was just my own insecurities coming out and wanting to do my best, which I always tried to do—give my best. And these were big shoes to fill. Diana and Jean—they were big shoes to fill, but I just went on ahead and jumped in there and didn't think about it. Every now and then, people would bring it up about Diana. You know, God bless her. She's fantastic. I can only do what I can do, and I'm a different person. It's just me—here I am!"

Despite their identity crisis, The Supremes entered the disco era with a splash. Their 1976 Holland-Dozier-Holland penned album, *High Energy,* was a major club hit with numerous songs (led by the Top-40 pop hit "I'm Gonna Let My Heart Do the Walking," which reached number 1 on the disco charts with its "Rock the Boat" style) finding favor in the clubs. But Payne views the album from a different vantage point. "I really didn't think of *High Energy* as our big entry into disco. I just thought we were being elevated to another level. Just going with the trend and being current with it. I was happy. I was back with the Hollands, and I felt like I was back home. And when Susaye [Greene] came into the group with her dynamic voice, it was just wonderful. Of course, I loved singing with Cindy and Mary. I listen back to some of those songs and think, 'Wow, we were really singing!' I just wished that Motown had gotten behind us and given us that big push. I didn't feel that they did, to be honest.

"I felt like, here I am finally with this fantastic group and with people I always admired, and I really wanted Berry Gordy's input—he had always been an active part of the group as far as nurturing and grooming and making decisions. I wanted that for myself because my mother had known his family, grown up in the same church, worked in his parents' store. He didn't travel with us as he had in the past, and that was disappointing. I don't know why Motown pulled back, whether it was the management or that they just lost interest. I really don't know—I wish somebody could tell me why. Previous Supremes had been worked with, groomed and developed for long periods of time. But they didn't do anything for me. If it weren't for Mary—I think she was the one that held it together; she was the glue because of her tenaciousness and perseverance. From the time I joined, from that first concert in New Mexico, there was really no input from Motown. There was no special attention as far as grooming of the act. Mary had to do everything on her own," asserts Payne.

She adds, "We probably were under some pressure to have bigger hits. Maybe I didn't realize it that much at the time. I was just excited that we would go into the studio and record other songs. I was happy to work with Brian and Edward. I guess there was more pressure to produce hit product on their part because they were the writers and producers." The Supremes finally disbanded in 1977 with a farewell concert in London in which founding member Mary Wilson announced she would embark on a solo career.

In 1982, Payne returned to the dance charts with a brilliant discofied version of the 10cc hit, "I'm Not in Love" on Altair Records in the U.S., which featured Payne's sister Freda and Mary Wilson on backup. The soaring anthem was a triumph and turned an unlikely rock ballad into a high-energy emotional storm. Scherrie's voice was at its finest. "It was all because of [producer] Rick Gianatos—I think he came up with that idea, and I've always loved the original song," she recalls. "So when Rick told me about it, I automatically said, 'Yes, yes, yes, I love it!' Then we brought in Freda and then Mary on backup—so I just loved every single moment of it. I wish it did better on the charts, but I'm telling you it's my all-time favorite. And I love performing it in the clubs. I always look forward to doing it! It was just a feel good song, and I just loved the arrangements. It was just magical for me. I don't think it took many takes to record it because I loved it so much."

Producer Rick Gianatos says, "Scherrie and I were both in love with the R&B ballad version that had been a hit by Dee Dee Sharp on her debut album for the Gamble & Huff team. Dee Dee's interpretation was mesmerizing. However, that was not what motivated me to record a dance version. I had been working at AVI Records, which was a leading independent dance label at the time, and I was in the A&R department. Along with mixing, I was always looking for new music to sign. We always had an eye out for music coming from overseas. I was—and still am—a great fan of Petula Clark, and I had gone to England and had found an album by her on CBS Records in one of the shops. She had a dance version of 'I'm Not in Love' on it, and I went crazy for it. It was more upbeat than what I created—more pop-dance than my eventual arrangement for Scherrie. AVI, at my insistence, tried to license Petula's version, but CBS would not respond to our requests. So I said the hell with them—I'll do my own version. I set up the recording at Sigma Sound in Philadelphia, arranged and conducted by John Davis, and the classic MFSB players were on it. I originally intended it for Shirley Bassey, who I had just produced a 12" dance single for. I played it for her, and she sniffed and said, 'Oh that is the rubbish Petula has been doing all over England on the telly. No thank you.' A mutual friend of Scherrie and I, John Whyman, was sure it was right for Scherrie. She lit up when we played it for her and, of course, we both had the same admiration for Dee Dee's rendition. Scherrie's vocal, the flavor and mood of it, was inspired by Dee Dee's beautiful work.

"The background vocals were incredible. Mary Wilson came in for the recording carrying a bottle of champagne to celebrate, as did Scherrie's sister Freda. The third vocalist, unknown to me at the time, was Edmund Sylvers [of the Sylvers], who was dating Freda at the time. It's funny, but I had never originally thought of Freda as a background vocalist. I don't know why. However, Edmund did the arrangements, and the three of them blended beautifully. Then, on the vamp of the song, he and Freda did some beautiful ad-libs back and forth in between Scherrie's bits. Edmund was an amazing person and so talented. Scherrie was, and still is, a one-take wonder. We went in and did the scratch vocal recording and, though I call it a scratch, it was basically the main-take you are hearing on the record," he says.

"The song hit the midsection of the dance chart, but I was working with one of the many independent labels of the time that ran out of money," Rick recollects. "The problem was they didn't have the cash to press the vinyl, so we had demand and no records — which is a very tough spot to be in. We had a big West Coast R&B station [KUTE 102] that was playing a lot of dance music, and Scherrie was in heavy rotation without any favors. And we didn't have any product in the stores. I was miserable! At the time, I also had the Gap Band's 'Early in the Morning' in heavy rotation, but the label had to grease a lot of palms to get that. I'm at least proud to say that I didn't have to do any favors to get 'I'm Not in Love' on the air. They really liked it. I'm very proud of that song and consider it among my best works."

The Broadway favorite "One Night Only" was next in line for Payne. Mixed in 1984 by Gianatos and DJ Will Crocker, Rick (once again producing) describes the track's evolution. "The Broadway show *Dreamgirls* was going over like gangbusters. Geffen Records was pushing 'And I'm Telling You I'm Not Going.' But every night on TV, commercials for the show were featuring 'One Night Only.' I thought it sounded like a hit and wondered why they weren't promoting it as a single. I was going to have a female member of my first group, d'Llegance — who had nice, tasty vocals that were kind of like Chic meets the 5th Dimension — sing the song. Linda Leilahni Brown had the goal of wanting to be another Diana Ross. Before I knew it, Linda had run off to New York City and replaced Sheryl Lee Ralph in *Dreamgirls*, first on Broadway, and then on tour and was then contractually unable to record for me. You would think I would have thought of Scherrie immediately, but as I had another track waiting in the wings for her, the song 'Hope,' I instead asked Freda to do it. Freda felt Scherrie should be doing it, and finally the light bulb went off— lead singer of the Supremes doing a *Dreamgirls* song? What had I been thinking ... it was a no-brainer!" Rick laughs.

"I had assembled another great set of 'Stars on Background'— Cindy Birdsong of the Supremes, Pat Hodges from Hodges, James and Smith and from the Honey Cone, Edna Wright," Rick says with pride. "They were brought together by good friend and makeup artist extraordinaire Rudy Calvo. These ladies were studio veterans who immediately blended well together, and it was magical. Altair Records was distributed by Megatone Records and the 12" single did very well in the clubs and on the *Billboard* dance chart. Our next project was going to be Scherrie's song 'Hope,' but, again, I found myself working with the problems of a small label. Megatone's president, Marty Blecman, couldn't come up with the advance, and the project got shelved. It sat in the can until it was finally released this year as a bonus track on Scherrie's 2012 single, 'Let Yourself Go.'"

Brainstorming in 1986, Scherrie teamed with Jean Terrell and Cindy Birdsong to develop a revival act for the Supremes. Birdsong left a short time after its inception and was replaced by Lynda Laurence. Says Scherrie, "My boyfriend at the time, Ronnie Philips, had the idea of taking Jean, Cindy and me, calling ourselves Former Ladies of the Supremes, but using the acronym, FLOS. We checked with lawyers and so forth. They said we could use FLOS, and so we put out a 12" single, 'We're Back,' and performed quite a bit in the late '80s. It might not have been the best name," she laughs, "because people kept call us the 'flows' or 'floss'—no it's F-L-O-S, the acronym."

When Ian Levine formed Motor City Records to work with many of the Motown acts not currently recording, Rick brought FLOS to the fold. Recording a number of covers and original tunes for the label, they were considered a premier act with Motor City—just as they had been at Motown. Gianatos says, "Jean, Scherrie and Lynda were a continuation of the Supremes sound as it was in the days with Jean—smooth, slick and stylish. Working with Jean was a new experience for me, and the minute she got behind the mike, it was remarkable." After the Motor City experience ended, Jean decided she didn't want to do so much touring, and Scherrie and Lynda continued FLOS with Linda's sister, Sundray, and later Freddi Poole. In the current line-up is Joyce Vincent (formerly of Tony Orlando and Dawn). Ironically, when Mary Wilson went solo, Joyce had been the choice to continue the group, until Motown made the decision to retire the name. FLOS is continuing to record and tour to this day.

While she is reserved about acknowledging her success, Scherrie is quick to identify one of her career highlights. However, the event was not without its challenges. "I never felt like I made it; I never did. But I had many great experiences. Every time I performed, I was always pumped up, even though I didn't always feel that good beforehand. The reunion tour with Diana Ross was probably the ultimate highlight of my career. It wasn't in the disco era, but that was my highlight and a fantastic experience, despite some of the difficulties." The 2000 Diana Ross and the Supremes Return to Love Tour was enveloped in controversy almost from the start with rumors of participation resistance from Mary Wilson, salary haggling and ego struggles. In the end, the Wilson and Cindy Birdsong deals were dropped. Lynda Lawrence and Scherrie Payne took their places.

Scherrie says, "Diana was just so gracious to Lynda and me and just concerned if we were happy and if there was anything we wanted or if there was a problem anywhere. It was just great, and she was very humble. Of course, she was aware of all the negative reaction that was going on. Many of the fans were upset because they were saying Diana Ross *was* the Supremes and we weren't. But we were—just not the Supremes *they* wanted. [When the tour was being planned] it was going to be the original line-up and I don't really know what happened, but I got called and they to asked me to join the tour. At one point, I had suggested we try to bring in all the other Supremes again, but they said no and 'blah, blah blah'—and that didn't happen unfortunately. The fans were mad at us, and we had nothing to do with it. It wasn't up to me. I was just happy to be there. I needed the work, and I certainly wasn't going to turn it down. When I would hear the negative response from some members of the audience, I thought, 'I'm just here, just glad to be here, and it's not my fault.'

"I did eventually get over it, but it did affect me. I mean, I wondered why some people didn't realize we had nothing to do with it. Absolutely nothing. I don't really believe it was because of a squabble with Mary Wilson like some thought. It's unfortunate because it could have been wonderful with all the singers—I know it should have included Mary and Cindy—Cindy is one of my dear, dear friends. It should have included them, but it just didn't work out that way for whatever reason. There's a reason for everything, and the show had to go on, absolutely."

Water has passed under the bridge since that event, and Payne, still a poised and beautiful woman, has no intention of letting fears of aging upset her outlook on life. "I refuse to get Botox or plastic surgery," she says. "It is what it is; I am what I am! I'm not a big fan of people getting compliments on the way they look when they've had work done. How can you say thank you, when it has nothing to do with your natural aging—because you had assistance from a doctor or plastic surgeon or Botox specialist or whatever. So, I'm just going to age naturally and am just thankful for life. My parents are no longer here, and I had breast surgery last year. I'm a survivor, and just grateful to God for being with me and choosing me. My mother passed away in '77 at the age of 56 from breast cancer, so I've gone way past my mother—so you know I'm cool. I just let Him do his thing and try to stay and feel as young as I can naturally. People can just look up on the Internet and see how old I am, so I'm not fooling anyone! Come on; be real! You just can't stay young forever. I have a wonderful daughter and a wonderful grandson and, hopefully, I'll have more grandchildren. I just want to enjoy life, enjoy my family, enjoy my friends, my church and just ... *enjoy.* I'm doing fantastic, and I can't complain."

Still working with producer Rick Gianatos, Payne has continued to release dance singles over the past few years, unleashing the highly lauded CD and digital hit "Let Yourself Go" in the summer of 2012 (which featured 14 club mixes, the long-awaited bonus track "Hope," and her first solo music video, which included a turn by her grandson, Shaun). "In recent years, I also started screenplay writing," she says with pride. "I really love doing that. I can't say if that was my passion all along. I know I love to sing, still do, and sometime when I am really happy or, to the extreme, really sad, I get on the piano and play and sing. It has always given me a release or comfort. So I know singing is my first passion—screenwriting is my second passion. I've been evolving. I'm learning more and more as I write, and I find out the mistakes that I've made along the way. I have written 17 screenplays—working on an 18th. I don't know how to get them out there yet. I have to work on getting an agent—it's such a

Scherrie Payne is exploring new avenues of creativity through writing while continuing to record dance hits like 2012's "Let Yourself Go" (courtesy Rick Gianatos).

competitive field. I am also putting on a play, which I adapted from a screenplay I wrote. We already held the auditions and cast it, and *It Always Rains on Sunday* was produced by my good friend and colleague Donald Welch." [Payne's play successfully opened in September 2012 to strong reviews].

Meanwhile, it doesn't seem as if Scherrie Payne will ever fully acknowledge her remarkable contributions to R&B and dance music. Those accomplishments are, however, memorable and significant, much like the artist herself. She'd like her legacy to be quite simple. "I want to be remembered as a good person, a loving person, even off the stage. Because some people act real nice on the stage but off of it they suck—I hope nobody will ever think of me that way!" she chuckles. "It's a lot easier to laugh than frown!"

Wardell Piper

The danceable funk sound that rallied alongside the sugar-coated energy of disco music in the late '70s was a specialized style that only a few artists were able to deliver with conviction. Their early brand of funky, danceable soul paved the way for the urban jams that followed in the '80s and beyond. One of the purveyors of this hybrid disco sound was Wardell Piper, whose biggest hit, "Super Sweet," boiled with a rhythm and vigor that took the artist to the top of both the disco and R&B charts in 1979 and 1980.

"I'm originally from Albany, New York, and I moved to Philadelphia when I was 14 in 1968," says Wardell. "When I was a child, my brother and sisters (Dee, Charlita and Glenn) and I sang in the church under the instruction of our mother, Lois." Even at such a young age, Wardell envisioned the progression of her music career. After seeing Diana Ross and the Supremes on *The Ed Sullivan Show* at the age of seven, Piper knew her calling was to entertain. "When I moved to Philadelphia, I went to Roberts Vaux Junior High, where I met Rochelle Fleming. We were in the choir when she heard me sing and asked me to join her group, The Debonnets, which later went on to become First Choice," she recalls. "Melanie McSears was already a member, and when Rochelle and I got to Overbrook High School, we met Annette Guest in the choir and asked her to join the group. We would do fashion and talent shows, and then Melanie decided to marry and start a family. This left me, Annette and Rochelle. 'This Is the House Where Love Died' was our first recording together, and the B-side was 'One Step Away.'"

With potential evident for First Choice, Piper says she wanted assurances that she would have chances to sing lead in the group. Feeling that she might not get as many opportunities to be as front and center as she'd like, Wardell decided early on (after recording "Armed and Extremely Dangerous," one of the group's first big hits) that it was time to explore other options. "I sang lead with my siblings in our group, so I guess it was natural that I always dreamed of having a solo career. Not that I had a problem with doing background," Wardell claims. "I loved to harmonize. I just didn't want my talents to be limited to that. It wasn't like we had a falling out—I just knew it was something I *had* to do. Two years or so ago, I ran into Rochelle while we were both in Lord & Taylor in suburban

Wardell Piper, flush with success following her disco funk hit "Super Sweet," and disco icon Sylvester converse at a Washington, D.C., concert, circa 1980 (courtesy Wardell Piper).

Philadelphia. I hadn't seen Rochelle in about 25 years! We talked for hours, and I thanked her for the experience I had with First Choice." She adds, "Being in the group molded and shaped me for my solo career, and for that I will be forever grateful to both Rochelle and Annette. I still love them like sisters and wish them all the best.

"When I left the group, I honestly didn't think that anyone would remember that I had even been in First Choice. I never got a chance to perform with the girls after 'Armed and Extremely Dangerous.' Periodically, I would run into them while we were both performing in Atlantic City back in the '70s. Many people never knew I was on the record, since I wasn't in any of the pictures with the girls, but you can hear my voice. I ended up marrying for two years and thought I would raise a family. After that didn't work out, I started my career again, doing little shows on my own," says Piper.

She soon began aggressively forging her own identity in the emerging disco genre. "I was introduced to Reuben Cross and John H. Fitch, who had written 'Shame' for Evelyn 'Champagne' King, through my girlfriend, Terry Jackson. They were looking for a lead singer for an all-female band. I auditioned, and they loved me! They called a gentleman named Jerald, as I remember, who was handling A&R for RCA in NYC at the time. Jerald didn't like the group concept, but he *did* like me. So Reuben and John decided to work with me as a single artist. We went into the studio and developed all of the songs that were eventually going to be on my first LP in 1978. The first company we went to see was Midsong, and they signed me immediately!"

Her funky first single, "Captain Boogie," remixed by Eddie O'Loughlin and Tony Gioe, got things off to a promising start as the track became a formidable dance and R&B

chart hit. "I grew up hearing all types of music and had a love for all of it, so it really didn't matter to me what I was going to sing, just as long as it was good quality music and popular. I was young and you want to do what's popular—that's the way I looked at disco then. I was ecstatic to be a part of Midsong Records, since I knew they had Silver Convention, Carol Douglas and they even had John Travolta! I will never forget when they told me that 'Captain Boogie' was a hit in the South! It's like when I first heard 'Armed and Extremely Dangerous' on the air—it blew my mind! Then, when 'Super Sweet' came out and took off, I was like, 'Wow, this is amazing!' I was so grateful, so excited! My mother and my family were so proud of me!"

As the even catchier follow-up single, "Super Sweet" (remixed by Jimmy Simpson), made a huge impact in the clubs and cracked the Disco Top 30, Midsong released Wardell Piper's self-titled debut LP. It was an instant attention-getter. With artwork featuring the singer's exotic, angular facial profile provocatively teasing a snake, the album scored points for edgy suggestiveness in the sex-charged disco market—but the depiction left the singer disturbed. "The record company asked me if I minded posing with a snake, and I told them I was okay with the idea," she recalls. "When we actually did the photo shoot, I had absolutely no idea they were going to do trick photography for the finished look. I wasn't happy about the way my album cover looked, since that wasn't the initial pose. I told Bob Reno [co-founder of Midland/Midsong Records] at the press party Midsong gave me (at a club named Some Place Else in Cherry Hill, New Jersey) that I wanted them to change it. Everybody that was anybody was at that press party, and I really felt humiliated since my boyfriend, grandmother, mother and my aunt and uncle were there. I never wanted to be depicted as a 'brazen temptress,' as one guy described me when I performed on Fire Island. After meeting me, that guy saw that I really wasn't that way at all. I was even ousted from the church that I belonged to. My mother, who was on the church board, told me [the other members] were planning to put me out. I now look at that album cover like it was just a marketing strategy, and the thing that makes me happy is that people tell me they love the album cover and, in turn, also say that they loved what I did with the songs and my voice. I appreciated that since I wanted them to buy my record because of my talents, not necessarily the cover of the LP. It was kind of embarrassing at the time, since I wasn't like that, but now, looking back, it's nice to be remembered—that's the way I look at the album today."

"Captain Boogie," "Super Sweet" and Piper's solo LP were dance club favorites and financially positive endeavors for the artist. However, she says the business side of her early success was of little concern. She admits, "To be honest, all I wanted to do was be able to entertain and perform. Many of us didn't really pay much attention to the business end of it unfortunately—we entrusted that to management. We would hear from the company that certain songs may or may not cross over and how many records we sold. I was just excited that people were hearing my records and they were buying them. I was grateful that I was gaining popularity and that I was performing. That's what I appreciate more than that whole competition thing—I just wanted to perform."

Wardell observes, "The majority of us made our money from when we would do appearances, which usually paid very well. As far as the record sales go, it was always kind of hit or miss because, unfortunately, when we were in the early years, the labels gave us certain budgets and producers went over the budget quite a bit. So, you know how *that* goes. Record companies wanted to ensure they got their money back first. They took good care of me though, even kind of spoiled me with the limos and all of the fanfare. So now, here we are 30 years later and what's nice is to be able to still collect on some of my efforts from that time period. I'm grateful for that. The Internet has really been like a godsend. For example, 'Captain Boogie' has taken off in Europe again. I was really, really surprised. They call it 'northern soul,' and it's really big over there.

"I have to say other countries have more respect for disco. Period! Disco is [still] huge, and they love it! They love the music that we contributed. It isn't like we all had to have the biggest mainstream disco hits—they just love us for what we did. On Facebook, I get a lot of messages and a lot of props and accolades from people all over the world. I can't believe, 30 plus years later, they remember who I am. It's amazing to me."

She recalls one particular event that became *the* highlight of her time in the spotlight. "Sylvester asked me to do a show with him in 1980 in Washington, D.C., at Constitution Hall! It was so exciting for me, since I was such a big fan of his—even my mother loved his music! And just the idea that he asked me to open up for him—oh, what an exciting moment that was for me! The record company forgot to send 'Super Sweet' on tape though, so I told the audience there was some sort of technical difficulty and that I would have to sing it a capella. I asked the audience to clap along with me, and I started singing the song from beginning to end. When I finished, the audience gave me a standing ovation and threw flowers onstage. When I went offstage, I saw Sylvester, who gave me a thumbs up just as he and Two Tons of Fun were about to perform. I couldn't believe it! After the show, I'll never forget how Sylvester and I engaged in conversation and he thanked me for being on his show! He was the most gracious person in this business I have ever met."

Traveling further along the path of the entertainment world, Piper quickly discovered the road was far from smooth. A second album was prepared, but the project hit a roadblock. She says, "John Davis [The Monster Orchestra, Carol Douglas] was the one who produced me after 'Super Sweet.' I had just finished a new album with him, and I had done a remake on it of 'Gimme Something Real' by Ashford and Simpson. Cissy Houston did background vocals on this project. The LP had been dropped in Detroit and was making waves. It actually was the album we were banking on to take us all the way. And to be honest with you, it was a beautiful album! The production that John Davis had done on it was amazing. Unfortunately, only a few got to hear it." Piper says the album was suddenly cancelled due to financial difficulties and upheaval at the Midsong label. The record company did manage to release "Gimme Something Real" as a single, with the "Power of Love" on the B-side.

"After Midsong folded," she says, "I did a song on Sam Records [in the U.S.] entitled 'Come on Back to Mama' that was also released in Paris and Amsterdam and was a hit in Sweden. The session was done in London in 1982 under the production of Victor Scott. I was also signed to Prelude Records in 1984, which released the song 'Nobody Can Take You from Me,' produced by James Batton, Dr. Perry Johnson and Hope Sullivan." Piper also released the club songs "Backtracking" and "Sweet Surrender" on the U.K.'s Roadrunner label.

Piper tried to keep the momentum going, despite the uphill climb. "I was also signed to Polydor Records under the production of the Parisian producer, Don Ray ("Got to Have Lovin'"), who unfortunately lost the contract due to personal issues he had at the time. While that experience wasn't the best, I have to acknowledge Berlin-Carmen Management, who represented so many artists then, along with yours truly. They, along with Midsong, really helped shape my solo career. Frankie Crocker also played a role in my success. Even though these hit or miss opportunities came and went, I still survived," says Wardell.

Today, Wardell is extremely grounded about her life and facing the realities that have come with it. She observes, "Well, actually I have to attribute my attitude and maturity to my faith. I really believe I was pulled out of that part of my life so I could find out what was the *reality* of my life. Listen, I was working a job before I had a record album, so when things got crazy, I just went back to work," she laughs. "I firmly believe in keeping a roof over my head, you know, and clothes on my back, food on the table. I was never that proud. During my hiatus, to stay grounded, I worked in a boarding home part-time, then I would go to New York City to perform. Nobody ever knew.

"I went back to school in 1981 and got licensed in cosmetology in 1983. I opened a salon and worked in that area for 15 years, following in my mother's footsteps. Although I am single today, I got remarried in 1992 and raised my ex's daughter from the time she was eight. Amber is 27 and her father, Ed Starr, is an awesome guitarist who I met while he was performing in my band. We did weddings, etc."

In 2000, Piper returned to music and was featured on a house record with the David Banks Project called "Good Lovin'" that was released in the U.K. The artist has continued to further her skills in the entertainment world since then. "Now I am in college majoring in music!" she proudly announces. "I am also currently working on an innovation through the Davison Company. They represent many idealists with their products and, hopefully, my innovation will be one that gets the attention like the infomercials you see on T.V. I also hope to one day initiate a 24–7 disco radio station that can be heard in several markets. I would love to see underground disco, disco-R&B, disco-funk and classic disco heard like all the other genres." Wardell also released a new CD in 2012 called *Pipergirl,* which featured all new material.

"A lot of us, and even younger generations, want to hear disco—the young want to know what it was like back in the disco era. I never thought, at this point in time, anyone would want to talk about disco. There are many who miss disco—I miss it!" asserts the singer.

With Wardell Piper's music and place in disco history assured, she warmly admits, "I am very grateful for all of my accomplishments in the recording business, and I'd like to let those who appreciated what I did musically know that I loved and appreciated them very much. Those who genuinely cared about me—thank you! They know who they are. My prayer is that everyone will seek the Lord and, one day, know Him as I do. He has been wonderful to me! Love to all!"

"I never thought, at this point in time, anyone would want to talk about disco. There are many who miss disco—I miss it!" says Wardell Piper (courtesy Wardell Piper).

The Ritchie Family, 1975–1978

Gwendolyn Wesley, Cassandra Wooten, and Cheryl Mason-Dorman

It's hard to imagine a more energized way to capture the excitement and array of hits the disco genre had amassed by 1976 than the juggernaut single "The Best Disco in Town." The song was a fast-flowing, super-charged medley of disco classics, from "Lady Marmalade" to "Lady Bump." Performed by the female trio known as the Ritchie Family, the song became a number 1 disco anthem and took the group to the Top 20 of the U.S. and U.K. pop charts. The invention of producers Jacques Morali, a Frenchman, Philadelphia's Richie Rome, and Morocco-born business partner Henri Belolo, the group was originally given form, substance, and vocal prowess by three beautiful black women: Cassandra Ann Wooten, Cheryl Mason Jacks (today known as Cheryl Mason-Dorman) and Gwendolyn Oliver (today known as Gwendolyn Wesley). Passionate about their contributions to disco's history, the ladies take a step back in time to speak about their remarkable legacy, which included 18 gold records and two platinum albums.

"Jacques Morali could not play any instruments, nor could he sing," says Gwendolyn, "but he was able to get a lot of people around him who were experts at what they did." Henri Belolo joined the mix a short time later as a producer and composer. Cheryl describes it as a great collaboration. "Jacques was very emotional. Henri was very easy going and he was able to calm him down and keep everything flowing and moving. Henri's whole demeanor really helped keep things smooth for a long time and we had a lot of respect for him. I believe he had a lot of respect for us too," she says.

At the outset, the group (whose moniker was derived from co-producer Richie Rome's name with an added "t") was simply a concept involving studio musicians and vocalists. Cassandra notes the group name was already in place when they came on board a bit later on, but they would have chosen a different one. "It didn't strike us as the type of name that was particularly en vogue at the time and they never gave us a clear rationale for it. Richie Rome was their point person and they worked it out with him," she says. Gwendolyn has a theory regarding the name. "I don't think [Morali] thought of the dilemma that everybody might think we were an actual family. I think he thought of the group as more of a musical family. It was funny because so many people thought Cheryl was white and they didn't understand how she could be in our black family!" she laughs. Cheryl chimes in, "Wherever we'd go, they would describe us as two black girls and one white girl. When I'd tell them I was black, they'd say, 'How, by transfusion?'" The ladies laugh.

Regardless of the unusual group name, the idea paid off for Morali. The largely instrumental first single under the Ritchie Family name was "Brazil," a disco-tinged remake of a vintage Xavier Cugat song. It was a solid hit for 20th Century Records, crossing from number 1 at the clubs to a respectable showing in the Top 20 of the pop chart. The song was nominated for Best Pop Instrumental Performance at the 1976 Grammy Awards, but lost out to the equally iconic "The Hustle" by Van McCoy. The *Brazil* album's irresistible '40s swing-disco style earned the act another dance chart hit, the combo "Peanut Vendor/Frenesi."

Tom Hayden was in charge of promoting the "Brazil" single and the group's debut album for 20th Century. "I never met any members of the studio group, but I did briefly talk with Richie Rome," he recalls. "I remember noticing how well 'Brazil' was doing in the clubs. We were getting huge sales out of New York and a few other cities without any radio play. We had distributed a promotional 12-inch single to the major clubs and they really picked up on it first. We had a guy named Billy Smith who was really great with club promotion and he played a big part in getting the song out there. It was a whole different way of promoting in 1975 because at that time the *Billboard* disco chart reflected just a tiny handful of clubs. Billy had especially good contacts with the New York hot spots and he'd personally take the single to them. I did the same thing on the west coast and mailed the single out to some of the other discos in different parts of the country. We never heard the response from them because it was a bit before the *Billboard* disco chart became more sophisticated and before the record pools had started. Tom Moulton was in charge of the chart at that time and the survey didn't utilize quite the methodology that developed a few years later with a broader range of reporters and clubs. We started promoting 'Brazil' to radio and it did well, but it wasn't quite as successful as the big hit from the Ritchie Family that would come later on."

The next major release from the entity (now signed to the pistol-hot Miami-based disco label TK/Marlin Records) would take the studio concept to the next level. Henri Belolo extended his role on the project as a songwriter, executive producer and business manager. Richie Rome and Jacques Morali co-produced. Rome, who had been working as far back as the '60s with the O'Jays and other acts, added his signature soulful sound to the beat. Lyricist and vocal arranger Phil Hurt also played a key role. And finally, three beautiful vocalists became the face of the Ritchie Family during this period: Cassandra, Gwendolyn and Cheryl.

Cassandra recalls, "Nadine Felder and I sang as Honey and the Bees and were asked to come to New York to do background work for a song that Jacques Morali was co-producing with Patrick Adams. Jacques told us that if he ever put together a girl group, he'd call us. We didn't think anything more about it. About two years later, Jacques did call us back, but Nadine was no longer interested in singing secular music. In the meantime, Gwendolyn had joined Honey and the Bees and Cheryl and I had been working together in a community theater group. The three of us had decided we wanted to do background work and we had just started practicing a few weeks before I got the call back from Jacques. As a result, in 1975 we all went down to Sigma Sound Studios and I reconnected with him. Henri was there as well. Though 'Brazil' was a success, session singers had recorded it and the Ritchie Family group didn't really exist. But now that the single was such a big hit, Jacques need a real live group. So we sang about two bars of 'Brazil' and he said we had the gig! After that, we started work on the *Arabian Nights* album in 1976, all as a result of that two-minute audition!"

In the beginning, the three women agree Jacques' concept of the group was a bit of a mystery. Says Cassandra, "He guided us more or less by *doing* as opposed to sitting us down and talking out a whole, full concept of what direction he wanted the group to go in. For instance, we were walking past an art gallery that actually specialized in costumes. He saw these incredible costumes, the ones you see on the cover of the *Arabian Nights* album, and he got them for us. They melded well with the concept of a lot of the music on the album — very exotic, very different. I think the group Labelle also influenced him. They were doing a lot of feathery costumes that were different from the norm. I think he was initially going for that kind of a look. But he changed direction often. On the second album, *Life Is Music*, we had a softer, more glamorous look. On *African Queens*, he again went back to a theme. We went to Eve's Costumes for the outfits on that album cover, Nefertiti, Cleopatra, and the Queen of Sheba! I'm not sure that Jacques knew exactly what he wanted over the long term. He would just push you in the direction he had in his mind at the time."

The first release from the ladies was the smash hit single, "The Best Disco in Town," an infectious dance music milestone. Essentially a fast-paced, nearly seven-minute medley of disco's earliest hits (including "That's the Way I Like It," "Love to Love You, Baby" and "Fly, Robin, Fly") mixed with snippets of original songs from the ensemble's forthcoming album, the single topped the disco chart, crossed to pop and became an international smash. The track served to announce — in no uncertain terms — that disco had truly arrived.

The Ritchie Family (Cheryl Mason, Cassandra Wooten, Gwendolyn Oliver) take a break from the 1977 photograph shoot for the *African Queens* LP cover. With the ladies are producers Jacques Morali (left) and Henri Belolo (right) (courtesy Cassandra Wooten).

"I believe 'The Best Disco in Town' was the first song we recorded for the album and we didn't yet know what the whole album concept was going to be," says Gwen. "We recorded the entire extended version of the song as one recording. Jacques would lay out the whole track and then he would teach us the song. He handled all his music this way. Whatever key the song was in, we'd have to sing it. All he had to do then was add our vocals. There were times you'd be singing and you have a momentum going and you'd have to break due to a vocal or technical glitch, but there was never any difficulty going from one part of that song to another. It wasn't a problem recording it or performing it live. That was the case for all our recordings. Once the song was released and it was such a big hit, it was like, 'Wow, we have to go in and do more tracks!' Instead of following up with other songs in the style of 'Best Disco,' he came up with a whole other theme."

"The male vocals that are heard in 'Best Disco' came in later," adds Cassandra. "We didn't know when we did our part that male voices would be added. When we heard the final cut, we heard the men singing. I liked it a lot, but it was pretty much that Jacques did things the way he thought it should be done with little input from us on any level. We used to refer to ourselves as glorified robots because he really had his own ideas about everything and he didn't want a lot of input. We were young and very opinionated, so you could tell there was a clash coming somewhere." The group laughs knowingly.

The trio agrees that performing such a diverse disco medley in the studio wasn't a difficult undertaking. Says Cheryl, "To me, the concept of the song was a bit like the mixing of records you'd hear in the clubs." Cassandra adds, "I never felt like we were encouraged to imitate the original records. We were able to sing the portion of 'Brazil' exactly like it had been recorded, but for the other tunes I just did what I felt sounded right and filled in each portion of it. It felt kind of automatic from a professional singing perspective; we just knew what to do. But Jacques didn't really coach in terms of 'Sing it this way; sing it that way.'" Gwendolyn admits they didn't want to make the track sound like brand new arrangements of the medley's songs and tried to stay somewhat true to each portion's original sound.

All agree the single sounded like a potential hit after recording it. The realization that they had struck gold was a profound moment for the trio. "I was working at a small college when this all started," says Cheryl. "To me, the success of 'The Best Disco in Town' was unreal. I was actually getting to sing songs that would be put out in the world. When I told the people where I was working why I needed to take off, they were really impressed." Gwendolyn says, "As much as we enjoyed all the little things that had come before, this was finally the moment where we had felt like we'd hit the jackpot and done something that had universal appeal. Except for Canada, we'd never been out of the country. Now the song was a hit in Austria, Italy, Australia, then South America! So it was incredible!"

Cassandra recalls the launch party for the *Arabian Nights* LP. "It was held at a place called Enchanted Garden in Queens, New York. They sent a limo to pick up Gwen and I in Philadelphia and flew Cheryl in from Ohio. It was a fabulous place built on a huge golf course. They had live elephants! It was incredible! There were beautiful people all around and an amazingly lavish spread. We met Steve Rubell there, who said he was going to open up a club in New York, which of course was Studio 54. It really set the tone for what was going to come for the Ritchie Family."

"They started preparing us right away and walking us through everything," recalls Cheryl. "They took us for the passports and visas. They got us the shots. They set us up in a dance studio to rehearse non-stop. It was so professionally done, you really felt like this was your life now." Cassandra adds, "We'd rehearse in New York all week and come home on the weekends. They paid for our tickets to go back and forth and had them couriered to us each week. They made sure we had all the right make-up and a hairdresser was hired to travel with us on the road."

The trio acknowledges their sudden fame, but they don't feel the spotlight ever went to their heads. "I was so involved in what I was doing and was paying attention more to that than the feeling of having 'arrived.' I just felt like we had a lot more to do," says Gwen. "I loved the accolades and the things we got to do," Cassandra adds, "but I was still Cassandra Wooten from North Philly and this was just something going on at the moment. I did think that I would be performing the rest of my life, but without the feeling of limitation that I was experiencing with the Ritchie Family. I couldn't see a long-term vision beyond what we were currently doing. I didn't feel like a star. I just felt I was still me. When people treated us like stars, it was great, but it wasn't me." Cheryl adds, "We sometimes felt like we were living someone else's life, but we were having a great time."

"There were several times that Jacques went way overboard and tried to make people put us on a pedestal," remarks Gwen. "I feel funny saying this, but he wasn't very nice to some people. And we felt like that wasn't necessary. After those people got to know us, they appreciated our attitude towards them. One time we were in Italy and Jacques called for a car and the best they could do was to send over a Chevy Impala. It was the best car they had; they didn't have a limousine. Jacques had a fit! He made the man handling the transportation feel so bad. It was just horrible. We were like, 'What the heck is going on?'" Says Cheryl, "Jacques would say to us, 'Oh darlings, how does it feel? You are stars now!' We'd say, 'We are?' We didn't feel that star thing so much."

When asked if they feel they were well compensated for their roles in the Ritchie Family, the answer is a resounding "No!"—all at once, from all three women. Cassandra describes the dilemma. "We had a royalty agreement, but our lawyers said we weren't in a great bargaining position. So the deal we had wasn't a very good one for us but it was excellent for Jacques and Henri. However, we really loved what we did and to be able to travel all over the world and wear beautiful clothes, it was like, 'Oh well!' We believed that if the hits continued, we would be able to re-negotiate our contract. But it was something that was going to bother us. It would become a point of contention going forward if we had stayed in that situation much longer. We realized we were worth more than what we were getting."

The less widely popular (but equally disco-oriented) albums *Life Is Music* and *African Queens* followed in 1977. Each garnered great favor in the clubs, with tracks like "Quiet Village" and "Life Is Music" topping the disco surveys, the latter a particularly strong track, rich in strings, bass and lush harmonies. The trio was voted Best Female Disco Group three times in a row by *Record World* magazine. Pop crossover success, however, became harder to come by and change was in the air. Richie Rome departed from the production team after the *Life Is Music* album. Says Gwendolyn, "We never thought disco would last. We came from an R&B background, so that was all we knew. Disco was so new and a lot of people in the industry didn't respect it. So we really didn't think it would be around forever. When we worked in Honey and the Bees, we were an extremely self-sufficient group and had our own creative ideas. In the Ritchie Family, we felt we were doing a good job, but we weren't showing all the talent we had."

"Disco seemed kind of lightweight," Cassandra opines. "I appreciate the music we did now more than when we actually recorded it [Cheryl and Gwendolyn chime in agreement]. I just felt like our music was lightweight in comparison to the people we really respected, like the Temptations and Aretha Franklin. Jacques had his way and he wasn't interested in our ideas or concerns. Yes, we enjoyed the disco, but we would have enjoyed it more if we had been allowed more creative input. But that wasn't to be. But you know, over time, truthfully, I can now appreciate Jacques talent and vision. A lot of what he created lasted a very long time and really impacted the music industry and if he were around, I'd let him know that."

"When I was singing, I used to refer to disco music as cotton candy music," says Cheryl. "It had this big, beautiful puffiness, but when you'd bite down on it, it would dissolve. That's how I thought back then. But over the years, I started appreciating disco more and the complexity of our songs, the orchestrations, the bigness of the music. It got to me even more when I was able to step back from it as opposed to sitting in the middle of all of it. When you're doing something non-stop, you don't have time to reflect on it. And like Cassandra said, Jacques wasn't interested in anything we had to say anyway. He never entertained any song ideas we had or anything we thought might work. That was difficult. We were artists as well the singers he hired and it was like he didn't want artists. He only wanted performers."

Cassandra adds, "We might have gone in a contemporary R&B direction with the group had we had any say. Maybe we would have had a hit, maybe not. But the thing is, we weren't very mature or sophisticated in our thinking at the time. We didn't think as broadly or globally as Jacques did. I think we all have to admit, Jacques' music still has international appeal and a lot of R&B music didn't crossover. The music we did with Jacques had definitely longevity and impact."

Says Gwendolyn, "I guess as far as the music goes, Jacques was right!" Cassandra and Cheryl agree with her assessment.

Despite their undeniable success in disco, the frustrations that had grown between the group and their producer reached a peak following the *African Queens* album. Gwendolyn describes her take on the situation. "I have to say, by that time I was tired of feeling like a puppet. I had given birth to a son just shortly before we started the Ritchie Family and I was missing being with him. I also had very bad asthma, which was sometimes affecting my ability to handle the work. I just had enough. For health and emotional reasons, I simply had to leave."

"Over the years we were with Jacques," says Cassandra, " the tension had increased to a point where we didn't have good feelings toward him and I guess he didn't feel good about us. We didn't know how much the situation had escalated until it was time to renew our contacts. Gwen was done. Cheryl and I still wanted to do it, but when we were called into the office, we were told they wanted to go in a whole other direction. It was hurtful, but we were very proud. I know in my case, I was like, 'Okay, fine.' Henri was the one who did the talking. Jacques wasn't there when we had that particular meeting. Henri said the press loved us, we were great, this, that and the other thing, but that they wanted to do something different. Surprisingly, Cheryl was given the opportunity to stay if she would agree to lose more weight and train the new girls. She did not believe she needed to lose any more weight and did not want to train any replacements for her friends and fellow group members.

"It was a sad day for us all," Cassandra concludes, her disappointment still evident. "Henri said, 'This is not personal. It is business.' Well, it was *very* personal for us!

"After thinking about it years later, I think the tension, our outspokenness, the differences of opinion, the back and forth with Jacques, is what really got us to that point. I think he was looking to show us that he owned the situation and that he could go and get someone else. I can't speak for Jacques, but that's how I felt when it went down. We felt like we were rather easily replaced and we didn't have much recourse. There was no social media back then and we thought that maybe the public really didn't care. There was nothing that we ever saw or read anywhere that indicated anyone wondered what happened to us or that they wanted us back. I personally felt like just slipping into a little corner. I didn't tell anyone for years that I sang. Over the years people would randomly approach me and ask if I used to sing and was I a member of the Ritchie Family or Honey and the Bees. It wasn't until 2010 with the explosion of Facebook and YouTube that I started noticing people were still interested in us and missed us. They wanted to know what happened. It was a huge surprise to all of us that the love was still there for us."

Jacques Morali reinvented his Ritchie Family in 1978 with a new trio of singers *(see the Ritchie Family, 1978–1982)* and continued producing dance music for several years. The original group members were not aware of Morali's passing from AIDS in 1991 until recently. "I'd really like to have told him, no matter what happened, we turned out fine. We didn't have a chance to reach him and I'm sad about that," says Gwendolyn. "We thought he was somewhere off enjoying life," Cheryl adds, "and discovering he had passed on was a shock." "Whatever else, Jacques enjoyed life," adds Cassandra, "and I am sure it was very difficult for him to be ill before he passed on."

Cheryl says that she and Cassandra tried to regroup following their departure from the Ritchie Family. A few years later, they became the background vocalists [with Michelle Simpson] on John Lennon & Yoko Ono's *Double Fantasy* album and were discussing going on the road with the legendary artist when he was tragically murdered. After that devastating setback, the ladies felt it was time to place new careers and family life at the front of the line. In the time that has passed since, they've matured and developed a philosophy for living beyond the spotlight. "I have no regrets about any of the things we did. None whatsoever," says Gwendolyn. "All the problems and such, that was just part of growing up. We did things that most people will never get to do in a lifetime. The funny part about it is our children are not impressed by any of it," she laughs. "I lead a quiet life now and I am very involved in my church. I am a saved person and Jesus Christ is my savior. I teach the bible now and I really enjoy that. When people find out what I used to do, they are amazed and enjoy hearing about it."

Cassandra is equally proud of her accomplishments. "I think I've been on every continent except Africa. When I look at the opportunity that came my way, how many people do you know had a chance like that? So I am eternally grateful for that experience. I would tell anybody, when you get an opportunity — embrace it; go for it! Give it your all! Time passes very quickly. However it turns out, at least you tried your best and you might do something wonderful. When I look back, I know we *did* do something wonderful with the Ritchie Family. Though Cheryl and I are mature now, we are singing again as the Ritchie Family [with new member Renée Guillory-Wearing] and I feel good about how we sound. Maybe if we had been singing all these years, our voices might have left us. I'm so glad that fans are able to enjoy our music again. I am always grateful to God for another opportunity!" Cassandra also earned a Bachelor's degree in Communications after she came off the road and will soon complete her work on a Master's degree in Instructional Technology Management.

"Being in the Ritchie Family was a chance that few people get to live," says Cheryl. "Not only did we get to travel and sing, but we did it in a style that a lot of people would

Gwendolyn Wesley, Cheryl Mason-Dorman and Cassandra Wooten say they have come to realize how many hearts were touched by their classic disco music (courtesy Cassandra Wooten).

envy because Jacques did *not* play around. Everything was first class! I mean, we were even the first western group to be seen on Soviet block TV in 1977. It was just fabulous. When it was over, none of us held any grudges or hard feelings toward anyone. We remained friends and just moved on with our lives in a different direction. After the Ritchie Family, I got a job in the School District of Philadelphia where I was a researcher. I was laid off after 17 years and was told if I wanted a job I'd have to be a teacher. I had to go get another masters degree in education and from there I eventually became an assistant principal. When I was a child, my mother asked me what I wanted to do. I said I wanted to sing, I wanted to dance—all of those things. She said, 'Well honey, you sing real good, but there's a lot of people who sing good. So you need to find something to fall back on in case singing doesn't work out for you.' I was angry because I thought she had no faith in me. But I followed her advice and got that degree and it helped me so much after the whole Ritchie Family part of my life ended. My philosophy is the more you can do, the better off you'll be. God has been good to me and he has taken me through a whole lot of things! I have seen Him turn the worst things that have happened in my life into the best things in my life. Many years ago I saw a sign in front of a church that said, 'Preach by your life!' I decided that was how I would live my life. I have followed my interests in music, art, and writing. I have continued my education and recently completed my Doctorate of Education."

The Ritchie Family was inducted into the Dance Music Hall of Fame by *Billboard* magazine at the Dance Music Summit in 2004. "Unfortunately," says Cassandra, "the award was only presented to one of the ladies from the later lineup of the group. Ouch!!" However, the honor serves to remind what a remarkable group this was and the historic distinction these women have earned as pioneers of the best disco music in town. They think about their musical estate and each member offers her optimism for how their legacy will be remembered. "I'd like our fans to say that our music was done well and that it was quality. That our music added something to popular culture that was lasting," says Cassandra. "I hope that we were able to show the world the value of living life, having fun, and not taking everything so seriously," says Gwen. Cheryl concludes, "I hope people continue to enjoy the beauty of our voices together. Sometimes the beautiful harmonies just sound heavenly to me. I hope we were able to touch people's hearts with our music and I want them to know that, in the end, we really *did* become a family after all!"

The Ritchie Family, 1978–1983

Theodosia "Dodie" Draher

Like disco music itself, some artists and acts linked to the genre were an evolution of ideas, images and themes brought forth by their producers. The Ritchie Family concept, which was personified by a trio of female singers amidst a storm of thumping beats, changed its line-up, look and sound as the ensemble's creators repositioned the act in the late '70s. Theodosia "Dodie" Draher (representing the Ritchie Family that reformed in 1978) candidly and enthusiastically relates her experiences with the energized assemblage.

Flush with success, producers Jacques Morali and Henri Belelo sought a modernized direction for their Ritchie Family project. They held auditions, seeking new performers to represent the group. "When I went to the audition, I knew nothing of The Ritchie Family background," remembers Dodie. "All I knew was that I was working for the telephone company at the time and I always got all the show business and backstage papers, and I saw that an internationally famous disco group was looking for singers. So I called in sick to work and went to the audition. They held the audition right here in New York City at what was then the Ed Sullivan Theater on Broadway. And there we were—300 other hopefuls and I doing our best—*but they all had to go home!*" she chuckles. "In March of 1978, I became a member of the Ritchie Family! Jacqui Smith-Lee had already secured her place as a member. Later, Ednah Holt became our third Ritchie."

"Our first album was *American Generation,* and they just took us in a whole different direction compared to the previous albums," Dodie observes. "I'm not sure why he didn't just create a new group with a new name, but I guess the Ritchie Family name was established, and they just wanted to continue along with it. Maybe they didn't want to go through all that rigmarole to establish a new group."

Dodie admits, "I had just been in New York for probably about a year and half when I became a member of the Ritchie Family. I had been attending the University of Colorado and ended up singing with a traveling Top-40 band based in Colorado. I wasn't New York material then—New York show business material—I wasn't seasoned at all. Not in this

The Ritchie Family (left to right: Dodie Draher, Vera Brown Pressley and Jacqueline Smith-Lee) was a Casablanca Records priority in 1979, when the group was actively touring with the Village People (author's collection).

whole new arena. This was a whole new ball game for me. [The recording session] was surreal. With all of the show business savvy that others there had, I was just overwhelmed. That was my first experience going into the studio! It was difficult. It was hard because Jacques Morali was very demanding—and I don't mean that in a derogatory way; he was very good! He knew exactly what he wanted, and he used whatever tools he had to get it. It was hard work, very hard, but it was an invaluable learning experience and, you know, I just had to grow into it. Retakes, being on pitch, long, long hours in rehearsal learning choreography and things like that. It was an easier process for Ednah because she had recorded before. It may have been an easier process for Jacqui because she had done some Broadway shows, the movie *The Wiz* as a dancer, recorded Broadway musical soundtracks and things like that. I can't say there was initially great chemistry between all of us. Me—I came in straight from the West Coast. So this was all 'college' for me. I remember thinking, 'Oh, hell, this is serious stuff! This is the real deal, Ms. Dodie!'"

It quickly became apparent to the singer that she had entered the big leagues. "We didn't know at that point if we were going to be successful. We just felt that, well, here's an opportunity—let's see where it goes. As we learned more about Jacques Morali, we realized that this was *big*; this was *huge*! This man knows what he's doing. He's had hit songs, and he's as serious as a heart attack. I think we all knew that something great was going to happen working with him. The *American Generation* album wasn't a big seller in the U.S., but I can tell you it was huge in Europe. Jacques really threw in that European influence into that LP, and I think Europeans connected with that sound better," she says.

The effort proved to be a noteworthy (if somewhat unheralded) stateside debut for the girls. As Dodie attests (and despite the album title), Morali and Belolo ironically switched from the previous American pop-soul-disco sound they had cultivated to a heavier Euro-disco style. The girls certainly looked domestic enough, however, playfully (and minimally) costumed in football, hockey and baseball gear and looking extremely fetching. The title track was a solid U.S. club hit as it reached the disco chart's Top 20, and it was suggestive of another Morali classic—Patrick Juvet's similarly themed "I Love America" (for which the Ritchie Family had done background vocals). The album marked the last time the group appeared on the TK-Marlin Records label, a Florida-based record label that had a long and prosperous history in disco with hit releases by KC & the Sunshine Band, George McCrae, Foxy and Anita Ward. "I can't remember that Marlin Records made much of an impression on me at the time," she says. "We came along and did *American Generation* towards the end of that relationship. So we didn't have that much interaction with the label people. The interaction came with Casablanca Records. That was just a *fabulous* label! [Our move there] was a business venture with Henri, Jacques and Neil Bogart. Neil Bogart, the head of Casablanca, was a fabulous man—a really, really nice man. Everybody there—it felt like family; it just really felt like family! They took a real interest in moving us to the next level. I think that Casablanca saw a huge potential with us as a group, and Henri and Jacques were very pleased with us—with their new children. So the label pushed us as much as they could. They had us doing everything. They would always be pushing for hits. I think they did a good job of promoting us, and they were especially happy with our first album for them—*Bad Reputation*. We did all the television there was to do back in the day, and we did some of the shows more than once—*The Dinah Shore Show, Mike Douglas, Merv Griffin, Dance Fever*. Ray Bolger [*Wizard of Oz's* Scarecrow] was my dance partner on *Dance Fever*. I think about [that event]—about actually being in his company, talking and dancing! I am in awe of everything we have done as a group and everything we continue to do!" Dodie says, almost breathless.

The Ritchie Family hit pay dirt with the group's move to Casablanca Records, the ultimate dance label of the day and then home to Donna Summer, the Village People and Cher. Vera Brown, now in the lead vocal position, replaced Ednah Holt, and the album *Bad Reputation* made its debut at the very peak of disco fever in 1979. It got plenty of attention. Village People front man Victor Willis handled the vocal arrangements. The single "Put Your Feet to the Beat" cracked the disco Top 20 once again. Recalls Draher, "Making the album *Bad Reputation* was a much different experience than *American Generation*. We recorded *Reputation* in Los Angeles at Rusk Sound Studios, which was a really nice facility to work at. It took about a week and a half to record the album. It was another growing experience, a learning experience. We had our highs and lows and we were sequestered, as one would say, quite a bit in the studio. Hours on end! It was similar on the next album, *Give Me a Break*. We wrote two songs on *Give Me a Break* and recorded the album at the same Rusk Studios.

"We would go in and lay down our vocals, then the next thing we'd do is the videos. We made videos for many of our songs — almost everything. I don't know if you remember, but before VH1 came into play, HBO used to play music videos in between movies and shows. A lot of our videos were shown that way. Then of course, VH1 came out and all the videos were played there. Making the videos was just wonderful. I mean *fabulous*! We had choreographers maybe eight hours a day teaching us moves five days a week. The moves were almost as important for us as the vocals. Remember that our generation of the Ritchie Family, in 1978, was a front-runner. No one was doing that kind of choreography; no one was dressing like we were — we had become, as Jacques Morali always said, 'trendsetters.' And that is exactly what we were! The videos did a lot to get our songs out there. Our video for 'Give Me a Break' did very, very well, and I think that 'Put Your Feet to the Beat' did really well also. 'Put Your Feet' was a really good one in my opinion. That was a very involved video to make, and it came out very well. I wish you could see them ... oh, wait, you can — on YouTube!"

The single "Give Me a Break" (not to be confused with a popular Italian import by singer Vivien Vee released around the same time) registered well in the clubs. The track was also in the running as a theme song for a program sponsored by New York City that promoted jobs for young graduates. "Give Me a Break" received more attention thanks to the girls' showcase of the track in the Village People movie musical, *Can't Stop the Music*, and its soundtrack album. The film, however, released days after the unofficial crash of disco, bombed miserably at the box office.

"It was still the experience of a lifetime making the movie — it was just awesome," Dodie says despite the critical bashing the film received. "First of all, you should understand that the Village People and the Ritchie Family were like brother and sister groups at the time because we worked together in so many productions and Henri and Jacques were both our producers. We opened concerts for the Village People and were able to do the world tour for the movie soundtrack and promotion of the film. Our world premiere was in Sydney, Australia, where we opened for the Village People, and then we would quickly go change clothes and sing backups for their portion of concert. We did all that, and then headed to Japan and did the same thing. We just learned so much watching the guys work, and it was just one hell of an experience. Okay, the movie wasn't that great, but making the movie was a lot of fun. Once the movie buzz was over, they broke us up a bit, and some of us went off to the northeast to keep promoting the music and to the South and to California."

Belolo and Morali left the comforts of Casablanca around the time when Neil Bogart had passed away from cancer. They took the girls to RCA Records for their next LP, *I'll Do My Best*. With co-production by Fonzi Thornton (an up-and-coming funk artist on the label) and Jacques Fred Petrus (who had scored numerous crossover disco hits with acts like Change and BB&Q Band), the album's title track was a dance-floor hit and did equally well on the R&B side. "We moved to RCA in 1982, and our sound changed to more of a funky dance/R&B style to reflect the times. Really, that was for survival because of that post-disco backlash effect. Luckily, we ended up having a lot of great hits on that album. RCA was a different experience. They promoted us well, but we were really spoiled by

Casablanca. Henri and Jacques were, again, the business people, and they just told us, 'Okay, this is what is happening and this is where we are going,' so I don't recall hearing that much about why we left Casablanca. We met the label executives and different songwriters, like the fabulous Eumir Deodato, a Brazilian pianist, composer, record producer and arranger most famous for his work with Kool & the Gang. Initially we spent some time with him, going through music and such. We thought he was going to be the primary writer for this RCA venture, so we were very, very excited about the possibility of working with such and incredible, successful musician. But then that never came to fruition."

Instead, Petrus utilized his longtime writing companion, Mauro Malavasi, and writers like James Herb Smith to compose the girls' latest songs. "We were very excited by the material they eventually came up with because now we got to do something different. We were able to use our abilities in another area, in another genre—and that made us very, very happy. I really love that album. 'I'll Do My Best (for You Baby)' crossed us over more into pop and R&B and we enjoyed having the chance to expand our audience. Had we stayed with the pure disco sound—that would have been fine too. Trust me—we would have made it work! But then the business heads didn't want to gamble on disco."

One more album followed on RCA in 1983, *All Night, All Right*, with Gavin Christopher handling much of the production and writing chores. The title track was a modest R&B and dance hit, but it was missing one thing—Dodie. "I had left the group before that last album to have a baby, and a lovely young lady named Linda James stepped in to take my place. I had a another boy, the third of three: Timothy W. Wright, Stephen S. Wright and Daniel Draher, who, by the way, is serving our country as an awesome Special Operations Marine, I am proud to say! I think the group lasted for six months after I left, and then that was the end of the Ritchie Family for some time." As for the group's founders, Morali added his name to disco's tragic statistics and unfortunately fell victim to complications from HIV infection in the mid–'80s, passing away in 1991. Henri Belolo, however, continues to produce music in France.

"I had decided I needed to get grounded and spend time with my family. We had [previously] been home for two weeks out of every year for the past five years or so. We worked our asses off! I'm not complaining, but it's really, really hard work. It's glamorous to those on the outside looking in, and they would say to me, 'Wow, you are so lucky.' And yeah, we were lucky to be able to work at what we love to do and experience so much—but it's grueling. I'm telling you—you had to be very much grounded and have your head screwed on right and not get into the drugs and such—where you could easily fall off the deep end.

"We were exposed to the drugs and the craziness all the time," Dodie says. "A club that was notorious—*notorious* for it—was Studio 54. I mean people were hanging off the rafters and just doing their thing. But despite that side of it, I just loved the disco era because it was the one time that I know of that people really cared about each other. You could let your hair down, and there was a new sense of freedom. There was some kind of camaraderie—I don't know how to explain it! I just thought it was a really great time and yes, Studio 54, places like that, there were often drugs everywhere, but those clubs were the best. Studio 54 was world renowned, historical and legendary, having been the playground to the famous as well as the not-so-famous. It was a real fun place in its day. I guess that is something that also comes with the sense of freedom. There were times we'd go on tour to, say, Venezuela and there was somebody always there offering you [some kind of drug], saying, 'Do you want this or that'—it was everywhere. That was the reality. But there were just as many good, incredible experiences too."

Dodie recalls memories of the group performing great shows in the Pines on Fire Island. "Jacques would rent a fabulous house there every summer. The shows were always off-the-hook incredible! With the huge gay following we had, the club [we'd appear at] there was always jam-packed! Cher even hung out in our dressing room one year! *Wow!*"

Called to appear in all corners of the globe at the height of the disco era, Draher remembers finding the group in another unusual setting. "Our first gig as the Ritchie Family was in Rabat, Morocco," she remembers. "We had just recorded the *American Generation* album, so it was towards the end of 1978. We went down there and played for the king and his brother, whose birthday it was. So, we go there and did our show at the palace in Fez and the staff—I don't know who they were really—would come with bowls of keif, probably like an organic type of drug—brown stuff in bowls—some kind of drug that they obviously did over there. They offered it to the males. They didn't offer it to us, which I thought was very interesting. But again, I'm right out of Colorado, so I don't know what to look for," she laughs. "Then, at one point during our concert, the king himself came walking towards the stage, and he had a platter with three glasses—and they didn't drink water. At least that's how it seemed. All they drank was Dom Perignon, and he came up on the stage and gave Jacqui, Ednah and myself each a glass of champagne, and then he proceeded to go back and play on the drums. We just had an awesome time! I'm talking about a birthday party held by a king! It was like all the rich people of the world were gathered there. To me, it's was one of the most awesome experiences I ever had. All these filthy, filthy, rich people there having a great time. Then, with a motorcade and police escort—the whole nine yards—he took us to a beautiful, secluded park in the forest for a huge picnic—shrimp as big as your fist and bottles and bottles of Dom Perignon. He presented each of us with necklaces made of rubies, sapphires, diamonds and emeralds. Incredible!"

"Then, to boot, he sent us and the band to Casablanca [ironically reported to be the birthplace of Henri Belolo] for seven days! He just sent us there on a luxurious bus and put us in this fabulous hotel. Then, out of that—check this out—there's a Texas oil magnate there and he saw us and he liked us, so he hired us to go perform at Princess Caroline's engagement party in Paris! We were flown over there in his private jet, and we performed at Maxim's, an elite club for the rich and famous! We thought the people might be stiff or uppity, but can I tell you—those people in the club had more fun than we did! They were all over the place! And oh, by the way, Princess Grace [Kelly] of Monaco was there, but her husband, Prince Rainer, didn't attend. He did not approve of Princess Caroline's fiancée, Phillipe Junot."

The artist holds firm to the conviction that disco made for a remarkable era and still has its place today. "It was such a great era, and it has so many great songs too. I'll tell you one song that I really would still love to do and that's Alicia Bridges' 'I Love the Nightlife' [she sings a few bars]. I love that song, and, hopefully, we are talking about putting a show together were we can do songs that we like and you don't hear performed much anymore, but were huge, one-hit wonders if you will. There are a lot of great disco songs out there! We all have our favorites we want to incorporate into our show and, who knows, maybe even re-record them! My favorite artist of all time was the late great Sylvester. There are still many people who go crazy for disco. Look at the Disco Ball in Atlantic City every year and all the people that come out for it. They are die-hard disco fans, and they know all the words of the songs! We did the show [in the summer of 2012], and the people came out in droves from ages 18 to 80. We did a state fair in Louisville, Kentucky, opening for the Village People again, and it was packed. You can be sure there are *plenty* of people who love disco!"

The First Ladies of Disco—The Ritchie Family, 1978–1983

"You know, it's funny, back in the disco era, a lot of artists that had big hits in other genres claimed they hated disco, but they knew disco music was hot and that was the way to go to get a hit song and stay out there. Rod Stewart, Barbara Streisand, the Rolling Stones for example—and the list goes on and on. They'd say disco was a joke, and then they would come out with a monster disco tune. Now, looking back, I'm sure they realize maybe disco wasn't such a bad thing after all. For disco artists today, it's still a bit of a challenge. You have all these things that interfere with what you would like to do. I'm speaking specifically to the [current] economy, making it really, really hard to put on the type of show that properly pays the artists and where people can afford the tickets. The economy has a lot to do with it—it kind of really messed things up," says Draher.

She and her fellow group members take the issues that surround aging in stride. "If there is pressure in aging, we put it on ourselves," she claims. "We know what Jacques raised us to be, and we try to carry that on. He was a blessing to our lives. He had a vision and he built that vision, and it's up to us to carry on with that legacy. It's very important for us to maintain our bodies, our looks, how we present ourselves, how we dress and things like that. And thank God we are able to do that! That's in the front of our minds—our image and looking like we take care of ourselves. Honestly, we don't want to be all out of shape where you can't move around well on the stage and things like that. Who wants to see that? We want to be a combination of what we were and what we are, and that's what we will continue to be!"

"I would say, for the Ritchie Family—and I know I can speak for Jacqui and Vera—we genuinely have a really great respect for each other. We don't fight. If something is on someone's mind, we speak about it, talk about it, get it out and it's done. I think that's key to longevity. The other thing is just being respectful to other artists and living well personally. Being the best person you can be and putting that out there with every opportunity that-

The second generation of the Ritchie Family (left to right: Dodie Draher, Vera Brown Pressley, Jacqueline Smith-Lee) say they'd like to continue to carry on the vision of their late producer, Jacques Morali (courtesy Dodie Draher).

comes our way — when you're on the stage, when you are talking to fans, when you do interviews — in all aspects of life. You just need to be honest, real and send a good message. I think that's what we definitely try to do. I just really believe in that. I believe that what you put out, you get back," she says firmly.

Ranking high among the elite of disco's female ensembles, the 1978 incarnation of The Ritchie Family played an important role in the genre's history. Dodie Draher looks at the legacy of the group with appreciation and cuts to the chase, simply saying, "Oh heck ... just remember us for giving people some fun times and good music! That we helped make it *party time*! That we were *fabulous* ladies and we made some good music!"

Barbara Roy (Ecstasy, Passion & Pain)

One of the first dance music compilations ever advertised on TV was released on Springboard-TVT Records. It was an LP called *Disco Hustle*, in which the top hits of the period were somewhat poorly sequenced (by today's standards) with no breaks — "just like you'd hear at the discos!" It was one of the best-selling disco collections of its day, and what stood out most on this album was an exceptionally pumping track called "Touch & Go" — the tale of a woman whose man keeps doing her wrong. The song was delivered with a soulful vibe by a group called Ecstasy, Passion & Pain. The vocals on this stunning, pioneering dance effort were belted out by a young Barbara Roy, who possessed a fierceness that could stand up against anything Motown had to offer. The song became one of disco's earliest classics. Roy, an accomplished musician and songwriter, says, "We performers don't get a chance to talk about those days often. We never did get our due, but we made do!" She is eager to share her thoughts about the faith and inspiration that she says was the root of her uplifting dance music.

Roy describes her beginnings in Kinston, North Carolina. "I came from a musically-inclined family," says Barbara. "My dad was a prayin' man, and my mom had the music side. I was the youngest of 13 children. I only weighed two pounds when I was born. Seven of us played guitar and all of us sang. Being the youngest, I wasn't able to travel around with the group my mother had formed in the family. They would go around to churches, venues and events and perform. I was a little thing, so I couldn't go. But I did become interested in guitar at the age of two, my family said. I remember when I was five years old, I could play a chord or two, and I stuck with it and it stuck with me. I didn't really learn to sing until was 11 or 12, but I kept trying and trying till I finally developed a little somethin' somethin'," she laughs. "The reason I say that is because one of my sisters had moved away to New York and she would come home to visit in North Carolina and would say to me, 'I see you're still tryin' to sing! Keep tryin', baby! You'll get it.' And I did. My mother would start to take me to the church, where I joined the junior choir, and that helped my voice even more.

"My niece Brenda and I became like sisters at an early age. We started to sing together, we'd do duets and we did pretty well! We'd write songs, I'd play guitar and we'd record them on this terrible little recorder. We entered elementary school contests and talent shows — and we won. We beat the 12th graders — can you imagine? We did [the Buddy Holly hit], 'Peggy Sue.' It was a gas! We did well later on, too. We called ourselves 'Barbara & Brenda'

An early formation of the group Ecstasy, Passion & Pain, which blazed the disco trail with the hits "Ask Me" and "Touch & Go" included (left to right) Joseph Williams, Jr., Bassist Carl (Teddy) Jordan, Ron Smith, Barbara Gaskins (Roy) and Alan Tiza (courtesy Barbara Roy).

and when we went to New York, we got a few jobs at places like the Apollo Theater, the Baby Grand nightclub and Illusion in Brooklyn. We were well known in the New York area."

The singer wasn't mindful of bigger aspirations during her earliest years in the industry. "At the time I was with Brenda, I didn't have a clear vision of becoming a successful singer on my own. We were planning to stay together and do this thing—that's what I had in my mind to do. Well, Brenda met a gentleman, and they fell in love and got married," she laughs. "Brenda quit the music, and I was on my own. But it was okay; I love Brenda to this day. But, you know, I was stuck with music because music was in my bones. But I needed another job. You may remember Inez and Charlie Fox—they had the 'Mockingbird' hit. I played guitar for them, and we toured the South, England. It was very nice working with them. After Charlie and Inez decided they wanted to cool it, here I was again without a gig. I had gotten with another group, and we were just doing local clubs—nothing big. The bass player told me they were forming a new group at a nightclub in New York. He was their bass player, knew they needed a guitarist and asked me if I was interested. By this time, I had met a beautiful man who became my mate, and I was carrying our son. I was seven months pregnant. He said, 'Oh come on, do the audition and after the baby comes you can do the work.' He talked me into it. When I went to the club, there were approximately seven to 10 men sitting around with their guitars, auditioning or waiting. Ronnie Smith was the organizer of the audition, and he asked me to do 'Let It Be Me,' an easy song. I started singing and playing my guitar, he accompanied me on an organ and I thought it was going very, very well. But I don't think I'd even done 10 bars before he stopped me and said, 'That's enough; that's it! You're hired! We need you!' What embarrassed me so much was he added, 'The rest of you guys can go home!' I didn't want him to say that to them like that. There's a way to do things, you know? But they hired me, and that's how Ecstasy, Passion & Pain was formed."

The evocative, soulful name the band branded for itself was the result of a group effort. Says Barbara, "We didn't have a name for three or four months, but we were still [out there] working. We had a meeting one night, and we all said we needed a name—people needed to know what to call us. We couldn't come up with one at that moment, so everybody went home and came up with a list of names that might fit the group. When we got back together again, everybody had a little list. One had ecstasy, one had passion and I think I had passion or pain—one or the other—and everybody liked those three names. During that time, three name groups were very popular—Faith, Hope & Charity, Earth, Wind & Fire, you know. We didn't really realize what we were putting together when we came up with that name until much later on—or that it could have so many meanings."

Roy and company scored a number of hits after their formation in 1972. They cracked the Top 40 with "One Beautiful Day" in 1973 and were a strong presence on the soul charts with songs like "Good Things Don't Last Forever." The group began its connection with disco during the genre's earliest days. The Roulette Records single "Ask Me" had powerful lyrics, Roy's gritty, earnest vocal delivery and a delicious hustle beat that made it an unstoppable force in the club environment. The track had a respectable pop and soul chart ranking but soared to number 2 in its extended version on the 1975 disco charts, turning the group into a dependable source for the vital grooves developing in the very early days of disco.

"I didn't realize exactly what was going on with disco," she admits. "It happened so fast, and before we knew it, we had crossed over the bridge. I liked it. Come what may, I was still going to be me and record what I felt was good. A song tells a story. Everything I ever recorded has had something to do with my life. And others' as well. I've written songs about other people, but somewhere in those songs, I was a part of it too. I don't have to like a song to do it, but whatever song I do, I have to do it in a way that's gonna help me to project it properly. When the music changed towards disco, it didn't really bother me. It was right up my alley, really.

"I was young and energetic, so I didn't feel disco was limiting. I felt wherever this genre was going, I wanted to see where it would take me. I wasn't going to eliminate it from our sound. And if it didn't do what it was supposed to do for me, then we'd try something else. Artists don't really belong to themselves — they belong to the fans, the people listening to our music. We're supposed to give the people what they want. There are many artists who did songs they didn't want to do, and many of those same songs wound up being big hits. Disco was an era, and you had to change with it. I would have been doing people an injustice if I hadn't changed with it.

"Hey, I mean some people called our music 'secular music,'" Roy adds. "The music of Ecstasy, Passion & Pain, I feel, was *not* secular music. The world liked it. They were clean stories, stories of people's lives. I believe the songs I wrote were given to me by God — if you can believe that. At the time of Ecstasy, Passion & Pain, I was a church girl, but I wasn't attending church regularly. I had the Lord working inside me, and I know he gave me those words to write. And do you know why I know? Because they have blessed people. When we were performing in South Africa, we did the song 'Don't Burn Your Bridges Behind You,' a song I had written for our album. After the show, this lady made her way backstage from the audience. I don't know how she did it, but she got back there and she made her way to me. She was crying and took me by the hand. In her dialect she said, 'Excuse me for crying. I just had to come and thank you for singing that song. Now I know what I have to do. I was going to leave my husband, and now I know that I can't. It's the wrong thing to do.' She was blessed, and she just thanked me and thanked me and cried. It was something I had never seen before in my life — [happening to me] on the other side of the world."

Barbara — whose professional career path positioned her as a woman of color in a man's world — didn't always find the road easy to navigate. "There were so many ways I, as a black woman, was discriminated against because of my talent and because I was a black woman. How can I put this ... even in my own race — men were jealous of my gift to play. They just couldn't seem to grasp it. They never saw a woman play a guitar like I played. I'm not bragging on myself, but I played guitar for God. I'm not messing around — I'm playing for God. Even back when I was a young child in school, I would play guitar back when you had morning devotions before school. I was so happy to do that. Well, I played, and this little girl came up to me and said, 'You play like a man!' Oh my, it hurt my feelings so much. I went home, and I never picked up my guitar again until my brother Howard came home from the army several months later. I told him what happened, and he explained that she probably meant I played as well as a man. He made me understand. When God gives you something, you've got it, a gift, and you use it for His glory. You forget all about that dumb stuff. It doesn't matter what people think. I'm still paying my bills with this gift."

The exhilarating 1976 single "Touch & Go" (mixed to perfection with a heated and soul-drenched vibe by Tom Moulton) became the one of the band's biggest hits and is often regarded as an essential of the early disco era. The song was a Top Five dance smash and cracked the Hot 100 on the pop side. "I didn't feel pressure to follow up the song with something equally big per se, but I felt if we continued to do songs like 'Touch & Go,' we would stay in the 'now'—that we would continue to cross over. We wanted to do the type of songs that would sell and people wanted to hear," she recalls.

With Ecstasy, Passion & Pain's formidable presence in the clubs and their records selling hot, Roy had to face the faith-challenging environment head on. "My sisters were in music long before me, and they warned me what to look for," says the singer. "They said, 'If you're gonna be in this music, in this world, then there's gonna be things that will happen that you shouldn't take part in. Because if you do, you're headed downhill. It's gonna hurt you big time.' Other than drinking a little alcohol—having a few cocktails—that's *all* that we ever did. *When* we did. And we didn't make it a point to do that; it was just to be social—dinners, interviews and that sort of thing. But to sit around and party and be a part of a drug-infested room or place ... *no*! I was a businesswoman out there. I had a godly background, and my parents taught us values. They taught us how to take care of ourselves—how to handle ourselves when tempted to do the wrong thing. Now, I wasn't perfect. I definitely did some things I should not have done, but I had my mother's voice inside of me and the spirit of God inside of me."

Amid appearances on *Soul Train*, *American Bandstand* and other television shows, Barbara's conspicuous talent and presence led to an evolution of the group's name and direction. "I had written several songs on our first album. I was the only singer, and I eventually felt it was time for me to elevate myself. So I talked to the group about calling us 'Barbara Roy and Ecstasy, Passion & Pain.' At that time, we had made some changes, adding people to the group—horns, some side-members—and so I approached our manager, Phil Braxton, and he didn't have a problem with it. The record company didn't want to change it, however, because our record had gone out under the original name, and they were selling it under that name—and I could understand that. To change it so abruptly might have hurt us. So, eventually, we figured we could go into it gradually. I think we did our tour in South Africa, and while we were there—around when 'Touch & Go' was released—they started introducing the group on stage as 'Ecstasy, Passion & Pain, featuring Barbara Roy.' Later on, I started recording with a label called Roy B Records. Most people think that was my own label, but it was really Roy Birmingham's label. When I recorded 'If You Want Me,' we made it under the name 'Barbara Roy with Ecstasy, Passion & Pain.'"

Forging a music career on the group's original recording label, Roulette Records, was not without difficulties. Says Roy, "I received my writer's royalties from BMI; I signed up with them when I first went into the business. So I would get my writer's royalties and my publishing. I still do, even today, after 30 years. The company I was recording for, Roulette Records, did not want to give me any publishing, but they had no choice. [I felt] if they wanted us to record, they were going to have to be somewhat fair. They didn't treat us fairly in many ways, but, you know, you gotta crawl before you walk. You can't start at the top—you know all those little clichés. Roulette Records was ... Roulette Records. Many artists were not happy [with the label], and I wasn't happy when I realized a few things. I wasn't happy at all. However, I had a contract to fulfill, and I did that to the best of my ability."

Among the challenges, there were also some remarkable highlights for Barbara and the group. "For me," she recalls, "a major one was when we played Madison Square Garden—it was incredible. The Spinners were on the show, lots of big acts. Such a long time ago. But Madison Square Garden ... oh man! It's where everything in the world happened. We were there, and my family came from North Carolina, D.C., Baltimore—they came from everywhere. It was absolutely wonderful. When the crowd would go crazy over our songs, I knew I was pleasing them, and they were happy! That was my aim. The audience—they're the ones who spent their hard-earned money to come and see us — and when they react to your music ... it just puts you on a cloud!"

The founding formation of Ecstasy, Passion & Pain disbanded around 1977, but the group's name (with personnel changes) endured into the '80s. "If You Want Me," a funky dance jam and club favorite that featured her nieces (Jocelyn Brown and La Rita Gaskins) on backup vocals (with a nod to Ecstasy, Passion & Pain), "Gotta See You Tonight" and "Gonna Put Up a Fight" successfully moved Roy into the new decade. She continued touring domestically and abroad as, primarily, a solo artist. The classic "Touch and Go" was remixed and re-released again in 1986 by Tony Smith and Danny Krivit.

"After 1990–91, I moved from Baltimore to Washington, D.C., to my brother's house," Roy says. "I wanted to go back to church. He needed me to help him in the music area of the church as well. So I helped him; he helped me. My mother had always taught us you can't straddle the fence, meaning you can't serve the devil and God too. You have to choose one or the other. You can't choose gospel music and secular music at the same time. It won't work. That was instilled in us. All my life I fought with that. When I moved back to D.C., I decided I would not sing secular music again because it was against God's will. At the same time, I was learning more and more about the Lord and building my relationship with him. And this thing I kept hearing in my head, 'You can't do this; you can't do this,' was a challenge for me. My niece Jocelyn wanted me to come to London to do some shows with her. I said, 'Joss, I can't,' and I turned her down because of this reason. And I wouldn't go to New York, where I had jobs waiting for me — people wanting to hire me. I wouldn't do it; I turned them down. Yet I had the urge to sing ... I *wanted* to do it. I finally said, 'Why I am feeling this way? Why do I want to do this so badly, if it's such a horrible thing to do?' I [prayed] and said, 'I want to do R&B music. You've given me the words to write; show me the right way to go.' Little by little, I began to hear His words, from good friends, family, Jocelyn. 'You *can* do it; you can do what you *want* to do as long as you put God first.' My brother, who was a minister (and is a bishop now), told me to just to make sure I didn't jump into anything without being sure it was the right thing for my life. It came to me one day, clear as a bell. The Lord showed me that he had to trust me in order for me to be able to do a song in a nightclub, where alcohol is served, where drugs are everywhere. Where temptation is going to be so intense. Well, when I thought about that, I *knew* there was no way I was going to turn away from God. I mean, you couldn't pay me to do that! There's not enough money in the world! And He knows my heart. So with that, I decided its okay to perform. 'Cause God said so. And when I opened up that door, I let everybody know I was available again. Jocelyn called, I did a show with her in London, and it was phenomenal! Three days of all *good*, on stage again — we had a ball! It was just something!"

Barbara is recording again in the 21st century, enjoying club and event dates and appreciating the recognition she is given today as an accomplished and respected soul, disco and gospel singer/musician. Looking back on the disco era, Roy feels good about the experience but acknowledges the evolution of the music was inevitable. She says, "Disco did what it was supposed to do when it was here and, actually, it never went away. The '70s and '80s era music never left. It was music people could relate to — it didn't degrade anybody; it didn't bring anybody down — if anything it would heighten you, lift you up and make you feel good. Anything that warms the heart like that is not going to go away. But it had to be pushed aside for a minute or two because the new thing came in, and that had to happen. Change is always going to happen. One of my church band members came to me the other day and said, 'I heard your song on the radio.' I said, 'You did?' He said, 'Yeah — Ecstasy,

Passion & Pain. I knew it was you ... your voice hasn't changed!' I asked what song they played, and it was 'Touch and Go.' On 102.3 — that is a major station here in Washington, D.C. It's not underground, not hip-hop. It's a major station that plays major music. It made me feel good to hear that!

"I'll tell you what change did bother me and still does to a degree today — when everything started going *technical.* You know, CDs, no more live bands on the stage and all that — life took a stab in the heart. First of all, it cost so many people their jobs — the very people that make the music that makes the world go 'round. The type of music that makes the old feel young. Musicians couldn't find jobs. There was a time when jobs were plentiful in the industry — singing, playing, writing, producing, arranging — whatever. But when technology came in, it seemed to just ice everything. But the true musicians, those who loved music at the heart — they're still around. Those who are still with us, they're doing what they can do ... and so am I. *So am I!*"

The powerful voice and talent of Barbara Roy is, without question, divinely inspired and contributed significantly to the quality and legitimacy of disco's very beginnings. Bar-

Looking back on her dance music legacy, Barabara Roy says, "Disco did what it was supposed to do when it was here and, actually, it never went away. The '70s and '80s era music never left" (courtesy George "Iz" Corriea).

bara again thinks of her devout faith when contemplating her musical legacy. "If you ask an artist how they want to be remembered, they usually say that they want to be remembered as a good person, that they helped people — that kind of thing. I want all that. Yes — everyone does. But I want people to remember me as a person who gave them something that turned their lives around and turned their lives to Christ — from bad to good. I want them to remember me singing a song on stage, and [after hearing me] they were ready to stop drinking, turn the drugs loose, stop being promiscuous. Ready to give their life to God — *and they did*! That's how I want people to remember me!"

Pamala Stanley

Pamala Stanley is proof positive of the tenacity of the women who pioneered disco music. After a well-received debut at the peak of the '70s disco explosion with the aptly-titled song and album *This Is Hot* (an album that burst not only with dance hits, but also with a plethora of well-crafted, hook-laden pop songs), Pamala found herself caught in the genre backlash, deserted by her label and left with little choice but to reinvent herself. She did so with spectacular results and would go on to be one of the '80s premier dance music artists. Her path to success has been a winding, unstoppable and adventurous journey—"magical" in her words—and it has served to bolster her already remarkably positive attitude.

Says Pamala, "I had a very talented family. For instance, my grandfather played piano, banjo, guitar, mandolin, ukulele and he would write silly songs. He didn't make a living at it, but he was always the life of the party, and I remember him making everybody very happy. My brother James taught my sister Sandra and I how to harmonize at age six, so by the time I was about eight, we were entering singing contests and winning. We actually got a recording deal when I was 10, and I just sang, sang, sang all the time. I didn't have a question as to what I was going to be in life. I didn't even prepare—like when people go to college and want to be able to have something to fall back on. That never even entered my mind. After I got older, I started analyzing that decision and thought, 'What was I thinking? You're just gonna sing and make a living at it?'" she laughs. "But I absolutely did! I would sing pop, oldies shows, rock. I sang every kind of music, and I made it my life."

"I will tell you I did *not* have a vision of being in dance music. I wanted to be on Broadway. I wanted to be in musical comedy. I think I was about 25 when I went to New York. I had been auditioning for a plays and working at a piano bar on 46th Street. A German producer, Karl Schmitz, happened to come in with a French artist, and they wanted to use the piano. He heard me and decided he wanted me to go to Germany and make a 'white Donna Summer' out of me. He said in a heavy accent, 'I think you'd do very good in Germany!' So they flew me over on Lufthansa, and I spent a week there singing and recording, just to see how I sounded. Then I was offered a record deal through EMI Germany—the *This Is Hot* album. And that's how I got into dance music. I was comfortable with disco. Singing is singing as far as I was concerned."

The song "This Is Hot," the lush and pounding title track from her EMI-Germany debut album, was a magnificent collaboration between producer and songwriter Joachim Heider and Stanley. Pamala recalls, "I wrote 'This Is Hot' and 'Heart of a Clown' with Heider and three songs—'Mr. Sunshine,' 'Only You Can Reach Me' and 'What I Like Is You,' with lyricist David Zippel. He also wrote the lyrics to songs from Broadway plays like *City of Angels* and *The Goodbye Girl* and was nominated for an Academy Award. I wrote two songs myself, 'You Are My Love' and 'That'll Be the Day.'

"They would sit me down with the arranger every day and ask me what I wanted from this song and that song. I learned quite a bit about writing from that album. I was completely involved the entire time. They would ask me what type of instruments I'd like in a song, and they'd add them. The Berlin Opera House Symphony Orchestra was used on a few of the songs. Forty-five pieces getting ready to do disco! Imagine! It was *great* back then!" she recalls with excitement.

"I was absolutely in awe of the whole experience," Stanley adds. "I have to say, the Germans were amazing! When I went there, we worked 10 A.M. to 7 P.M. every day. Nobody was allowed to work later. No matter what point you were at, that's the end of the day. You never worked on a Sunday. They treat their music exactly like a job. It's very interesting! I have to say, though, they have very odd record jackets over there. Check out the European version of the album. I mean, to me, the jacket picture of me on the back looked like I had just been hooking all night. It's hysterical!"

"This Is Hot" became a big hit in Germany and throughout Europe during the spring of 1979. A lavish production with a powerful Euro-disco sound, the record caught the ear of EMI-America, who enlisted DJ and producer Rick Gianatos to enhance it for domestic audiences. "It was so unbelievable! I remember the first time I was back in New York, and I was in a record store and a man walks in. He's got my 'This Is Hot' 12" single in his hands, and he's getting ready to buy it. So, [laughing] I said, 'Oh you're buying "This Is Hot."' He says, 'Yeah, my daughter wants this record.' I asked him if he wanted me to sign it because that was me. He says, 'Yeah, right! Get away from me!' Well that's New York! The song first did well in Europe, and I was on all the pop charts— Amsterdam, Germany, England. I did some major T.V. It was fantastic. Rick Gianatos remixed the album for the U.S., and he was amazing. It was a beautiful record, but when Rick got ahold of it, it was really incredible. It was fun to sit in with him on some of the mixes. Then they re-did the cover, and I loved the U.S. version. I thought the 'This Is Hot' [layout] with all the red was really cool."

Pamala Stanley, seen here in 1986, made her recording debut at the height of disco in 1979 and went on to become one of the '80s most successful dance music performers with the hits "Coming Out of Hiding" and "If Looks Could Kill" (courtesy Pamala Stanley).

The promotion of the album in the U.S. gave Stanley the opportunity to hone her club diva skills, and it a started life-long connection with gay fans. "The label gave me this great guy named Joey Palmentieri, who is not with us anymore," she says, "and he was my promo exec. A fabulous gay man! He started booking me in gay clubs. I had never done that before. I had worked gay piano bars in New York City, but not the discos. I remember he booked me at some place called the Red Parrot or something on Santa Monica Blvd., and they didn't even have stages in those clubs. They would put a piece of plywood over the pool table, and I would hop up there and you'd have to sing around the [overhead] lamp and not knock your head on it. Sometimes they'd just pile up beer boxes in front of the deejay booth, and he'd hand me a little microphone and the cord wouldn't even go that far. Some of the jobs I did were absolutely hysterical. But it was fun. It was the start of live disco acts in the clubs."

Pamala had no problem assimilating into the club stomping ground or handling the nightlife. "I never got involved in drugs at clubs. I didn't even drink alcohol at that time. The clubs treated me well. They would always ask what I needed, and I'd say orange juice and Perrier. It was that easy for me. I never even realized half the time that people were doing drugs. I knew they did poppers—I could see that when I was singing—and I knew they had back rooms and naked dancers on the bar in some of the clubs, but I was never bothered or affected by it. They had their business, and I had mine. I loved the gay community, and they have always been good to me. I'm not sure I'd have the career I have if it wasn't for them. There weren't a lot of live performance opportunities in Europe at the time. I remember I played the Lido in Amsterdam, and the reception was incredible. But that was just a pop audience. When I got to L.A. and started playing for the gay community, they were so demonstrative, warm and receptive—I probably felt more comfortable here."

The wave Stanley rode was short-lived as the decade drew to a close and the tide of popularity turned against disco. Label support for Stanley ground to a sudden halt. "I had a manager who screwed up my opportunity to record a second album for Europe," she says. "My manager had delusions of grandeur about her promotion career here in the U.S., and so I never knew I had an offer to stay with Europe and do another album. I didn't find that out until much later. Also, what happened was the *This Is Hot* LP came out in September of 1979, and I was up to number 13 on the club charts with the song. In November, the big headlines were, 'Disco is dead!' EMI in the U.S. totally closed down its dance operations. I was out on the road promoting the record, and I tried to call Joey and was told he didn't work at EMI anymore. I asked to speak to someone in the disco department and they told me, 'There is no disco department.' They left me on the road in Miami in the middle of my tour. I was literally abandoned. And then they didn't renew my contract."

Pamala had a knack for perseverance, however. "It was quite a shock. I wasn't sure what I would do. But then I got a job down in Ecuador performing, and I got my album released down there. As soon as I got down there, I had EMI South America call EMI America, and they made the deal. I got my album released in a week. I even got my own Christmas special on TV. I went down there and had a ball! I was like the American Charo because my Spanish was all broken. It was incredible. My mother always said my guardian angel must be exhausted!

"After I left Ecuador, I got married to my second husband, Frank Mandaro, and I decided to quit the business. I stopped singing as a recording artist for a few years, and I had my baby. I would sing at a little piano bar once in a while, and I had my little house. I was happy. Then someone asked me to sing in Dallas, where my husband was working with an oil company, and we had relocated. So, I went and did this live show, and my husband saw it and asked me why I wasn't back out there using my voice. We started to put together a record company with two wonderful men who owned a record store in Dallas—Ray Cooper and David Hilzandager." She laughs, "Even my gynecologist wanted to invest in it! I have to give credit where it's due. My husband, Frank, pushed me out there. His father had died some time before, and I think he was realizing that life is short and you have to go for it!" she says.

With Pamala's energy recharged, she began her second foray into dance music and successfully emerged as one of the genre's most revered vocalists. It began with a 1983 track called "I Don't Want to Talk About It," first released by Komander Records, which became a Top-20 dance hit. She remembers, "My brother, James Lee Stanley, had written a country song called 'I Don't Want to Talk About It,' and he had sent it to me. I was in my car and Michael Jackson's 'Beat It' and 'Billie Jean' came on. I heard the beat and, for some reason, I started singing 'I Don't Want to Talk About It.' So we hired a producer to try and build on that song as a dance vehicle. But all he did was copy the groove of 'Billie Jean.' Once again, my husband stepped in and told me to get in there and produce it and fix it up. So, that's what I did! We put it out, and I thought it would just be this little record in Texas. Never knew it would go worldwide! You know, at the time you don't always realize what you have. You're just trying to make something good. Then it started hitting the club charts."

Momentum building, Stanley felt her next song should pay tribute to the fans that had supported her career. "I started playing a lot of gay clubs again, and I decided I needed a really good song for the gay guys — because they had been so great to me. So, I called my brother again and said, 'I want a gay anthem!' My brother is straight and said, 'Gay anthem? Okaaaay....' About six weeks later, I get this song from him called 'Coming Out of Hiding' and I go, 'This is amazing!' I called him and told him how incredible the song was and asked him how he came up with it. He said he wasn't even sure why it came into his mind. It's not like he studied the gay community, but that phrase came to his mind. He wrote it not realizing he captured exactly what the gay community wanted to do. Isn't that wild? Frank and I produced it, and it was huge!" The song, initially released by the prolific high-energy label TSR Records, became Stanley's biggest dance hit and, she says, her most commercially successful record worldwide. It also became an astonishingly rallying force for a community struggling against the damage of AIDS and fighting for the right to come out of the closet.

TSR's Tom Hayden says, "Pamala was always a pleasure to work with. We had a lot of fun on 'Coming Out of Hiding.' She brought it to us, and the production was just great on it. It had a fullness that sounded great in clubs and had a slight 'delayed' sound on it that she and her team were insistent on using to the fullest. And I think that really helped the record. It was an easy one to promote. It started exploding immediately after we released it, and then it moved onto the pop charts. I got a call from Jerry Greenberg at Atlantic Records because, at the time, we were also handling all the independent promotions for that label. We did probably 60 percent of the club records that were coming out on Atlantic, and they were putting out four or five a week. He called me and said he was dreaming about Pamala's record and wanted it for Atlantic. It had already hit the pop charts, and he said they could take it all the way up the chart if we would license it to them. I believed they were going to make it a top priority. I had discussed it with Pamala and her husband, Frank, and we all felt it would be a great opportunity [for her to be with] a major label. All deals have to be good for both parties; it can't just be a one-sided situation. So we gave it to them as a license for a couple of years, but they kind of dropped the ball as far as the pop charts were concerned. We had taken it Top Five on the dance charts, and, with Atlantic, it didn't get much further up on the pop chart than where we'd gotten it. They had about five or six other major records that were tied to big albums, and they ended up putting those at the top of the heap and pushed ours down the list. I called Jerry about it a year or two after he'd licensed it and told him I really needed to get it back in the TSR catalog because a lot of people still wanted the 12" single of 'Coming Out of Hiding' and their label hadn't done a good job of marketing it. The week we got it back, we sold 10,000 singles just from back-orders of everybody who wanted the record, but couldn't get it on Atlantic!"

Stanley, producing songs that were well-timed to the demands of the marketplace, had a knack for craftsmanship and a sense for detail that were essential elements of her recording success. "Every section of 'I Don't Want to Talk About It' and 'Coming Out of Hiding' was carefully planned," she says proudly. "I would say, 'Does this section thrill me?' And if it didn't, I'd keep working on it. Let me tell you, we remixed 'Coming Out of Hiding' three times before that was released. We'd mix it, listen to it in a club — it wasn't right. Went back in — 'What's missing, what's missing?' I worked that song over until I heard it, top to bottom, and every measure worked."

The artist's greatest cross-genre success would follow with 1985's "If Looks Could Kill," covered later by the rock band Heart. Credited to both Pamala and husband Frank as producers (and Chris Barbosa and Mark Liggett — the formulators of Shannon's 1983 breakthrough "Let the Music Play" — on an alternate version), Stanley says it was her version that made the charts. A pop-style rendition of Stanley's song appeared in the Arnold Schwarzenegger film *Raw Deal*. "It's one of those thrills of a lifetime," Stanley observes. "They just called — Orion Pictures got in touch and asked if I'd allow it to be in the movie. I was like, '*Yeah!*' We couldn't wait to run and see the movie. I still have the movie on a VHS tape; that's how old it is. Then we saw the scene and heard the intro to the song and saw Arnold walking all around the club. They swooped in, and there was a drag queen lip synching to my song — I roared! I thought, 'Well, that's appropriate!' Because I was always in the dressing room with them, and I made more drag queen friends! I always got tips from them — they taught me to put eyelash glue under your shoulder pads to keep them in place! I learned that and lots of thing! It was so funny!"

Despite the thrill ride, the artist's life was not immune to the pain of loss that many in the industry had experienced. "I've worked with so many great performers: Vicki Sue Robinson, Loleatta Holloway, The Pointer Sisters' June Pointer, Sharon Redd and Viola Wills — another good friend of mine. It's so sad. Donna Summer and Whitney Houston — two of our greatest. There's so many gone now. Sylvester ... oh my God, I hated when he went. Paul Parker nursed Sylvester. Literally — Paul was a nurse. He would carry him back and forth to the bed. He was an angel, and he was really amazing. Paul and I recorded 'Running Around in Circles' and 'Strangers (in a Strange Land)' after we met at the Backstreet Club in Ft. Lauderdale. We've also lost so many club owners. They were the owners of the biggest clubs, and they were the first to go at the beginning of the AIDS crisis. Some of them — they had the money to buy the drugs, and I think that compromised their immune systems. I always knew the ones who usually went first were the heavy druggers, the heavy partiers. And nobody knew why they were dying ... it was scary in the beginning."

However, the good far outweighed the bad for Stanley, and she fondly recalls a number of more pleasant career highlights. Her voice becomes warm with pride as she recounts some memorable moments. "Having the video for 'Coming Out of Hiding' become a worldwide hit—that's a pretty amazing thing. To turn on the television and see your video playing! Or when I was in Boston and heard 'I Don't Want to Talk About It' on the radio for the first time, driving down the street. The first time you hear your song on the radio is pretty thrilling. I think playing Washington, D.C.'s gay pride at the monument with thousands of people ... *that* was a big deal. They were there for a bigger reason, but they are also screaming for me—it was just incredible. I think singing the National Anthem at the L.A. Rams–New Orleans Saints game—that was pretty amazing. Singing at Lee Iacocca's retirement party in Vegas. It actually feels surreal, as if you're standing on the outside watching. You're performing, but you're in awe because you're so thankful that you're there. It's a love affair. It's like lovemaking in the purest form—a true love affair between your audience and yourself. Imagine being madly in love—that's what it feels like. When you perform, it's like going out on a first date every night. And each audience is a new being," she warmly opines.

Stanley looks back on the women who pioneered disco and dance music. "I feel that we paved the way for dance artists today like Lady Gaga. We were the beginning. I have to tell you, honestly, when I read stuff about me on Wikipedia or wherever—about me being a dance music innovator—I had no clue. You're just trying to make good music. I think Madonna opened it up for everybody. I had hits around the same time as when she began. I wish I had been as smart as she was in planning. I look at what she's done, and I respect the woman for how she marketed herself. She just blew it wide open. My son is 29 and his friends have all my music—and they love the stuff. They are rediscovering this dance music of ours, and it's really great!"

If remixes are the sincerest form of flattery, Stanley might have a swelled head at this point in time. "Almighty Records did a pretty good job on remixing 'Coming Out of Hiding,'" she says. "Almighty's remixes of the song are probably the only ones I've liked. There was another one that came out that I liked, but it's rare. I always say, 'Make it better!' I don't care; show me up! Don't come out with a mediocre remix. You gotta blow it up. Just do my songs better than me, and I'm okay with that. As long as it's all above boards. I have some songs out all over the world where I've never made a cent off them. I will hear versions I had no idea even existed, but you get used to it. You know what's amazing? That nobody took the song 'This Is Hot' and ever re-recorded it. I guess I should re-do it because I'm always thinking of ways I can update a song!"

Stanley is mindful of the aging process. She says, "I went through a period where I had to deal with the fact that I'm getting older. I'm not going to have the in-shape body I once had, and I felt you make a trade with that. I saw Frank Sinatra perform in Vegas in the early '90s, and I never saw a performer with such ease before an audience. He was very comfortable, and he didn't try. When you get that experience, you trade the years that you have for the comfort of being in that moment. It's okay if you make a mistake; it's okay if you're not perfect. It's okay if your voice cracks, which mine does sometimes, because your audience is always rooting for you. They *want* you to do well. I got to the point where I look at it as—I go on stage and I'm having a party in my living room. It's just a party in my living room. And you're in my house, and I'm going to be the best host I can be. My job is to bring you joy. That's all I care about. If you come to my show and you leave happy and joyous, I'm good. I've had 21-year-olds and 80-year-olds come to my shows, and both are in love with my performance. If they could get in under the age of 21, I'd have 'em even younger. It's not about me; it's about them. All I do is have fun. When I do a show, I also don't just do my own stuff. When I do a show, I do Lady Gaga. I'll do Laura Branigan, or a song like 'It's Raining Men.' Maybe something by Adele. You have to do that. Don't just stick with yourself. Other people make good music. But sometimes, I'm on stage laughing doing 'Coming Out of Hiding' almost 30 years later. Not laughing at people or the song — I just get a kick out of it. Thirty years later, I'm still doing it! Don't take life too seriously ... from now until death, it's about fun!"

Today, Pamala continues to record. In recent years, she released a greatest hits compilation through her own label called *Looking Back: The Disco Years 1979–1989*, *Live and Cookin'*, a beautiful album of standards called *It's All in the Game* and *Seasons of the Heart*, which showcased her versatile pop vocals and prolific songwriting skills. She remains a remarkable live performer. As evidence, one need only check out her hilarious video rendition of "Is There a Straight Man in the House," one of many examples of her talent floating about on YouTube. Almighty Records in the U.K. unleashed new mixes of her perennial hit "If Looks Could Kill" to rave reviews in 2012, and Stanley is currently developing a new version of "Suspicious Minds." which will solidify her ranking as a premier dance music artist in the 21st century.

Pamala Stanley enjoys looking back at her achievements. "I'm on stage laughing doing 'Coming Out of Hiding' almost 30 years later. Not laughing at people or the song — I just get a kick out of it. Thirty years later, I'm still doing it!" (courtesy Pamala Stanley).

Pamela Stanley keeps doing what she does best, and her exquisite vocal contributions as one of the original ladies of disco will resonate for years to come. When her extraordinary musical legacy is reflected upon, she'd like "to be remembered as a great singer and a joy-bringer. I'd also like to be known as a good producer and a fun person to work with. But to bring joy — that's *really* what I want to be remembered for. Singing well and bringing joy — I'm happy!"

Evelyn Thomas

Something as dazzling as the song "High Energy," an explosive, game-changing dance music anthem, doesn't come along often. The song's pounding beat and euphoric sound stunned audiences back in 1984. With its success, Evelyn Thomas became an international star. Raising the bar with her unrestrained, powerhouse voice, "High Energy" not only became a club and radio smash, it ushered in a whole new type of dance music that would bridge the fire of old-school disco with the harder-sounding, warrior drive of the mid-'80s and beyond. It was the *must-have* single of its year and defined a genre of music that endures to this day. For Thomas, who earned both gold and platinum records, it would be a remarkable career highlight and the experience of a lifetime.

Evelyn's beginnings were not unlike those of many young vocalists of the day. She describes her early days with a warm, humorous sense of nostalgia. "My mother was a singer and also a CPA. She sang for the church. My grandmother was a soprano and had a gorgeous voice. She could really lay it down! We had music in our house 24–7; that's just the way it was. I discovered singing when I was seven years old, and I had no doubt — I just knew I had no option to do anything else. I had been practicing and doing everything a person can do to hone their craft as best I could from that age. When I was about 14 years old, looking very much like I was 18 — with the makeup and all that stuff — I used to sneak out of the house. I don't suggest that young kids do that, but I did it, and I would go to a club called the Green Onion in Chicago. There were members of Earth, Wind & Fire there, the Chi-Lites, different singers that all became huge. We used to sing with each other all night long till about five in the morning. I just really caught the bug! When I was about 16, I got with a band called the Mood Mixers, and we traveled all over Chicago doing jazz and R&B everywhere. We never did any dance music, but we did plenty of R&B and jazz. That's when it kind of started for me.

"I absolutely had a vision I would be successful, and I *still* have that vision! No vision — you can't go anywhere. I just had a passion for music and anything creative, and I still have that passion today," she says.

"There were two gentlemen in the Mood Mixers band, one named 'Pumpkin'— and I don't remember this boy's real name to this day, we just always called him 'Pumpkin'— and L.J. Johnson. One particular evening, Pumpkin said to me he was going to try out for a recording contract. So I went with him and L.J. for the ride, and we went to [well-known recording engineer, guitarist and session player] Danny Leake's house in Chicago. Ian Levine was there, and he was looking for a male artist. So Pumpkin tried out and Ian loved his voice, but for some reason he didn't think Pumpkin

Evelyn Thomas' monumental "High Energy," its 1984 American 12-inch single cover seen here, launched an entire subgenre of pounding disco music (courtesy Tom Hayden/TSR Records).

had the right look or whatever. So he just didn't hire him. Barbara Pennington was also there, and that was the first time I had met her. Pumpkin said, 'Evelyn, why don't you try out for it.' I said, 'No, no,' because at the time I thought Ian was pretty obnoxious, to be honest with you. I wasn't used to that type of person with his kind of personality. He was very ... scary. I was about 20 years old, and I had just had my daughter at age 19. But I got up the guts and asked him if I could audition, and he just said he wasn't looking for any females. I said, 'Well, maybe in the future you might need one.' He just said, 'No, no, no, no females.' I felt kind of bad because I got up the nerve to ask him, and he turned me down. So then Danny took Ian in the back and talked to him—and to this day I don't know what he said to Ian—but then they came back and Ian said, 'Okay, go ahead, but I'm only giving you a few minutes.' I sang Gladys Knight & the Pips' 'Neither One of Us' a capella. Before I could finish with the whole song, Ian jumped off the couch and told me how wonderful I was. He said, 'I would have never dreamed something like that could come out of someone like you!' I was like, 'Really?'" she laughs sarcastically, imitating her tone at the time. "I hadn't been dressed for the audition; I just had on jeans and a funny little t-shirt, little jeans cap—I wasn't dressed to meet anybody."

Thomas observes, "I'm pretty knowledgeable about the business today, and had I known then what I know today, I would have changed a lot of things. Especially when it came to the business end of it, okay? As soon as Ian discovered I could sing and everything was wonderful, he said, 'Would you like a recording contract?' I said, 'Absolutely!' And he said, 'Well come back here in the kitchen and sign this contract.' I signed it. And that was the beginning of everything. I think about it sometimes, and it was kind of dumb, but, you know, you're young and excited and you're not thinking of the business end of it. This is what I tell young artists today, 'Honey, I love that you can sing, but you know today singers come a dime a dozen. There are a lot of people singing. There's a lot of talent in this world—period. You *must* learn the business end of it. That's what's gonna keep you going. Perfect the craft, yes, but find out what you're in. Find out what publishing is all about. Find out about copyrighting—whatever. You need to be well-rounded in this business. You have to have passion for this business or you can't stay in it.' That was it for me—and I'm still in it!"

Levine's instincts about Evelyn's voice were on the mark and her zippy 1976 debut as a professional recording artist yielded stellar results, much to her surprise. "The first song I did with Ian was recorded in Chicago and was called 'Weak Spot.' I thought 'Weak Spot' was the silliest song I had ever sung in my whole entire life! I thought nobody would like that song. I thought it was insane!" she admits.

The song ended up a major pop hit with a disco flavor in the U.K., but its success and this new musical direction were a challenge for Thomas. "Okay, you're talking to a black girl who did nothing but jazz and R&B. Then comes along this producer with a whole different outlook on music—period! He asked me to take my jazz intonations and the way I did R&B and put it in this dance thing. This music was music that I was really unfamiliar with. But, you know, it worked and it went to number 5 on the British charts. I was in London and I did *Top of the Pops,* and it was fascinating meeting these television personalities. It was so '*for real*,' and it was the biggest show you could do over there. Honey, let me tell you, I felt like Granny on *The Beverly Hillbillies.* You know it was a good time. I was young—you're not afraid of anything; you try everything! There were times, though, they'd be talking to me over there and I couldn't understand anything they were saying with those accents.

"It was overwhelming," she says, "but so much fun. I didn't mind the dance music so much. Some of it wasn't bad, but it just wasn't always me. You know? It kind of became a music that actually had to grow on me. After 'Weak Spot' came the real disco. They were calling this kind of music northern soul—it wasn't called *disco* yet. Then came disco and then high energy [music]—that's where I really came in."

Thomas was professionally linked to Levine for a considerable time, but the partnership hadn't yet created its ultimate moment. An album on Casablanca Records, *I Wanna Make It on My Own*, and scattered singles like the Rick Gianatos-remixed "My Head's in the Stars" garnered modest attention but failed to propel the singer's career much further. "I wanted to work with other people, but I was contractually tied down to Ian. After my contract was up, I did work with Bill Curtis and Jerry Thomas of the Fatback Band. I did a lot of gigs traveling all over the world. Then Ian got back in touch with me in 1984. Our split-up had been ... well, let's say he was the type of producer who would do a project with you and after it was over with, you didn't hear anything else from him. It's like you didn't exist. I didn't like that. I'm being right upfront! I'm sure he was busy with other artists—in fact I know he was—but I never received, business-wise, what he was supposed to deliver. He just didn't deliver. He let me down. So, he calls me in 1984 and says, 'Let's try this thing one more time.' Right? He wanted to do this song called 'High Energy' and I agreed, and we went back into the studio. [Producer and composer] Hans Zimmer, who would later be famous for movie scores, was very instrumental in making 'High Energy' sound the way it did. Because this guy was a master at sound—period! Ian had called him in to help produce it, and when I went into [the studio] to do it, I knew it was going to be something special. I gave that song *everything* I had inside of me! I think that it was really amazing—it was one of those songs you could really lay out and have some fun with it. It was great! We changed a whole genre of music! It was a mega-hit in the U.S.—number 1 everywhere! Even more so in Europe—absolutely huge!"

"High Energy," co-written and co-produced by Ian Levine and Fiachra Trench, made it to number 1 on the U.S. dance charts and crossed over to the lower regions of this country's pop charts. The song didn't just coax dancers to the floor—it yanked them out there. It was handled domestically by TSR Records' Tom Hayden. "Evelyn's record came out about six months after Miquel Brown's 'So Many Men.' We had such great success with Miquel, and with all the money we had paid Record Shack, I think they wanted to give us this record," Hayden recalls. "I think Ian Levine capitalized on the high energy music that was out there and popular in the clubs. The terminology 'Hi-NRG' was already in the clubs, and I think Ian had the foresight to observe that and title the song 'High Energy.' It was right in line with what was happening out there. By the time we had signed the deal, it was becoming a huge hit overseas, and we had it out here in the States within a week. It had only about a one-week release jump on us in the U.K. We had sent test pressings out to all the *Billboard* reporting agents, and, within a week, it was already on the charts. Within three to four weeks, it was number 1. It was a very big song for us, and we sold a whole lot of 12" singles. It was dominating the clubs, and we got a lot of airplay in Florida, all the New York stations, L.A. and all the major cities."

Thomas' song, with its pounding, almost marching-style music beat and euphoric vocal crescendo, was particularly well-received in Europe, where it trampled the competition to reach the number 1 spot on the German pop charts and number 5 in the U.K. Evelyn has a deep affection for her overseas fans and an appreciation for the reception they gave her music. "As an artist, we don't realize the impact we have on people with our music really. Europe always embraced me more. Europe was very different. They respect their artists, and they remember their artists. They support them to this day. That's just what they do. I love them for that. I might have made Europe my home. The only reason I didn't was that I had my daughter in the United States, and I didn't want the girl growing up here not knowing I was her mother. And my grandmother was in the States and at the time she wasn't that well, so I had to look after her too. It was family ties that kept me here. I really believe, had that not been the situation, I would have definitely moved to London. I love it over there! I love Paris. Just take me to Paris and feed me! I love it!" she enthusiastically announces.

"When something like 'High Energy' happens, I try to savor every moment of it. When I stood on stage — and there were [thousands of] people in some of the places I appeared — I was more in awe of those people than they were of me. I'm standing there and saying, 'I cannot believe this — that I am here, doing exactly what I dreamed I could do — thank you God!' It was just so surreal and beautiful. I just wish that at the time — it happened so fast — that I had some people that were true friends that I could have shared it with more. Even though you're in front of all these people doing what you want to do, I felt like I was on my own. But it was okay; it was okay. I enjoyed myself; it wasn't a negative thing at all. I'm just being honest. I'm the type of person that likes to share. That was the only downside to the whole thing. That song was good for me. Every artist has their 'just for them' song, and that was it for me!"

Thomas confesses there was a lot of pressure to have a successful follow-up to such an enormous song. "Absolutely! That song was so big that I could probably have taken a vacation for four years. It was *that* big. It was huge! I personally thought they should have come out with a ballad afterwards. They went for the song 'Masquerade,' and that song didn't do it. They should have come out with something more funky or a ballad like 'How Could You Be So Heartless' — you know, change it up a little bit. Or they could have found someone to produce or write something different. At the time, they wouldn't let me write; they were doing all the writing. I just felt like we should have come back with something else, but nobody listened," she laughs. "We milked it for everything it was worth, and they're still milking it today. It was a great thing though; it's what put me on the map. I was on the map a little bit with 'Weak Spot,' but 'High Energy' just changed the whole thing. I can't erase 'High Energy,' and I wouldn't. I love it! 'High Energy' — are you kidding? Sometimes, I listen to it and I can't believe that's me singing! That was a great song then and it still is today, so I don't mind at all that it's considered my signature song!"

The artist pauses and adds, "I regret the fact that I didn't get to write more. Well, actually I *did* write back then, but I didn't get credit for it for some reason. Writing is very important — it's the core of the business. It gives you a chance to express yourself. And a chance to get paid!" she laughs. "As far as vocals go, the Record Shack label paid me $16,000. I never received another dime for 'High Energy' or anything else I did. I've sometimes heard [the song has sold as many as] seven to 11 million copies and is still selling. I didn't get a dime for any of [those sales] after the $16,000. Any money I got was from doing my gigs and making other things happen. With the ups and downs of this industry — I'm telling you — you have to really love it."

Issues surrounding color did not manifest themselves often in the singer's experience she reports, but Thomas was not immune to prejudice entirely. "Well, if anyone did have prejudices against me, I didn't notice it," she laughs. "But on my album covers they would always make me look really light; they would change my skin color and stuff. So, in Germany, nobody really knew what I looked like. One day, I hit a German stage for the first time, and I'm telling you—all I saw were these stunned faces. They were looking at me like I was a ghost, like I really wasn't Evelyn. One guy actually pointed to his skin and held up and pointed to my album cover asking, 'Is that *really* you?' because they thought I was white. Okay? My first album cover, it was with the Casablanca label, they didn't even do a photo of me. They said they didn't like the pictures that were taken of me, so they did a cartoon. Here I am—a cartoon with all this long flowing hair—*come on*! I guess it didn't bother me at the time because—it just didn't bother me. I have to say that because in my family we have Jewish white people, Indian and African American. I was raised with all that, so it didn't bother me. I didn't even think about it really. I suppose it could have hindered me from a few things I could have gotten, but I never let it bother me."

The artist's formidable gay following was, and remains, a natural audience for her to embrace. "I loved having a gay audience," she says. "There were times where my audience was quite diverse—it just depended on where you went. The gay community embraced me, and I embraced them. I loved them, and they *still* support me. My audience now is a little bit more diverse today because of some of the songs I'm singing, you know. But let me tell you something—my sister is gay. And I love her with everything in my body. She taught me about all of it. And I learned about it from her friends when I was little girl. She was always my sister and she was always gay, so I never saw anything different. Her name is Diane—they call her 'Red.' I'm not religious—I'm spiritual. You either know God or you don't. There's no condemnation in going out [to clubs]. I've been going to the clubs since I was yay high, and I'm still going. If people want to get into that bible thing, well, where did Jesus go? He hung out with us. That's where he was. I know who God is, and I know He knows who I am. And that's a personal relationship that I have—nothing to do with anybody else. So, everybody has their opinion, and I'm entitled to mine. That's where I stand with that!

"With the clubs, I can't say I didn't party, because I did!" she adds. "I mean, not the way some people did. But I didn't sit there and judge anybody. You mind your own business in this business. And if that's what people wanted to do, then that's what they did. I'm a quiet person you know; I would just do my shows and pretty much disappear. I would be in my hotel room lookin' at some TV thing or whatever. Or having dinner. I was just one of those people who, after the show was over and I did autograph signing, most of the time we would go out to dinner, and then I'd head back to my hotel room and get ready for the next day. I just stayed to myself, and it was really all just about business to me. A lot of people liked to stay up and have a lot of fun with each other, which I would do just once in a while. However, it was time to go to bed when you knew you had to be up and on the circuit at 7 A.M. There's a lot to singing—you can't just jump up on the stage and start singing. Physically, you have to be ready for that stuff."

Following her tremendous success, Evelyn remained a presence on the club charts for several years, with "Heartless" crossing onto R&B charts in the U.S. and "Reflections" (a Supremes cover) and "How Many Hearts" scoring on the dance side. After a break from recording for several years, the artist returned to the studio in the late '90s. Her revival of "High Energy," via a 2005 remix, was well received in gay clubs throughout the world. The singer reunited with Ian Levine for the single "Pounding the Pavement." In recent years, Thomas recorded the progressive and addictive songs, "Stick to the Plan" and "Missing the Target" and teamed with producer Laurent Wolf for the Anton Wick hit "That's It," a lyrically savvy floor-filler written by Thomas and released by Sony in 2011.

She reflects on her history, dance music and maturing in the industry. Her tone is positive, and her attitude about flexibility is clear. She says, "I was sitting here the other day and I was thinking, 'Where did all the years go?' I can't say I've been disrespected being a dance artist. I don't know — different types of music — it goes in and it goes out. Then it comes back around again. You have to respect that times change, people change, new generations come and with them come new ideas. So music is gonna change too. As an artist, you try to be in there with that. You don't have to change; you can remain true to yourself. But you should always be working towards creating —*always creating*. If you have the passion for music and that's what you want to do with their life, you can't have problems with change.

"As far as aging goes, well, one thing I do is I work out. When I got in my 50s, I started to go up and down with this yo-yo weight thing. Because after 50, your body starts saying, 'I'm gonna do it *this* way,' and you say, 'No, I wanna do it *that* way!' So you gotta stay in the gym; you gotta stay alert. And I have a business now called Evelyn Thomas Enterprises (evelynthomasenterprise.com) and it keeps me busy every day. I have a great partner, Chuck Stewart, and my husband, Anthony Simpson, he works with me. We do children's educational programs, animating them, writing the music, doing voices, working on movie soundtracks. So my career has evolved into something else, other than just singing and doing dance music — which I still do. Now I am at the point where I also do jazz and get my band together — so I'm just doing everything I wanna do. I have my hands in all the things I like. I'm just having fun being creative. I'm working on a charitable foundation as well. It's wonderful. Listen, I know I'm much older and I can't do everything the way I used to — but its okay. I can still do my thing!"

Evelyn Thomas' place in dance music history is safely secured with "High Energy" and her powerhouse vocal gift continues to set the bar. But the artist has little desire to rest on that accomplishment, and she wants to be remembered for much more. "I still have never said that '*I've made it.*' The 'High Energy' thing was great, but — to this day — I never thought, 'I've made it.' There are a lot of things I would still like to do, so much more I would like to do and so much more I would like to leave as a legacy. I'm

"You have to respect that times change, people change, new generations come and with them come new ideas. So music is gonna change too. As an artist, you try to be in there with that," professes Evelyn Thomas (courtesy Evelyn Thomas).

working on that. The best is yet to come! I'd like to be remembered as somebody who gave to people—something happy, fulfilling—and someone who brought something positive into their lives. I'm not finished, and I want to leave a legacy for all people who want to be in the industry. Young people that I work with now—I want to help them get educated so that they can sustain themselves and not have to scrape the money together to survive just to be who they are. My passion in life is to use my music, which I love, to make *other* things happen. My passion is for people!"

Jeanie Tracy

An artist whose career included a close friendship with (and extraordinary backup vocal work for) the legendary disco icon Sylvester, three number 1 *Billboard* hits and a string of immortal '80s club tracks might have reason to brag. Add in session work with the likes of Celine Dion, Patti Labelle and Aretha Franklin (and a remarkable voice that remains a major club force in the 21st century), and that artist might get a swelled head. Yet one would be hard-pressed to find a more unaffected, grounded and charming performer than Jeanie Tracy. She has enjoyed all of these accomplishments and experiences and many more. She possesses a remarkably sincere way about her, and when one hears this artist reflect on her life, it's impossible to remain unmoved by her candor. Jeanie has seen it all, lived to tell about it and continues to warmly embrace the dance-music fan community that has recognized her talent from the very start.

"I grew up in kind of a farming town between San Francisco and Los Angeles," says Jeanie. "It was a wonderful town, and I still have lots of friends there. Early on, my mother decided I would play a musical instrument, and she asked me what I'd like to play. She said that she would get me lessons. But, she said if she was going do this, I'd have to be really serious and [learn] it! So I chose the piano—we had one in our house, and it had just been sitting there because nobody played it. So, I took piano lessons from age six to about 17. I studied classical piano from Bach to Beethoven, and my mother decided I was going to be this classical pianist—*that I never became*," she laughs.

"I was really good at it, though. But what really interested me was singing, because my aunt (Jackie) was a singer. My aunt taught me many songs. When I got into the church, there was a minister who needed someone to play a piano there. I knew nothing about playing for the choir and such, so I asked my teacher to teach me how to play by ear. My teacher taught me a lot, and I became very good. I started to travel at a young age playing for the choir, and I began singing as well," says Tracy.

Her earliest career plans were, she admits, somewhat modest. "I really just wanted to be a school teacher and teach music. That's what my youthful sights were set on. But what ended up happening was a TV station in the area, KYNO, would do these big shows. Somehow, I met the DJs there and I got on a few of the shows, and I started rubbing elbows with some of the big stars that would come and perform on their programs. While there, I got an offer from a guy who had seen me play and sing, and he asked if I would join his

A stellar line-up of performers from the first days of disco mingle in the studio, circa 1978. Left to right are Izora Armstead, Dionne Warwick, Sylvester, Martha Wash and Jeanie Tracy (courtesy Jeanie Tracy).

band. I [turned him down] because I didn't know anything about being in a band. He called me a couple of times, and I still said, 'No!' He came by my house one evening and said he really needed me to help him because [one of his band members] had become ill. He grabbed me up and told me to just play what I knew and they'd follow. So that's what happened, and I played what I knew. Mostly Etta James and Aretha Franklin."

Tracy's talent and reputation began growing, and her stars aligned with those of Harvey Fuqua, a West Coast record producer and lead singer of the group Harvey and the Moonglows. He was a progressive music man who had been instrumental in the formation of the Motown label. "Harvey came to see me at a club I was playing at," recalls Tracy. "By then, I was just singing, and a local radio DJ had told Harvey he should hear me. It was a beautiful club. Harvey liked me and was very nice. I was really excited. I started going out to Harvey's studio, which he had converted from a big old Safeway store where he was working with his associate, Nancy Pitts. They had turned it into offices, studios—that kind of thing. Harvey wanted me to start writing songs for a choir he was producing. So I did that, and then I started to write songs for myself. Harvey wanted to form a family like Motown. [He was involved with] a big, rising performer named Sylvester, and Harvey invited me to go see him and the Two Tons of Fun—Martha Wash and Izora Armstead. Martha looked so familiar to me, and we were all backstage there laughing and talking. I discovered that Martha's brother, Ralph, had once been my lead guitar player. He had always told me, "Jeanie, you remind me so much of my sister! She's bad; she's really bad!' Martha and I hugged, and the reason I had thought she looked so familiar was that she looked just like Ralph! The girls and I became fast friends. Martha and I are very close to this day, and I [was friends with] Izora until her passing a few years ago. I even went to Germany a couple of times to be a Weather Girl!"

These new connections laid the foundation for a close friendship with Sylvester, who was poised to become one of disco's hottest and most unusual acts — thanks to his magnificent falsetto voice, great music material and flair for the flamboyant. His powerful backup girls were adding to the momentum. Jeanie recalls meeting the fascinating artist. "One day, I was over at the studio, and I could see Sylvester arrive. But when I first saw him, he looked like a woman. He wasn't in drag or anything like that. He just had bracelets and a tunic or something. Harvey invited me into the room where Sylvester was and I was listening, and Sylvester was throwing his hands all in the air," she laughs. "They said, 'Jeanie, this is Sylvester.' I said, 'Sylvester? I thought you were a woman!' I said, 'Oops, I'm very sorry.'" Jeanie changes her voice to a softer whisper to imitate Sylvester. "He said, 'Oh no girl, that's okay!'

"We hit it on and we started to chat and he ended up giving me this long beautiful blue sequined dress he had made. Things moved along, I went on singing and would go to their shows. They were still just a city-wide hit, and then Harvey started recording them. They initially signed with Honey Records and then Fantasy. I had not signed on yet, but I was in the wings. Harvey's Motown-style plan was going to be [to launch] Sylvester, then the girls, then [singer] Eric Robertson and then me. [Sylvester] had started to become really big with the first hits 'Dance Disco Heat' and 'Mighty Real,' traveling and that kind of thing.

"I opened for Sylvester in San Francisco. He really loved me and the girls — we really loved each other too. The girls were very big on telling Sylvester what they wanted, and they were very instrumental in letting him know they wanted *me* with them! It was also in Harvey's plan to have me sing with Sylvester. So Sylvester, when the money was right and everything, hired me to sing with the girls. But then they didn't know what to call us. They were calling us 'Tonage.' I wasn't a big woman at that time — I was curvy. It annoys me that some people try and erase me out of the group, but honey, *I was there*! When I came into the group, he used Martha and me quite a bit. Martha and Izora eventually left and later became the Weather Girls."

Jeanie adds, "I'm not [singing] on 'Dance Disco Heat' or 'Mighty Real.' Later on, I came in on all the albums after that — like the *Too Hot to Sleep* album, which included a song that was a duet between us. The song 'Here Is My Love' was a big New York hit. I'm on 'I Need You' as well. Sylvester hired another girl after the Tons left. He did a call out and hired a girl named Debbie and then another girl named Emma Jean. Debbie eventually left because she said she felt like a 'sixth finger'— those were her words. I guess [she felt] that Sylvester wasn't close enough to her — I'm not really sure what it is she wanted. I explained to her that when I came along with Martha and Izora, I had to work hard! [Martha and Izora] were friends and they wanted me there, but I had to work for it. I just had to find my little niche. Martha and Izora had theirs, and I had to find mine. Sylvester had been singing backup and lead — and having me freed him up from doing backup work so he could concentrate on the lead. Those were some of the most amazing times of my life!"

Though occasionally eclipsed by the original Tons' fame and not always given her due credit as a principal player in Sylvester's musical lineup, Tracy persevered. She asserts, "When I was singing with Sylvester, it was like singing gospel, and I was very comfortable with that. I loved doing it. The gay community was so accepting — they saw my face and heard my voice. That's why I get annoyed when people leave me out of singing with him. There were quite a number of people that sang with Sylvester before Martha and Izora, but they were the ones that gained notoriety with him — and I was part of *that* group, I'm proud to say!"

Jeanie starts to sing "Can't You See," a glorious, if unheralded, disco track off the *Too Hot to Sleep* album. "That's Maurice Long and I on that track," she says. "Maurice was a magnificent tenor. 'Give It Up' [also features] me singing lead, and I wrote the lyrics to that song. Sylvester is singing backup with me. I had gone to an interview at a Philly radio station and the DJs—who were fine looking I might add—were looking at me and asking, 'What about your stuff?' I said I was working on my solo album. Well, they asked if there's anything on Sylvester's album that featured me. I said, 'Yeah, "Give It Up."' They start playing it! When I got home, I got yelled at by Sylvester's management because the new single was going to [have to then] be 'Give It Up.' I got a little upset because those DJs asked me what I sang, and I just told them. I guess [if I had been part of Sylvester's management] I would have been upset too, but Sylvester was fine with it! 'Give It Up' was a hit, especially in the bathhouses and such," she laughs.

Tracy does not recall encountering many difficulties resulting from racial prejudice or sexism during her recording career. "It wasn't that difficult. The only thing I felt that held me back was being full-figured. When I was smaller, my career was soaring. It wasn't until I hit the gay community or when I went to Europe that I was accepted as full-figured. But in the mainstream, when I was smaller, I was doing fine. So, I have experienced downfalls, but you know what? I said, 'I'm just going to keep going!' There have also been times where I said to a club or show organizer, 'I'm a woman of color, and I'm a very large woman. Is that okay?' And they've said, 'Oh, that's just what I'm looking for!' That's always really nice. But being a woman of color—I did not experience those problems. Or if I did, they never let me see it."

Jeanie caused a stir with her beautifully rendered *Me and You* solo album for Fantasy in 1982. Produced by Fuqua, the collection favored an R&B sound and featured "I'm Your Jeanie" (with Sylvester doing low-voiced back-ups) and the title cut single. She remembers, "As time went on, Harvey was dealing with Marvin Gaye, and I didn't have a deal with Honey anymore and nothing was happening. That's when Tim McKenna, Sylvester's manager, came into my life. Sylvester had left Harvey and Nancy's management and went on to Megatone Records. And that's when, rightfully so, I went on to hire Timmy as my manager. I didn't want a manager, but my husband said I needed one and Tim was asking me—and that's how I got with him. And I loved him! I stayed on with him until he passed. I adored him and, to this day, I have not found anyone who has been close to the way Tim was with me. When I went over to Megatone Records, James 'Tip' Wirrick (Sylvester's musical director) called me and said, 'Jeanie I have this song, "Time Bomb," for you.' Marty Blecman, Megatone's president, talked to Timmy about me doing it. I heard the song, liked it and we did it. Sylvester is in the background and so is Martha Wash. Oh God, we were singing so high you could get a nose bleed! Because I was Sylvester's protégé, he was absolutely willing to come over and help me."

Tracy's connection and professional relationship with Sylvester worked both ways. She adds, "I had a song called 'I'm Your Jeanie' on my solo album, and there's this part that [is about letting one funk with emotion]. Sylvester said, 'Girl, you wrote that?' He thought it was brilliant! And he really sung the heck out of that part on my song. So he moves onto Patrick Cowley and they write 'Do Ya Wanna Funk?' which became a big hit. I said to him, 'You owe me money!'" she laughs. "It's all about timing!"

"I was the demo queen for Patrick Cowley and that crew," Tracy says. "I used to do all their demos. I remember Harvey didn't want me to do their demos when I was getting ready to release my own album. 'Sing Your Own Song' was one of those demos. The Tons had wanted it, but I decided I wanted it for myself. So, I did 'Time Bomb,' which was a very big hit, 'Sing Your Own Song' and 'Don't Leave Me This Way.'" More than just a footnote, Jeanie's riveting remake of Thelma Houston's "Don't Leave Me This Way" became an underground smash with its gospel-fused power and artistic variation of the Thelma Houston version. "I love Thelma Houston, and I still love her today! And I love the song. I wanted to do a good song like that because I didn't have a lot of songs in my repertoire at that point," she says.

"Later on, I did a song called 'Manhunt,' which Tip had written for me. I did it under the name 'Silhouette.' That's me. Some fans got mad saying, 'We know that's Jeanie Tracy's voice! Why are you calling it "Silhouette?"' I went onto to do 'I Found Love' and 'Feel Like Dancing' with Freddie Hubbard. I had done his album, *Splash,* and I had asked him if he would do my record. He gave us a really good deal! I also did 'Let's Dance' for Megatone."

Tracy's hits made her a regular on the gay club scene, but the artist says the sex and drug elements of nightlife weren't often on her radar. Tracy admits, "[I saw some things] a couple of times — it was in the back that some sexy things were going on. I was mostly on stage or in the dressing room and, you know, it was fine. Only a couple of times did I ever witness some things where I was like, 'Oh no!' — [things] that you don't see in the straight clubs. But I embrace the gay community, and it was the experience of a lifetime. I fell in love with all of that. The way they embraced me, treated me, the whole experience. It was just fabulous — *it is just fabulous!*" Jeanie says beaming.

Sylvester had contracted the mysterious illness that hovered over these times. Many artists and gay men had fallen ill to the (then quite fatal) disease that eventually became known as AIDS. The magnitude of the epidemic was only just being realized. The contrast between the bliss of his success and the stark realities of his gradual loss of health was not lost on Jeanie, but she looks back at that time, at least on this particular day, with a warm sense of emotion. "When I would sing with Sylvester and the girls," she says, "those were some of the best times of my life — I'm telling you! Martha and Izora were so much fun, and I adored them and I adored Sylvester. One time Syl and I were walking down the street in New York going to a store, walking in the snow and people were leaping out of their cars into the streets. By the time we got in the store, the place was mobbed. When we walked out, I said, 'How does that feel?! Did you ever think that you would be *this* big?' He said, 'Yes girl; I always wanted it!'" Jeanie laughs. "For me, he and I became so close because we liked so many of the same things. He liked my flair for fashion. He thought I dressed fabulously and that kind of thing. He liked my style, so we had a lot in common. At the time he got sick, he was just Sylvester though. Because we had become so close, he wasn't this icon. He was a good friend and my brother.

"At the time [he became ill], I thought people had abandoned Sylvester. But a writer, who I had worked with on a biography of Sylvester, said he had had chosen who he wanted to be around him. I thought everybody should be coming to see him. I brought Patti Labelle to see him. He had been very sick and lost a lot of weight. She thought he looked like a little old man. She was at Narada Michael Walden's studio, and I was doing some vocal work with her. She asked how Sylvester was, and I said he was doing well. But she looked at me like I had two heads. What you have to realize is, he was living with AIDS, and sometimes you were really ill and sometimes you'd pop back like nothing's wrong and at *that* moment he *was* doing really well. I told her she should go see him. She agreed, and I told her this would make his day — his year — but I had the feeling she was kind of iffy about it. She called me one night, and I sensed she might be getting nervous or having second thoughts, so I said, 'Patti, he's so excited, you don't know what this is going to do for him. It might extend his life! Sometimes you have to be more than a singer; you have to be a missionary.' She then said, "Okay, I'm gonna do this!" I told her, 'Do *not* cry! He wants you to *dish*! Go in there and laugh and start dishin' about folks!' So she dished about a couple of people, and it was all in good fun. Later, she admitted to me, 'I never do that—saying just okay to someone! "*Okay Jeanie; I'll do it?*"' We laughed!

"He was funny till the end. He would make us laugh even in his misery. I saw him cry once—only once. He cried, and I hugged him and told him it's okay to cry, but then he should let it go. He had no regrets. I took care of him and cooked for him. It was hard to manage it all. I liked cooking at his place so he could smell the food. He'd go, 'Girl, you cook fab! I never thought my taste buds could enjoy this again.' "He called us all in to talk to about his last wishes. I remember I had a white Cadillac once. He had asked Patti Labelle if I had driven her [over in it] to see him. He said, 'Jeannie was so nice to bring you ... oh, you rode in the white refrigerator!' Oh my God, he was so funny, even when he was so ill. But as soon as they got out of his room, those tears came."

Sylvester's death on December 16, 1988, was a huge blow to the Hi-NRG music community (which embraced his later music strongly), a somber moment in disco history and a source of heartbreak for Jeanie. "He was buried in a red kimono and a pearl casket because he said, 'I don't wanna look like I'm buried in no white refrigerator,'" she says with a smile. "I kind of put my music on hold for a bit. I never did really grieve. But when I came back, I was ready to write and throw myself into it."

Tracy still had much to accomplish, and eventually she threw her career into high gear. She became a force to be reckoned with throughout the '90s, with club hits that included a popular take on Frankie Valli's "Can't Take My Eyes Off of You" (a Top-20 dance chart smash in 1999) and "Keep the Party Jumpin'" which hit the Top Five the same year. She kicked off the 21st century by scoring a number 1 dance hit, "The Power," joined by the DJ-duo Rosabel. She continues to enjoy a large and enthusiastic fan base that grew out of (and beyond) those early days with Sylvester, and having so many members of the LGBT community supporting her career is just fine with her. "I was mainstream at one time, but I never really thought about the limitations of having a primarily gay audience because they treated me so well. Going around straight clubs was okay, but you always had to pull teeth to get money and that kind of thing. And so, for me, these [gay] men would put you on a pedestal, pay you well, give you drag stuff and were so ... accepting. [Just] like the Europeans. The Europeans just treated us like royalty. I used to say, 'What are we doing here in the United States?' So, for me, once or twice I might have thought about going more mainstream, but I realized I was happy. You don't bite the hand—you know what I'm saying?"

The artist observes there have been some changes in the entertainment industry over the years. "You have to know that the gay clubs were paying great money back in the day," Tracy claims. "I'm not talking $200 or $500. I'm talking about thousands of dollars to do two or three songs. That's what's disheartening about what is going on now, even in the gay community. They're not hiring a lot of live performers, except for the big events or Pride. The clubs are saying they can't afford it. They just use DJs, and that's really, really sad. A lot of the divas are going to other genres of music. I still stay pat, because I haven't had a bad run of it. But it's slower now because of the times.

"I have to tell you what the sad thing is—the [major] record companies all bitch about how they don't make any money because of the Internet and such, but I don't feel sorry for them. Because guess what—*they took all the money!*" Jeanie alleges. "I don't know if it's true or not because I didn't hear it myself, but I was once told that [a record executive] said, 'It's a good thing that these people can't afford to sue me.' I'm not saying who it was or what company it was, but that's what I was told."

In retrospect, Tracy is positive about disco's place in pop-music history and the level of recognition it has received, but qualifies her thoughts. "I think [disco was respected] because it did very well. So much so, the rock stars got pissed and couldn't get airplay. But the mainstream people got more play than the disco artists. Our music was just as good. A lot of the songs we did [still] get played on Sirius and things like that, but mainstream radio — today they're only playing artists like Jennifer Lopez. You know, I hear them doing songs that sound an awful lot like ours, and they aren't doing anything but copying our music and putting it out there. Now the mainstream artists are jumping on our chart. The dance chart was [meant] for us! The disco and club divas who weren't able to cross over to the pop charts. So, now you've got all these companies putting their stuff on the dance chart, [using] remixers that I work with, and getting them all over it. You've got Jennifer Lopez, Beyonce, Rihanna on the dance chart and with two songs each sometimes. There are only 50 slots — *come on*! *Billboard* is not [fair] to us because they are so busy entertaining them. Which is okay, but be fair to *all of us*! You were fair to us before; be fair now. I'm looking at the *Billboard* charts, and we can't get to number 1— and we can't even hope to get there. I'm sure those large record companies are putting out a few pennies for that. Payola is still alive and well probably. I'm not looking at anyone's bank account, but that's just the way I feel."

Jeanie, like her fellow sisters in disco, has also faced the challenges of maturity. She says, "I'm grounded through an attitude that makes you do certain things. My faith in God — it all keeps me grounded. Maturing is something you have to become comfortable with. Sometimes the powers that be don't allow you to mature or to grow old. They can be ruthless. I feel like I've come into my own. Occasionally I may say, 'Oh my God, am I too old for this?' But you know what? I have such young fans that come up to me and say, 'Miss Tracy, please don't stop singing!' And I'll turn around and say, 'Did I tell someone I was gonna stop singing?'" she laughs. "Honey, as long as you guys enjoy it, then I'll keep doing it! And when I don't enjoy it anymore, then I'll just do something else. One thing I am going to do is

Jeanie Tracy (seen with her pooch, Taco) says, "I have such young fans that come up to me and say, 'Miss Tracy, please don't stop singing!' And I'll turn around and say, 'Did I tell someone I was gonna stop singing?'" (courtesy Jeanie Tracy).

go back to my adult contemporary roots, like the Luther Vandross love songs, R&B, jazz and that kind of thing for a new album. But I'm never going to abandon my dance audience, because I love them!"

So far, there's been no need for Jeanie to modify her successful formula. The artist, who says she would liked to have covered the song "Love Train" back in the day ("I thought that was a great one!"), can take her own material or the classics of others and still stir up the masses like a cyclone. "I was at an AIDS function, and they catered mostly to theatrical people," she remembers. "They had all these people singing very theatrical songs. The crowd was good, but they were only responsive at the end of each performance. I told my girlfriend, 'Oh, this is gonna be one of those nights. They're gonna just sit there!' Well honey, I started off behind the curtain singing the opening of 'Last Dance,' and I walked out into the light on stage and the song kicked in! I joined it with one of my songs, 'Everybody Up!' A woman who hosts a show about movies in the Bay area, Jan Wahl, and the mayor, Willie Brown, got up and came up to the stage dancing! People were dancing in the aisles and in their seats! I said to the crowd, 'Oh, y'all wanna party?' It was so much fun, and I was told in the 20 years the event has been taking place, nobody had ever gone crazy like that! It was a great feeling for me!"

In recent years, she has been busier than ever. Tracy won a Grammy for her work on Celine Dion's "My Heart Will Go On," (from the movie soundtrack to *Titanic)* and another for her collaboration with Carlos Santana on his *Supernatural* CD ("The Calling" featuring Eric Clapton). In 2010, Tracy appeared on the *Unsung* program to help tell the story of Sylvester. The year 2012 has seen the artist's work recognized with a prestigious induction into the West Coast Blues Hall of Fame and an artist award presentation from the Just Circuit Award Hall of Fame. She released the songs "Getcha Hands Offa My Man" and "We Will Be Free Tonight" and has continued to travel throughout the world to perform for audiences that receive her with astonishing enthusiasm.

Jeanie Tracy's heart and voice have earned her a well-deserved place of honor in disco's history, and she doesn't see her participation in dance music coming to an end anytime soon. However, when people remember her, Jeanie hopes they will say, "She loved to motivate and make people feel good! With my music, I try to do uplifting songs to make people just forget about their problems for that moment in time and then, when they leave, I want them to be encouraged and have hope about whatever they're going through!"

Anita Ward

What made the song "Ring My Bell" such a phenomenally huge disco sensation in 1979? "Probably just the simplicity of it! One thing I've learned over the years is that the simplest of songs can be really something if you can sing along with it. Who can't sing 'Ring My Bell,' you know?" conjectures Anita Ward, the warm and charming vocalist who made the song into a disco and pop classic over three decades ago. Everyone may be able to sing it, but Anita made it something everyone wanted to *hear* with her well-pitched, sweet and engaging vocal style. A survivor of her monumental music achievement and her adventures in disco, Ward's story is as surprising as it is remarkable.

"Let's put it this way — I liked to sing," Ward says of her early years in Memphis with an engaging Southern accent, "but I didn't know how successful I would come to be. I was told by my parents and my late grandparents that I used to walk around with a bottle in my hand, pretending it was a microphone, and I would be singing into it. My late grandmother told a story of when I was only two years old and we were on a train going to Arizona to see my parents. She said I sang all the way there. The people on the train called me 'little songbird.'"

Ward found her career suddenly taking wing by the time she'd earned her college degree. "I went to Rust College, located in Holly Springs, Mississippi, and they were doing a play, *Godspell*, and one of my friends suggested that I audition for it. So, I actually did do that, and I did get a part. However, in the meantime, there was a gentleman, Chuck Holmes, who happened to be an administrator at the college and someone who dabbled around in the music business. He heard me singing during my audition and he asked if I would like to become a recording artist. That's how it all got started. We actually did a demo and shopped it around through the people he knew, and that's how we hooked up with Frederick Knight, who had an independent label [Juana Records] that was distributed through T.K. Records out of Florida. The 'Ring My Bell' record came out one year after I graduated from college, and I was waiting around with Chuck to see what would happen with it. I started substitute teaching in the meantime because I figured if anything goes, or if it doesn't, being a teacher would allow flexibility in my schedule. That's why they promoted that I was a teacher back then. I did teach for four months, and then I got a phone call on a Thursday. My producer told me that he had great news for me — the record had gone gold after only two weeks!"

"Ring My Bell" (written by the song's producer, Frederick Knight, and mixed by Richie Rivera) was an infectious smash. It had been originally composed (reportedly) with the youthful pop-R&B singer Stacy Lattisaw in mind. Instead, the song fell into the lap of the unknown Ward, whose unique falsetto interpretation helped the song to catapult to number 1 on the U.S. dance, R&B and pop charts (and take the same position at the top of the U.K. pop chart). Clubs relentlessly played the cut as throngs of dancers fired their fingers into the air in unison with the percolating sound of this highly distinctive hit. The song became one of the best-known of the entire era. "Suddenly, the label wanted me to do *The Midnight Special* and they flew in two dancers and a choreographer from New York. This guy worked parts of my body I didn't even know I had!" she laughs. "Yes, it all happened very quickly!"

She recalls, "It was very exciting. I had been singing all my life locally here in Memphis and in different places. In church, of course — I always sang in church. But I had never even been inside of a club. It was definitely an experience for me. I don't remember being afraid until I had an appearance to do — I think it was in California — and I was meeting all these celebrities! I just couldn't believe it was happening. I just kind of broke down for a moment. I was in my hotel room, and I just had to call my manager and said, 'I guess it's just finally hitting me!' So I got my eyes opened very quickly. If you love performing, once you are on stage and there's an audience giving you a little positive feedback, you'll get over it — but it was kind of a shock at first."

Anita confesses that she had some misgivings about "Ring My Bell." "Well, I'll tell you — everything gets out. It's true; I did not like 'Ring My Bell' at first because I wanted to be, you know, a ballad singer. I wanted to be this great balladeer, doing the serious type of music, and I thought this was just so silly. Honestly, I thought the song was just so silly — but over the years I definitely realize by thinking that way, I had really put my own foot in my mouth. That's what I actually was doing because this song has proven to be a classic! People love the song. It's been in 13 movies. So, I guess I was the only one who didn't initially like the song. That was a long time ago. Let me clear it up now — it's no more ... no more! I love it just like everybody else! It's fun! Today, it reminds people of fun and happy times — it was just a clean song. It was great to dance to and nothing to get offended by," she says.

Identifying the song's qualities, which resounded so strongly with a pop-hungry and dance-crazed public, is easy for Anita. "Just that simple lyrical hook line was very important," she observes. "Another thing that helped was probably the sound of the syndrum and the 'woo-woo' [making the song's laser-gun popping sound]. Actually, I think my song was probably one of the first to come up with that sound, and then later came Shalamar's 'The Second Time Around.' Of course, since then a lot of folks have used it. I think again that was surely the fun part of it because people liked that sound the most."

Anita Ward strikes an innocent pose for a 1979 publicity shot with little idea of the disco roller-coaster ride yet to come as the song "Ring My Bell" climbed the charts to number 1 (courtesy Anita Ward).

"I was new to the business and, keep in mind, that's probably why I thought, 'Oh, I don't know if I like this song.' I didn't think the song had any potential — no, I really didn't. I didn't understand fully that you have to put out what the people need right at that time. What's going to capture their attention? Actually the song came up mostly because Frederick Knight was so focused on it. We were doing the album, and it was like one of the last songs that we did. That's the one he just kept working on — so he sensed something probably that the rest of us didn't know. It was the only song to come out off the album that was going to capture everyone's attention and get a buzz," she observes. In retrospect, Knight was right. The album, *Songs of Love,* was a Top-10 smash, but the infectious single was the only hit to come off the set. The rest of the LP comprised material written by Knight and Ward's mentor, Chuck Holmes. The clubs and radio largely failed to embrace any of it.

However, the wave created by such a powerful single was enough to keep Ward front and center for some time. The singer remembers the excitement of being so prominently in the spotlight. "I was up there with Donna Summer, and my goodness, she was the queen — the disco queen along with Gloria Gaynor. Having this hit is why I got to meet a lot of these people. Unfortunately, I actually did not get to [personally] meet Donna Summer, but I did get to meet a lot of other great people because we were all in that same era. Like Amii Stewart of 'Knock on Wood'—God, that song was so great! I used to like it a lot! So I really was overwhelmed! I could not believe these were the people that I had seen watching *American Bandstand*—which I appeared on as well—and *Soul Train*. As a matter of fact, when I went to do the Wolfman Jack show, *The Midnight Special*, Melba Moore was also recording the show. I just couldn't believe it—it was very, very overwhelming.

"For me, another highlight was going overseas. I was traveling overseas more than I was going places in the States—and it's also a phenomenal thing that the song became a hit everywhere. I didn't ever get to Africa, but I was in demand and made it to places that I never thought I would get an opportunity to see. I remember going to Paris, which I went to many times, and I saw Sophia Loren just walking down the street! *Now, I could just not believe that!* I think I screamed! I think she had actually recognized me! I had gone into a store; I think it was Christian Dior. It was a shoe store. And she just looked at me and bowed her head and I thought, 'My God, I think she knows me!' or knew of me or figured I was somebody—so that freaked me out. I wouldn't dare go up to her. I was just too alarmed to go up and say, 'Ms. Loren would you give me your autograph?' I didn't do that. But just [having the actress] look at me and bow her head just made me feel like I had died and gone to heaven!"

However, the whirlwind of attention that had engulfed Ward shifted directions. "As big and fast as a success as 'Ring My Bell' was, that's how equally quickly the negativity started. I think it was Deniece Williams and Johnny Mathis that sang 'Too Much, Too Little, Too Late,' and I started to feel like that [song's title]. The success was huge, but maybe it was really just too much. If you are going to have a big hit, maybe it shouldn't be your first release. I started to feel like, okay, the pressure is really starting to [increase]. Especially when the relationship between my producer and I was no longer so charming and wasn't as it should be. I think because—you have to understand—he, too, was dealing with something he had never experienced before. Then my manager, Chuck Holmes, ended up dying in Mexico City while I was on tour. You know, he was sick at the time the record was actually produced and released, and he just became more and more ill. So when he died, the relationship between my producer and I—it was not all that cool. It just kind of phased out as well. I later had an injunction placed against me by Frederick—you know, it was just all these negatives starting to happen. So, for a minute, I didn't care to be singing, heard or around people because it was just an awful lot on me. This was the part that was not as attractive. It wasn't all, 'Oh gosh, this is the lady that did "Ring My Bell!"' all the time—wow, no! It sure wasn't that!"

The *Sweet Surrender* album followed later in 1979, and it featured the single "Don't Drop My Love," a catchy track, but one highly derivative of the "Bell" formula. Though it cracked the dance Top 30, it never made it past the lower regions of the pop chart. Still, some pundits said the album was a preferable showcase of Ward's talent when compared to her first LP. However, the singer says the chemistry between her and her producer had been lost. "We went into the studio, Frederick and I, to make the second album," Anita sighs, "but it wasn't with as much passion, you know, or care or concern. We were just doing it because this is what we were supposed to do in the contract—that's sort of how I felt. That is why it's ironic when I hear people say they liked *Sweet Surrender* even better than the first album—that's really interesting. Sometimes people work well under pressure, so maybe I can say that's what it was. Yeah, things just didn't go quite so well. So, I left singing for quite a while, and it wasn't until probably seven to 10 years ago that I started to actually feel much better about it. Now I'm getting residuals for 'Ring My Bell' because my former manager, bless his soul, had it in my contract to receive a percentage of what it earned in case anything happened to him and, Lord, was that not a great decision? I didn't see this coming—so now, because 'Ring My Bell' has become such a classic, things are not quite as difficult for me financially as they had been for a while. It's just turned out to be a real blessing."

It may seem surprising that Ward and Knight encountered so much friction soon after the success of the first album. "I agree that it might seem odd, but I'm going to tell you this," she says. "You see, Frederick Knight was also a singer—he put out a couple of songs like 'I Betcha Didn't Know That' and 'I've Been Lonely for So Long,' so, somehow, I think what may have happened is that he might have been under pressure from his peers. Maybe it was a little bit ego—or maybe a huge ego—but I think he saw himself as the person who 'made' Anita Ward. Sometimes producers and managers will do that—'I made her and created her.' If it had been anyone else who had done that song, I think he still might have felt that and I think he wished he himself had sung it. I think he may have started to feel a little jealousy—I know it sounds crazy, a little immature and silly, but I kind of picked up that some of that may have been going on. It didn't have to be that way. This second album was the time to jump right into it and try to create something as close to the success of 'Ring My Bell' as possible, but it just didn't happen that way."

When the heat began to wane from Ward's pop and disco career, she says she was grateful for the support system she had in her life. "I'll tell you one thing—I'm grateful for my parents," Anita says. "Unfortunately, my mother is dead, but my father is still alive, and I feel they gave me the strength and the perseverance to go on, no matter what happened. I was able to because of what they taught me and how they let me know about God. You know, some people don't believe, but I know I believe because I've been through a lot of things—not all good, some bad—and I'm still here. Miracles have happened in my life as well, so I know there is a God, and I think if I had not had that faith, I would have just given in like, unfortunately, some of the wonderful artists from the disco genre have. You feel the phone isn't ringing as much, you're not as popular, you don't have as much money—how am I going to pay my bills? You might start to turn to drugs as an answer—and that was never an answer for me because I didn't need that to get high to perform. My high was my natural high. I was high just being overjoyed and elated to be on a stage. I think because of my belief in God, it wasn't meant for me to have it all for my entire life—like that was my moment. And so, that is the way I sort of look at it all now.

"I'm not saying I always felt this way because I'm still a human being like everybody else. You know, I had some weak moments. But my parents—thank God for them and now my husband—got me through them. I have a daughter that is attending college, so that's my life and that is my family. I just thank God for everything—I'd be nothing without His strength and my belief in Him. And faith! When you can't see the concrete thing, and faith is something you can't see, you still have to have it—and that is what I held on to," Anita says with a firm voice.

While attempting to stay active with performance gigs, Ward experienced more of the grimmer realities of the business, especially for women. "My record was an overnight success—I mean [it happened] immediately! Here's a woman that would fly the Concord airplane all over the world doing some big time stuff as soon as my record came out. However, after the song started dying down, the calls were fewer and I wasn't being recognized as often. That's when I went into a [negative] circuit for a time. There was a gentleman who had a band — not the greatest sounding or looking band — but we traveled and tried to do a show. In the process, we might be in places that were really a hole in the wall, okay? Or maybe two steps above a hole in the wall. Sometimes, in these environments, I wasn't respected because I was a woman. I wouldn't get paid. I think at that time it had to do with the class of people I was meeting up with who didn't have a lot of scruples about being kind and nice. Sometimes, I would have some of them approach me in a way I definitely wasn't interested in. It was business to me, and that's the only time I felt disrespected — after the time of the big success. But other than that, at least I can say I was never treated badly in my career."

The stall in Ward's career was but one of a series of challenges the artist faced. "I actually did become a teacher later, a full-fledged teacher as well," she recollects. "I had been in a car accident, which had created some kind of leakage in my brain over time, which I knew nothing about. Then, much later on, working around kids, you are susceptible to getting colds and the sniffles, and I would get sick because the bacteria would back up into my brain. I developed meningitis, not once, but twice! And if you know meningitis, you know I'm telling you that I'm a walking miracle to be here today. I did have surgery about eight to 10 years ago. The doctor wanted to work on my head to stop the leakage, but I was very reluctant. You know, 'Oh God, no doctor, not on my head,' but that is what he had to do to stop the problem. It has never reoccurred since then, but in the meantime, I did discontinue teaching because I felt, for health reasons, I needed to put that to the side right now. I just know that I have something to be grateful for. It's not just being in the limelight and that's all. I'm just grateful to be alive and for being here. I am truly honored that I was thought of to be in this book. I almost didn't [participate]. I thought, 'I don't have as great a story to tell as maybe the other women,' but then I was like, 'Wait a minute, it *did* happen and nobody can take that away from me!' So why not talk about my life?" she says with a tone of assurance.

Reflecting on the era and the disco genre, Anita observes, "My records came out in '79, and you know the '70s was when most of the disco artists were hot. But I hit in '79, right before they started talking negatively about disco. I think if my former manager hadn't died and my producer and I had a better connection, I feel — when things did start to calm down in the early '80s — I could have evolved with the music. But all of a sudden, 'disco sucked.' Over the years, I think people got over that, and the music was something you could have fun with and dance to again. That's why it's called dance music now. I think our music is kind of coming back, but it's not called disco. Maybe disco didn't get its fair share of respect, but I think things are probably trying to change now. I think people want to hear it again."

She adds, "I'm more open to things now more than I used to be. I don't go along with guys or girls who sing songs about wanting to go under someone's dress; you know what I'm saying? I still can't go for that yet. I don't think it's needed if you are going to be a real performer. I was recently looking at *The Today Show*, and they had Aretha Franklin on there. She was doing a little cooking segment, and she was saying that she and Clive Davis have come together. She's trying to get with Babyface and some others, and they are going to come out with some music for her. So I said, 'Well, you go girl!' People still love her and, like her, many of us have that history. I think sometimes the media is only interested in the young ones. The music to which people are exposed seems to be the tiniest amount possible, and the less information you know about the business, the more they can take advantage of you. So yeah, Aretha's not over, and maybe it's not the end for any of us. Most of my work today, believe it or not, actually comes from overseas. I get called to do work from Europeans much, much more than I have from the United States. I think it is because they aren't [as inflexible] as we Americans sometimes can be. They are much more open to real music from my era, and they always have been. That's the truth!"

Recently, Ward was featured on a new release called "It's My Night." Says Anita, "Actually, with that song, the gentleman who produced it is a young guy, and it needed to be funded and marketed better. I rewrote it, so that's probably why you hear some of that old school stuff in there. I've had a few people tell me that they like it, but I'm not sure that it [will be successful] because you really have to have money. Clive Davis is going to have to pick it up!" she chuckles. "So, I just keep saying, 'Just keep hanging in and maybe something will come along.' I was in Paris, and I did a TV show there earlier this year. I've been made offers to go to Syria and Beirut, but I just don't feel comfortable going there. I have a daughter in college and need to help out as much as possible, so I work a regular job just like everyone else. That's what I do. People can't believe I actually do that—but I do. Because I believe that if one thing doesn't work out, you just try something else. I don't make a lot of money, but it's something. So I guess sometimes it may seem like a humbling experience, but, hey, I didn't always have 'Ring My Bell' in my life. I think I know how to survive and manage. I think I've actually managed to do pretty much okay."

Anita Ward says of her remarkable career in disco, "My philosophy is—if it's meant for you, no one can take it away from you" (courtesy Anita Ward).

Ward seems at ease with her life experience and the maturation process she has navigated. Her advice is "to keep praying and just keep God in your life. Stay away from the drugs. I've been told that I look good for my age, and if I do, it's because of what I put in my body. If you don't abuse your body, you can pretty much live a good life. My philosophy is—if it's meant for you, no one can take it away from you. Just believe in God and take care of yourself, inside and out."

She is an artist with remarkable resilience and a woman who possesses no grand notions about her tremendous signature hit or her time in the spotlight. While her place in pop and disco history is unshakable, so too is her attitude about life and the future. Anita Ward would like to be remembered as "someone who earned respect and who tried to respect everyone else. I know that's probably not a long enough statement. I know that 'Ring My Bell' just happened to be something that occurred in my life, and I'm not trying to take that lightly now because it caused me to meet a lot of people and to go to a lot of places I thought I would never see. But beyond that, I would like to be remembered as someone who believed that if you respect yourself, others will respect you. If you have that solid grounding, you are going to make it no matter what you do. That's what I believe; that's what is really important!"

Martha Wash

Many female vocalists in disco music had the power to motivate, but when a singer with the celebrity of Martha Wash commanded attention, it was cause to listen up! Martha, whether shaking it up with partner Izora Armstead or going it solo, supplied the high-octane fuel that made one certain no roadblock, however daunting, was insurmountable. Wash's determination to make her way in the world of entertainment, a world that did not often warmly embrace plus-sized women, was not to be underestimated. Prejudicial appearance standards were no match for the astonishing vocal gift this hardworking woman unleashed on audiences across the globe. From her indispensable smashes with Sylvester, to her huge club hits under the Two Tons of Fun banner (think "Earth Can Be Just Like Heaven"), to the incomparable "It's Raining Men" (which practically defined the '80s) and beyond, she has proven to be an extraordinarily gifted vocalist with an astonishing command of any song to which she lends her voice. It's undeniable — you've never seen glamour quite like this before!

"I started singing when I was three years old with my godmother," Martha recalls. "I was sitting in the back seat of the car, singing and playing. She told my mother about it, and my mother was also a singer. She sang in the church choir and all that. She's the one who really helped me to sing. Growing up in churches and singing in them is really how I got my start."

"I always knew I wanted to sing," she continues, "but I didn't know in what kind of genre I would sing. My mother, bless her heart, wanted me to sing only gospel. Growing up as a child, it was the only type of music that was allowed in my house. So I grew up listening to Mahalia Jackson, Clara Ward, James Cleveland, the Staple Singers, Roberta Martin — those folks. And as I got older and became a teenager, I would listen to a local radio station in San Francisco, the rock stations and the soul stations, that kind of thing, on my transistor radio. Under my pillow!" she laughs. It was also not an easy time for the young girl, who knew the harsh realities of being bullied and taunted for her large appearance. Singing in the church provided a refuge from that, and it was there that Martha honed her remarkable voice. She emerged from the chaos of adolescence as a young woman possessing more than a few emotional battle scars, but determined and ready to take on a professional entertainment career.

In the latter half of the '70s, Martha was at the beginning of her backing vocal partnership with Sylvester James, who was then gaining popularity in San Francisco clubs and drag bars. She and Sylvester eventually crossed paths with producers Harvey Fuqua and Nancy Pitts (who had formed Honey Productions) and made history. "I met Harvey and Nancy, and I went to their studio in Oakland. They had a kind of a recording studio and rehearsal-space combination. I went over there to meet them to audition as a background singer — sort of a studio singer. I spoke with him and auditioned and told them I was singing with a guy named Sylvester. I told Harvey and Nancy to check out our show, which they did. From that, Harvey and Sylvester hooked up and Harvey ended up signing Sylvester to Honey Records. Izora [Armstead] came on board a short time later, and immediately it all kind of clicked. It all took off from there!" Sylvester and Two Tons of Fun became a vivid reality.

Martha Wash and Izora Armstead as the Weather Girls, circa 1982, announce to the world, "It's Raining Men" (courtesy Martha Wash).

The trio's chemistry was like a house on fire. A cross-dressing lead singer and two plus-sized powerhouse backup vocalists was a new kind of team on the music scene, and they got attention. Sylvester (performing under his first name only) and the girls recorded the 1978 classic *Step II* LP, which yielded two of disco's ultimate extravaganzas. The tracks "Dance Disco Heat" and the James Wirrick-composed "You Make Me Feel (Mighty Real)," became among the most beloved songs of disco's feverish peak days. Sylvester, Martha and Izora (and later Jeanie Tracy), conjured up irresistible music with infectious melodies and a gospel spirit that made their performances a religious experience for many. "Dance Disco Heat" brought the ensemble straight to the Top 20 of the U.S. pop chart.

Moving from church-based gospel to disco didn't seem like much of a stretch to Martha. "I certainly didn't have a problem with it — but my parents did," she says. "When I started singing background for Sylvester, I can't say they were pleased, and they kind of got flack from the church members. They came around to supporting me as much as possible. If we were doing concerts, they would sometimes show up. They weren't necessarily thrilled, but they were still supportive of what I was doing—especially when I started traveling quite a bit. I would call them and they'd be, 'Let me talk to her! No, let me talk to her!' That kind of thing," she laughs. "I was comfortable with disco. I liked the disco music and the artists—some of them—at the time. I was a fan. And look, honestly, I was happy to just get in this business. I guess you could say I was just happy to work as a background singer and do all these shows and start traveling. We wanted to sing; it's just really what we were doing."

Martha adds, "With Sylvester, I would work during the day and sing with him at night, and there came a point where I had to make a decision to do this full time. The point came when Sylvester was offered a job in Sao Paulo, Brazil. He was going to be there for two weeks. Now, I was still working a regular job during the day, and I had just signed up to become a permanent employee in a part of the University of California Hospital in San Francisco. I was working in the nursing department in their clerical pool. Although I was a temporary, I had been working there a year or so. They offered me a full-time position, and I said yes. Then I get the news that Sylvester was going on a two-week tour of Brazil, so I had to make a decision whether to go on the road or not. I had to decide whether to work or step out on faith and go on the tour. Well, three days later I had to tell the hospital that I could not take the position. So, I went on the road. When I came back, I was, of course, without a job," she laughs, "so I went back to temp work. If the work doesn't come in, you still have to do something to keep a roof over your head. Back then, you prayed not to get sick! I mean, even with health insurance *today*, you pray not to get sick! I know I didn't have any at the time. Honey, I thank the Lord I didn't get sick much. Later on we were in AFTRA because we were doing TV shows and things like that, so we were kind of making enough in the union to get the health insurance from them. It definitely helped. But the part-time work was important and afforded me the time off that I needed when we'd start traveling again."

Martha and Izora, collectively billed as Two Tons of Fun, unashamedly capitalized on their larger-than-life visage. "There's always been a debate about who actually named us Two Tons of Fun," Martha alleges. "Izora said it was her. My former manager said he did. So I kind of stayed out of that whole situation. I guess the name did add to the novelty aspect of the group—two large women. A cheeky kind of thing! It kind of grabbed your attention immediately! But as time went on, we wanted to prove that we weren't a novelty act—that we were really out there doing our thing. I guess people ultimately didn't care what the name was. They just enjoyed the music."

The girls' eventual split from Sylvester was probably an inevitable "step two" in their careers, even though their initial pairing had been a left-field smash success. "I guess maybe it was a natural progression," Martha says. "Sylvester wasn't too happy about it though. Harvey was the one who suggested Two Tons of Fun record [their own] album. We said, 'Okay, cool!' So he got Eric Robertson to write most of the songs on the first Two Tons albums. It worked out very, very well for us. We had quite a few hits. It was great! We were really stepping out from being background singers to being lead singers, a lead act. We wanted it to be as good as possible and Harvey, as well, said, 'This is your chance.' In a way you had to really prove yourself because I think initially when we came out it was like, 'There's a group called Two Tons of Fun. What are we going to do with them? How are we going to market them?' That kind of thing. And we were considered basically a novelty act. But the *real* novelty was—we *could* really sing. Yeah, we were two large black women—

but we *could* sing! There's something I've really come to realize, probably in the last couple of years or so. When you think back to that time, and possibly before that time we came out, you did not see large women singing background — period! Maybe in the last 10 years or so you are seeing large women singing background. But back then, it was unique."

Performing in discos was a staple of the girls' career. Providing a rousing soundtrack for the evolution of the club scene was more on Martha's mind than any of the excesses for which the venues had often been notorious. However, for all the notoriety the scene endured, it left little impression on Wash. "I saw some things going on, but it didn't bother me. I was there to do my job. We saw some things, as far as drugs were concerned, mostly on the dance floor. During that time, there was a lot of amyl nitrate around — people doing poppers. Things like that. Although we knew all about drugs and all the different kinds, I wasn't a part of any of that stuff. That wasn't for me, and it didn't bother me. I was there to do my job and be a background singer for Sylvester. And when it came time for Two Tons of Fun to do their thing, neither Izora or I was into the drug scene, and Izora didn't drink, period! I would drink every now and then, but alcohol wasn't something I cared for. We were just going there to do what we were supposed to do, go on home and you know — whatever. The drugs were something we just didn't bother with."

The gay community was tremendously responsive to the Tons and would remain a significant following for Martha's entire career. She observes, "The connection I had with gay men just really kind of evolved. It goes all the way back to singing with Sylvester. We were doing a lot of the gay clubs in San Francisco and across the country. It evolved with Sylvester, then it became Two Tons of Fun, then it became the Weather Girls. So we've had that fan base for decades. And they have been loyal followers, and I definitely appreciate that. The whole LGBT group has been very loyal and enthusiastic!"

The AIDS crisis of the '80s impacted nearly everyone in the music business, and Martha was no exception. Seeing associates like Patrick Cowley (the producer and innovator of such iconic hits as "Menergy" and "I Wanna Take You Home") stricken, one by one, and then by the dozens, was sobering. "On the personal side, it was very sad to see Sylvester affected by it," she says. "That was the thing — and so many people we had known, especially back in San Francisco. Like one of our other band members, Patrick Cowley. He was one of the first ones that passed from AIDS. And then some years later, Sylvester was affected by it. But by the time Sylvester had really gotten sick, I had moved to New York. We were talking on the phone, and finally one day he called and said, 'I've got it.' And I was like, 'Damn, one more!' There came a point — I'm trying to remember — there was a point for almost two weeks that we got a phone call just about every day hearing about somebody who had just passed. It got to a point — like the phone would ring and you'd look at it and you'd say, 'Okay, who's going to be calling next to say somebody has gone?' It had really gotten to that point! I want to say it was really so sad and really unnecessary. Really, really sad! We lost a lot of people in the industry — a lot. In the dance music industry — managers, agents, DJs, performers, everyone. It was surreal," Martha says, releasing an exhale of emotion.

Those who embraced disco's culture and forged careers in the music were forced to trudge their way through the AIDS epidemic, but somehow the music went on. Despite the sobering realities of life and death that intruded on dance music for many years, several career highlights were also on the way for Martha. Two Tons of Fun crossed paths with a remarkable new song in 1982 and, in doing so, changed their name to the Weather Girls. Not since the Village People's "Macho Man" had a song come along to lionize masculinity like "It's Raining Men." This was one of those sensational, game-changing compositions whose opening chords, accelerated by some thunderstorm effects, sent people scrambling to the dance floor *instantly*—and in droves! Written by the composer of Donna Summer's "Last Dance" (Grammy-winner Paul Jabara), the tune celebrated, with unbridled enthusiasm, all things male!

"It wasn't a song we wanted to grab immediately, not at all," confesses Martha. "We just laughed at him. When Paul brought the song to us, he played it and said he wanted us to sing it. I would say the song was basically finished when we were approached. It just didn't have any vocals. He played the song, and we laughed and laughed and laughed some more. We said, 'You've got to be kidding!' He said, 'No, I'm serious. I need you to record this song!' When I hear that people can't imagine anyone else singing that song, it is kind of true. Stop and imagine Barbra Streisand singing that song—or Donna Summer or Diana Ross. Those were the ones who turned down the song, according to him. So, I guess we were like his last hope, you know? I didn't think it would be necessarily a hit, and I wasn't thinking of the gay community slant of the song. So it must have been like a day or two later we went into Larrabee Studios in L.A., and we recorded the song in about 90 minutes. We walked out of the studio and said, 'Okay Paul, see ya!' That was it! Paul was really the one who took that song club to club, walking around with acetate and begging the DJs to play it. So, in essence, the song was a big hit in the clubs long before radio picked up on it.

"'It's Raining Men' was a pop song really and the gay community just snatched it," Wash laughs. "They made it their anthem. But the thing is, over the decades, it's become a song that *everybody* loves—and I mean straight people, gay people, kids, grandparents. They love the song because it's such a fun song. So it has crossed the boundaries and all age groups!"

Follow-up singles like "I'm Gonna Wash That Man Right Out of My Hair" pressed on with the fun spirit, along with the show-stopping and suitably titled cut "Success," which seemed to joyfully revel in the girls' newfound fame. "That song is absolutely from Paul's background—Broadway and things like that. He wanted a big theatrical type of song and 'Success' was definitely that!" she says. However, nothing that immediately followed matched the unprecedented reception "It's Raining Men" enjoyed and the Weather Girls, at least the formation that included Martha, disbanded between 1990 and 1991. Izora later reformed the group, pairing with her daughter.

Wash had few, if any, thoughts about going out on her own. "At that point, I really wasn't tripping on going solo. Even while we were signed with Fantasy, we would go in sometimes and sing background on other artists' projects, so I was kind of satisfied doing that and it was fun. Sometimes people think a backup singer longs to be in the spotlight by themselves, but that's not necessarily true. Some people are happy just doing background work. It depends on their lives. They may, you know, have families and other types of obligations, and it kind of just suits them."

Instead, Martha lent her unmistakable voice to projects by other artists. To do so on her terms was one thing, but to have her voice used in recordings without credit, or worse, to have her voice appearing to come out of a woman who looked like a Victoria's Secret model, was another story. The latter scenario was a bitter reminder of the singer's earliest days experiencing emotional abuse that centered on weight issues, something not easily forgotten despite all the success that had followed. Martha took legal actions that drew attention to the issues. The controversy sprang from contemporary chart-topping acts of the day using the singer's vocals on songs that had become huge pop hits (most notably C+C Music

Factory's "Gonna Make You Sweat" and tracks by Italian upstarts Black Box) while failing to give Wash credit. The insult was further exacerbated by a Black Box promotional music video ("Everybody, Everybody") featuring a slim, sexy woman appearing to be the vocalist. Wash's resulting lawsuits eventually led to legislation that made proper, accurate credits mandatory on compact discs and videos.

"They were satisfying victories," she claims, "although you'd probably have to ask my attorney about that because he was the one that really fought for trying to make the person that is responsible accountable. You know, if you're gonna sample someone, you need to give the person you are sampling the credit. Whoever it is; it doesn't matter. But the other thing is—it doesn't just happen in the entertainment business. It can happen in any kind of field of work. If somebody lays claim to the work that you've done, then it's wrong. You wouldn't like it, right? I mean, it's done all the time. But it's wrong. I had the same situation, but it was magnified because it was on a song. And the thing is, why would you try and take someone's voice and put another person's face out there in the public and expect the public to buy it? That was the main thing—it was false advertising! I used to hear from other people in business that they were glad I did what I did, that it was wrong in the first place. They were glad that I won. So, yes, it was very satisfying experience," she says.

Wash reflects on the subject of residuals, another sore spot that so many dance artists have had to wrestle with in their relationships with some record labels. She concedes, "Unfortunately, that's usually how it works. I think years ago, with the record labels, they could slice, dice and chop up the songs. Remember that 30 years ago, you had singles, cassettes and the album itself. You can slice and dice those entities. And when you talk about the sale of those things, I think the record companies got away with a lot. You know, with the Internet, I think it may be even worse nowadays. As for overseas, there are some organizations that protect you and collect those royalties, but it depends on the country. However, all countries don't have agreements with the United States, so it can be very, very hard."

Adding to her requital, Martha's legal victory happily set the stage for a well-received and long-awaited solo single on RCA Records in 1992, "Carry On," which reached number 1 on the dance chart. A self-titled, full-length album the following year yielded more massive club hits. Still, the road was not always smooth as the singer mourned the death of her manager and dearest friend, Doug Kibble, and was forced to find her way without his valued guidance. In the years that followed, Wash persevered and continued to lend her voice to numerous dance hits, teaming with producers like Todd Terry and artists ranging from Jocelyn Brown to RuPaul. Songs like "Keep on Jumpin'" and "Catch the Light" became, as expected, club smashes. She teamed with Tony Moran for "Keep Your Body Workin'" and, in 2011, Wash released an unexpected single, a mesmerizing soft jam called "I've Got You." In 2012, the spotlight was aimed on the 30th anniversary of "It's Raining Men" and early in 2013 the artist released her first new album in 20 years. Titled *Something Special*, the collection was widely praised and the irresistible first single, "It's My Time," appeared almost prophetic. As she continues touring and committing to philanthropic and humanitarian work, including tireless efforts on behalf of AIDS organizations and work on autism awareness projects, she has also been working on her autobiography.

Martha is quick to acknowledge the blessing of being such an in-demand performer and the opportunities that still present themselves. She speaks warmly of her loyal domestic following and is equally appreciative of her overseas fans. "I would say I've received a good reception here in the U.S., and I have great fans here," she states, "but I think as far as

Europe goes, you have to remember that's a whole lot of countries. I think the fans in Europe tend to stick with the artists who have been around for a long time. There are a lot of artists that you don't hear from anymore in the United States that are making a wonderful living over in Europe. They've moved there — lock, stock and barrel — and they've told me I need to live over there too. They've been there for years and years and years, and they are thriving! The only other thing about that is artists who live and work in Europe are the first to admit they also want to get their music broken back in the U.S. There's always that idea that if you can conquer the United States, then you've got it made. Well, all I know is, there are a whole lot of great artists who have gone over there, and they have not looked back. And the fans are true fans over there! They love you if you have one head or if you have 10. It doesn't matter."

If you ask Wash what event in her vast experience made her feel as though she'd made it, she's quick to recall a very domestic celebration. "Singing at the White House!" she says without hesitation. "It was during President Clinton's administration in his last year. He was getting ready to leave office, and it was during the Christmas holiday. I had been watching Mrs. Clinton doing a tour of the White House on television, and I loved it. And previously, you know how you say one day you'd like to do this and one day that? Well, I had said, 'One day I'd love to sing at the White House!' And I'm sure a lot of artists have said that! I then got a phone call and the person asked me, 'Would you like to sing at the White House?' I said, 'Uh ... yeah!' They told me the Clintons' Christmas dinner was coming up *that* weekend and this was a Tuesday. By that Saturday, I was at the White House. They had the dinner on the lawn, inside tents, and about 500 people attending. A group of us came in by train. I always loved coming into D.C., Baltimore, Boston on the train — it's fun for me —, but we got there in really awful weather. It was me, Sister Sledge and a third performer. We did the sound check and we were basically set and headed over to White House for the reception. I'm amazed like a kid. Because I'm looking at all the things I had seen on TV, and now I'm seeing them in person. That was such an amazing thing. I met with politicians, entertainers — a big mix of people. We were shuttled over to the dinner and the Clintons came in, and it was amazing. Sister Sledge performed, I sang 'It's Raining Men'— that's what they wanted and I said, 'Okay fine!'— and they had a great time, clapping and smiling. Naturally, when it was over, everyone wanted pics with President Clinton and we made our way in and we got to meet them, and it was just a surreal time."

Martha Wash, the picture of glamour, enjoys a huge worldwide legion of followers and remains one of disco's most in-demand performers (photograph by Sean Black, used by permission. All rights reserved).

There's a tone of experience carefully mixed with caution and humility in her voice when the artist analyzes her career and accomplishments. She's come to have a solid personal philosophy that keeps her grounded. "Don't believe the hype; don't believe your own hype!" she says. "Because people want to put you on a pedestal, tell you how good you are — this, that and the other thing — but they also can turn around and tear you down so quickly it will make your head spin. I have always viewed my career as — I'm a working woman. This is what I do for a living. It takes up a lot of my time. It's not a 9 to 5 — at times, it can be a 24-hour thing. I just don't let the media get to me. We need them for promotion and such, but they want to paint you in a certain way. Honey, I never wanted to be a star. Because I've seen the stars, and what people report to me as the stars, and it's taken their lives — literally — being a star. I'll just be a celebrity; that's fine!" she laughs. "You have to pay so much to be a '*staaaar*,' you know what I'm saying? You can lose yourself. I didn't take the hype seriously."

Surely among the most respected, revered and beloved of disco's original groundbreakers, Martha Wash has earned the diva and legend titles. As for being remembered, Martha says, "I would like my fans to say they liked my music — that they got something from it. That it touched them, that they'll always remember it with a smile on their face. I'd like to be remembered as someone who tried to give some of myself and my time to charities and in ways that could help people. Some interviewer once said to me, 'Do you know you are an institution?' I said, 'Well, sometimes I think I needed to be *institutionalized*!' I said, 'Okay, institution? Fine, I'll take that!' I just *never* trip on it!"

Carol Williams

The *'Lectric Lady* album by Carol Williams was one of the most colorful and eye-catching on the bestseller walls of record retailers in 1976. Its beautiful portrait photograph of Carol, mike in hand and singing in the neon glow of a discothèque, was irresistible. Anyone dropping the needle on the cuts "More" and "Love Is You" and hearing her vibrant vocals was destined to become a Williams devotee. "I've opened up for James Brown, Dizzy Gillespie and Ray Charles. I've had the pleasure of being onstage with the very best disco artists, male and female, back then and still today. It was — and is — a great era to be remembered for!" Carol says most genuinely. Williams' beautiful voice, energy and connection to the pulse of dance floors made her a true early pioneer of disco, and today she is one of the genre's best spokespersons.

"I always knew I wanted to be a singer," says Carol, "from the time my father took me to the Apollo Theater on Sundays. I was an only child, and we went horseback riding and fishing a lot. I think he thought I was boy because we used to do different things like that." She laughs. "One particular Sunday when I was eight or nine years old, he took me to the Apollo and when I saw that show, I *knew* this is what I wanted. To be up on that stage! To be an entertainer! I learned to sing with a couple of girl groups, and eventually I went out on my own as Carol Williams."

Williams recalls one of the first ensembles she joined. "I worked with a group called the Geminis, and we recorded for RCA. We had a hit with the song 'Get It on Home.' We also had a song out that I wrote called 'The Price of Our Affair' on the Brunswick label. These songs all made it onto *Billboard*'s airplay list, and the vinyl records are still sought after out there today." Carol sang with her own band for years prior to connecting with the legendary Salsoul record label, but her association with the iconic record company proved to be essential to the artist's career. "I got with Salsoul because my husband at that time, DeVerne Williams, was Wilson Pickett's musical director, and he was told by Pickett's road manager that Salsoul was holding auditions for a girl singer. They wanted someone similar to Gloria Gaynor, because, at that time, Gloria was having big hits with 'Honey Bee' and 'Never Can Say Goodbye.' So they were looking for a fresh, new disco singer, and I gave it a shot. There must have been about 200 or 300 singers who auditioned, but I got it! The deal was initially going to be for one song, but when they saw that I actually had a band and was an artist who had been out there for a while and touring, they signed me up for a whole album deal."

The result was 1976's *'Lectric Lady*, an album produced by Salsoul's legendary composer and arranger, Vincent Montana, Jr. The record was prime dance material in its day (when LPs were also fashioned with a diverse, carefully-crafted selection of songs and less filler), and Salsoul aggressively marketed their new star. "The album took almost a year to record at Sigma Sound in Philly," she says. "I was working six nights a week with my band at that time — it was called Carol Williams & Fantasia — and I was always performing. I was still previously contracted to be in certain places when I got the Salsoul deal. When I was finished singing at night, I would go down to Vince's place, and I would pick the songs out. It takes a long time when you first start out with an album. You're not recording; you're finding out what songs you want to do. We'd go over what songs we thought would be best. I had written three songs on the album, he wrote some, and it just ended up taking a year to get it all together."

Backed by the Salsoul Orchestra, Carol's auspicious single debut, "More," was one of the very first commercially-available 12" singles and was a smash, reaching the upper regions of the disco charts in 1976. With her club-targeted and similarly themed follow-up tracks, "Love Is You" and "Come Back," Williams became an in-demand disco performer. "I came up with the idea of singing 'More,'" she says of the discofied remake of Kai Winding's 1963 hit from the movie *Mondo Cane*. "I was sitting home one day, and I was very aware that people were taking old standards and doing them over, like Gloria Gaynor's 'How High the Moon.' I told Vince my idea and how I wanted to sing it and asked what he thought of it. He liked it and built the arrangement around it, and that's how we came up with it. I remember when we finally completed the album, and Salsoul agreed that 'More' would be the first single. I still had engagements and was up in Canada, where the song had just come out as an import. Meanwhile it was breaking big in New York. I had to stay up in Canada, so I wasn't even hearing it starting to get airplay on New York radio and in the discothèques. I couldn't believe when they told me how well it was doing down in the States, and I was stuck up in Canada!"

"More" quickly became an early classic of the genre, around the same time as The Andrea True Connection's "More, More, More" was making waves. Recalls Williams, "I would have loved to have met Andrea because a lot of people used to say to me, 'Oh you're the lady that did "More, More, More."' And I'm sure they were saying to her, 'You're the lady who sings "More!"' I really didn't anticipate my song would be such a big disco hit. I mean, after I heard it and they made the long version of it, you just don't know what's going to happen. I finally realized it had made a big impact when I came back from Canada and I heard it on the radio and everywhere. My parents went on a trip to Puerto Rico, and they called me from the airport and told me, 'Your record is playing all over the airport!' That was when I really had the sense that I had a record that was big — and big all over the world. It was so exciting!"

Williams is passionate about the sound of disco, enthusiastically recalling the charm and quality of production those songs possessed. "I loved disco! I was comfortable with it because of the beautiful tracks. I loved it, and I still do. I think the reason the songs I sang were such big hits was because of their sophistication. I believe that disco brought back standard songs in a big way. They were taking these big band hits from back in the day and, through disco, they brought back beautiful string lines, you heard wonderful orchestrations and they had this exciting disco beat. You had live horns; you had live strings, real drums — those were real drums that Earl Young was playing on everything that came out of Sigma Sound. It's not heavily synthesized. Disco brought out the full, beautiful orchestration and composition of these songs. When you talk about an original disco song, you're talking about at least 30 to 40 people playing behind it. Vince was playing the xylophones, then you had the congas added in — you had so many people involved in the making of the song so that is sounded so full. You had great singers and background singers. So, you had songs that were several times more elaborate and lush than, say, the same song that was recorded in the '30s or '40s."

Carol Williams was already singing and touring professionally prior to being discovered by Salsoul Records, which released her first hit, "More," in 1976 (courtesy Carol Williams).

She adds, "At the beginning of the disco era, I remember we didn't do tracks. We had bands. I remember the Trammps and my band were both scheduled to appear at two different clubs in Brooklyn on the same night — the Odyssey and some other place. I'd do the Odyssey first and then head over to the other club. We agreed to leave our equipment and instruments, and the Trammps would use them and we'd use theirs. If you knew other acts and had that kind of rapport with them, you could do two or three clubs that way in one night."

During the height of her Salsoul label success, Carol identifies the moment she knew she had hit it big. "I think I felt like a star when the Salsoul Orchestra performed with me, Double Exposure and some other acts at Roseland, a huge venue with a huge stage. The Salsoul girls were on stage with me singing 'More,' Vince [Montana] was conducting the orchestra and it was really something! They filmed all the performers as part of an advertisement for a record compilation Salsoul would be promoting on television. They were selling a record that featured all of us artists, and the ad would play on TV at 12 or one in the morning. I could turn on the TV and see myself in clips singing. That commercial must have been run for almost a year. I could see myself, what I had on, singing with the girls — and when I saw that, I just knew I had made it. I think that was *the* highlight of my career," she declares with excitement in her voice.

There are more pleasant memories from the era for Carol. She recalls, "My great friend, Loleatta Holloway, asked me to put a band together for an appearance she was making at the Apollo many years ago. I used some of my band members and my son DeVerne, who was only 12 at the time, to play the drums. Loleatta knew he played the drums, but she was blown away when she heard him play all of her hits in rehearsal. She was astonished! When we did the show, we had to have a platform built to bring him up higher so the audience would be able to see him. Loleatta's two sons were her dancers. Junior Walker and the great Bobby Womack were on the show as well, and Loleatta was in rare form! That night she sang all her dance hits with her wonderful clear diction and powerful delivery. I was part of her backup, along with Sheila Tolbert, a singer named Cassandra and two male singers. Because of that show, my son became the youngest professional musician to ever work the Apollo!

"One more highlight that I can't leave out," she adds, "was doing background vocals with the great Melba Moore in the studio at my house. It was for her song 'Lean on Me.' She guided a male vocalist named Hafise and me. It was a really wonderful experience. Melba is one of my favorite singers, along with Gloria Gaynor and Donna Summer."

Carol's time at Salsoul was relatively short, despite her successful debut with the label. "Love Is You" (a song Williams claims she may have performed even more often than "More") was nearly as big as her previous hit. Meanwhile, her record label was also moving up in the world. "The clubs played a few more tracks off the *'Lectric Lady* album," she remembers, "but 'More' and 'Love Is You' were the big radio play hits. At the time, Salsoul and Goldmine Records were starting to work with a lot of different people. They had Loleatta Holloway, Double Exposure, Claudja Barry, First Choice, Charo and several others, and I felt that they weren't paying particular attention to any one artist. I felt that it was time to go to the next level, the next label where I could have a little more say in what I wanted in my songs and albums. We parted ways fine, with no problems, but I went my way and they did their thing."

By 1979, Williams, in fine vocal form, was back on record store shelves with another LP released through Canada's Quality Records. It featured the lushly orchestrated disco hits "Dance the Night Away and "Tell the World About Our Love." Williams remembers, "I did that second album, which was called *Reflections of Carol Williams,* on a label subsidiary of Roy B. Records. Tony Valor handled the production. I felt if my band was good enough to do gigs with me, they should have been good enough to be on my album. I insisted that the musicians that worked with me on stage be in the studio with me. We had full creativity, and I was able to even include two slow songs. I think I wrote nearly every song on that album, and I was able to collaborate with my musicians on some and my husband, DeVerne, as well. He did all the arrangements of every song. I remember him writing all the string lines out, all the horn lines, in our dining room, everything. And we rehearsed the rhythm sections in my house as well. We recorded it at Sigma Sound in New York. With Salsoul, we had been at Sigma Sound in Philadelphia. Everything on that album was me—what I wanted to sing. After that, I worked with a group called Lady Ritz, and we also did a disco album. We did a song called 'Green Eyes.'"

The early '80s were an equally creative period for the artist, who was still a staple of the club charts. She began working with Darryl Payne, who had produced major dance artists such as Carol Douglas, France Joli and Tavares. "I signed with Vanguard Records. I never did a whole album with them, but I did several singles, including 'No One Can Do It (Like You),' which Shep Pettibone remixed and which was a big club hit, 'Can't Get Away (from Your Love),' which did very well and was more of a funky, dance-R&B type of song, and 'You've Reached the Bottom Line.' The sound was really different from what I had done with Salsoul. Darryl had more of a black, urban dance feel in his producing style." "Can't Get Away (from Your Love)" kept the singer on the dance charts for several weeks in 1982.

Carol continued to keep her presence known on the dance floor with more Payne-influenced tracks, including 'One More Time,' released on an Atlantic Records subsidiary label, and numerous other club hits like "Queen of Hearts" for Prelude Records. She laughs, "It's funny how you think back and you forget all the things you've done, but I guess I never stopped recording. Of course, when you first hear your records playing on the radio, you'd love to have that continue. I had that experience with my biggest hits. It makes you feel great when more people are hearing your music. But I never stopped performing. I performed before I ever had a hit record and even when I was in between record companies. I was always out there with my band."

The club environment was, as Williams puts it, "where it was all happening." She vividly recalls the nightclub landscape and all the drama that went with it. "I remember being at Studio 54. I was at a big affair for Frankie Crocker, his birthday I believe, and Madonna was there, and he rode in on a white horse. I was there as a guest. I was aware of what was going on with drugs and such, especially since I wasn't performing. You see what's going on. As a performer, though, you go in, you go backstage, you do your show. You're not really conscious of what's going on. I never participated in any of that stuff. My thing was—people are happy; this is what they chose to do. It wasn't *my* thing. I've been like that since I was a teenager performing at the Apollo—when I was still young and there were people there drinking, gambling, you know. You just let people do their thing, and you do your thing. It wasn't about being stuck up or anything; everybody just needs their space to do whatever they choose to do. It just was never my thing. When I finished singing, I went home. For me, it was a job—it was really that simple. It was a career that I enjoyed very much, but when it was over, I came home and went back to being a regular housewife," she laughs.

Carol Williams was part of a disco diva show that made the rounds throughout the '90s. "It was a happy time," she says. "I remember Carol Douglas and I doing a show at the Limelight in New York, and I think we didn't come onstage until like 4 A.M. on a Monday morning. We had arrived around midnight Sunday night. I'm telling you the place was packed! If you didn't know it was four in the morning, you'd have thought it was 11 or 12 on a Friday or Saturday night. The club was huge, and I'll never forget that it looked like a cathedral and saying to Carol, 'I can't believe these people are still partying and dancing at this hour. This is a Monday morning! Don't they have jobs to go to?' I'll never forget it! I was there a number of times, for several shows with Loleatta Holloway, Vicki Sue Robinson, Sharon Redd and Carol. You're in it at the time, but until you look back at it, you don't realize *what* an era it was. My God, the clubs in New York: Limelight, Studio 54, Zanzibar, Bonds, the Paradise Garage, Broadway International. There had to be 20 or 30 big clubs in Manhattan alone. I don't know how it is today, but back then, it was incredible!"

Though Williams enjoyed numerous hits, there was the *one* that got away. However, there's little tone of regret in her voice as she relates the story. "Darryl Payne and I had done 'No One Can Do It' and we were trying to figure out what was going to be the follow-up song," she says. "I'll never forget we were up at Vanguard Records—I think they were up on 23rd Street in New York—and we went upstairs. I recall one of the writers of the song was there. Darryl wanted me to hear this writer's song that was on a cassette. What I heard was somebody on a keyboard and Jocelyn Brown singing 'Over Like a Fat Rat.' Nothing like the way Fonda Rae [eventually] did it, though. I'm sure Jocelyn's melody was the same, but when you just have a basic version, to my imagination, I really couldn't put it together and said I didn't like it. I said I didn't want to sing about a rat. I kept hearing [the song title and lyrics]. What is that? I am a songwriter myself, so I guess I didn't understand the concept. Anything I am singing has to make sense to me and tell a story. It has to have a melody that is catchy to me. I didn't hear any of that. Darryl kept telling me to look beyond just hearing the keyboards and someone just singing. He said I wasn't hearing the bass line and all the stuff that would go around it and that it would be very funky. But I said no, and I turned it down. The next thing I know Fonda did it, and she did a *fantastic* job. The way they arranged it—it was amazing. When you heard it in the club it was just so funky and catchy. But to this day, I just have to say I didn't hear it at the time. I know what the hook is, but I still haven't gotten into the lyrics of the song, the verses. I can't say it *wasn't* the right song for me back then, though. Had I heard it the way the production ended up being, I probably would have wanted to do it. But from the way I heard it originally, it was nothing like the final production or the way Fonda sang it. But, you know, my song 'Can't Get Away' kind of had the same feel as 'Fat Rat'—it kind of fell into the same category of music. So I got to do something like it."

Williams continues to perform today and music remains her passion. As she's matured, she's had to face the same issues of aging that many divas have, and she relates her philosophy with ease. "We don't sing as much as we'd like to. But disco—that's somebody's era. That's the music they grew up with and enjoyed. Thank God in the heavens above that it's still relevant. I think that being in the music business, my philosophy for matur-

Carol Williams traveled to Paris for a special show in 2012 and says, "The anticipation of this show was unbelievable for me, and it was a big success. I almost felt like it was the rebirth of Carol Williams" (courtesy Carol Williams).

ing in it—and the belief I have about it is—that you have to kind of remember that old adage, 'the show must go on.' When you have a show, you put yourself in a different frame of mind. You don't want to bring any of your problems with you when you're on stage. You have to be in that joyful mode. Nobody wants to see someone up there acting like, 'Oh, I'm just here. Let me just sing the song.' Nobody wants to see a performer like that! Singing puts me in a *very* happy place. And even though I get older and I may not be able to do some of the things I would like to do on stage, I still always try to give it my best and to look my best. And I *have* to do my best! To me, it keeps me young.

"I recently visited Paris to do an hour-long show," she says. "I had never been there before. I had slept, dreamed, rehearsed and worked on this show like never before. I wondered why I hadn't been there 15 or 20 years ago! They recently reissued two of my older songs for the first time there—'What's the Deal' and 'Have You for My Love'—songs I never performed that much. I had stopped doing those songs in my show. Now *that* was a challenge—I had to learn those songs again, but I was ready and really looking forward to it. It was exciting; there was a fresh kind of nervousness and the thrill that I was going to Paris was incredible! I sang 'Last Dance' as a memorial tribute to Donna Summer as well. The anticipation of this show was unbelievable for me, and it was a big success. I almost felt like it was the rebirth of Carol Williams." Recalling her vast musical journey, she adds, "You know, when you have a successful career in music, you realize that many people are to thank for it. I will always want to thank Lee Wade, John Weber, Sheila Seigal, Lou Gurino, Tony Valor, Johnny D, Mike and John, Ron, Carl, Eric and all the wonderful artists I've had the pleasure to work with."

Though the road is far from fully traveled for Carol, she's confident about how she'd like others to remember her well-spent time here. She says, "I want to be remembered as a person who gave her all and her best in what she loved to do—to sing and be an entertainer. I'd love to be recognized and known for the fact that when I did my shows, I always did them to the best of my ability. I'd like to have reached everybody, but if I got the attention of one person—touched the heart of just one person—then I'm happy. That's what I want to be remembered for. I think any artist is glad to have signature songs—and I was lucky enough to have had 'More' and 'Love Is You!' They are very positive songs with a very positive message. I feel very blessed that I've had the privilege to sing those songs and that people know and recognize me for them!"

Jessica Williams

Few songs brought the extraordinary work of backup singers into focus the way the Motown hit "Love Hangover" did. As mesmerizing as the song's arrangement and Diana Ross' extraordinary lead vocals were, the listener couldn't help but be drawn to the enticing female voices singing, subtly cavorting and playfully mingling in the background as this sexy musical cocktail spilled from the turntable. Jessica Williams was one of the backing vocalists who helped provide that slow boil. She added her remarkable vocal gift to an astonishing, nearly uncountable number of iconic disco productions, as well as her own solo masterpiece, "Queen of Fools." Williams is, unquestionably, one of the most accomplished artists in the history of disco.

"My whole family was in music," says Jessica. "I started singing in the church and high school [and headed] straight over to Motown. I got signed there in early 1973 — me and two other girlfriends. We had just been rehearsing, and we decided to call a girlfriend who worked at Motown Records. We missed her, but we got a Motown representative instead, and he asked us if we could sing. Of course we said yeah, and he set up an interview for us! We went up there and met Hal Davis, who was a producer of the Jackson 5 and lots of artists at the time. We did our introductions with him and got all excited. He ended up grooming us at 'MoWest.' That was when Motown moved out west to Hollywood on 6400 Sunset, at the corner of Wilcox. So we were going up there every night, rehearsing, and Hal was actually buying us clothes! We would go with him and buy clothes, and he would make us try them on up in his office — *uh oh*!" she laughs. "We would have to try on the clothes in front of him! I wasn't married, so it was cool. He wasn't interested in me that way anyway," she chuckles.

"He was preparing us for a big audition at Motown, and, when it finally was time, it was held at the Motown Sunrise Recording studio. We had just a piano player and all the executives sitting around with Suzanne de Passe [creative assistant to label founder Berry Gordy]. We did the audition, and Davis called us that evening and had the champagne ready. I was really a kid at the time, and when he said, 'You guys got it!' well, we were all wide-eyed and we were thinking we're bad-asses now! I was signed to Motown under the name Jessie Richardson. It meant you could *really* sing if you were signed at Motown! Back then, it was really hard to get tied to the label."

Williams recalls, "Being in the presence of Smokey, Diana, Gladys, The Four Tops — it was amazing. At that time, they had all kinds of people. They had Thelma Houston, too. I was a fan of hers, and I used to see her shows. At that time, she was wearing afros and no shoes on stage! She was up there, and I used to see her, The Commodores and Michael Jackson, when he was a little tiny boy. I started doing demos for the Supremes, Mary Wilson and Diana Ross. I got to meet them, and that's how I learned mike technique — all that kind of stuff.

"One of my girlfriends in the group got pregnant, and she decided she was going to move to Texas, so that was the end of our group. We had done two albums of our own, but they were both canned. When they shelved albums, it was like a tax write-off for the label. When they spent money on you and didn't put your product out, they'd just use it as a tax write-off. And if they were over-budget on some of the other artists, they would charge the expenses to the artists like me. They would charge different songs by other artists to our account, and we would end up paying for it. But I ended up staying there at Motown and doing a lot of background sessions, and that's how I ended up being on so many records. I think I worked with just about everybody who was on Motown at the time."

Williams' experience at Motown gave her the opportunity to sing on two of disco's biggest hits ... *ever*! The seminal, number 1 pop and disco classics "Love Hangover" and "Don't Leave Me This Way" both feature Williams on background vocals. The songs became iconic dance masterpieces thanks to the melding of a soulful essence with lush and skillfully executed orchestration — not to mention the legendary vocals of Diana Ross and Thelma Houston respectively. "Don't Leave Me This Way" landed Houston a Grammy award and "Love Hangover" earned Ross a nomination. Jessica says, "My background work on Diana

Fred Sawyers, Jessica Williams and Jerry Scott (left to right) made up the group Arpeggio, whose percolating hit "Love and Desire" sent crowds rushing to the dance floor at the height of the disco era (courtesy Jessica Williams).

Ross' 'Love Hangover' was one of those Motown session jobs. We had to be social with the producers. And the recording sessions would always be late at night, 12 or one at night. We'd all be very dressed up, like we were going to a party. Dressed real nice — nails were perfect, we had jewelry on, sometimes mink coats, and we had heels on. We did *not* come to the studio wearing tennis shoes or without makeup. *Never!* It was the standard that all L.A. singers had at the time. We all looked good! And everybody dressed the part. You got called back on sessions because you looked good. You might not have been the best singer, but as long as you could sing your part and looked good, you could be in that clique. 'Cuz the other girls would pull your coattails if you were singing stupid. After a couple of tries, if you didn't get it right, they would call you out of the studio.

"You'd also have to be able to handle a couple of drinks," she remembers, "at least a little bit, with some of the producers — because they'd try to make the session fun. Hal Davis was the producer on 'Love Hangover.' Singing in the background was me, Brenda Sutton and I can't remember who the other singers were. It was late at night, and the way he got that sound out of us and out of Diana was through a drink called the 'Motown Slush.' I wasn't a drinker, so I would always try to sit where I could pour mine into a flower pot. It was just about every liquor [Davis] had in his cabinet. He had a bar that had all kinds of booze. So when it got down to a certain level, he would just mix it all together with what I guess was a mai-tai mix, and it would be all the rums, the vodkas, the scotches — every kind of drink you can imagine. He'd pass the glasses around to the four or five people in there. Sometimes we'd be drinking for money! He'd give us $100, $50. 'Here, I'll give ya $100 — down this,' he'd say. He'd be getting us looped!" she laughs. "So, that's how he got that [playful, lazy, late-night] sound. Diana was a little buzzed! We all were! That was Motown. It's the truth! He wanted to loosen us up because the song was like that. He wanted that slurred sound so he could get to the gist of the song. We were loose, but we weren't drunk. Everybody was loose, but not so intoxicated where we wouldn't be able to remember our parts.

"I knew it would be a hit," says Jessica, "because everything he produced was a hit. He had the Jackson 5, Thelma Houston and more. I knew Thelma before she was on Motown, when she was on the Sunshine label. Brenda Sutton had given me a call to come work on 'Don't Leave Me This Way' and Hal Davis was again the producer. I loved that song and Thelma was one of my favorite singers. We had to sing all the way down the long versions of those songs. You would have to sing all of that — the whole song. Today you don't have to do that, but back then you did. It made me feel great to be a part of these songs. Many of them are like anthems, especially in the clubs, and it was a great experience!"

She continues, "After that was over, I ended up doing shows with Lainie Kazan, who is still one of my best friends, and I met my husband, John B. Williams, through her. She was working at the Playboy Club on a regular gig, and I worked that with her. Then I went over to Polydor Records. Pattie Brooks was there, and she really brought me over there. She was a session singer and one of the producers, Simon Soussan, asked me if I could sing lead. I said, 'Of course!'"

Performing under the name Jessie Williams, her collaboration with Soussan produced a string of disco classics in which her powerful vocals were an integral element of each project's success. Her voice can be heard on "Mr. Big Shot" by the Simon Orchestra, "Dance My Way Into Your Heart" by Romance and on the feverishly percussive hits of Arpeggio, which Soussan launched through his Harem Records (and Polydor). "The first time I started singing lead was with the group Arpeggio," she says. "We did 'Love and Desire,' 'Breakout,' 'Saturday Night.' 'Love & Desire' was one of those long songs to sing too. Sometimes it would take days or a week to do a song, but it wouldn't matter because you were being paid. Sometimes you could get a song out in a day or you would break it up. They brought the speed up on that one, but I sang it in a lower, more comfortable key. It was cool singing it on *Soul Train* and shows like that. That way your family could see you. 'Cuz if you're on TV, you've made it. If not, they just think you're jivin'! We did *The Midnight Special* when Linda Clifford was hosting the show. Doing shows like that was really validation. That was a highlight for me, because the disco years were the only days the work was really in the spotlight."

Williams finally scored a major disco hit under her real name a short while later. A Top-20 dance classic that stayed on the chart for nearly half of 1980, "Queen of Fools" became an energized smash on the club scene. A track that exploded with Soussan's electrifying synthesizer and percussion work, Jessica describes her signature song as "the highlight of my career! That's what started me! They were giving me the words to 'Queen of Fools' right out of the control room. And I'd sing it. I didn't even like the song at first. I was like, 'What kind of song is this?' Because I was an R&B singer, and R&B was a lot different from disco. 'Queen of Fools' had a lot of lyrics, and it looked like it went on forever. They would write a verse and tell me how the verse goes and they'd say, 'Now sing this part, now that part, now this part.' It took us a week to finish that song because it was so long."

Williams' studio recording work was a true education for the artist. "It was very enlightening for me and, with having had no formal training, being in the studio was just how I learned how to do it. When I started out, I had no kind of training and only knew I could sing. But you still needed technique, because you can't sing the way you would live when you do a recording. When you sing live, you can sing full voice, you can ad lib and do different change-ups, participate with the audience, alter the way you stand at the mike and you have fun. You have fun in the studio too, but it's still tense. Every little crack, pitch, everything had to be perfect back then. A lot of people think it was easy, but I had to go through different takes, three or four times. You get stuck — and you get mad at yourself. Then you have to wait and take some deep breaths. Sometimes you'd start to think you can't sing because they're telling you what to sing most of the time. With recording, it's very structured. You've got people telling you what to do, and you've only got the headphones and yourself and the music. That's scary! In front of the mike recording, it's all on you. By the time I was with Soussan, I was more polished."

It should come as no surprise that gay clubs were huge supporters of Jessica's "Queen of Fools," and the artist had no problem embracing the community. "I was secure with myself and maybe that's why I had no problem with disco, going into the clubs and making lifetime friendships with club owners and their friends. Neither did my husband, John. He would go with me a lot. When he'd escort me to the stage, he'd get pinched sometimes," she laughs. "I told him, 'Well stop wearing those leather pants!' He would say, 'What am I gonna do? Fight everyone in the club?' It was a compliment as far as we were concerned. He had no problem with it, and neither did I. Sometimes even my daughter would be with me in the club on some occasions, and she was about 17. Of course, I had to keep an eye on her and make sure she stayed out of trouble. But the club environment didn't affect me, and I'm still married to the same man for 34 years. I never indulged in drugs and such. I didn't knock people who indulged, but they all knew I didn't do it — outside of smoking a little pot. Drugs, coke — I wasn't into any of that.

"You know what I will tell you? I loved those gay club owners! We would go down on a Thursday and come home on Monday. We'd hang out at the club owner's homes and on their yachts. We had a great time. I never had any problems with money in gay clubs! They would always give us our money! I'd take that money and put it right down there where my pussy was! And ain't nobody going down there but my husband! Before I'd go on stage, sometimes I'd get up there with a pussy full of money! I'd have twenties comin' through my panties. That money would be wet by the time I'd get home!" Jessica says with a roar of laughter.

Williams' solo album, also called *Queen of Fools*, was prime material for disco fans and DJs during dance music's tricky transitional period in 1980. The album yielded another hit, "Gambling on Your Love," which gave Jessica's name additional star power in the clubs. But the project failed to be as lucrative as the singer might have hoped. "I didn't make any money off my album — the record company took everything," she says. "I never received any royalties. You see, my problem was that I was signed to the producer. When you're signed to the producer and not to the label, the money comes through the producer. The producer is supposed to disperse the royalties to you. Well, Soussan had so many projects — he had like six or seven a year — and he would put the money back into those projects and the rest he would spend on himself and his lifestyle. But I was on every album and single that was on his label, under different names. He would change the names and put different people's names on the recordings and call it a day. I was on records by Romance, Simon Orchestra. Oh God — I can't even recall all the names of all the acts, so-called artists, but it was me. I did all the singing. I was the only girl on the label. Many people recognized that I was the real singer on so many songs. People at the clubs would say, 'Isn't that you on this song or that song?' They knew it was me, but he would put different faces on the songs, his girlfriend and his momma even. I'm serious! I took legal action at one point. He said, 'You're suing me, but you should be suing Polydor.'

"Well, there was eventually a statue of limitations, and it was all off. I made money from the actual up-front advance for the recording. I had to get paid at least union scale. Personal appearances — that's the only way I made money. You know, I was doing these recordings for five straight years and I made pretty good money, and I didn't even think about royalties at the time. I just automatically thought I was gonna get them. So I didn't think about it. When I'd ask about the royalty statement, Soussan would say, 'Well, this is not the time for the royalty statement,' or 'This is not the quarter' and 'Well, it didn't sell that many records' and all that kind of bullshit. He was a snake. If you don't have a manager or agent or attorney watching your money, you don't end up getting what you deserve."

She adds, "I was with [Soussan] for about 16 years, and I'll tell you — it was like a marriage when we broke up. It was really hard for me when we went our separate ways, even though he screwed me out of a lot of money. He had me recording all the time, just putting out singles, and I had no reason to go anywhere else. You know, I was recording every day. I was calling friends and family to work with me, so it was really comfortable. And it was right in town. I could call the shots. If I didn't feel like recording one day, I could say lets do it tomorrow. After he realized how many records I was selling, I could pretty much call the shots like that."

Jessica takes a broad perspective of her career when looking back. "It bothers me sometimes that I didn't get the royalties and recognition on the songs that I did record, but then I let go of it," she says. "God had more things down the road for me to do than cry over spilled milk with Simon. I've done lots more things and worked with everybody. I worked with Helen Reddy. The movie *Trick*. That's me singing 'I Am Woman.' I sang a duet called 'Friends' with Helen on her *Center Stage* CD. I did some work on tracks for the movies *What's Love Got to Do with It*, *Clueless* and *Addams Family Values*. I've worked with Engelbert Humperdinck, Connie Stevens, Arsenio Hall. I was the background singer for Arsenio's show — and my husband was the bass player, but he played *everything* on that show. For the stars that didn't bring their background singers with them, I would be the background singer. I worked with Ringo Starr, Martha Wash, Lonnie Gordon — a whole bunch of people. Ringo was the only one who asked for my resume. I said, 'Fine, you want my resume? Here it is!' He was like, "I should be backing you!' I was like, '*Yeah!*' But who wouldn't want to back the Beatles? I've done a lot of things. I never minded doing the backup thing. I learned from doing the side work with big celebrities, people you could walk on stage with. You do your thing, collect your check and go home," she laughs.

The artist reflects on her remarkable life, the personal and professional gains and losses (including the passing of her daughter not long ago — a deeply personal tragedy for the artist and mother) and where she's at with life today. "My daughter, Vetia Gaye Richardson, passed away a few months ago, so I am now raising my grandchildren, and I'm just getting myself back. I'm getting stronger. I never knew I had that many emotions in my body. You go through different stages when dealing with something like that. But I'm okay. I have my friends like Lanie, Connie and Cynthia [Manley], and they call me and make sure I'm okay. And my husband is wonderful. I don't know what I would have done without him. He is such a good man. He kept me in the business, he kept me up and he kept me in the state I needed to be. You know?

"I know I've been blessed. I've been working as a singer all my life. That's it. That's all I've done. So I'm still doing things that I enjoy, that I want to do. I recently did a song called 'Mingle with the Night' on Paradax Records, and I have another dance project that I'm getting ready to do. There are no record deals anymore. People just do them and put them out for downloading. All the technology has wiped the labels out." Jessica also recently released a slick and ethereal version of Donna Summer's "Sunset People," a production helmed by Rick Gianatos.

Williams' personal approach to maturing doesn't include a whole lot of dwelling on the subject of aging. "I never even thought about aging," she says. "I just kept going—I never stopped. I never stopped to look back and reflect or anything. I always did what I wanted to do, so I really couldn't tell you about how I handled aging. I still look good!" she laughs. "I still look *very* good, and I still get calls to do stuff. And I stayed flexible about it. I never thought of myself as, 'I'm a big star, and I'll only do what Jessica Williams did on her records.' I would go and work for all kinds of people, not just stay in one category. I'd do country & western, blues, jazz, gospel, you know. I got to do both R&B and disco. I didn't feel slighted in any era because I was doing everything. I would be doing four different projects at any one time. You can't do just one thing if you want to work. I just kept working at my craft."

The astonishing singing career of Jessica Williams is as much a testament to her tremendous talent and durability as it is to the disco she loaned her voice to, if not always her name. The performer has still more to reveal when the time is right, but she is less concerned about her legacy as an artist than as a person. She says, "I just want to be remembered as a caring person, a talented person, a flexible person, a God-fearing person — that can do good shows. I wanna be known as a good mother and a good wife and a good performer who enjoyed a very full life — that's always been first for me. That's how I am!"

Jessica Williams reflects on her music career and says, "I just kept going—I never stopped. I never stopped to look back and reflect or anything" (courtesy Jessica Williams).

Norma Jean Wright

Few groups from the disco era had the star power that the band Chic wielded following the success of their 1977 album debut and crossover megahit "Dance, Dance, Dance." Likewise, the group's creators, Nile Rodgers and Bernard Edwards, became among the most sought-after producers of the time, thanks to their extraordinary vision and ability to create a sophisticated disco sound unlike any other material of the day. Norma Jean Wright was one of the first vocalists to work with the duo as a lead singer for Chic (and, no less, as a stellar solo performer), and her sweet, stylish voice seamlessly blended with her producers' scintillating dance-floor rhythms. Together, they created some of disco's finest moments. She candidly discusses the highs and lows of life under the disco ball.

Norma recalls her transition from Ohio girl to New York sensation. "A friend of mine that I went to high school with moved to New York City to become a fashion model. I stayed in touch with her and, soon after graduating from Ohio State, I told her of my plans to relocate there to pursue my singing career. Over the phone, she introduced me to Curtis Knight, a music manager known for having worked with Jimi Hendrix. He was launching a soul-rock band called ESP and was still looking for an additional female vocalist. I sent him some footage of me singing, as well as photos, and he offered me the gig—if I was willing move there and put in the required rehearsal," Norma remembers.

"In June of 1976, I moved to New York and started rehearsing with ESP. Several months later, I met guitarist Nile Rodgers through my roommate and friend, Lynna Davis. She had previously worked with Nile and knew that he and bass player Bernard Edwards were developing a band and searching for a female lead to record some of their original music. I decided to audition, and they hired me."

Chic's early development mixed some remarkable vocal talent with stellar, hook-driven music arrangements, and the combination produced some monumental results. "The first song I recorded with them was 'Everybody Dance,'" Wright says. "Once my vocals were laid, they tested the song out at a local dance club, and the crowd loved it! They worked on another song, 'Dance, Dance, Dance,' with session singers Luther Vandross, Alfa Anderson, Diva Gray and David Lasley. It was initially released on Buddah Records, but due to some contractual loophole, Buddah lost the single and it was quickly

Norma Jean Wright segued from a successful turn as a lead singer in the seminal disco group Chic to solo star with the hit single "Saturday" in 1978 (courtesy Norma Jean Wright).

picked up by Atlantic. On board with Atlantic, we went back into the studio to add my voice to 'Dance, Dance, Dance,' and while it was catapulting up the charts, we tweaked 'Everybody Dance' for the follow-up single. We soon started working on the album. A highlight for me while recording the album was working with Luther Vandross. My favorite song on the album is an R&B ballad entitled 'Falling in Love with You.' Luther and I sang the chorus of this song as a duet, and his vocal is as smooth as butter. Oh my God, as far as vocalists go — he was the cat's meow!"

The self-titled debut album from Chic was a certified smash. The rollicking single "Dance, Dance, Dance" made it to number 1 on the disco chart and made the Top 10 on the pop side. Its hook, an old-time, jazz-based cheer of "Yowsah" (repeated three times) proved irresistible to audiences everywhere. "Everybody Dance" followed as a Top-20 R&B hit and Top-10 smash in the U.K. The string and beat-heavy sound Rogers and Edwards created became their signature through the remainder of the disco era, and their productions were largely heralded as sophisticated, nearly instant disco classics. They'd expand their horizons with Sister Sledge's stupendous anthem "We Are Family" and the crowd-pleaser "He's the Greatest Dancer." The team later kicked off the '80s by providing adrenaline to Diana Ross' career with their highly identifiable style on the album *Diana*, which included the landmark singles "Upside Down" and "I'm Coming Out" (though the artist was reported to have initially disliked the sound).

Evidence of an evolving process, the Chic debut LP oddly featured a pair of fair-skinned women's faces posed with suggestive eyes and pursed lips. "These two faces graced the album cover for a reason," asserts Norma. "They added an element of mystique, and it gave many radio programmers the impression that these girls were members of the group. Nile and Bernard felt that by displaying these beautiful women (one a fair-skinned black girl and the other white), that it might encourage pop radio programmers to play Chic's music faster — if they thought the group was mixed. Although Chic's sound had crossover appeal, I believe they feared that if the group had been depicted as an 'all-black act,' that some Top-40 programmers might not have played our music. It was common for black acts to be pigeonholed, and their music was targeted only to urban programmers."

With the onslaught of Atlantic's publicity campaign, the world eventually became familiar with the actual members of Chic. "Our first publicity shot captures the four of us. I'm wearing a white, floor-length gown and Bernard, Nile and Tony [Thompson, another founding member and the group's drummer] wore designer suits. I was proud of our image and happy to be the lead singer, but I felt isolated at times, being the only female in the group. I missed working with ESP, where I traded leads and backgrounds with co-member Luci Martin. She and I became comrades, and I missed that. As we prepared for our tour, auditions were held [to add] another girl. Luci auditioned, and she became the fifth member of Chic."

Wright describes the unique dynamic between herself and her producers and the challenges of participating in the development of Chic. "The chemistry between Bernard, Nile and Tony was tight. There was something special about them as a unit; it was magical. Sonically, it was a melting pot of sorts, with Bernard's background in funk and R&B, Nile's classical training and Tony's studies in jazz. All of them were native New Yorkers. However, I grew up in the Midwest, listening to Motown, gospel, pop and R&B. I had honed my skills early on, starting out by singing in my church choir, and, by 16, I was performing regularly with live bands. I caught a break when I was asked to accompany the Spinners on several spot dates and sang lead on their hit, 'Then Came You,' which they had recorded with Dionne Warwick.

"Working with Bernard and Nile on the album was tedious at times," she confesses. "The ballad came easy. Once Bernard gave me the basic idea, he pretty much let me run with it. They were pleased with the outcome, and so was I. On the up-tempo tracks, my lead vocals are syncopated, playing cat and mouse around Bernard's beat-driven bass lines. With 'Everybody Dance,' I combined a mixture of chest voice with falsetto, and on the ballad, they preferred my 'damsel in distress' technique — which was sweet and airy in texture. The most challenging song for me was 'Est-Ce Que C'est Chic' because the key was way too high. For the most part, while singing with Chic, I used my soprano and upper register. It was the lighter side of my voice, and I kept it sweet, seductive and sexy. This is what they wanted. When our songs took off, I was blown away! Here I was living in New York City for less than a year and the lead singer of a hit-selling group. It was a dream come true, and I was ecstatic. I had taken their direction very well on the Chic songs, and later, with my album, I finally had an opportunity to utilize my natural alto range, which was rounder and a little huskier in tone."

Once Chic's album was certified gold, Bernard and Nile began brainstorming plans for Norma's solo endeavor. "They informed me that several labels had expressed interest in doing a spin-off deal with me," the artist recalls. "Many of them had heard 'Falling in Love with You,' which piqued their interest even more. It was agreed that I'd do a solo album, with Bernard and Nile as producers, and I would continue on as the lead vocalist of Chic," she says.

The LP *Norma Jean* was released in 1978 on Bearsville Records, a subsidiary company of Warner Bros. The solo album gave the singer a Top-20 R&B hit with the single "Saturday," which also was a major club hit. Numerous tracks on the collection were dance-floor hits, including "Having a Party" and "Sorcerer," all featuring the trademark Chic sound that had become the rage. "I enjoyed doing the album," she reflects. "[Nile and Bernard] allowed me to step out a little more than on the *Chic* LP. I wasn't allowed to be as creative as I would have liked, but we managed to find a balance, and I was pleased with the final product. While recording my album, there was less pressure, but there were still some frustrating moments. Bernard and Nile had a formula that worked for Chic, and they didn't like to veer away from it. As a result, often they appeared to be inflexible, and [that] even caused them to initially bump heads with Sister Sledge and Diana Ross."

She goes on, "As talented as they were as musicians, they were still developing their skills in the area of vocal production. For instance, with Chic's first album, they didn't check to discuss the best keys for my voice, and on ["Est-Ce Que C'est Chic"] in particular the key was way too high and uncomfortable to sing. I mentioned this to them, and never once did they consider a key change. Instead, I was told, 'I could do it,' and I had to make do. At least by the time we started my album, they checked to make sure the keys were in my range. Occasionally, they even loosened up a little, allowing me insert ad libs here and there. For the most part, I followed their dictates, but there were moments where they let me run with an idea that they loved."

While Norma's album was making waves, she says, "They had started writing the second Chic album, *C'est Chic*. My album was released on Bearsville, and Albert Grossman owned the label. He was highly respected in the industry for having managed Janis Joplin, and he had artists such as Todd Rundgren signed to his label. I was the only dance artist signed, and outside of his interest in a making a profit off the dance market, it was apparent that he had no real love for dance music. Eventually, he had creative differences with Bernard and Nile and decided not to do any heavy marketing and promotion for my album. For some reason, he didn't seem to respect them as producers and complained that their fees were too high. He finally said that if he committed to a second album, that he wanted me to move more towards soul music and he wanted to enlist Al Green's producer, Willie Mitchell."

Wright says she dealt with other complications. "After the fallout between Albert and Bernard and Nile," she recalls, "I encountered another problem prompted by my album cover. The photo I selected for the cover had sort of a girl-next-door flavor to it, and it worked for me, but Bernard and Nile had major issues with it. They ridiculed my choice and said they wanted me to portray more of a sex kitten image. I really wasn't comfortable with the sex kitten angle and moved forward with my choice. Ultimately, I think their issues with Albert Grossman, along with the album cover, caused them to throw in the towel. I can only speculate and give my take on it. I was never contacted or informed by them directly that I was no longer with Chic. I heard this news through the grapevine, first from Luci. She was told by them that it was my decision to leave. Needless to say, I was hurt and felt betrayed."

Alfa Anderson took over Norma Jean's role and Chic continued onward for the somewhat limited duration of the disco era with great success, unfazed to all outward appearances by Norma's departure. The number 1 anthemic crossover smash "Le Freak" went on to become one of disco's best-selling and most famous tunes, dominating radio and the clubs for several months. The monster summer jam "Good Times" followed and became a radio, disco and roller-rink staple. "Nile and Bernard were running the show — and that was okay — they were the founding fathers," admits Wright. "They were never the best at being good communicators, and with Albert Grossman, he wanted to try another genre besides dance music because disco music was in and out so quickly. It didn't even last for a decade, so I understand his desire to look at other options."

Norma took the difficulties she encountered with her producers in stride and remains pleased with the direction her life has taken since those days. "Some people in the music industry have tragic stories to tell where they've hit rock bottom or where they were strung out on drugs, robbed of publishing, etc.," she says. "I've never experienced any of that, and for this I'm grateful. The music industry is a tough field to be in, especially for women. It's tough on men as well, but women often take the biggest hits. I took a few, but I'm still standing and I've rebounded. My solo album went on to become successful, selling well over 300,000 copies! It's now

"The name changed from disco to dance. That's the thing that amazes me — no matter what you call it, some 30-plus years later, it's still alive!" exclaims Norma Jean Wright (courtesy Norma Jean Wright).

a collector's item, and it's been reissued several times. I continue to perform and own a management company housing the talent of dance artist Reina. I also oversee the careers of young producers like Black the Beast and LT Thomas. Original Chic members [Luci Martin, Alfa Anderson and I] are developing a new project together. I've been fortunate enough to have worked with Spike Lee, Madonna, Aretha Franklin, Michael Jackson and a host of others. I am blessed!" Wright also co-wrote a song with Kenny Burke called "Rising to the Top" which has been recorded by LL Cool J, Mary J. Blige and Nas. She actively tours in disco revival shows, singing her many hits.

She looks at maturity with grounded acceptance. "You know what? It hasn't been difficult—at least not yet," Norma asserts. "Aging happens. It comes with the territory. I've never been one that was so hyper-focused on it. That's another reason why I didn't want to play heavily into the sex kitten image. Maintaining that type of image is too much work. I'm not afraid of aging. And, so far, Mother Nature has been kind!"

Having survived the peaks and valleys of a career in disco, Norma seems to feel fondly about the music of the era. She affectionately says, "There are many great songs from that time, and A Taste of Honey's 'Boogie Oogie Oogie' is one of my favorites. I would love to have done a rendition with Bernard Edwards playing the bass line. As far as the music goes—it is still very much alive today! It never died! There are the baby boomers who still love the music, and there are younger people who are now being introduced to it—and they're embracing it. So this is encouraging! Dance music hasn't gotten the respect that, say, rock 'n' roll or R&B has, but it hasn't gone anywhere. Back then, when there was a backlash and they had the mantra claiming 'disco sucks'—that was unfortunate. They tried to snuff it out, but you know what? They couldn't! The name changed from disco to dance. That's the thing that amazes me—no matter what you call it, some 30-plus years later, it's still alive!"

Norma Jean Wright had the unique privilege of being one of disco's originals and helped pioneer the distinctive Chic sound with her beautiful voice on the group's earliest classics and on her own stellar solo hits. She embraces her status as a legendary diva in the genre's proud history. "I hope that I'm remembered for my music and that my music inspires people in some form or fashion to feel uplifted—and that it makes them want to get up and dance!"

Afterword
by Harry Wayne Casey (KC)

KC & the Sunshine Band danced their way into the pop music scene more than 35 years ago and are often credited with introducing disco music to mainstream culture. Harry Wayne Casey, KC for short, developed a highly unique fusion of disco, R&B and funk (with a hint of a Latin percussion groove) that gave the world a string of crossover hits. "That's the Way (I Like It)," "Boogie Shoes," "Get Down Tonight," "Keep It Comin' Love," "I'm Your Boogie Man" and "Shake Your Booty" topped the pop charts and sent dancers scrambling to the floors of the era's discos. With sales of more than 100 million records, nine Grammy nominations, three Grammy awards and an American Music Award, KC and his band are among disco music's most successful and popular original stars. KC's songs have appeared in more than 75 major movies, and the artist has been honored with a star on the Hollywood Walk of Fame. In 2012, he continued to tour worldwide (with no intention of stopping), as his Flashback with KC & the Sunshine Band *CD remained a top-seller on* Billboard's *dance and electronic albums chart for well over a year. An innovator, supporter and true pioneer of the genre, Casey offers his thoughts about disco and the women who sang it.*

Women vocalists have always played an important role in all kinds of music, and they always seem to garner more recognition than their male counterparts. Disco was no exception. Let's face it — it was just a great recipe. You took those great songs from the '70s and early '80s, you added those powerhouse female voices — women who had come into their own with this amazing new sound called disco — and *bam*! You had the perfect cake!

I don't think just anybody could have sung those wonderful disco songs everyone loves. I think those songs were meant for the women featured in this book, and they were hits because these particular women sang them. Maybe it was destiny. They were great songs and productions, but the vocal skill and style of these ladies was an integral part of each record's success. I don't think a man could have sung "I Will Survive" with the conviction of Gloria Gaynor. I don't know that a man could have really pulled off "I Love the Nightlife" the way Alicia Bridges nailed it. I'm not sure a man could belt "More, More, More" with quite the same kind of passion that Andrea True gave it. The productions of so many songs were amazing, but the first ladies of disco had what it takes to make you *feel* and *believe* those songs.

During the years when disco was exploding, I was overwhelmed with my own projects and working 24–7 — not even paying attention to what was going on outside of my studio for almost 12 years. I would hear their songs on the radio, but I didn't have the connection to these women that I would have liked. I have always felt that many of them didn't get a fair shake in the business, and I felt they were sometimes held back by the number of crossover hits they had. It was not a reflection of their talent. They had the voices, but in an industry driven by so many other factors, sometimes talent alone wasn't enough. You needed a lot of luck. I had several hits and was luckier than some performers in the disco era. Maybe because I was writing and producing for myself, so I had more control over my career. Still, I wrote a huge smash for George McCrae ("Rock Your Baby"), but we never could get him those follow-up hits.

I was an innovator of disco and I am very proud of that today, but I was never allowed to change — and that probably happened to a lot of these women. I know there were other styles they could sing, and each of these ladies had their own idea of who they wanted to be as entertainers. The industry — and sometimes the public — often had trouble seeing them beyond their disco hits. Every time I tried to change,

Seven-inch single label for "Get Down Tonight," KC & the Sunshine Band's first hit to make the Billboard Disco Chart in 1975 (author's collection).

they'd say, "That doesn't sound like KC & the Sunshine Band." What did they mean? *It was KC! It was me!* I would say, "Let me change; let me grow!" Easier said than done. The so-called disco backlash didn't help either. It was really one person in one city doing one publicity stunt. I really don't think the whole nation burned their disco records. It was publicized by the media to look bigger than it was. This person actually apologized to me many years later and told me how awry his original plan had gone. He told me he was fired from the job he held because of it. The truth is — I don't think he did anything but kill the word disco.

You can't be more disco than Culture Club, Madonna, Paula Abdul, Jennifer Lopez, Lady Gaga and all the acts that followed in the wake of the disco era. The clubs just continued to get bigger and bigger. Bigger than any of the discos I had ever been to in my life — packed to capacity with lines out the door! Instead of two in Miami Beach, there were 20 of them. Today, almost everything you hear on pop radio is dance music. A few decades ago, it would have been called disco. So I don't know how anyone can still say disco died!

As for the first ladies of disco, it's almost 40 years later and we still remember and love the songs they gave us. And we are still talking about them. It's very simple — these women delivered the soundtrack to each and every one of our lives ... beautifully. That speaks volumes!

What more do I need to say?

The Flip Side: Recommended Listening

The following is a somewhat random and extremely small sampling of some noteworthy disco tracks generally released between 1974 and 1984 by artists not prominently featured elsewhere in this volume. Primary recording labels are indicated. Some are well-known classics, some are a bit more obscure and some may have been completely missed by disco aficionados the first time around. However, all are significant products of the disco era by important female vocalists and worthy of a spin.

[Note: The vast majority of songs mentioned throughout this book are available in original, extended, remix and re-recorded form (in CD and digital download formats) from all the major legitimate Internet platforms. In some cases, the artists themselves offer the tracks through their personal websites.]

Shame, Shame, Shame—**Shirley & Company** (Platinum)
Get Up & Boogie/Fly Robin Fly/Save Me/No No Joe—**Silver Convention** (Midland)
Rockin' Chair/Have a Good Time—**Gwen McCrae** (TK)
This Is It/The Greatest Feeling/The Way You Make Me Feel/You Stepped Into My Life/Pick Me Up, I'll Dance—**Melba Moore** (Buddah/Epic)
Car Wash—**Rose Royce** (MCA)
Don't Leave Me This Way/Saturday Night, Sunday Morning/Love Masterpiece/96 Tears/Working Girl/Just Like All the Rest—**Thelma Houston** (Motown/Casablanca/RCA/MCA)
Never Gonna Be the Same—**Ruth Waters** (RCA)
Doin' the Best That I Can—**Bettye LaVette** (West End)
Magnifique—**Magnifique** (Ariola)
Je Survivrai—**Regine** (Prism)
Knock on Wood/Light My Fire/Jealousy/137 Disco Heaven/The Letter/Where Did Our Love Go/Save This Night for Love/Working Late Tonight/Beginning of the End/That Loving Feeling/Fever Line/Friends—**Amii Stewart** (Ariola/Handshake/RCA Germany/RCA Italia)
Heaven Must Have Sent You/Free Me from My Freedom/Can't Help Myself (Sugar Pie Honey Bunch)/Your Touch/Heaven—**Bonnie Pointer** (Motown/Private-1)
Take Me Home/Hell on Wheels—**Cher** (Casablanca)
Ain't Nothin' Gonna Keep Me from You—**Teri DeSario** (Casablanca)
Come to Me/Heart to Break the Heart/Gonna Get Over You—**France Joli** (Prelude)
Groove Me/Let the Good Times Roll—**Fern Kinney** (Malaco)
Trouble Maker/Love Power/Oh Happy Day—**Roberta Kelly** (Casablanca)
Want Ads—**Ullanda McCullough** (Ocean)

Sinner Man—**Sarah Dash** (Kirshner)
Work That Body/Heartbeat—**Taana Gardner** (West End)
This Time Baby/Helpless—**Jackie Moore** (Columbia)
Cherchez La Femme/Pow Wow—**Dr. Buzzard's Original Savannah Band** (RCA), **Cory Daye** (New York International)
Dancing in My Feet—**Laura Taylor** (T.K.)
God Don't Like Ugly—**Roberta Flack** (Atlantic)
Dance with You/Keep Smiling/It's Not What You Got, It's How You Use It—**Carrie Lucas** (Solar)
Look Up/Haven't You Heard/Never Gonna Give You Up/Forget Me Nots/Breakout—**Patrice Rushen** (Elektra)
Spacer—**Sheila & B. Devotion** (Carrere)
Hit 'n' Run Lover/Mercy/High Cost of Loving/Get On Up & Do It Again (as **Suzi Q**)/Touch 'n' Go Lover—**Carol Jiani** (Ariola/Matra/Streetwave)
Release—**Patti Labelle** (Epic)
Cry Me (a Million and One Tears)/First Be a Woman—**Leonore O'Malley** (Polydor)
The Runner/Giving Up, Giving In/Set Me Free/Red Light—**The Three Degrees** (Ariola)
Get on Up & Do It Again/Tonight/Get on Up—**Suzy Q** (Atlantic)
Bustin' Out/Do What You Wanna Do—**Material featuring Nona Hendryx** (Island), **Nona Hendryx** (Warner)
Love Don't You Go Through No Changes/We Are Family/Thinking of You/Got to Love Somebody/You Fooled Around/All American Girls/He's Just a Runaway/Jackie's Theme (There's No Stoppin' Us)/Get You in Our Love—**Sister Sledge** (Atlantic)
Take My Heart, Take My Soul/I'm So Excited/Automatic/Jump/Neutron Dance—**The Pointer Sisters** (Planet)
Hold on I'm Comin'/Love Me Tonight/Set Me Free/Clean-Up Woman—**Karen Silver** (Arista/Quality)
Can't Fake the Feeling/It Doesn't Only Happen at Night—**Geraldine Hunt** (Prism)
Too Through—**Bad Girls** (**Jocelyn Brown**) (BC)
Give Me a Break/Pick-Up/Let Him Go—**Vivien Vee** (Fuscia)
Do You Love Me/Every Home Should Have One—**Patti Austin** (Quest)
Blood & Honey/Follow Me/Oh Mother, Look What They've Done to Me/Gold/Hollywood Is Just a Dream/Diamonds/Fever/Love Your Body/Darkness & Light/Tam-Tam/Assassino/Stato d'Allarme—**Amanda Lear** (Ariola/WEA)
My Heart's Not in It—**Brenda Jones** (Wave)
I Specialize in Love—**Sharon Brown** (Profile)
I'm Starting Again—**Grace Kennedy** (Profile)
You're Love Still Brings Me to My Knees/Love Sides—**Marcia Hines** (Mercury)
Wir Fliegen Zu Den Sternen—**Nicole** (Jupiter)
Begging for More—**Monica Neal** (Sam)
Do It Again—**Paulette Reeves** (Dash)
Love Is the Drug/Best Part of Breaking Up/Spies—**Roni Griffith** (Vanguard)
Can't Believe—**Nancy Martin** (Atlantic)
Upside Down/Dynamite—**Vanessa** (Dureco)
Calling All Boys/Passion/Jukebox (Don't Put Another Dime)—**The Flirts** (O Records)
Jump Shout/Rocket to Your Heart—**Lisa** (Moby Dick)
Give It to Me/Murphy's Law—**Cheri** (Venture)

Recommended Listening

Whatcha Gonna Do —**Stephanie Wells** (Tojo)
Groove Patrol —**High Inergy** (Motown)
Let the Music Play/Give Me Tonight —**Shannon** (Emergency)
Save the Overtime (for Me) —**Gladys Knight and the Pips** (Columbia)
You Should Hear How She Talks About You/My Boyfriend's Back-Runaway —**Melissa Manchester** (Arista)
Too Much Mister —**Natalie Cole** (Epic)
Holiday/Burning Up —**Madonna** (Sire)
Rush Rush —**Debbie Harry** (Chrysalis)
Body Rock —**Maria Vidal** (EMI)
Bette Davis Eyes/You Make My Heart Beat Faster —**Kim Carnes** (EMI)
Robert De Niro's Waiting/Cruel Summer —**Bananarama** (London)
Belle of St. Mark —**Sheila E.** (Warner)
Don't Leave Me This Way —**Slip** (Proto)
Why Me/Breakdance —**Irene Cara** (Geffen)
Happy Station/Colour My Love/Give Me Your Love/Tell Me —**Fun Fun** (TSR/Teldec)
Walk Into the Daylight/White & Black —**Taffy** (Ibiza)

Index

American Bandstand 65, 67, 79, 220
Anderson, Alfa 244, 247
Armstead, Izora 38, 211–212, 224–228
Arpeggio 239–240

Barry, Claudja 3–5, 57–64
The Bee Gees 33, 92
Belolo, Henri 16, 175–188
Black Box 32, 229
Bowie, David 140
Boys Town Gang 143–148
Branigan, Laura 31, 132–133
Brontein, Troy 13
Brooks, Pattie 24–25, 64–71
Brown, Miquel 71–75

C&C Music Factory 228–229
Cara, Irene 32, 80
Casey, Harry Wayne 249
Chambers, Marilyn 50–51
Chic 244–247
Christopher, Gavin 187
Clapton, Eric 90–91
Clifford, Linda 75–85
Correia, George "Iz" 13
Cowley, Patrick 227
Cross, Reuben 124, 171

Davis, Clive 102
Davis, Hal 238–240
Davis, John 86–87, 173
Dean, Hazell 13, 74
Deodato, Eumir 187
DeWalden, Christian 134
Diamond, Gregg 43–45, 48–50, 55–56, 103–104
Diamond, Joel 108
Douglas, Carol 75, 83–89, 235–236
Draher, Dodie 183–190

Ecstasy, Passion & Pain 190–196

Edwards, Bernard 244–248
Elliman, Yvonne 89–93

Fekaris, Dino 105–107
First Choice 93–100, 170–171
Fitch, John H. 124, 171
Fleming, Rochelle 93–100, 170–171
Ford, Stephen 14
Friederich, Jean-Claude 118–122
Fuqua, Harvey 211–213, 224, 226

Galetovic, Sandy 41–42, 49–50, 54, 56
Gaynor, Gloria 25, 29, 100–110
Gianatos, Rick 14–15, 67, 69, 198
Glass House 165

Harris, Norman 31, 94, 102
Hayden, Tom 72–73, 105–106, 122, 176, 200–201, 206
Hayes, Isaac 80, 162
Hernandez, Patrick 24
Holloway, Loleatta 31, 88, 99, 236
Houston, Cissy 23, 52, 173
Houston, Thelma 20

Jabara, Paul 34, 67, 228
Jacobs, Debbie 111–117
Jones, Grace 19, 27, 113, 149
Jones, Quincy 34
Juvet, Patrick 185

Kane, Madleen 117–123
Kashif 127
Kass, Art 45, 48, 50
Kaczor, Richie 106
King, Evelyn "Champagne" 28, 123–130
Kirshner, Don 41

Knight, Frederick 218–221
Korduletsch, Jurgen 57, 60

Labelle, Patti 214–215
Landers, Audrey 130–137
Lane, Suzi 137–143
Levine, Ian 72–73, 154, 204–207
Life, Theodore (T-Life) 124–127

Manley, Cynthia 143–152
Marie, Kelly 152–155
Mason-Dorman, Cheryl 175–183
Mayfield, Curtis 77–78, 80
Montana, Vincent, Jr. 232, 234
Morali, Jaques 16, 175–188
Moroder, Giorgio 34, 120–121, 138–139
Motley, Bill 144–146, 148
Moulton, Tom 15–16, 45–50, 97, 102–103

Nightingale, Maxine 156–163

O'Loughlin, Eddie 85–87, 171
Orlando, Bobby 60

Parker, Paul 114, 121, 201
Payne, Scherrie 163–170
Perren, Freddie 90, 105–107
Piper, Wardell 94, 170–174

Rae, Fonda 236
Ray, Don 173
Ritchie Family 175–190
Robinson, Vicki Sue 32, 100
Rome, Richie 175–176, 179
Rose, Felipe 16, 54–55
Ross, Diana 87, 168, 237–240, 245
Roy, Barbara 190–196

Sabu, Paul 111–112
Saturday Night Fever 21, 86, 89–92
Schatz, Warren 32
Sebastian, Lana 118–119
Sebastian, Paul 118–119
Sinitta 71
Smith, Carlton J. 50
Soul Train 66, 95, 240
Soussan, Simon 65, 240–242
Stanley, Pamala 197–203
Stephens, Ian Anthony 121
Stewart, Amii 71, 220, 251
Stigwood, Robert 80, 91
Stock-Aitken-Waterman 14, 34, 154
Summer, Donna 33–36, 59, 66, 78, 83, 104, 139

The Supremes 165–166
Sylvester 25, 147, 171, 201, 210–215, 224–227

Tams, Paul 154
Thomas, Evelyn 203–210
Thompson, Tony 245
Tracy, Jeanie 210–217
True, Andrea 41–56, 232

Village People 16, 22, 24, 29–30, 186

Ward, Anita 217–223
Wash, Martha 211–212, 224–231
Wesley, Gwendolyn (Gwendolyn Oliver) 175–183

White, Jack 31, 132–134
Williams, Carol 231–236
Williams, Jessica 146, 237–243
Wills, Viola 36–37, 114
Wilson, Mary 165–167
Wirrick, James "Tip" 16, 213–214
Wooten, Cassandra 175–183
Wright, Norma Jean 244–248

Young, Karen 37, 100

Zager, Michael 16–17, 50–52

www.ingramcontent.com/pod-product-compliance
Lightning Source LLC
Chambersburg PA
CBHW060258240426
43661CB00060B/2831